RHINEGOLD

D0917631

WORLD CONSERVATOIRES

AN INTERNATIONAL GUIDE TO MUSIC STUDY

RHINEGOLD DIRECTORIES

First published in 2009 in Great Britain by
Rhinegold Publishing Ltd
241 Shaftesbury Avenue
London WC2H 8TF
United Kingdom
+44 (0)20 7333 1761

British Library Cataloguing in Publication Data.
A catalogue record for this book is available from the British Library.
ISBN 978-1-906178-74-1
ISSN 2040-2449

Printed in Great Britain by Headley Brothers Ltd, The Invicta Press, Queens Road, Ashford, Kent TN24 8HH

Contents

Foreword

Welcome to the first edition of *Rhinegold World Conservatoires*, a brand new annual book from the UK's leading publisher of magazines, reference books and educational study guides, Rhinegold Publishing Ltd.

Our aim has been to provide an easy-to-read, easily carried guide to the world's major advanced music training establishments, those places whose goal is to produce performing musicians for the classical music stage (universities which focus on academic education do not fall within the scope of this particular book). These go by many different names depending where you are in the world – music colleges, conservatories, music high schools, music academies, music universities and so on. But to keep things simple here, we have chosen to use the word 'conservatoire' throughout to refer to an institution providing that kind of high level training to university-age students.

Although the practice of travelling abroad to study has become increasingly easy in recent years, thanks in particular to the Erasmus exchange scheme, deciding where to go should not be done lightly. This is especially so for music students for whom poor technical advice, for example, or a study environment which they find unpleasant, can set them back in their professional training. That is why this guide should be only a starting point for the potential traveller, giving an idea of the number of institutions worldwide and the kind of choice available, and an indication of the scope of the courses on offer.

In fact, it is not our intention to point students in the direction of specific institutions. One of our key principles in the book is that we know there will be many factors influencing the decision about where someone will decide to visit – climate and quality of life come into it too. This explains our choice of geographical classification, for example. It is also why we devote a large amount of space to giving a flavour of the cities and countries where conservatoires are located, with particular attention to the musical and cultural life of a place – it is not only or necessarily the biggest cities which are the most active musically, after all. Wherever we can, we have given details for tourist information offices; why not take a trip or two to get a sense of the atmosphere of a place before making your final decision?

Indeed, as with any decision bearing on your education, there can be no substitute for detailed research and that includes making enquiries at the institutions themselves. Although information in *Rhinegold World Conservatoires* has been compiled from various sources, including details provided by the conservatoires, it is inevitable that the quality of information available will vary from place to place. (One could even argue that the conservatoires which provide the most information in the most easily accessible form are the ones who are keenest to attract students from overseas, the ones most likely to make you feel welcome.) And for various reasons, the guide does not aim to be exhaustive, so not every institution in the world, nor every country, is represented. We will doubtless address this in future editions, just as we will be exploring ways to make the book an even more useful tool. You can help with this – tell us what you would like to see included next time by emailing us: directories@rhinegold.co.uk.

Studying abroad – some practicalities

Why study abroad? Well, if travel broadens the mind, then a period of studying overseas can blow your mental horizons wide open. For a musician, studying abroad offers many opportunities for professional and personal development. British string players, for instance, may want to head to Vienna and pianists to Moscow to immerse themselves in an approach to technique and style that's quite different from anything they will encounter in British conservatoires. Brass and wind players, too, will find Germanic and Scandinavian musical cultures have a lot to offer in exploring different, often enlightening approaches to teaching and performance. Few singers will be able to make a good career if they stick purely to home territory, and the networking opportunities offered by taking courses overseas will stand them in good stead for developing future strands of professional work in different areas of the world.

Studying overseas helps musicians to connect to areas of the music industry that are not easily accessed from the UK. Promoters, artist managers, auditioning panels and casting directors all operate differently n different areas of the world, and some familiarity with how other cultures go about their business can be an invaluable asset to any musical career.

For some, studying abroad will be merely an adjunct to getting to know another culture and being immersed in a totally new tradition. It's unlikely that a classical musician who has trained in earnest in the UK will gain much in the way of professional career development by going to areas of the world where interest in western classical music is either or non-existent at best nascent. However, for encounters with other musical traditions, and an opportunity to exchange experiences and skills with musicians from very different backgrounds, a stint of studying music in places such as India or Africa can be extremely rewarding at a personal and creative level.

Using study as a means of engineering an extended recreational visit to another country is a risky tactic. A genuine interest in the chosen course of study is usually a prerequisite to building towards a career in music. Otherwise, staying motivated while coping with an unfamiliar culture might be difficult. Often this motivation will come from connecting with a respected teacher or being given opportunities to become involved in a professional forum such as a renowned orchestra or opera house.

To get the most out of studying abroad, careful preparation is vital. Unrealistic expectations at the planning stage can lead to misery and money down the drain further down the line. On the whole, studying music abroad will involve the same rigours that go into becoming a professional musician in your home country, but with added challenges such as cultural unfamiliarity and the need to be unusually self-sufficient. Below are some of the factors you should consider if you are planning to embark on such an endeavour.

What is your motive for studying abroad?

- If you want to go purely in order to advance your instrumental (or vocal) skills, then your priority should be to vet the institutions you will be applying for thoroughly. Look at who is on the faculty and make enquiries as to their professional reputation and their teaching methodology. If you are at a UK conservatoire, there may well be exchange schemes whereby teachers are accredited in partner organisations and the period spent abroad will contribute to your overall degree or qualification.
- The likelihood is that you will be going abroad because there is someone specific with whom you want to study. In this case, be aware that you will also need to be comfortable with the culture around you and well prepared for your new surroundings. Russia and the former Soviet states, for example, may have fine traditions of music teaching, but local languages are difficult to learn and teaching methods are often prescriptive and disciplined to an extreme degree.

How will you survive financially?

Studying is one thing, but how do you keep body and soul together in a context where you have no support system? First, you must research the costs of living in your chosen destination thoroughly. A scholarship or grant may look decent on paper, but big, international cities can be exorbitantly expensive to live in anywhere in the world, and finding decent accommodation can take time and effort. As far as possible, do a recce to set things up before you start your course and to get a realistic idea of how much your living expenses will be – some institutions are very helpful in this, providing estimated living costs on their websites, for example. Pump the locals for information as much as possible and take advantage of any resources and connections that your new place of study can put your way.

A few things to consider when it comes to finances:

- Transferring money and setting up bank accounts overseas can be much more complicated than you expect. Make sure that you have easy access to your bank account at home (hole-in-the-wall cards are very useful) as it could take a long time to set up accounts abroad. The US is especially notorious for this.
- Always have contingency funds to cope with unexpected events. There's nothing worse that feeling stuck miles from home without the wherewithal to return whenever you need to. Book air tickets that give you flexibility on return dates.
- UK passport holders studying in the EU can take part-time employment to fund their courses (some conservatoires don't officially allow this). Remember, however, that in many countries outside the EU, UK citizens on a student visa will be forbidden to take paid jobs, so don't count on being able to work – and that includes teaching and giving concerts – to support yourself through your studies.
- Some UK conservatoires offer exchange programmes with overseas counterparts, and sometimes these include free or subsidised board and lodging. Opting to take a well-trodden institutional path will be off-putting to those who want to study overseas out of a sense of adventure; for others it provides a reassuring way of living and learning in a new context.
- One major advantage of studying in the USA is that there are a number of generous grants and scholarships available, particularly for postgraduates, many of which cover travel, accommodation and fees. Competition for places is fearsome, but once you are in, US conservatoires and music academies go out of their way to make overseas students feel welcome and well looked-after.
- There are areas of the world such as the Baltic countries and eastern Europe where the cost of studying and living is considerably cheaper than in the UK, but where music education exists to a high standard. As mentioned above, however, the challenges of language and cultural differences are ever present.

Before you go

- Outside the EU, most UK students will require a special visa to study abroad. In most cases, these visas are reasonably easily obtained from the relevant consulate, but often a raft of documents to support your application will need to be sent by the organisation where you will be studying. Make sure you know exactly what is required in advance, otherwise you will waste a lot of time waiting in queues only to be sent away for more documents at the final hurdle.
- Regulations for obtaining US study visas have tightened considerably since the 9/11 terrorist attacks. Anybody visiting America to pursue a study course of more than 18 hours a week is now required to travel on student visa. There is a useful and comprehensive official website at http://educationusa.state.gov/
- In most Asian and Middle Eastern countries, overseas students are required to register with the police and with their local consulate on arrival – a wise thing to do in the unlikely event of emergencies. Take print outs of scans of your passport with you, as they may be required for official purposes.

- A good, comprehensive insurance policy is vital – particularly for medical coverage and emergency repatriation. Make sure your policy covers study overseas and that coverage for your instrument is valid for abroad.
- Health issues may be of some concern to students planning extended stays in developing countries. The Foreign Office website generally has all the information you will need to take the right precautions: www.fco.gov.uk
- Consider what steps you might need to take to make sure your instrument remains in good shape if you are heading for exotic climes. Conditions such as extreme humidity in the tropics or excessive heat and dryness can have a disastrous effect on your priceless Strad.
- Taking your instrument on an aircraft needs planning. It's a good idea to discuss the airline's policy towards musical instruments when you book your ticket. If you are a cellist or a double-bass player, you will almost certainly have to book an extra seat if you want to carry your instrument in the cabin. Excess baggage charges may apply to large, heavy instruments being checked in as hold luggage.

The most comprehensive source of information on studying abroad can be found in the country specific information, where you will also be able to find information on studying in particular countries. In addition, embassies are a useful source of information. Project Visa has a searchable directory of contact details for many of the embassies around the world (http://projectvisa.com).

Learning languages – a door to personal and professional development

If you have the urge to spend a significant period of time living in a foreign country, particularly if you have not made your mind up where to go, the question of language is bound to crop up. Of course, if you have already studied a language, this may be one of the reasons why you are looking to travel abroad. But if not, you will need to realise that a tourist's level of knowledge will probably not be enough to allow you to negotiate day-to-day life in a strange country. You will need to be able to manage your finances, arrange accommodation, socialise and so on, not to mention follow classes.

Doubtless, this prospect is one thing which puts people off the idea of living abroad, or at least encourages them to choose countries which speak the same language as them. But learning a foreign language brings all kinds of benefits, certainly benefits that outweigh the difficulties.

The first thing to recognise is that being able to use a language on a daily basis, so much so that it becomes part of your everyday life, is not the same as trying to learn grammar and vocabulary in a classroom. Although this kind of study is certainly helpful in enabling students to gain a deeper knowledge of how a language works, nothing compares to the practical application of it – musicians more than anyone know the difference between written analysis and actual music-making, or the relief of performing compared with the repetitiveness of technical work. You could even say that, for a music student obsessed with practice and perfection, learning a language is a way to use your brain doing something different; and having an ear for sound should help you with the aural side of speaking and communicating.

In fact, just as there are captivating performers who are more timid away from the concert platform, there are those who find they can express themselves more adventurously in a foreign language. Partly this is because, if you are a visitor making an honest effort to communicate with people in their own language, you are not only more likely to be welcomed, but your linguistic clumsiness will also be excused. This in turn will help your confidence, and you will inevitably find yourself trying to find new ways to say things … thereby improving your language skills in turn. And if you find yourself living or working in a small town, or in a particularly close professional community (like music), it's possible to stand out in a way you might not back home.

The various organisations promoting foreign language learning all point to the communicative aspect as being one of the main pluses. As an individual you find yourself with new people to interact with. But you also play your part in promoting understanding between cultures, in promoting a less insular outlook on the world. And if that sounds idealistic, there are other advantages that can benefit you personally, as those same organisations argue: it's an additional skill you can put on your CV; travelling overseas to learn a language can open doors in other countries; by learning on your own initiative, you are demonstrating to future employers your self-motivation.

These advantages are relevant to musicians in particular. Say you are a member of a string quartet and you are beginning the process of promoting your group, think how much wider you can spread the word if each of you could speak a second language. Or imagine you want to build up your teaching portfolio; you could offer classes in another language; indeed, it would make it easier to establish your teaching in another country. Take a third scenario: you don't want to take on any more teaching or playing (perhaps it doesn't fit with your domestic arrangements), but you do want to earn some income another way; if you become really proficient and are prepared to take a few more exams, there are opportunities for freelance translation and interpretation work. And with so much demographic movement, particularly within Europe, if the language you learn is a less widely spoken one, this is even more so.

The final thing to realise is that most conservatoires offer assistance in language-learning, often through associated universities, but many expect non-native speakers to be able to show their abilities have reached an acceptable level as part of the application process. So make enquiries about language classes at your home institution, nearest university or college, or at a cultural office in your home country of the place you are visiting (organisations like the Goethe-Institut, for instance).

Powodzenia; or should that be *boa sorte!*

Specialist early music courses

In compiling a list of conservatories offering Historical Performance (HP) I have divided this into 3 areas: Europe excluding the UK, UK, the rest of the world.

The study of Historically informed Performance (HiP) has certainly moved forward in the last 15-20 years and there are numerous conservatories now offering full time courses for students wishing to specialise in this area. There have always been a few instruments represented in most established conservatories (namely harpsichord and recorder), but now more and more institutions are employing specialist professors to teach period instruments with disciplines covering voice, strings, wind, brass and keyboard. In addition it is more common to have classes on specific topics or areas of study based on repertoire from the medieval times through to the classical repertoire and beyond.

In Europe there are numerous conservatories offering students the opportunity to study period instruments at a principal study level with well-known professional players and teachers. Among some of the more established institutions for Historical Performance (HP) are conservatories in Amsterdam, Barcelona, Basel, Bremen, Brussels, Geneva, The Hague, Hamburg, Lyon, Trossingen and Verona. In addition to 1-1 teaching many of these institutions offer well-organised courses including baroque orchestra and opera productions, studies in chamber music and different national styles. In addition a new initiative, Nominem, has recently been formed to create a joint Nordic Masters Programme in Early Music linking the Royal Danish Academy of Music, The Sibelius Academy in Helsinki and the Grieg Academy in Bergen.

In the UK we have 8 music conservatoires, four in London alone — The Royal College of Music, The Royal Academy of Music, Guildhall School of Music and Drama and Trinity College of Music. No other city in the world offers this number of top level conservatoires, so there is plenty of choice for prospective students. Each institution runs a department for HP in various guises and with different levels of activity. Here the professors tend to be UK-based and involved in the UK early music movement. Each of the institutions has a full roster of professors teaching period instruments.

Since taking over as Head of HP at the RCM in 2006 I have been developing a curriculum for studying HiP which I hope will enable the student to cover, in detail, a wide range of styles in music. In addition to 1-1 lessons on all period instruments we encourage our students to attend regular classes ranging from medieval chamber music to late classical and early romantic orchestral projects with, among others, Sir Roger Norrington. All of our HiP classes and lectures are open to both period and modern instrumental students who can select these classes through various electives and pathways. In this way modern string players experience baroque string classes, pianists have lessons on harpsichord and fortepiano, wind players have the opportunity of trying period wind instruments etc. Thus we actively encourage our students to study these related instruments, resulting in many of them pursuing period instruments as a second or joint principal study. Our principal study period instrument students are expected to follow all the classes and lectures in HP and take an active role in the numerous performances within and outside the RCM.

As I have mentioned already many institutions worldwide do offer the opportunity of studying period instruments (especially recorder and harpsichord) and America has numerous Conservatories with well established HP departments. These include Boston, Eastman, McGill, Oberlin, Yale and even Juilliard has just launched a new department for HP under the direction of Monica Huggett. My co-founder of Florilegium, Neal Peres Da Costa, is currently running a very successful programme for HP in Sydney, Australia

In the end the enormous number of institutions promoting HP is drawing on a small pool of interested students and so they must offer a wide range of related studies to attract the highest calibre of student. Most of the professors teaching 1-1 have established reputations in HP and this is certainly an important aspect leading to student choice. However in my experience more and more students want to gain a broader knowledge of HiP whilst studying and feel the need to be part of a community of like-minded students at conservatory who have similar goals and aspirations. Therefore the HP department, and how it is run, becomes increasingly important in creating this community. In addition, institutions must encourage more research based performance activities, and a number of these institutions (like the RCM) do combine a high level of research and practical performance through their departments of HP. This is vital for the continued growth and development of any conservatory and especially for the future progress of historically informed performances.

Ashley Solomon ARAM, HonRCM
Professor of Recorder & Head of Historical Performance
Royal College of Music, London

Opera studies abroad

Any long, successful career in opera is bound to have an international dimension, and a period of studying and developing skills abroad should be considered as a vital component in preparing for the profession.

Studying in conservatoires overseas offers the opportunity to work with particular teachers – perhaps even an operatic legend, such as soprano Renata Scotto who heads the young artist programme at the Verdi Institute in Parma. In the case of European study courses, there's also a chance to develop language skills along with insights into the variations in professional norms that singers are bound to encounter when they travel the world.

Often a conservatoire will be affiliated to a local opera house, with all the resources that come with such an association. For example, if you join the Vocal Arts and Opera course at the Juilliard School in New York, you'll work with the likes of Stephen Wadsworth – an influential director at the Metropolitan Opera – and James Levine, the Met's music director. Regular access to these key artistic figures at the Met can do a promising young career no harm.

In America, opera study courses often attract generous financial support from wealthy patrons and foundations. One of the most important opera study centres in the USA, the Academy of Vocal Arts in Philadephia, offers around £50,000-worth of free training per participant each year for a full four-year study course in opera.

Meanwhile, Opera Studio and Young Artists Programmes are a vital stepping-stone from conservatoires into the wider profession, allowing young artists aged typically between 24 and 34 to experience the working life of a professional company while still developing and honing their skills. Studio artists are given opportunities to interact with professional singers, conductors, directors, designers and technicians of national and international acclaim, and to follow a standard rehearsal and production schedule within a major opera company. Many studios arrange auditions for their young artists throughout the year with artist managements, visiting general directors of other opera companies, guest conductors and directors. There are also opportunities to take small roles on the main stage, performing alongside major international figures in opera.

As with conservatoire courses, several US Young Artist Programmes come with substantial grants from philanthropic sources which allow selected participants to study for free. In the case of San Francisco Opera's famous Merola Program, the opera house covers all travel and living costs as well as offering a stipend to participants over a period of 11 weeks. The Merola's generosity even extends to post-program career development, with former participants eligible for further grants up to five years after leaving the programme. Competition is stiff, however. The Merola, which counts Thomas Hampson and Deborah Voigt among its distinguished roll-call, typically accepts 24 singers, five assistant coaches and one stage director each year from around 800 people who audition.

Founded in 1977, the Houston Grand Opera Studio in Texas has a good track record for producing rounded opera professionals – its alumni include Bruce Ford, Denyce Graves and Joyce DiDonato. The programme provides eight to 12 young artists each season with the opportunity to study and perform under a distinguished professional staff of teachers and singers. Studio artists commit themselves to an intense study programme while in residence in Houston from September to May, including classes in voice, acting, stage movement, diction and languages. Individual coaching sessions are a key part of the programme, along with career counselling and the personal development of the artist.

Other major programmes that overseas applicants might consider in the US include the Lindemann Young Artist Development programme at the Metropolitan Opera, New York , Santa Fe Opera's Apprentice Program and Seattle Opera's Young Artist Programme which has been ably shaped under its director Peter Kazaras.

In Europe, Zurich Opera's International Operastudio (IOS) is a leader in this field (alongside the Jette Parker programme at the Royal Opera House in London). Modelled along American lines, with an added emphasis on German language and repertoire, the IOS provides a season-long programme of intensive training, geared around staged productions of opera. Living expenses of participants are covered by grants. The programme provides excellent career development prospects, with its links into the German-speaking opera world and good relationships with agents and opera managements in the region.

In Germany itself, opera houses have a long tradition of nurturing young talent within their professional ranks. The German 'Fach' system is a tried and trusted method for building up a solid repertoire of roles in a particular voice-type. While developing their Fach, young singers become part of an ensemble where skills and professionalism are passed down from within the company through an ethos of apprenticeship. Young artists are gradually introduced into main-stage productions as they graduate from small, comprimario parts to principal understudying and finally gaining the spotlight in major roles.

In fact, Germany, with its 150-plus opera companies, remains the world's operatic powerhouse and familiarity with the German opera world is almost a pre-requisite to fast-tracking an international operatic career.

A selection of Opera Studios and apprenticeships is given in the Appendix, on p.268

+2 +3 +4 +5 +6 +7 +8 +9 +10 +11 +12

APRIL 2009

Mon	Tue	Wed	Thu	Fri	Sat	Sun
		1	2	3	4	5
6	7	8	9	10	11	12
13	14	15	16	17	18	19
20	21	22	23	24	25	26
27	28	29	30			

MAY 2009

Mon	Tue	Wed	Thu	Fri	Sat	Sun
				1	2	3
4	5	6	7	8	9	10
11	12	13	14	15	16	17
18	19	20	21	22	23	24
25	26	27	28	29	30	31

JUNE 2009

Mon	Tue	Wed	Thu	Fri	Sat	Sun
1	2	3	4	5	6	7
8	9	10	11	12	13	14
15	16	17	18	19	20	21
22	23	24	25	26	27	28
29	30					

JULY 2009

Mon	Tue	Wed	Thu	Fri	Sat	Sun
		1	2	3	4	5
6	7	8	9	10	11	12
13	14	15	16	17	18	19
20	21	22	23	24	25	26
27	28	29	30	31		

AUGUST 2009

Mon	Tue	Wed	Thu	Fri	Sat	Sun
31					1	2
3	4	5	6	7	8	9
10	11	12	13	14	15	16
17	18	19	20	21	22	23
24	25	26	27	28	29	30

SEPTEMBER 2009

Mon	Tue	Wed	Thu	Fri	Sat	Sun
	1	2	3	4	5	6
7	8	9	10	11	12	13
14	15	16	17	18	19	20
21	22	23	24	25	26	27
28	29	30				

OCTOBER 2009

Mon	Tue	Wed	Thu	Fri	Sat	Sun
			1	2	3	4
5	6	7	8	9	10	11
12	13	14	15	16	17	18
19	20	21	22	23	24	25
26	27	28	29	30	31	

NOVEMBER 2009

Mon	Tue	Wed	Thu	Fri	Sat	Sun
30						1
2	3	4	5	6	7	8
10	10	11	12	13	14	15
16	17	18	19	20	21	22
23	24	25	26	27	28	29

DECEMBER 2009

Mon	Tue	Wed	Thu	Fri	Sat	Sun
	1	2	3	4	5	6
7	8	9	10	11	12	13
14	15	16	17	18	19	20
21	22	23	24	25	26	27
28	29	30	31			

JANUARY 2010

Mon	Tue	Wed	Thu	Fri	Sat	Sun
				1	2	3
4	5	6	7	8	9	10
11	12	13	14	15	16	17
18	19	20	21	22	23	24
25	26	27	28	29	30	31

FEBRUARY 2010

Mon	Tue	Wed	Thu	Fri	Sat	Sun
1	2	3	4	5	6	7
8	9	10	11	12	13	14
15	16	17	18	19	20	21
22	23	24	25	26	27	28
26	27	28	29	30	31	

MARCH 2010

Mon	Tue	Wed	Thu	Fri	Sat	Sun
1	2	3	4	5	6	7
8	9	10	11	12	13	14
15	16	17	18	19	20	21
22	23	24	25	26	27	28
29	30	31				

	Australia	Austria	Belgium	Canada	Denmark	Finland	France	Germany	Israel	Italy	Ireland	Netherlands	New Zeland	Norway	Portugal	Spain	Sweden	UK	USA
April 2009	10, 11, 13, 24, 25	12, 13	12, 13	10, 13	9, 10, 12, 13	10, 12, 13	13	13, 12, 13	9, 15, 19	12, 13, 25	10, 12, 13	10, 12, 13, 30	10, 13, 25	5, 9, 10, 12, 13	10, 12, 25	10, 12, 13	9, 10	10, 12, 13	
May 2009		1, 21, 31	1, 21, 31	18	8, 21, 31	1, 21, 31	1, 8, 21	1, 21, 31	29	1	4	21, 31		1, 17, 21, 31	1	1	1, 21, 31	4, 25	25
June 2009		1, 11	1	1, 5	20		1			2	1	1	1	1	10, 11		6, 20		
July 2009			21	1			14											13	4
August 2009	15	15					15			15	3				15	15		3, 31	
September 2009				7					19, 20, 28										7
October 2009		26		12	31		3	3, 10				26	26		5	12	31		12
November 2009		1	1, 11	11			1, 11			1					1	1		30	11, 26
December 2009	25, 26	8, 25, 26	25	25, 26	25, 26	6, 25, 26	25	25, 26		8, 25, 26	25, 26	25, 26	25, 26	25, 26, 28	1, 8, 25	6, 8, 25	25, 26, 28	25, 26	25
January 2010	1, 26	1, 6	1	1	1	1, 6	1	1		1, 6	1	1	1, 4	1	1	1, 6	1, 6	1, 4	1, 18
February 2010														6					15
March 2010									30		17			28		19		17	

Country	Code	Country	Code	Country	Code
Albania	335	Greenland	299	Nicaragua	505
Algeria	213	Guedeloupe	590	Nigeria	234
Argentina	54	Guatemala	502	Norway	47
Armenia	374	Haiti	509	Pakistan	92
Australia	61	Hong Kong	852	Panama	507
Austria	43	Hungary	36	Paraguay	595
Bahrain	973	Iceland	354	Peru	51
Bangladesh	880	India	91	Philippines	63
Belguim	32	Indonesia	62	Poland	48
Belize	501	Iran	98	Portugal	351
Bolivia	591	Iraq	964	Romania	40
Bosnia, Herz.	387	Ireland	353	Russian Fed.	7
Brazil	55	Isreal	972	Saudi Arabia	966
Bulgaria	359	Italy	39	Senegal	221
Cameroon	237	Japan	81	Sierra Leone	232
Canada	1	Jordan	962	Singapore	65
Cape Verde	238	Kenya	254	Slovakia	421
Chad	235	Korea (South)	82	Slovenia	386
Chile	56	Kuwait	365	South Africa	27
China	86	Latvia	371	Spain	34
Colombia	57	Lesbanon	961	Sri Lanka	94
Congo	243	Libya	218	Sudan	249
Costa Rica	506	Leichtenst.	423	Sweden	46
Côte d'Ivoire	225	Lithuania	370	Switzerland	41
Croatia	385	Luxembourg	352	Syria	963
Cuba	53	Macedonia	389	Taiwan	886
Cyprus	357	Madagascar	261	Thailand	66
Czech Rep.	420	Malaysia	60	The Gambia	220
Denmark	45	Maldives	960	Tunisia	216
Dominican Rep.	1809	Malta	356	Turkey	90
Ecuador	593	Martinique	596	Ukraine	380
Egypt	20	Mexico	52	Utd. Arab Emirates	971
Estonia	372	Micronesia	691	UK	44
Fiji	679	Moldova	373	USA	1
Finland	358	Monaco	377	Uruguary	598
France	33	Morocco	212	Venezuela	58
Germany	49	Namibia	264	Veitnam	84
Ghana	233	Nepal	977	Yemen	967
Gibraltar	350	Netherlands	31	Zambia	260
Greece	30	New Zealand	64	Zimbabwe	263

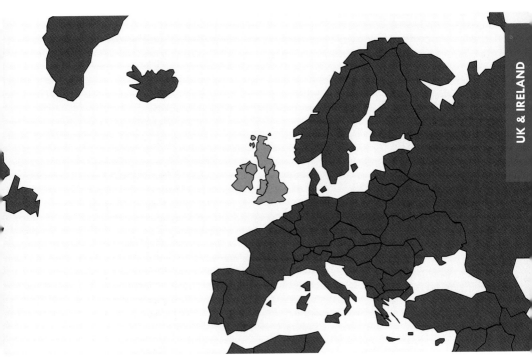

UK & IRELAND

United Kingdom and Ireland

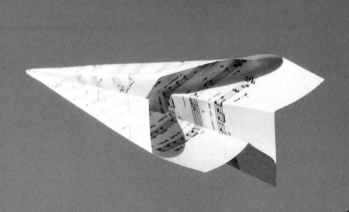
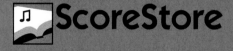

United Kingdom and Ireland

For a country labelled 'the land without music' at the beginning of the 20th century, the UK has certainly developed since then into a thriving musical location. Perhaps music in Germany is more deeply embedded at a local level – outside the main UK cities, high quality performance is harder to find; perhaps it has been more heavily funded in other countries, with the UK falling between the US model of private funding and the European model of central/municipal funding. But in those cities – London, Glasgow, Manchester, Birmingham, Cardiff, in other words, the very cities where the conservatoires are based – there is a huge range of well organised, well promoted concerts to hear. In addition, the country has two other strong traditions that others may not. Perhaps because of the concentration of high profile music in a few cities, there is a wide network of local music festivals, some prominent, others more locally orientated. Secondly, the level of music-making at an amateur level is second to none, and this includes instrumental participation as well as singing.

Students will be attracted to Ireland for other reasons, perhaps for the traditional Irish music rather than classical. The country is famed for being both relaxed and welcoming, forward-looking as well as having a strong sense of history and tradition. And being part of the Eurozone, it is an attractive location for many in Europe. In fact, the country's appeal is wider thanks to an Irish diaspora in North America and Australia that identifies strongly with it – it is a country with friends around the world.

UNITED KINGDOM
The UK's conservatoires all award degrees which are accredited by universities, and course structure and content is conceived along university lines, albeit with a focus on practical performance. The closeness of the systems means that many students do first degrees at university, only auditioning for postgraduate courses after that. Undergraduate degrees are generally awarded after 4 years' study, with postgraduate courses (masters or postgraduate diplomas) after a further 1 or 2 years.

Conservatoires are partially funded by government and are theoretically independent when it comes to curriculum and course content, although institutions' funding is in part subject to satisfactory results in quality control exercises so there is some measure of central control. A proportion of funding is also dependent on a conservatoire demonstrating that a certain percentage (75%) of its graduates are employable within music.

IRELAND
Ireland operates a 2-cycle system with a 4-year undergraduate period leading to bachelors degree (BMus or BA, depending on the institution and course content) followed by 1-year or 2-year postgraduate (MMus or MA).

BIRMINGHAM

City in central England, sometimes known as 'England's second city' thanks to the importance it gained in country's industrial development. Although industrialisation has left its mark, this is not all unpleasant – city is the location for one of the early model towns, Bournville, built for workers at Cadbury's cocoa and chocolate factory; also, many canals pass through it, linking it to the attractive surrounding countryside. Architecture largely reflects 18th and 19th century importance, with new developments replacing some of the uglier post-war constructions. Well connected to other cities in the UK, both north (Manchester, Glasgow) and south (Oxford, London).

Musical life

Over past 20 years, has developed a strong musical identity through the City of Birmingham Symphony Orchestra (and its associated chorus). Orchestra's main venue is Symphony Hall, renowned for its good acoustics; sister venue is recently renovated Birmingham Town Hall (both have non-classical performances). Orchestra is actually based at CBSO Centre with 300-seat performance space and rehearsal facilities. Orchestra of the Swan is nearby chamber orchestra based in nearby Stratford-upon-Avon with frequent concerts in Birmingham and surrounding counties. Contemporary music from Birmingham Contemporary Music Group. Adrian Boult Hall is conservatoire's hall but public concerts held there. Ballet at Birmingham Hippodrome (English National Ballet); no city opera house, but Birmingham Opera Company specialises in performing opera in unusual locations. Concerts at Birmingham Cathedral and Barber Institute of Fine Arts; close to Warwick Arts Centre in Coventry for further classical concerts.

Other cultural information

Birmingham Repertory Theatre and Old Rep Theatre are main venues for drama; also the Alexandra and Hippodrome receiving venues. Several galleries and exhibitions – main city museum and gallery has large collection of pre-Raphaelite paintings; art deco Barber Institute for early 20th century art; jewellery quarter has its own museum. Also botanical gardens.

Festivals and events

Early music festival in autumn, jazz festival in Jul. ArtsFest is a weekend in Sep of free performing arts events across the city. City's multicultural population reflected in various community festivals.

Tourist information

www.visitbirmingham.com; +44 121 202 5115

BIRMINGHAM CONSERVATOIRE

Paradise Place, Birmingham B3 3HG.
t: +44 121 331 5901 f: +44 121 331 5906
e: conservatoire@bcu.ac.uk w: www.conservatoire.bcu.ac.uk

Courses Undergrad courses in music and jazz, both with option to include PGCE; bespoke undergrad, conversion and postgrad jazz courses; postgrad performance-only courses (inc part time, intensive and professional level). Postgraduate Diploma and MMus combine advanced study in performance, jazz, composition, community music or musicology with academic programme. MPhil/PhD offered full-time, part-time or distance learning. Joint courses offered in popular music, music tech and digital arts in performance. *Application requirements* All candidates: English language skills equivalent to IELTS 6.0, except PGCert (Specialist Performance) (IELTS 5.5) and MMus (IELTS 6.5). All applicants auditioned and/or interviewed. Undergrad: practical skills equivalent to ABRSM gr 8 (distinction), plus academic qualifications suitable for entry into higher education in home country. Postgrad: first degree plus practical skills. *Term dates* Late Sep-mid Dec (autumn term); mid Jan-mid Mar (spring term); mid Apr-end Jun (summer term). *Application deadline* 1 Oct via www.cukas.ac.uk; late applications accepted until 31 Aug for courses/areas with vacancies (please contact if applying after 1 Feb). *Fees* £3145 pa for UK undergrads, subject to confirmation; £12,500 pa for full time overseas students (undergrad and postgrad). *Scholarships* Variety of scholarships available, awarded on merit. Further details available on website. *Exchange details* Exchange partnerships with Vienna University of Performing Arts, Koninklijk Conservatorium (Belgium), Prague Academy of Music and Performing Arts, Lyon Conservatoire, Paris Conservatoire, Leipzig Hochschule fur Musik und Theater, Weimar Hochschule fur Musik,

Royal Welsh College of Music & Drama
Coleg Brenhinol Cerdd a Drama Cymru

NATIONAL CONSERVATOIRE OF WALES

This year the Royal Welsh College of Music & Drama will celebrate its 60th birthday by hosting a year long calendar of prestigious events including a masterclass with Sir James Galway and a performance of Beethoven's 9th Symphony led by Sir Charles Mackerras. The College will become the first All-Steinway Conservatoire within the UK as it takes delivery of 62 new pianos.

2010 will see the opening of the £22.5 million new campus with a suite of world class training and performance facilities. Be one of the first to experience these new facilities and perform in the 450 seat concert hall.

Undergraduate Programmes

BMus (Hons)
BMus (Hons) Jazz

Postgraduate Programmes

PGDip in Music
MA Music Performance
MA Choral Conducting
MA Jazz
MMus
MMus in Creative Music Technology
by Distance Learning
MPhil/PhD Music

discover more at **rwcmd.ac.uk**

Norwegian State Academy of Music, Krakow Academy of Music, University of Music Bucharest, Malmo Academy of Music; also Crane School of Music (USA). *Language requirements* English (as per entrance requirements). *Music facilities* 520 seat Adrian Boult Hall, Recital Hall (set up for performance with live electronics), 6 recording studios, music library. Extensive events run by the conservatoire as well as other organisations. *Accommodation* Some assistance available through Birmingham City University accommodation services dept; see www.bcu.ac.uk/accommodation for full details. *No of students* 548 students, of whom 57 from EU countries, and 39 outside EU.

CARDIFF

Welsh capital on the south coast of the country with a population of over 300,000. Developed as a port, particularly servicing the once dominant Welsh coal industry. Although that industry has declined, city has remained prosperous, with recent redevelopments on Cardiff Bay (including the Welsh Assembly building) and city centre giving it the appearance of a smart modern place. This has helped give the city a lively nightlife, popular among students and young people.

♪ Musical life
Centre for musical activity is the dramatic sea-front Wales Millennium Centre. Includes opera house, home to Welsh National Opera (main theatre and 2 smaller spaces) and Wales's main orchestra BBC National Orchestra of Wales in recently completed Hoddinott Hall (350-seat space) plus studio, practice rooms and backstage facilities. Music Theatre Wales produces range of contemporary opera and staged music for touring. Main concert hall is St David's Hall, staging a range of live entertainment as well as classical music. University's concert hall has regular classical performances from visiting soloists and ensembles as well as student performances. National Museum Wales has various music projects alongside its art exhibitions. Wales (though not Cardiff in particular) has strong choral tradition, especially male voice choirs. Also lively rock scene: International Arena venue for large-scale rock and pop.

🏛 Other cultural information
Chapter is a modern arts venue focusing on film and theatre/dance performance (there are 3 theatre spaces), plus workshop spaces. The Gate is a smaller venue based around a 350-seat performance space. National Museum covers art, history and archaeology, especially focusing on Wales. Sherman Theatre for standard theatrical productions. For many in Wales, the main national cultural activity is rugby, and the national stadium (the Millennium Stadium) is close to city centre.

🎟 Festivals and events
Cardiff Singer of the World one of the most important international events (biennial, odd years). Annual Welsh Proms at St David's Hall features orchestras from Wales and beyond.

ℹ Tourist information
www.visitcardiff.com; visitor@cardiff.gov.uk; tel: +44 870 1211 258

ROYAL WELSH COLLEGE OF MUSIC & DRAMA
Castle Grounds, Cathays Park, Cardiff CF10 3ER.
t: 02920 391361 *f:* 02920 391305 *e:* music.admissions@rwcmd.ac.uk *w:* www.rwcmd.ac.uk
Contact Jennifer Grey, admission officer. *Courses* BMus (Hons) music, PGDip in music, MA in music performance, MMus, MMus in creative technology (by distance learning), MPhil/PhD; also MA in music therapy. *Application requirements* For PGDip a good honours degree or equivalent (not necessarily in music). For MMus and MA, upper second class degree in music with significant practical or creative component, or university degree plus significant practical diploma in music. Overseas students require appropriate level of English proficiency (see website for details). *Term dates* Sep 2009-Jul 2010 *Application deadline* 1 Oct. *Fees* £2680-5130 (UK and EU students), depending on course (MMus in creative music tech, to be confirmed); £2030 for MA in music therapy. *Scholarships* A number of scholarships available to outstanding applicants on the basis of audition. Worth up to full value of tuition. *Music facilities* Open-air courtyard performance space, 3 recital rooms, 50 practice/teaching studios containing a large number of upright and grand pianos; collection of period instruments; recording studio; library including

internet, audio-visual facilities, Sibelius score-writing workstations. *Accommodation* Halls of residence nearby; student services dept provides one-to-one service to help all students find suitable accommodation. *No of students* 640 students in total (inc overseas students).

GLASGOW

Scotland's largest city, though not its capital, on river Clyde towards the country's west coast. Formerly a major shipbuilding city (further downriver at the city's port) and trading port. From 1960s onwards, decline in traditional industries led to downturn in fortunes, but from 1980s on, investment brought about significant regeneration. Now shipbuilding still active, alongside service, high tech and research industries. City is birthplace of art nouveau designer, architect and artist Charles Rennie Mackintosh; many examples of his characterful buildings across city in among numerous other Victorian buildings. In general, local sandstone of buildings give a distinctive character to the place.

Musical life

Although not the Scottish capital, has many advantages over Edinburgh as far as classical music goes. Well-regarded Scottish Opera housed at Theatre Royal. The 2 main symphony orchestras based there: Royal Scottish National Orchestra has Royal Concert Hall as its home; BBC Scottish Symphony Orchestra based at renovated City Halls and has radio studios for broadcasts. Scottish Ensemble is smaller group; city also receives visits from Edinburgh-based Scottish Chamber Orchestra; contemporary music from Paragon Ensemble. All perform in venues around Scotland.

Other cultural information

Centre for Contemporary Arts is home to Scottish Ensemble, but has a wider cultural remit to promote new and experimental performance and film. Various places where Charles Rennie Mackintosh's work (buildings and interiors as well as artefacts) is on display. One of these buildings, the Lighthouse, now a centre for architecture and design. Kelvingrove gallery and museum and Hunterian museum 2 major institutions.

Festivals and events

City shares festival of British Youth Orchestras with Edinburgh. Celtic Connections a major celebration across the city at the start of the year of Scottish music in its various forms. Jazz festival in Jun; comedy festival in Mar.

Tourist information

www.visitscotland.com; tel: +0845 22 55 121

ROYAL SCOTTISH ACADEMY OF MUSIC AND DRAMA

100 Renfrew St, Glasgow G2 3DB.
t: +44 141 332 4101 *f:* +44 141 332 8909
e: registry@rsamd.ac.uk; s.hallam@rsamd.ac.uk
w: www.rsamd.ac.uk
Contact Sherelyn Hallam, international student advisor *Courses* Bachelors courses including music, Scottish music, music education, musical theatre, modern ballet; postgrad courses, including music, opera, musical theatre; research degrees (MPhil and PhD) validated by University of St Andrews. *Application requirements* 3 subjects at higher grade or passes in 2 at Advanced HIgher or appropriate Scottish Group award, or passes in 2 A Levels or recognised equivalents. Audition dates to be confirmed, usually 2 week period at start of Nov. *Term dates* Late Sep-late Jun 2010. *Fees* £1542-9000 (UK students, depending on course); £5922-13,824 (overseas students). *Scholarships* A number of entrance scholarships awarded as part of the audition/selection process on the basis of merit *Exchange details* Exchange programmes run through Erasmus. *Music facilities* Wide range of fully equipped teaching facilities, rehearsal and practice rooms, organ room, classrooms and lecture theatre, recording studio, electronic music workshop; concert hall (360 seats), recital hall (100 seats). *Accommodation* Academy keeps a list of private accommodation; halls of residence nearby. *No of students* 656 home and EU students; 128 international students.

UK & IRELAND

LEEDS

West Yorkshire city which grew into importance due to the range of industries based there in 17-19th centuries. Prosperity of the city at this time reflected in monumental buildings such as town hall, but also its characteristic ornate shopping arcades in the city centre. Now home to several higher education institutions and a popular city for students to stay.

Musical life

Principal music performing organisation is Opera North, based at the Grand Theatre and Opera House. Acts as 2 organisations in one as the opera orchestra also performs widely at concert series in the city (Leeds International Concert Season) and the region. Howard Assembly Room features wide range of music from classical to folk. Classical and contemporary dance at Northern Ballet Theatre (tours widely).

Other cultural information

Henry Moore Institute sculpture centre includes collections and changing exhibitions; City Art Gallery also has substantial sculpture collection among its collections. Saltaire, just outside city, is Unesco world heritage site, includes art gallery (Salt's Mill). For theatre, West Yorkshire Playhouse very highly regarded.

Festivals and events

Leeds piano, conducting and Lieder competitions (one a year in rotation) are major events in musical calendar. Shakespeare Festival in Jul; annual film festival in Nov. Leeds Festival weekend of rock at end of Aug.

Tourist information

www.leedsliveitloveit.com; tourinfo@leeds.gov.uk; tel: +44 113 242 5242

LEEDS COLLEGE OF MUSIC

3 Quarry Hill, Leeds LS2 7PD.
t: +44 113 222 3400 f: +44 113 243 8798
e: enquiries@lcm.ac.uk w: www.lcm.ac.uk
Courses Foundation degrees in music production for film and TV, and commercial music production; bachelor's in music, jazz, popular music studies, music production; Application requirements Applications through CUKAS. Audition for performance courses; overseas auditions possible

in China, Hong Kong, Japan, Norway, USA. Fees £1570-3900 (home/EU), £1832-9800 (international), depending on course level. Scholarships Various awards available; see website for details. Music facilities 350-seat concert venue, extensive library, 24-track digital recording studios and edit suites, computer composition studio, Cubase lab, learning resource centre, large collection of instruments (including Indian andCaribbean), archive of jazz and pop. Accommodation Accommodation for new students provided; accommodation office advises on housing for others.

LONDON

Capital city whose importance dates back to Roman times. Location on river Thames gave it great significance as trading port, and this in turn attracted people from around the world to work there. Today has become one of the most international cities, not only in terms of business and trade, but the variety of nationalities and cultures represented. Conurbation itself (Greater London) is home to over 8 million people and spreads over a number of local districts many of which have distinctive characteristics. Large number of students (approx 200,000) from all over the world at various institutions.

Musical life

5 major symphony orchestras based there (London Symphony, London Philharmonic, Philharmonia, Royal Philharmonic, BBC Symphony Orchestra), but plenty of smaller ones too; 2 opera houses (Royal Opera and English National Opera), and various venues. Barbican Centre and Southbank Centre are all-round arts centres, the latter with 3 concert halls of different sizes; Royal Albert Hall stages large-scale popular classical music and opera as well as orchestral concerts; medium sized venues such as Cadogan Hall and St John's Smith Square, plus smaller halls for prestigious recitals and chamber music, eg Wigmore Hall, LSO St Lukes and newly opened Kings Place; regular performances of music in churches, especially in City of London, but also West End (eg St James's Piccadilly or St Martin-in-the-Fields) and in local districts.

Other cultural information

As well as theatre and dance events at the Southbank (National Theatre) and Barbican, West

British & International
The most comprehensive classified

British & International
Music Yearbook **09**

NEW
EDITION
OUT NOW

RHINEGOLD
PUBLISHING

CADOGAN HALL
London's Award Winning Concert Hall

Cadogan Hall in Chelsea is fast becoming one of the UK's principal concert venues with a reputation for presenting world class orchestras, artists, ensembles, gala shows and events in an intimate, critically acclaimed and award-winning environment. The hall has a 900 seat auditorium, comfortable reception rooms and is very easily accessed by public transport, being only a short walk away from Sloane Square tube station and close to Victoria mainline station.

Student tickets are available at £10 or less for most concerts. Please call the Box Office for details.

Highlights of the 2009/10 season include:

Prague Symphony Orchestra
Tallis Scholars
Orquesta Nacional de España
Norwegian Chamber Orchestra
The King's Singers
Czech Philharmonic Orchestra
Royal Philharmonic Orchestra
and many more recitals, semi staged opera and contemporary and world music events.

Please call the Box Office on **020 7730 4500** to order the latest brochure or go to our website: **www.cadoganhall.com**

Cadogan Hall, Sloane Terrace, London SW1X 9DQ

Royal Academy of Music

'an outstanding disc'
Gramophone, February '09

'surely a glimpse of heaven'
Evening Standard, February '09

'excellent young talent'
The Times, November '08

'an immense achievement'
The Guardian, November '08

'performances were excellent'
Sunday Times, February '08

Study at Britain's senior conservatoire

President: **HRH The Duchess of Gloucester** GCVO   Principal: **Jonathan Freeman-Attwood**

www.ram.ac.uk   Marylebone Road, London NW1 5HT   Telephone 020 7873 7373

The Royal Academy of Music — Britain's senior conservatoire

The Royal Academy of Music is synonymous with the best in British music. Since 1822 many of the world's most distinguished performers and composers have studied here. Our teaching represents a gold standard which was recognised in our role as Britain's 'pre-eminent conservatoire' in Beijing's Olympics celebrations.

Academy graduates work with leading orchestras, opera companies and chamber ensembles; have major careers in television and the media; contribute vitally to musical theatre, pop, music for film, television and the web, world music, and cross-over genres. Over 90% of recent Academy graduates are actively making their living in music.

The Academy's ever-expanding list of distinguished alumni includes Sir Richard Rodney Bennett, Sir Harrison Birtwistle, John Dankworth, Lesley Garrett, Dame Evelyn Glennie, Sir Elton John, Philip Langridge, Annie Lennox, Dame Felicity Lott, Joanna MacGregor, Nicholas Maw, Michael Nyman, Sir Simon Rattle and Jean Rigby. Alumni from previous generations include Sir Arthur Sullivan, Sir Henry Wood, Dame Myra Hess, Dame Eva Turner, Dennis Brain, Sir John Barbirolli, Sir Clifford Curzon and Dame Moura Lympany. Recent graduates include the music director of English National Opera Edward Gardner, chart-topping soprano Katherine Jenkins, and singer/pianist Myleene Klass. Appointments in early 2009 include Denis Bouriakov, Principal Flute Metropolitan Opera in New York; Dominic Seldis, Principal Double Bass Royal Concertgebouw Orchestra, Amsterdam; and Adam Walker, Principal Flute London Philharmonic Orchestra.

Our student body is an extraordinarily rich mixture of gifted individuals from over 60 countries. In the 2008 National Student Survey (NSS), the Academy was ranked second in the whole of the UK for student satisfaction. The 2008 Research Assessment Exercise rated 70% of the Academy's research activity as either 'world-leading' or 'internationally excellent', while a further 25% was rated as 'of international significance'.

The Academy hires the very best musicians as teachers: recent recruits include Dame Felicity Lott, Chevalier Jose Cura, Pierre-Laurent Aimard, Jane Glover and Sarah Walker. Sir Colin Davis, Sir Charles Mackerras, Dame Kiri te Kanawa, Barbara Bonney, Trevor Pinnock and other international stars have recently worked at the Academy.

We would be delighted to introduce you to the Academy in the best way possible: at one of our exceptional performances. To find out more, visit **www.ram.ac.uk**.

Professor Jonathan Freeman-Attwood
Principal, Royal Academy of Music

End is an area of central London with large concentration of theatres covering range of styles from new writing to musicals. Large range of galleries: National Gallery for all-round collection, riverside Tate galleries (one focusing on modern, one on British art); Royal Academy for high-profile changing exhibitions. Also museums focusing on various subjects from London history, British and world culture (British Museum) to design (Victoria and Albert), science and nature.

Festivals and events
BBC Proms (throughout summer) is one of world's largest classical music events; Spitalfields Festival (Jun and Dec) and City of London Festivals (Jun) both in historic centre of the capital. Various specialist events, eg Lufthansa Festival of Baroque Music (May); chamber music at London String Quartet Week; KlezFest for various aspects of Jewish music. Festivals in different boroughs: Hampstead and Highgate Festival in north (May); Chelsea Festival in west (Jun); Dulwich Festival in south (May). Many events arranged celebrating different cultures living in London.

Tourist information
www.visitlondon.com

GUILDHALL SCHOOL OF MUSIC & DRAMA
Silk St, London EC2Y 8DT.
t: +44 20 7628 2571 f: +44 20 7256 9438
e: music@gsmd.ac.uk w: www.gsmd.ac.uk
Courses BMus, MPerf, MComp, MMus, PGDip, DMus, MMA/DMA, MA in Music Therapy. Application requirements See website for full application details and course content. Term dates Mid Sep-early Dec; mid Jan-early Apr; late Apr-mid Jul. Application deadline 1 Oct. Fees See website for details. Scholarships See website. Music facilities Practice facilities within school, plus annexe with 46 further practice studios; theatre equipped for opera production. As part of Barbican Centre, school has developed links with London Symphony Orchestra, with opportunities for school's performers to give concerts in the hall. Accommodation 178 places in school's hall of residence; advice on other accommodation available. No of students Approx 40% of total students from overseas.

LONDON COLLEGE OF MUSIC, THAMES VALLEY UNIVERSITY
t: +44 20 8231 2304; +44 20 8231 2706 (international office) f: +44 20 8231 5646
e: music@tvu.ac.uk w: http://music.tvu.ac.uk
Courses Courses in music (performance/composition), Sikh/Indian classical music, popular music performance, music technology, sound engineering and production, composing for theatre, composing for film/TV, artist management, media health, audio technology.

ROYAL ACADEMY OF MUSIC
Marylebone Rd, London NW1 5HT.
t: +44 20 7873 7373 f: +44 20 7873 7374
e: registry@ram.ac.uk w: www.ram.ac.uk
Contact Edward Kemp-Luck, international admissions officer. Courses BMus (undergrad), MA, MMus, PhD. Application requirements RAM is not member of CUKAS; see website for full application details. Term dates Early Sep-late Nov; early Jan-mid Mar; mid Apr-end Jun. Application deadline 1 Oct, except 7 Jan for MPhil, conducting, choral conducting, and for N America auditions. Fees BMus: £3145 (home/EU), £15,500 (international); MA: £7600 (home/EU), £16,200 (international); MMus: £7600 (home/EU), £16,500 (international). For other fees, see website. Scholarships Many scholarships available; see website for details. Exchange details Exchange partnerships with many conservatoires across the world, both under Socrates-Erasmus scheme, and also individual arrangements with institutions in N America, Australia, Japan and Europe (non Socrates-Erasmus). Music facilities 100 teaching and practice rooms, Sir Jack Lyons Theatre, concert room, recital room, electronic studios, creative technology lab, well-stocked library. Main concert hall is Duke's Hall (seats 400). Accommodation Student accommodation primarily for 1st year students No of students Approx 650 students, inc about 50% from overseas.

ROYAL COLLEGE OF MUSIC
Prince Consort Rd, London SW7 2BS.
t: 020 7589 3643 f: 020 7589 7740 e: info@rcm.ac.uk; international@rcm.ac.uk w: www.rcm.ac.uk
Contact Darren Clark. Courses BMus(Hons), integrated Masters programme (including Masters

UK & IRELAND

and PG Dip), artist diploma in opera studies, graduate diploma (singer), artist diploma, DMus. *Application requirements* Extremely high standard of performance at audition. A Level (or equivalent) music at grade C or higher plus one other subject; for EU/overseas students, equivalent home qualifications accepted. For Grad Dip/Masters programmes, bachelors degree or equivalent required; for Artist Diploma, postgrad qualification with distinction. For DMus, taught Masters required. EU/overseas students whose first language is not English must gain IELTS at Level 6 (or acceptable equivalent) before beginning studies. *Term dates* Mid Sep-mid Dec (autumn term); mid Jan-late Mar (spring term); mid Apr-mid Jul 2010 (summer term). *Application deadline* 1 Oct . *Fees* £3145-8726 pa depending on course (home/EU students); £8665-15,780 pa depending on course (overseas students). *Scholarships* All applicants who audition in person will be considered for a scholarship; scholarships (up to full value of tuition fees) awarded based on standard of performance. *Exchange details* Exchange partnerships with Conservatorium van Amsterdam, Hochschule der Künste Berlin, Koninklijk Muziekconservatorium Brussels, Hochschule fur Music Köln, Koninklijk Conservatorium den Haag, Musikhochschule Karlsruhe, Norges Musikkhogskole Oslo, Conservatoire de Paris, Academy of Performing Arts Prague, Universität Mozarteum Salzburg, Kungliga Musikhogskolen i Stockholm, Staatliche Hochschule fur Musik und darstellende Kunst Stuttgart, Hogeschool voor de Kunsten Utrecht, Universität für Musik und darstellende Kunst Wien, Lietuvos Muzikos ir Teatro Akademija, Lemmensinstituut Leuven, Conservatoire de Lyon, Manhattan School of Music, New England Conservatory, Eastman School of Music, Sydney Conservatory of Music, Queensland Conservatory of Musi. *Music facilities* 2 concert halls, opera theatre, electroacoustic and recording studio, museum housing and displaying college's collection of historical instruments, large number of teaching studios and practice rooms, 3-manual Walker organ; library and reading room, listening facilities. *Accommodation* 180 places in hall of residence; student services advise on other accommodation available. *No of students* 340 national and 349 international students.

TRINITY COLLEGE OF MUSIC

King Charles Court, Old Royal Naval College, Greenwich, London SE10 9JF.
t: +44 20 8305 4444 *f:* +44 20 8305 9444
e: enquiries@tcm.ac.uk *w:* www.tcm.ac.uk
Courses Foundation degree in musical theatre; bachelor of music performance; bachelor of music, Indian music; various flexible courses possible from pre-undergrad to postgrad level, tailored to personal interests and needs of individuals; PGCE 'Musicians in Education'; master of music performance/composition/creative practice; postgrad advanced diploma *Application requirements* Most courses available for online application via CUKAS. *Application deadline* 1 Oct. *Fees* £700-7200 (home/EU), £700-14,700 (overseas), depending on course. *Exchange details* Exchange partnerships with institutions in Austria, Czech Republic, Denmark, France, Germany, Italy, Netherlands, Norway, Spain, Sweden. *Music facilities* Practice facilities; Blackheath Halls college's own concert venue. Library and resource centre, audio-visual facilities, Sibelius software. *Accommodation* Guaranteed place in halls of residence for all 1st year students; warden's office and students' union provide advice on finding private accommodation. *No of students* Approx 600 students.

MANCHESTER

Vies with Birmingham for unofficial title of England's 'second city'; located in north west of England. Like most major UK cities, its history linked to industrial revolution; in Manchester's case, city a centre for the country's textile industry, and city linked closely to political development of the country from then on (it was home to the young Engels, and his experiences there helped shape his radical political ideas). Also as with other cities, it went into decline only to undergo significant regeneration projects. Large number of students attracted to its major higher educational establishments not to mention its legendary nightlife

♪ Musical life

Very active city musically. 3 major orchestras: Hallé, based at Bridgewater Hall (over 2300 seats), is one of Britain's most respected groups; BBC Philharmonic is the broadcaster's northern England orchestra, based in the city and performing at

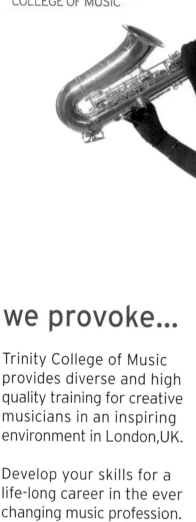

TRINITY
COLLEGE OF MUSIC

we provoke...

Trinity College of Music
provides diverse and high
quality training for creative
musicians in an inspiring
environment in London, UK.

Develop your skills for a
life-long career in the ever
changing music profession.
www.tcm.ac.uk/study

TRINITYLABAN
conservatoire of
music and dance

'Trinity College of Music will help you become the very best musician you can be. Whether you aspire to be a soloist, chamber musician, member of an orchestra or a portfolio musician, our experienced teachers and coaches will guide and nurture your musical development in what is surely one of the most beautiful locations in the world. This combination provides our students with a truly inspirational environment in which to study; a vibrant, supportive and above all happy musical community.'
Nic Pendlebury, Head of String Faculty at Trinity College of Music

Why study in the UK?
- Gain recognised,respected qualifications
- Improve your English
- Study in the way that suits you best
- Gain the skills and qualities employers want
- Enjoy a multicultural experience

Why Trinity?
We offer a variety of unique courses at undergraduate and postgraduate level, with every programme focused on developing Principal Study skills to the highest possible standard whilst enabling students to develop complementary skills.

As a student at Trinity College of Music you become part of an exciting, vibrant and supportive community of musicians. In its unique setting of the Old Royal Naval College, students benefit from beautiful surroundings whilst having the advantage of being only 30 minutes away from the bustle and vibrancy of central London.

Greenwich is a bustling town with a cosmopolitan atmosphere. With numerous restaurants, shops, and historical sites, as well as a thriving market and a royal park, it delights both locals and tourists at all times of the year.

London is the UK's most diverse and multicultural city with 300 languages spoken among its 7 million residents. The inclusive environment of Trinity College of Music provides students with a sense of community within a cosmopolitan city. With twice as many museums as Paris or New York, 120 historic buildings, 150 theatres, 8,000 acres of parkland, 37,000 listed buildings and four world heritage sites (including Trinity's own building and surroundings) you will never be short of things to see and do.

Over 85% Trinity College of Music Graduates are currently working as professional musicians, with 90% overall employed in the arts, education or community work.

For more information on all of our courses and life at Trinity College of Music, please visit our website:
www.tcm.ac.uk/study

Feel the passion for musical creativity

To find out more about RNCM Life
Visit our website www.rncm.ac.uk
Come along to an Open Day
Call +44 (0)161 907 5297 for a Prospectus

RNCM

ROYAL NORTHERN COLLEGE *of* MUSIC

Studio 7 concert hall studio; Manchester Camerata a chamber orchestra giving concerts in various venues in the city and the region more widely. Opera comes mostly through tours to the Lowry Lyric Theatre in nearby Salford. Various concert and recital series at these and other venues (eg Manchester Cathedral). As well as to the senior music college, city is home to specialist music school, Chetham's, whose students give regular performances in and around the city.

Other cultural information

Royal Exchange Theatre for drama (unusual in that main theatre is in the round venue; also 2 smaller spaces). Cube is city-based museum exploring Manchester's architectural history; Whitworth Art Gallery has substantial collection of British watercolours among other artworks, and received numerous changing exhibitions; Manchester Art Gallery located in Victorian building. The Lowry is an arts centre in nearby Salford, with 2 theatres and performing arts studio alongside art exhibitions.

Festivals and events

Wide range of events with musical side. Manchester International Festival is a broad arts festival consisting entirely of new work (biennial, odd years). Manchester International Piano Competition an annual event combining competitive element with showcase for young performers.

Tourist information

www.visitmanchester.com; touristinformation@ marketing-manchester.co.uk; tel: +44 871 222 8223

ROYAL NORTHERN COLLEGE OF MUSIC

124 Oxford Rd, Manchester M13 9RD.
t: +44 161 907 5200 *f:* +44 161 273 7611
e: admissions@rncm.ac.uk; international@rncm.ac.uk *w:* www.rncm.ac.uk
Contact Tatyana Yekimova, international officer. *Courses* Bachelor degree in music, foundation degree in popular music practice (session musician); postgrad masters degrees and diplomas in performance and composition; professional courses leading to RNCM international artist diploma (solo course, chamber music course, opera studio); MPhil and DPhil; PGCE in music with specialist instrumental

teaching. *Application requirements* High level of performing/composing ability; for overseas students, standard of general education comparable to UK candidates, and high enough standard of English. *Term dates* Mid Sep-mid Dec (autumn term); early Jan-end Mar (spring term); mid Apr-early Jul (summer term). *Application deadline* 1 Oct, but some flexibility for international students in particular. *Fees* £3145-7150 (UK & EU students, depending on course); £13,150-14,300 (Isle of Man, Channel Islands and non-EU students). Note that figures are for 2008-09 year, and are reviewed annually. *Scholarships* Some scholarships available to those demonstrating outstanding ability and potential at audition. Postgrad and non-EU applicants may apply for limited number of bursaries towards fees and maintenance, made on the basis of need; students expected to undertake activities for benefit of the college. *Exchange details* Links with institutions throughout Europe and in Australia, China, Japan and USA. Full list available on website. *Music facilities* Opera theatre; concert hall with Hradetsky organ; extensive library with IT, listening and video facilities; over 80 tutorial spaces and practice rooms; over 120 pianos. Professional development dept arranges external work for students. *Accommodation* 316 rooms in halls of residence; help available finding private accommodation. *No of students* 495 UK students, 51 EU students, 99 overseas students, 9 from islands.

MUSIC FESTIVALS

4th British International Male Voice Choral Festival Cornwall 1 Gloucester Rd, Sawtry, Huntingdon. *t:* 01487 830089 *e:* peter.davies@ abcd.org.uk *w:* www.cimvcf.org.uk *Contact* Peter Davies, festival dir. The largest male voice choral festival in Europe with competitions, symposia and workshops. Over 60 male voice choirs from the UK and across the world participate in concerts and festival activities all across Cornwall, at Truro Cathedral and at the Hall for Cornwall.
Abbotsbury Music Festival PO Box 5968, Abbotsbury, Weymouth. *t:* 01305 871475 *e:* info@ abbmusic.org.uk *w:* www.abbmusic.org.uk; www.st-catherine.org.uk *Contact* Barbara Laurie. Outdoor professional opera in a hotel garden in Abbotsbury, a village of mainly 16th C houses situated on the heritage Jurassic coast in W Dorset. Picnics allowed.

Aberdeen International Youth Festival Custom House, 35 Regent Quay, Aberdeen. *t:* 01224 213800 *f:* 01224 641122 *e:* info@aiyf.org *w:* www.aiyf.org *Contact* Stewart Aitken. One of the world's largest young people's multi-arts festivals with perfs and w/shops attracting up to 1000 participants from the UK and around the world. Participation is through application; all art forms and music genres considered. Events in Aberdeen city, Aberdeenshire and across the NE of Scotland.

Aberystwyth Musicfest - International Festival and Summer School Aberystwyth Arts Centre, Penglais, Aberystwyth. *t:* 01970 622338 *f:* 01970 622883 *e:* musicfest@aber.ac.uk *w:* www. abermusicfest.org *Contact* Sophie Bennett, co-ord Bursaries available for summer school, applications by May.

acoustICA Series at the ICA London c/o CAE/L, PO Box 27838, London. *t:* 07962 521330 *f:* 0870 051 7527 *e:* info@caelondon.org *w:* www. caelondon.org *Contact* Rachel McCarthy, admin; Sinan Savaskan, artistic dir.

Adur Festival Adur District Council, Civic Centre, Ham Rd, Shoreham-by-the-Sea. *t:* 01273 263274 *f:* 01273 263027 *e:* pamela.driscoll@adur.gov.uk *w:* www.adurfestival.com *Contact* Pamela Driscoll, artistic dir. Community-based with a balance of high quality professional and amateur performances and events.

Aldeburgh Festival of Music and the Arts Aldeburgh Music, Snape Maltings Concert Hall, Snape, Saxmundham. *t:* 01728 687100 *f:* 01728 687120 *e:* enquiries@aldeburgh.co.uk *w:* www. aldeburgh.co.uk *Contact* Hettie Hope, artistic admin; Marc Ernesti, head of mktg & media.

Amersham Festival of Music Ranmoor, Croft Rd, Chalfont St Peter. *t:* 01753 884628 *w:* www. amershamfestival.org *Contact* Iain Ledingham, artistic dir; Lynda Weiss, chair.

Annual Festival of New Organ Music. *w:* www. afnom.org Festival for composers to submit compositions for performance, discussion and sale.

ArtsFest Environment & Culture - Events Section, House of Sport, 300 Broad St, Birmingham. *t:* 0121 464 5678 *e:* Elise_duncan@birmingham.gov.uk *w:* www.artsfest.org.uk *Contact* Elise Duncan, festival co-ord Annual event produced by Birmingham City Council. All activity within city centre, indoors and outdoors. To help break down barriers to the arts, all events free, with no pre-booking, usually lasting only 30 mins.

Ashbourne Festival St John's Community Hall, King St, Ashbourne. *t:* 01335 348707 *e:* info@ ashbournearts.com *w:* www.ashbournearts.com *Contact* Ann Rosser, vice chair, Ashbourne Arts. An eclectic mix of performances and exhibitions.

Autumn in Malvern Festival 42 Worcester Rd, Great Malvern. *t:* 01684 569721 *e:* petersmith@ musicinuk.com *w:* www.malvernfestival.co.uk *Contact* Peter Smith, artistic dir. Classical music-based with strong literary and visual arts element. Features established and emerging artists.

Bangor New Music Festival The School of Music, University of Wales, Bangor. *t:* 01248 382181 *e:* g.j.cotterill@bangor.ac.uk *w:* www.bangor.ac. uk/music/festival

Banstead Arts Festival Little Hilden, Park Rd, Banstead. *t:* 01737 352098 *w:* www.bansteadarts. co.uk *Contact* Stephen Oliver, artistic dir, chair; EA Smith, sec; Gerald Baines, treas. Annual festival featuring lunchtime concerts, exhibitions, walks, talks, coach visits and a wide variety of evening events and music from jazz to chmbr music.

Barmouth Arts Festival 1 Epworth Terrace, Barmouth, Gwynedd. *t:* 01341 280392 *w:* www. barmouthartsfestival.co.uk *Contact* Mair Jones, sec. Annual festival of varied programme.

Bath International Music Festival Bath Festivals Trust, Abbey Chambers, Kingston Buildings, Bath. *t:* 01225 462231 *f:* 01225 445551 *e:* info@ bathfestivals.org.uk *w:* www.bathmusicfest.org.uk *Contact* Joanna MacGregor, artistic dir; Nod Knowles, CEO. International festival of classical, jazz, world, contemporary, traditional and electronic music, featuring collaborations and commissions.

Bath Mozartfest 110 Gloucester Ave, London. *t:* 020 7483 2681 *f:* 020 7586 5343 *e:* sarah. gordon@easynet.co.uk *w:* www.bathmozartfest. org.uk *Contact* Sarah Gordon, admin; Amelia Freedman, artistic dir. 10 day festival of chmbr, orch and choral works by Mozart and akin composers.

BBC Proms Room 330, Henry Wood House, 3-6 Langham Place, London. *t:* 020 7765 5575 *f:* 020 7765 2031 *e:* proms@bbc.co.uk *w:* www.bbc.co. uk/proms *Contact* Roger Wright, artistic dir; Rosemary Gent, artistic admin. Takes place over 2 months every summer at London's Royal Albert Hall.

For every concert, up to 1400 'Promming' (standing) tickets are held back for sale on the day at £5 each.

Beaminster Festival The Yarn Barton Centre, Fleet St, Beaminster. *e:* beamfest@btinternet.com *w:* www.beamfest.org.uk

Beaumaris Festival 6 Lon-y-Celyn, Cardiff. *t:* 01248 810134 *e:* anthony@beaumarisfestival. com *w:* www.beaumarisfestival.com *Contact* Anthony Hose, artistic dir. Music, visual arts, talks, drama, poetry.

Beverley & East Riding Early Music Festival National Centre for Early Music, St Margaret's Church, Walmgate, York. *t:* 01904 632220 *f:* 01904 612631 *e:* info@ncem.co.uk *w:* www. ncem.co.uk *Contact* Delma Tomlin, dir.

Beverley & East Riding Folk Festival The Stables, Westwood House, Main St, North Dalton, Driffield. *t:* 01377 217569 *f:* 01377 217754 *e:* info@ beverleyfestival.com *w:* www.beverleyfestival.com *Contact* Chris Wade, dir. 3-day event offering perfs and w/shops in folk music, world music, contemporary music, dance, comedy, literature and storytelling in historic town of Beverley. Camping facilities and festival village inc a variety of stalls and perf marquees. Esp suitable for families and young people.

Beverley Chamber Music Festival Springfield, Colton, Ulverston. *t:* 01229 861325 *e:* gaildudson@ colton2.demon.co.uk *Contact* Martin Roscoe, artistic dir; Gail Dudson, mgr.

Birmingham Early Music Festival PO Box 9442, Birmingham. *t:* 0121 427 1509 *f:* 0121 427 1511 *e:* Bryce@Somerville2.f9.co.uk *Contact* Bryce Somerville, chair. Brings internationally renowned period music specialists into venues across the city, staging concerts based on an annual theme.

Birmingham International Jazz Festival PO Box 944, Birmingham. *t:* 0121 454 7020 *f:* 0121 454 9996 *e:* festival@bigbearmusic.com *Contact* Jim Simpson, artistic dir; Tim Jennings, asst dir; Steve Kelly, mktg mgr.

Bledington Music Festival 9 Jackson Rd, Bledington, Chipping Norton. *t:* 01608 658669 *e:* enquiries@bledingtonmusicfestival.co.uk *w:* www. bledingtonmusicfestival.co.uk *Contact* Rodney Beacham, festival org; Thomas Trotter, pres; Catrin Finch, vice pres. At St Leonard's Church, Bledington.

Blyth Valley Chamber Music The Box Office, Marshwinds, 32 Saxmundham Rd, Aldeburgh. *t:* 01728 453193 *e:* info@concertsatcratfield.org. uk *w:* www.concertsatcratfield.org.uk

Brechin Arts Festival 34 Park Rd, Brechin. *t:* 07757 888233 *e:* info@brechinartsfestival.org *w:* www.brechinartsfestival.org *Contact* Ruth Leslie Melville, chair. Scotland's largest small-town festival covering both performing and visual arts, but with emphasis on classical and trad music.

Brecon Jazz Lion House, Bethel Sq, Brecon. *t:* 01874 625511, also fax *e:* info@breconjazz. co.uk *w:* www.breconjazz.co.uk *Contact* Catrin Slater, festival admin.

Brighton Festival Festival Office, 12a Pavilion Buildings, Castle Square, Brighton. *t:* 01273 700747 *f:* 01273 707505 *e:* info@brightonfestival. org *w:* www.brightonfestival.org

Brinkburn Music Summer Festival Foundry Lane Studios, Foundry Lane, Newcastle upon Tyne. *t:* 0191 265 7777 *e:* contact@brinkburnmusic.org *w:* www.brinkburnmusic.org

Bromsgrove Festival 10 Evertons Close, Droitwich. *t:* 01905 779852 (home); 01527 575441 (work) *f:* 01527 575366; 01527 574651 *e:* andrewh@ lgharris.co.uk *w:* www.bromsgrovefestival.co.uk *Contact* AD Harris, hon sec.

Buckingham Summer Festival 1 Poplars Close, Preston Bissett. *t:* 01280 848275 *f:* 01280 847363 *e:* robert_secret@fastmail.fm *Contact* Robert Secret, artistic dir. Festival of chmbr music, inst and vocal recitals. Fully professional morning and lunchtime recitals with evening celebrity concerts.

Bude Jazz Festival PO Box 32, Bude. *t:* 01594 516834, also fax *e:* rachelmhayward@yahoo.co.uk *w:* www.budejazzfestival.co.uk *Contact* Rachel Hayward, artistic dir; Jean Manuel, Diana Ohlson, admin.

Bury St Edmunds Festival Borough Offices, Angel Hill, Bury St Edmunds. *t:* 01284 757630 *f:* 01284 757631 *e:* nick.wells@stedsbc.gov.uk *w:* www. buryfestival.co.uk *Contact* Nick Wells, artistic dir. Takes place in a variety of locations. Festival has strong music focus, esp classical and jazz; the programme covers a wide range of art forms inc dance, drama, comedy, walks, talks and exhibitions.

Buxton Festival 3 The Square, Buxton. *t:* 01298 70395 *f:* 01298 72289 *e:* info@buxtonfestival. co.uk *w:* www.buxtonfestival.co.uk *Contact* Andrew

Chetham's International Summer School & Festival for Pianists

Artistic Director: Murray McLachlan

Chetham's
School of Music

Week One: 15-22 August 2009
Week Two: 22-29 August 2009

The Friendliest Piano Summer School in the World!

Faculty includes: Philip Martin, Peter Donohoe, Philippe Cassard, Christopher Elton, Hilary Coates, Song Wen Li (China), Thomas Hecht (USA), Bernard Roberts, Graham Scott, Joan Havill, Radoslav Kvapil (Czech Republic), Vladimir Tropp (Russia)

With daily concerts, masterclasses, lectures, intensive one-to-one coaching, composition, duets, improvisation, jazz, organ and musical appreciation.

For further information call +44 (0)1625 266899
or email info@pianosummerschool.com
www.pianosummerschool.com

The 2nd Manchester International Piano Concerto Competition for Young Pianists
15-22 August 2009

Chetham's School of Music & Royal Northern College of Music

CATEGORIES:

- **16-and-under**
- **22-and-under**
- **Ernest & Ellen Corby** transcription prizes

EMINENT JURY OF INTERNATIONAL CONCERT PIANISTS

under the Chair of Murray McLachlan

PRIZES

24 semi-finalists perform for £3,500 prize money, a debut solo recital disc and an impressive series of engagements in the UK and abroad.

In association with

Rhinegold Publishing
Steinway and Sons
The Michael Corby Foundation

FINALS ACCOMPANIED BY
Manchester Camerata

Chetham's
School of Music

www.alink-argerich.org

MANCHESTER CAMERATA

Manchester EveningNews

RHINEGOLD PUBLISHING

STEINWAY & SONS

For further information call **+44(0)1625 266899**
or email: **info@pianoconcertocompetition.com**
www.pianoconcertocompetition.com

Greenwood, artistic dir; Glyn Foley, chief exec. Opera, music and literature in a stunning Peak District setting.

Cambridge Music Festival 10 Gurney Way, Cambridge. *t:* 01223 350544 *e:* director@cammusic.co.uk *w:* www.cammusic.co.uk *Contact* Gillian Perkins, festival dir. Theme of music and evolution.

Cambridge Summer Music Festival (Cambridge Summer Recitals) 8 Horn Lane, Linton, Cambridge. *t:* 01223 894161 *f:* 01223 892945 *e:* info@cambridgesummermusic.com *w:* www.cambridgesummermusic.com *Contact* Juliet Abrahamson, artistic dir. About 50 concerts in many historic venues, inc Music for the Kids series. Also runs other concerts during the year, and Spring Concert Series in May.

Canterbury Festival Festival Office, Christ Church Gate, The Precincts, Canterbury. *t:* 01227 452853 *f:* 01227 781830 *e:* info@canterburyfestival.co.uk *w:* www.canterburyfestival.co.uk *Contact* Rosie Turner, festival dir. International arts festival offering 200 events in 2 wks across the art forms of music, theatre and visual arts.

Carducci Festival *e:* info@carducciquartet.co.uk *w:* www.carducciquartet.co.uk Annual festival of the Carducci String Quartet in Highnam.

Carlisle International Summer Festival 6 The Abbey, Carlisle. *f:* 01228 547049 *e:* miccarlisle@btinternet.com *w:* www.carlislefestival.org.uk *Contact* Jeremy Suter, chair of Carlisle Festival Ltd

Castleward Opera Festival Unit A, 280 Comber Rd, Lisburn. *t:* 028 9263 9545 *f:* 028 9263 9588 *e:* info@castlewardopera.com *w:* www.castlewardopera.com

Celtic Connections The Glasgow Royal Concert Hall, 2 Sauchiehall St, Glasgow. *t:* 0141 353 8080 *f:* 0141 353 8026 *w:* www.celticconections.com Over 300 concerts, ceilidhs, talks, free events, late night sessions and workshops in 14 venues across the city.

The Chantry Singers Bach Festivals 19 Belgrave Crescent, Bath. *t:* 01225 333527 *e:* info@chantry-singers.org.uk *w:* www.chantrysingers.org.uk *Contact* Elizabeth Bates, artistic dir.

Charleston Manor Festival 15 Birchwood Ave, London. *t:* 020 8444 1065 *e:* admin@charlestonmanorfestival.com *w:* www.charlestonmanorfestival.com *Contact* Robert Cohen,

artistic dir. Annual festival; Robert Cohen invites friends and colleagues, some of the most outstanding classical musicians, to join him for intense yet congenial music-making.

Chelsea Festival The Crypt, St Luke's Church, Sydney St, London. *t:* 020 7349 8101 *e:* info@chelseafestival.org *w:* www.chelseafestival.org.uk *Contact* Stewart Collins, artistic dir.

Cheltenham Jazz Festival 109-111 Bath Rd, Cheltenham. *t:* 01242 774400 *f:* 01242 573902 *e:* sophie.winstanley@cheltenhamfestivals.com *Contact* Tony Dudley-Evans, artistic dir; Sophie Winstanley, festival mgr. In association with Radio 2.

Cheltenham Music Festival Cheltenham Festivals, 109-11 Bath Rd, Cheltenham. *t:* 01242 774400 *f:* 01242 256457 *e:* music@cheltenhamfestivals.com *w:* www.cheltenhamfestivals.com

Chester Festival Ltd Festival, 4 Abbey Sq, Chester. *t:* 01244 320722 *f:* 01244 341200 *e:* kate@chesterfestivals.co.uk *Contact* Andrew Cornall, artistic dir; Kate Sawallisch, festival mgr. 2 wk festival with classical music at its core, focusing on the voice.

Chetham's International Summer School and Festival for Pianists Chetham's School of Music, Long Millgate, Manchester. *t:* 01625 266899, also fax *e:* info@pianosummerschool.com *w:* www.pianosummerschool.com *Contact* Murray McLachlan, artistic dir; Kathryn Page, admin. Recitals, lectures, intensive tuition, m/classes by world-class concert pianists.

Chichester Festivities Canon Gate House, South St, Chichester. *t:* 01243 785718 *f:* 01243 528356 *e:* info@chifest.org.uk *w:* www.chifest.org.uk *Contact* Amanda Sharp, dir.

Chobham Music Festival Dingle, Castle Grove Rd, Chobham. *t:* 01276 858552 *w:* http://festival.chobham.org *Contact* John Parry, festival dir; Dale Chamber, musical dir. Annual festival featuring classical music, jazz, br bands, children's events etc.

Church Stretton and South Shropshire Arts Festival 3 Cunnery Terrace, Church Stretton. *t:* 01694 722257 *e:* gandrwalker@talktalk.net *w:* www.strettonfestival.org.uk *Contact* Richard Walker, artistic dir.

City of Derry Jazz and Big Band Festival Derry City Council, 98 Strand Rd, Derry. *t:* 028 7137 6545 *f:* 028 7137 0080 *e:* jazz@derrycity.gov.

uk w: www.cityofderryjazzfestival.com *Contact* Johnny Murray, contact.

City of London Festival Fitz Eylwin House, 25 Holborn Viaduct, London. *t:* 020 7583 3585 *f:* 020 7353 0455 *e:* admin@colf.org *w:* www.colf.org *Contact* Lindsey Dear, gen mgr. Concerts in various venues throughout the square mile; also free outdoor events in the City's open spaces and Hampstead Heath.

Clacton Jazz Festival Tendring District Council, Clacton, Essex. *t:* 01255 686650 *f:* 01255 686411 *e:* rfoster@tendringdc.gov.uk *Contact* Bob Foster, artistic dir.

Clandeboye Estate *e:* info@camerata-ireland.com *w:* www.camerata-ireland.com Festival of classical music set in the Clandeboye Estate, featuring established and the next generation of Irish musicians and Camerata Ireland.

Cleckheaton Folk Festival 84 Pyenot Hall Lane, Cleckheaton. *t:* 01274 879761 *e:* dave@cleckheatonfolkfestival.org *w:* www.cleckheatonfolkfestival.org *Contact* Dave Minich, festival dir. Friendly w/end of folk music and entertainment for all ages.

Coleraine Community and Arts Festival Flowerfield Arts Centre, 185 Coleraine Rd, Portstewart, Co Londonderry. *t:* 028 7083 1400 *e:* info@flowerfield.org *w:* www.flowerfield.org *Contact* Malcolm Murchison, arts offr & centre mgr. Small-scale events, music and community participation, inc schools w/shops etc.

Corbridge Chamber Music Festival addressall. *t:* 020 7736 5268 *e:* penny@mneary.co.uk *w:* www.gouldpianotrio.com *Contact* Penny Neary. 10th anniversary programme. Chief festival artists are founders of the festival: Gould Piano Trio, Robert Plane (cl) and guests.

Corsham Festival The Pound Arts centre, Pound Pill, Corsham. *t:* 01249 701628, also fax *e:* info@corshamfestival.org.uk *w:* www.corshamfestival.org.uk *Contact* Nicholas Keyworth, festival dir.

Cotswold Early Music Festival Atkyns Manor, South Cerney, Cirencester. *t:* 01285 860395 *f:* 01285 862449 *e:* info@cotswold-emf.co.uk *w:* www.cotswold-emf.co.uk *Contact* Mark Venn, festival dir.

Coventry Jazz Festival c/o CV One Ltd, 1 Castle Yard, off Hay Lane, Coventry. *t:* 024 7660 7020 *f:* 024 7660 7001 *e:* jazz@cvone.co.uk *w:* www.coventryjazzfestival.com

Dante Summer Festival Festival Administrator, 4 Pempwell Cottages, Challington. *t:* 01579 370589 *e:* brian.champness@btinternet.com *w:* www.dantefestival.org Festival run by the Dante String Quartet with guest artists. Quartet concerts, w/shops and special events for children in ancient churches and traditional barns. Focus in 2009 on French music, plus Haydn, Beethoven and much more.

Dartington International Summer School The Barn, Dartington Hall, Totnes. *t:* 01803 847080 *f:* 01803 847087 *e:* summerschool@dartington.org *w:* www.dartington.org/summer-school *Contact* Gavin Henderson, artistic dir; Becka Rickard, producer; Sam McCaffery, registrar; Maisie Hunt, admin. 3 concerts every day, plus w/shops and m/classes.

Deal Festival of Music and the Arts Festival Office, The Pines, St Andrew's Gdns, Shepherdswell. *t:* 01304 830443 *e:* irondraw@btinternet.com *w:* http://dealfestival.co.uk *Contact* Mrs Willie Cooper. Concerts in Deal, Sandwich and Dover.

Denbigh Midsummer Festival 79 Stryd y Dyffryn, Dinbych, Sir Ddinbych. *t:* 01745 816080 *e:* philmorris@croeso.com *w:* www.visitdenbigh.co.uk/midsummer2.html

Devizes Festival Bachelor's Mead, Horton, Devizes. *w:* www.devizesfestival.co.uk *Contact* James Harrison, chair.

Dorset Opera Witchampton, Dorset. *t:* 01258 840000 *f:* 01258 840946 *e:* info@dorsetopera.com *w:* www.dorsetopera.com *Contact* Roderick Kennedy, artistic dir; Jeremy Carnall, mus dir; William Relton, production dir. The world's foremost opera summer school, with full professional orchestra and famous international soloists.

Dulwich Festival PO Box 26999, London. *e:* info@dulwichfestival.co.uk *w:* www.dulwichfestival.co.uk

Dumfries and Galloway Arts Festival Gracefield Arts Centre, 28 Edinburgh Rd, Dumfries. *t:* 01387 260447, also fax *e:* info@dgartsfestival.org.uk *w:* www.dgartsfestival.org.uk *Contact* Annette Rogers, admin sec. A multi-genre festival with national and international performers.

East Neuk Festival 29 Regent St, Edinburgh. *t:* 0131 669 1750, also fax *e:* info@eastneukfestival.co.uk *w:* www.eastneukfestival.com *Contact* Svend Brown, artistic dir. Music and readings in intimate venues.

Edinburgh & Glasgow - Festival of British Youth Orchestras NAYO, Central Hall, West Tollcross,

Edinburgh. *t*: 0131 221 1927 *f*: 0131 229 2921 *e*: admin@nayo.org.uk *w*: www.nayo.org.uk *Contact* Susan White, gen mgr. Youth orchs and ens in NAYO membership are given the opportunity to take part in the Festival in Central Hall, Edinburgh and the RSAMD, Glasgow. Forming part of the Edinburgh Fringe, many leading youth orchs and ens make regular return visits. Also guest youth choirs and int orchs/ens.

Edinburgh International Festival The Hub, Castlehill, Edinburgh. *t*: 0131 473 2099 *f*: 0131 473 2002 *e*: eif@eif.co.uk *w*: www.eif.co.uk *Contact* Jonathan Mills, festival dir. 3 weeks of world class theatre, dance, opera and music in Scotland's capital city.

Edinburgh International Harp Festival *t*: 0131 478 8446, also fax *e*: administrator@harpfestival. co.uk *w*: www.harpfestival.co.uk *Contact* Lindsay Robertson, admin. 5 day festival devoted to all harps and their music - traditional Scottish, Irish and Welsh, classical, Paraguayan, jazz and much more. Classes for everyone from complete beginners to advanced players.

Edinburgh International Jazz and Blues Festival 29 St Stephen St, Edinburgh. *t*: 0131 225 2202 *f*: 0131 225 3321 *e*: mikehart@ edinburghjazzbluesfest.com

Egerton Festival *t*: 01233 840630 *e*: ljanecarr@ btinternet.com *w*: www.egertonmusicfestival.co.uk Triennial festival; other musical events held each year throughout the year.

English Haydn Festival, Bridgnorth *w*: www. haydn.org.uk *Contact* HC Robbins Landon, artistic dir. Orch concerts, chmbr music, choral music, recitals and opera. Period insts.

English Heritage Picnic Concerts Series IMG, Pier House, Strand on the Green, London. *t*: 020 8233 5000; 020 8233 6400 (information) *f*: 020 8233 5001 *e*: concerts@imgworld.com *w*: www. picnicconcerts.com *Contact* Tania Meek, exec producer. Concerts take place in Kenwood, Hampstead; Audley End, Essex; Marble Hill, Twickenham; Battle Abbey, Sussex.

The English Music Festival 36 Forest Rd, Kew, Richmond. *t*: 020 3274 1054; 07808 473889 *e*: em.marshall@btinternet.com *w*: www. englishmusicfestival.org.uk *Contact* Em Marshall, mgr & artistic dir. Annual festival featuring works by British composers of all periods, focusing on the early 20th C. World class artists and a range of events from solo recitals through to full orch concerts.

Exeter Autumn Festival 4.46, Civic Centre, Paris St, Exeter. *t*: 01392 265205 *f*: 01392 265366 *e*: val.wilson@exeter.gov.uk *w*: www.exeter.gov.uk/ festival *Contact* Val Wilson, festival mgr.

Exon Singers Festival (Tavistock & Buckfast) 6 Ashlake Rd, London. *t*: 020 8677 0882 *e*: secretary@exonsingers.org.uk *w*: www. exonsingers.org.uk *Contact* Graham Wood, sec. Recitals, concerts and services (inc compline) in Tavistock's 13th C parish church; broadcast of choral evening prayer from Buckfast Abbey

Finchcocks Festival Finchcocks Musical Museum, Goudhurst. *t*: 01580 211702 *f*: 01580 211007 *e*: info@finchcocks.co.uk *w*: www.finchcocks.co.uk *Contact* Katrina Burnett, dir; Richard Burnett MBE, artistic dir.

Florestan Festival c/o Florestan Festival at Peasmarsh, Strawberry Hole Oast, Ewhurst Lane, Northiam. *t*: 01797 253178 *e*: enquiries@ florestantrio.com *w*: www.florestantrio.com *Contact* Sue Schlesinger. Annual chmbr music festival curated by The Florestan Trio. Includes perfs by The Florestan Trio, invited guests, and a major concerto concert at St Mary's church Rye.

Forbesfest Music Centre, Younger Hall, North St, St Andrews. *t*: 01334 462226 *f*: 01334 462228 *e*: music@st-andrews.ac.uk *w*: www.forbesfest.com W/end viola festival recognising the centenary of one of the most celebrated viola players of his generation, born and brought up in St Andrews. Includes Michael Kugel, Brodsky Quartet and international viola competition.

Garsington Opera Garsington. *t*: 01865 368201 *f*: 01865 361545 *e*: office@garsingtonopera.org *w*: www.garsingtonopera.org

Gateway International Roots Music Festival Brewery Arts Centre, Highgate, Kendal. *t*: 01539 722833 *e*: admin@breweryarts.co.uk *w*: www. breweryarts.co.uk *Contact* Mike Chadwick. Primarily features new roots musics (trad non-classical music forms) from around the world, for which it is a national showcase. Features established and emerging artists.

Glyndebourne Festival Opera Glyndebourne, Lewes. *t*: 01273 812321; 01273 815000 (info) *f*: 01273 812783 *e*: info@glyndebourne.com *w*: www.glyndebourne.com *Contact* David Pickard, gen dir. New productions and revivals.

Gower Festival Cruachen, Reynoldston, Swansea. *t:* 01792 390404, also fax *e:* gowerfestival@f2s. com *w:* www.gowerfestival.org *Contact* Gareth Walters, artistic dir.

Grassington Festival Riverbank House, Threshfield, nr Skipton. *t:* 01756 753357 *e:* arts@grassington-festival.org.uk *w:* www.grassington-festival.org.uk *Contact* Amelia Vyvyan, festival dir.

Greenwich + Docklands Festivals The Borough Hall, Royal Hill, London. *t:* 020 8305 1818 *f:* 020 8305 1188 *e:* admin@festival.org *w:* www.festival. org *Contact* Bradley Hemmings, artistic dir; Mathew Russell, exec dir.

Greenwich International Festival & Exhibition The Old Royal Naval College, Greenwich, London. *t:* 01274 288100 *f:* 01274 596226 *e:* enquiries@ earlymusicfestival.com *w:* www.earlymusicfestival. com *Contact* Peter Booth, dir. Major international early music exhibition held at the Old Royal Naval College, Greenwich, London. Around 100 exhibitors over 3 days. Concerts, m/classes, w/shops, demonstration recitals.

Guildford International Music Festival c/o Dept of Music & Sound Recording, University of Surrey, Guildford. *t:* 01483 689690 *f:* 01483 686501 *e:* p.b.johnson@surrey.ac.uk *w:* www.guildford internationalmusicfestival.co.uk *Contact* Pauline Johnson, artistic dir; Patricia Grayburn, exec dir. Professional and community festival with established and emerging artists, covering a wide range of musical genres.

Guildford Spring Music Festival *w:* www.gsmf. co.uk *Contact* Alan Dewey, hon sec Biennial festival.

Guiting Festival Langley Lodge, Langley, Winchcombe. *t:* 01242 603912 *e:* guitingfestival@ talktalk.net *w:* www.guitingfestival.org *Contact* Duncan Westerman, artistic dir. Classical music and jazz in a rural Cotswold setting.

Gwyl Gregynog Festival Gregynog, Newtown, Powys. *t:* 01686 650224 *f:* 01686 650656 *e:* post@gwylgregynogfestival.org *w:* www. gwylgregynogfestival.org *Contact* Rhian Davies, artistic dir; Susan Jones, admin. International arts event in a magnificent setting.

Hampstead and Highgate Festival PO Box 59221, London. *t:* 020 7435 5965 *e:* george@ hamandhighfest.co.uk *w:* www.hamandhighfest.co.uk *Contact* George Vass, artistic dir; Megan Campbell, development dir. Annual festival based around classical music but with some literature, visual art and cinema; takes place in small-scale venues in and around the twin N London villages of Hampstead and Highgate.

Hampton Court Palace Festival IMG Arts & Entertainment, Pier House, Strand on the Green, London. *t:* 020 8233 5000 *f:* 020 8233 5001 *e:* concerts@imgworld.com *w:* www.hampton courtfestival.com

Harrogate International Festival Raglan House, Raglan St, Harrogate. *t:* 01423 562303 *f:* 01423 521264 *e:* info@harrogate-festival.org.uk *w:* www. harrogate-festival.org.uk *Contact* William Culver-Dodds, chief exec; Sharon Canavar, operations dir.

Harrogate International Youth Music Festival Perform Europe, One Jubilee St, Brighton. *t:* 01273 810742 *f:* 01273 693148 *e:* sales@perform europe.co.uk *w:* www.performeurope.co.uk

Hebden Bridge Arts Festival New Oxford House, Albert St, Hebden Bridge. *t:* 01422 842684 *e:* hbfestival@gmail.com *w:* www.hebdenbridge. co.uk/festival *Contact* Rebecca Yorke, festival co-ord. Annual 2-week event celebrating art, literature, drama, music and all other art forms.

Henley Festival 14 Friday St, Henley-on-Thames. *t:* 01491 843400 *f:* 01491 410482 *e:* info@ henley-festival.co.uk *w:* www.henley-festival.co.uk *Contact* Stewart Collins, artistic dir.

Hexham Abbey Festival Hexham Abbey Parish Centre, Beaumont St, Hexham. *t:* 07979 866303 *f:* 01434 606116 *e:* festival@hexhamabbey.org. uk *w:* www.hexhamabbey.org.uk/festival *Contact* Graham Coatman, artistic dir. 10 days of classical, early, choral, contemporary, jazz, world and folk music, supplemented by Young Artist Platford; commissions, community & educ projects, exhibitions, film, street theatre etc.

Honiton Festival Hollick, Yarnscombe. *t:* 01271 858249 *f:* 01271 858375 *e:* eucorch1@aol.com *Contact* Ambrose Miller, mus dir.

Huddersfield Contemporary Music Festival Room TC/09, University of Huddersfield, Huddersfield. *t:* 01484 472900 *e:* hcmfinfo@hud. ac.uk *w:* www.hcmf.co.uk 50 events over 10 days, inc jazz, classical, electronic and improvised music, music theatre, film and multimedia events, installations, free workshops, drop-in events and a diverse educ programme. Attracts composers, performers and an audience from across the UK and around the world.

Iford Festival Iford Arts Ltd, The Gatehouse, Iford. *t:* 01225 868124 *f:* 01225 867471 *e:* debbie heyden@ifordarts.co.uk *w:* www.ifordarts.co.uk *Contact* Judy Eglington, artistic dir; Deborah Heyden, admin. Site-specific opera productions in the cloister; jazz and world music promenades.

International Choir Festival of Jersey Le Catel Farm, La Rue de la Falaise, Trinity, Jersey. *t:* 01534 864014 *e:* nickcabot@localdial.com *w:* www. internationalchoirfestivalofjersey.com *Contact* Nick Cabot, musical dir. Biennial festival.

International Classical Guitar Festival and Summer School West Dean College, West Dean, Chichester. *t:* 01243 811301 *f:* 01243 811343 *e:* short.courses@westdean.org.uk *w:* www. westdean.org.uk *Contact* Marcus Martin, course organiser; John Mills, course dir. Fully residential, inc full teaching programme and series of public recitals.

International East Anglian Summer Music Festival 3-5 Bridge St, Hadleigh. *t:* 01473 822596, also fax *e:* thomas.mcintosh@minstrelmusic. co.uk *w:* www.minstrelmusic.co.uk *Contact* Thomas McIntosh, artistic dir; MHV Reckitt, admin. Classical chmbr music. All concerts at The Old School, Hadleigh.

International Guitar Foundation and Festivals Newton Park, Newton St Loe, Bath. *t:* 01225 875522 *f:* 01225 875495 *e:* phil@igf.org.uk *w:* www.igf.org.uk

International Organ Festival at St Albans PO Box 80, St Albans. *t:* 01727 844765 *f:* 01727 868941 *e:* info@organfestival.com *w:* www. organfestival.com *Contact* David Titterington, artistic dir; Hilary Crook, admin sec. Biennial international music festival with org competitions for interpretation and improvisation at its heart. Also concerts, recitals, an exhibition of small orgs and an awayday visit to Eton College, Reading Town Hall and Douai Abbey. Special events in 2009 to celebrate 25th festival and the restoration of the Harrison & Harrison cathedral org.

International Ralph Vaughan Williams Festival Music at Woodhouse, Woodhouse Copse, Holmbury St Mary, Dorking. *t:* 01306 730956 *e:* info@ woodhousesounds.com *w:* www.woodhousesounds. com

Jewish Culture Day at the Southbank Centre Jewish Music Institute, SOAS, University of London, PO Box 232, Harrow. *t:* 020 8909 2445 *f:* 020 8909 1030 *e:* jewishmusic@jmi.org.uk *w:* www.jmi. org.uk *Contact* Geraldine Auerbach MBE, festival dir. Centred around a day at Southbank Centre, the festival includes music of the Jewish diaspora from Klezmer to cabaret, classical, cantorical, choral and the music of Oriental communities, with exotic insts and songs in many languages.

Jewish Song Summer School JMI, SOAS, University of London, Thornhaugh St, Russell Sq, London. *t:* 020 8909 2445 *f:* 020 8909 1030 *e:* jewishmusic@jmi.org.uk *w:* www.jmi.org.uk *Contact* Laoise Davidson, dir. Exploration of the repertoire, interpretation, style and pronunciation of Jewish songs in Jewish languages of Yiddish and Ladino in w/shops and m/classes for professional and amateur singers. Directed by Shura Lipovsky of Amsterdam with an international faculty inc Polina Shepherd. Runs parallel with JMI Klezfest London.

Keswick Jazz Festival Theatre by the Lake, Lakeside, Keswick. *t:* 01768 772282; 01768 781123 (jazz office) *f:* 01768 774698 *w:* www. theatrebythelake.com *Contact* John Minnion, programmer; Sophie Curtis, admin.

King's Lynn Festival 5 Thoresby College, Queen St, King's Lynn. *t:* 01553 767557 *f:* 01553 767688 *w:* www.kingslynnfestival.org.uk *Contact* Ambrose Miller, artistic dir; Joanne Mawson, admin. General arts festival featuring orch and choral concerts, classical recitals, talks, literature and exhibitions.

Kingston Early Music Festival 10 Viking Court, Beaver Close, Hampton. *t:* 020 8941 4917 *e:* williamsummers@uwclub.net *w:* www.lokimusic. co.uk *Contact* William Summers. Overall theme of 'Requiem', around All Souls/All Saints dates. Monthly chamber concerts in the Lovekyn Chapel, a medieval chantry chapel.

KlezFest London JMI, SOAS, University of London, Thornhaugh St, Russell Sq, London. *t:* 020 8909 2445 *f:* 020 8909 1030 *e:* jewishmusic@jmi.org. uk *w:* www.jmi.org.uk *Contact* Laoise Davidson, dir. Hands-on learning experience with luminaries of the Klezmer revival from Europe and America, focusing on the style, ornamentation, rhythm and repertoire of eastern European Jewish music, song and dance in w/shops, ens playing and m/classes. For amateur and professional instrumentalists, singers and dancers.

Lake District Summer Music International Festival Stricklandgate House, 92 Stricklandgate,

Kendal. *t:* 0845 644 2505 *f:* 0845 644 2506 *e:* info@ldsm.org.uk *w:* www.ldsm.org.uk *Contact* Renna Kellaway, artistic dir; Andrew Lucas, exec organiser; Rebecca Perkins, admin offr; Cliff Dixon, mktg. Widely spread music festival offering chmbr mus, opera, orchs, m/classes, talks and exhibitions in over 50 events against the backdrop of the Lake District.

The Late Music Festival 18 Glen Ave, Heworth, York. *t:* 01904 426372 *e:* steve.crowther@gn.apc. org *Contact* Steve Crowther, admin.

Leamington Music Festival Weekend Northgate, Warwick. *t:* 01926 497000 *e:* richard@leamington music.org *w:* www.leamingtonmusic.org *Contact* Richard Phillips. Annual 5 day festival of music over 1st bank holiday w/end. Theme for 2009: Haydn bicentenary and music in Vienna.

Leeds Lieder+ Festival Office, Leeds College of Music, 3 Quarry Hill, Leeds. *t:* 0113 234 6956 *e:* info@leedslieder.org.uk *w:* www.leedslieder.org. uk *Contact* Jane Anthony, founder; David Hoult, chair; Lord Harewood, pres; Elly Ameling, hon patron; Julius Drake, artistic dir. Biennial festival of art song in central Leeds venues. Recitals and other events inc m/classes, w/shops, world premieres, talks, composers and poets forum.

Leicester Early Music Festival 126 Shanklin Drive, Leicester. *t:* 0116 270 9984, also fax *e:* mail@early musicleicester.co.uk *w:* www.earlymusicleicester.co.uk *Contact* John Bence, dir. Festival has a strong family target and associated events such as guided walks, wine tasting, dance choral and jnr workshops.

Leicester International Music Festival New Walk Museum, 53 New Walk, Leicester. *t:* 0116 225 4916, also fax *e:* musicfest@btconnect.com *w:* www.musicfestival.co.uk *Contact* Nicholas Daniel, artistic dir. Classical chmbr music festival with an ens of international soloists playing chmbr music, inc contemporary and commissioned works. Different composer in residence each year, inc Thea Musgrave, James Macmillan, Nigel Osborne, Dobrinka Tabakova and Richard Dubugnon. 2009 composer: Tansy Davies.

Leith Hill Music Festival 59 Eastwick Park Ave, Great Bookham. *t:* 01372 458811, also fax *e:* maytime59epa@talk21.com *w:* www.lhmf.co.uk *Contact* Brian Kay, artistic dir; Liz May, hon sec.

Leominster Festival 183 Godiva Rd, Leominster. *t:* 01568 611553, also fax *e:* ajemattwood@aol. com *w:* www.leominster-festival.co.uk

Lichfield Festival 7 The Close, Lichfield. *t:* 01543 306270 *f:* 01543 306274 *e:* info@lichfieldfestival. org *w:* www.lichfieldfestival.org *Contact* Richard Hawley, artistic dir. Multi-arts festival with strong classical music content plus jazz, world, folk, centred on Lichfield Cathedral, Lichfield Garrick Theatre and small church and other venues around Staffs.

Lincoln and Lincolnshire International Chamber Music Festival Greetwell Place, Lime Kiln Way, Greetwell Rd, Lincoln. *t:* 07757 708858 *e:* licmfoffice@ntlworld.com *w:* www.licmf.org.uk *Contact* Rebecca Lee, mgr.

Lincoln Early Music Festival 45 Cecil St, Lincoln. *t:* 01522 543788 *e:* Helen@lemf.org *w:* www.lemf. org *Contact* A Helen Mason, dir; Colin Rout, treas.

Little Missenden Festival 3 Mill End Cottages, Little Missenden. *t:* 01494 864686 *e:* contact@ little-missenden.org *w:* www.little-missenden.org

Liverpool Summer Pops CMP Entertainment, 08 Place, 36-38 Whitechapel, Liverpool. *t:* 0151 708 6050 *f:* 0151 707 0400 *e:* info@cmplive.com *w:* www.cmplive.com *Contact* Chas Cole, mgr dir. Held at Liverpool Echo Arena.

Llandeilo Fawr Festival of Music 129 Rhosmaen St, Llandeilo, Carmarthenshire. *t:* 01558 823294 *e:* juliajones.heelappeal@tesco.net *w:* www. llandeilofawr.net *Contact* Julia Jones, festival dir. Internationally renowned singers, instrumentalists and choirs visit one of Wales's loveliest towns for a week of intensive music-making.

Llangollen International Musical Eisteddfod Eisteddfod Office, 1st Floor, Royal International Pavilion, Llangollen. *t:* 01978 862000 *f:* 01978 862002 *e:* info@international-eisteddfod.co.uk *w:* www.international-eisteddfod.co.uk *Contact* Mervyn Cousins, exec dir. World-renowned festival of music, song and dance. Competitors from more than 50 countries; concerts each evening by world-class artists.

Llantilio Crossenny Festival of Music and Drama Treadam Farm, Llantillio Crossenny, Abergavenney, Monmouthshire. *t:* 01600 780233 *e:* llantilio@btinternet.com *w:* www.llantiliocrossenny. com *Contact* Robyn Sevastos, mus dir; Eleanor Farncombe, artistic dir.

London Bach Society's Bachfest Bach House, 73 High St, Old Oxted. *t:* 01883 717372 *f:* 01883 715851 *e:* lbs@lonbachsoc.demon.co.uk *w:* www. bachlive.co.uk *Contact* Margaret Steinitz, artistic dir. Annual festival. Participation by invitation, but artist info/biographical material welcome (professional forces only).

London Festival of Chamber Music 44 Gondar Gdns, London. *t:* 020 7435 6232 *e:* office@londonfestival.co.uk *w:* www.londonfestival.co.uk *Contact* Luciano Iorio, exec & artistic dir.

London Festival of Contemporary Church Music St Pancras Church, Euston Rd, London. *t:* 020 7388 1461, also fax *e:* office@stpancraschurch.org *w:* www.stpancraschurch.org *Contact* Christopher Batchelor, artistic dir. Principal aim is to showcase perfs of recent and contemporary liturgical music and org music at the very highest levels, both in the context of services and concerts.

London Handel Festival Horton House, 8 Ditton St, Ilminster. *t:* 01460 53500, also fax *e:* c-hodgson@btconnect.com *w:* www.london-handel-festival.com *Contact* Laurence Cummings, mus dir; Denys Darlow, founder cond; Catherine Hodgson, festival dir.

London Jazz Festival in association with Radio 3 51 Kingsway Place, Sans Walk, London. *t:* 020 7324 1880 *f:* 020 7324 1881 *e:* claire@serious.org.uk *w:* www.londonjazzfestival.org.uk; www.serious.org.uk *Contact* John Cumming, David Jones, Claire Whitaker, artistic dirs.

London New Wind Festival c/o Catherine Pluygers, 119 Woolstone Rd, London. *t:* 020 8699 1101 *f:* 020 8699 2219 *e:* catherinepluygers@hotmail.com *w:* www.londonnewwindfestival.org *Contact* Catherine Pluygers, artistic dir. 8-10 concerts. Specialises in promoting new music for ww insts.

London Song Festival Flat 1, 42 The Crescent, London. *t:* 020 8879 0323; 07973 292992 *e:* nigelfoster@londonsongfestival.org *w:* www.londonsongfestival.org *Contact* Nigel Foster, dir. Promotes the song repertoire through an annual series of concerts and m/classes. Each year a different theme is explored; well-known and rare repertoire presented in innovative programmes featuring the finest UK recitalists.

London String Quartet Week 8 Woodlands Rd, Romford. *t:* 01708 761423, also fax *e:* info@playquartet.com *w:* www.playquartet.com *Contact* Ruth Wheal, gen mgr. Various diverse events celebrating the art of the string quartet. Includes London International String Quartet Competition.

Longborough Festival Opera Longborough, Moreton-in-Marsh. *t:* 01451 830292 *f:* 01451 830605 *e:* admin@lfo.org.uk *w:* www.lfo.org.uk *Contact* Martin Graham, dir; Alan Privett, artistic dir. 4 operas produced.

Lower Machen Festival 46 Richmond Rd, Roath, Cardiff. *t:* 029 2048 2183, also fax *e:* Lower.Machen.Festival@pjr.demon.co.uk *Contact* Peter Reynolds, artistic dir; Rosie Edwards, admin.

Ludlow Festival The Festival Office, Castle Sq, Ludlow. *t:* 01584 875070 *f:* 01584 877673 *e:* info@ludlowfestival.co.uk *w:* www.ludlowfestival.co.uk

Lufthansa Festival of Baroque Music 70 Overstone Rd, Harpenden. *t:* 01582 763494 *e:* info@lufthansafestival.org.uk *w:* www.lufthansafestival.org.uk *Contact* Lindsay Kemp, artistic dir; Lucy Bending, mgr. International festival featuring 17th-18th C music performed by the world's leading artists and ensembles at St John's Smith Square, Westminster Abbey and other venues in the Westminster area. Approx 10 fully professional concerts.

Machynlleth Festival Y Tabernacl, Heol Penrallt, Machynlleth, Powys. *t:* 01654 703355 *f:* 01654 702160 *e:* info@momawales.org.uk *w:* www.momawales.org.uk *Contact* Raymond Jones, admin.

Malvern Songfest *t:* 01684 578009 *e:* william.coleman-bar@virgin.net W/end festival of song.

Mananan International Festival of Music and the Arts Mananan Festival Office, Erin Arts Centre, Victoria Sq, Port Erin, Isle of Man. *t:* 01624 835858 *f:* 01624 836658 *e:* information@erinartscentre.com *w:* www.erinartscentre.com *Contact* John Bethell MBE, artistic dir. Annual music festival, in association with BBC Radio 3.

Manchester International Festival 3rd Floor, 81 King St, Manchester. *t:* 0161 238 7300 *f:* 0161 832 7047 *e:* info@mif.co.uk *w:* www.mif.co.uk International festival of original, new work and special events.

Manchester Jazz Festival 226 Ducie House, Ducie St, Manchester. *t:* 0161 228 0662, also fax *e:* fanny@manchesterjazz.com *w:* www.manchesterjazz.com *Contact* Steve Mead, artistic dir; Mick Waterfield, producer. Contemporary jazz festival featuring primarily new work by NW-based artists.

Marsden Jazz Festival 10 Peel St, Marsden, Huddersfield. *t:* 01484 846969, also fax e: mjfoffice@tiscali.co.uk w: www.marsdenjazz festival.com Contact Barney Stevenson, festival chair. International stars from the world of jazz; around 60 live music events, over 40 of which are free of charge. Takes place over 3 days each Oct in the picturesque Pennine village of Marsden.

Mary Wakefield Westmorland Festival 6 Summerhill, Kendal. t: 01539 736193 e: rosemary. howell@virgin.net w: www.mwwf.co.uk Contact R Howell, sec. Biennial festival with full range of adjudicated classes for all ages, schools w/shops, presentation days and concerts, culminating with a major choral concert.

Mendelssohn on Mull Festival Druimfin, Tobermory, Isle of Mull. t: 01688 302828 e: administrator@mullfest.org.uk w: www.mullfest. org.uk Contact Trish Haworth, admin; Levon Chilingirian, artistic dir; Marilyn Jeffcoat, chair.

Midsummer Music t: 01271 858249; 01789 298197 f: 01271 858375 e: eucorch1@aol.com; stratmusicfest@btconnect.com w: www.stratford musicfestival.com Contact Ambrose Miller.

Milton Abbey Music Festival 22 Binghams Rd, Crossways, Dorchester. t: 01305 852489 e: fatmangre6br@tiscali.co.uk w: www.milton-abbey-music-festival.co.uk Contact F Greenslade.

Minehead and Exmoor 'Sidella', Whitegate Rd, Minehead, Somerset. t: 01643 702353 e: david@ yates2446.fsnet.co.uk Contact David Yates, chair. The Festival Orchestra is made up of professional musicians from all over the country, providing W Somerset with 3 different programmes in a week. Artistic dir & cond: Richard Dickins, dir of music at Imperial College, London and principal cond at RCM jnr dept.

Music at Leasowes Bank Leasowes Bank Farm, Ratlinghope, nr Shrewsbury. t: 01743 790769, also fax e: musicatleasowes@googlemail.com w: www. leasowesmusicfestival.co.uk Contact Frances Williams, festival dir. Series of concerts covering a wide range of music. New commission each season.

Music at Paxton Paxton House, Paxton, Scottish Borders. t: 01289 386291; 07752 570389 e: music@helenjamieson.co.uk w: www. musicatpaxton.co.uk Contact Helen Jamieson, festival mgr. 10-day festival of chmbr music featuring international musicians alongside young and locally based artists.

Music at Restoration House Restoration House,

Crow Lane, Rochester. t: 01634 848520 e: robert. tucker@restorationhouse.co.uk Contact Robert Tucker, artistic dir. Period music on early insts in 17th C great chamber. Baroque, classical and early romantic specialities.

Music at the Priory Kingston House, Leonard Stanley, Stonehouse. t: 01453 822299, also fax w: www.leonardstanley.org.uk Contact Robert A Hutchings, chair.

Music from a Foreign Land Stricklandgate House, 92 Stricklandgate, Kendal. t: 0845 644 2144 f: 0845 644 2506 e: worldmusic@ldsm.org.uk w: www.ldsm.org.uk Contact Andrew Lucas, dir. Music and musicians from around the world in creative w/shops and perfs.

Nailsworth Festival Millbank House, George St, Nailsworth. t: 01453 833270 e: festival@ nailsworthfestival.org.uk w: www.nailsworthfestival. org.uk

National Festival of Music for Youth Music for Youth, 102 Point Pleasant, London. t: 020 8870 9624 f: 020 8870 9935 e: mfy@mfy.org.uk w: www.mfy.org.uk Contact Vicky Walker, festival mgr. 2009 event in Birmingham.

Newbury Spring Festival 1 Bridge St, Newbury. t: 01635 32421; 01635 528766 f: 01635 528690 e: info@newburyspringfestival.org.uk w: www.newburyspringfestival.org.uk Contact Mark Eynon, festival dir; Zoe Seenan, festival mgr; Emma O'Donnell, mkt mgr; Jane Pickering, festival sec. Fortnight of world-class music in Newbury and surrounding villages. International symphony orchs, ens and soloists, jazz legends, world music artists and the classical music stars of tomorrow.

Norfolk and Norwich Festival First Floor, Augustine Steward House, 14 Tombland, Norwich. t: 01603 877750 f: 01603 877766 e: info@ nnfestival.org.uk w: www.nnfestival.org.uk Contact Jonathan Holloway, festival dir; Clare Lovell, gen mgr; Daisy Turvill-Petre, press & mktg offr. Classical and choral music, jazz, world music, dance, comedy, outdoor spectaculars, left-field events.

The Northern Aldborough Festival The Festival Office, Aldborough Manor, Boroughbridge. t: 01423 324899 f: 01423 323761 e: festival@ aldborough.com w: www.aldboroughfestival.com Contact Dawn Seymour, festival admin. Music festival in the heart of N Yorks. Perfs inc 2 operas, pno recitals, quartets, cabaret night and last-night open air picnic finale. Morning concerts in stately

Northern Chords: The North East Chamber Music Festival e: tom@northernchords.co.uk w: www.northernchords.co.uk Contact Tom Rowley, business dir.

North Wales International Music Festival (St Asaph) Festival Office, Irish Sq, Upper Denbigh Rd, St Asaph. t: 01745 584508 e: admin@northwalesmusicfestival.co.uk w: www.northwalesmusicfestival.co.uk Contact Ann Atkinson, artistic dir; Katy Morgan, festival co-ord; Sian Rackham, festival admin asst.

Opera Holland Park Central Library, Phillimore Walk, London. t: 020 7631 2049 f: 020 7361 2317 e: press@operahollandpark.com w: www.operahollandpark.com Contact Michael Volpe, gen, mkt & publicity mgr; James Clutton, producer; Clarinda Chan, asst mkt & publicity offr; Katharine Camiller, asst producer. Summer festival of operas featuring 6 productions every year in Holland Park, with grade I listed Holland House as a backdrop. Resident orch is City of London Sinfonia.

Oundle International Festival 4 New St, Oundle. t: 01832 274919, also fax e: information@oundlefestival.org.uk w: www.oundlefestival.org.uk Contact Patricia Ryan, festival dir. Mainly classical music, featuring professional chmbr, orch, choral and organ music, with some jazz, open-air theatre and occasionally community opera.

Oxford Chamber Music Festival St Hilda's College, Oxford. t: 0845 652 0762 e: office@ocmf.net w: www.ocmf.net Contact Clare La Roche Salter, admin.

Oxford Contemporary Music Richard Hamilton Bldg, Oxford Brookes University, Headington Hill Campus, Oxford. t: 01865 488369 f: 01865 488317 e: info@ocmevents.org w: www.ocmevents.org Contact Scott Cridland-Smith, gen mgr.

Oxford Early Music Festival 33 Binswood Ave, Headington, Oxford. t: 01865 751928, also fax e: festival@charivari.co.uk w: www.charivari.co.uk Contact Susanne Heinrich, artistic dir; Kah-Ming Ng, mus dir.

Oxford May Music 48 Great Clarendon St, Oxford. t: 01865 273323 f: 01865 273417 e: admin@oxfordmaymusic.co.uk w: www.oxfordmaymusic.co.uk Contact Jack Liebeck, artistic dir.

Oxford Philomusica International Piano Festival & Summer Academy Templeton College,

Kennington Rd, Oxford. t: 0870 606 0804 f: 020 8208 4239 e: pianofestival@oxfordphil.com w: www.oxfordphil.com Contact Marios Papadopoulos, artistic dir.

The Pembroke Festival Foundry House Community Centre, Orange Way, Pembroke Commons, Pembroke. t: 01646 680090 w: www.pembrokefestival.org.uk Contact Elvira Adams, chair. Festival of music and the arts showcasing local talent.

Pennine Spring Music 24 Northgate, Heptonstall. t: 01422 843995 e: jean@richux.plus.com w: www.penninespringmusic.co.uk Contact Jean Leach, chair. W/shops and rehearsals for members - application open to all age groups, pref gr 6+. Orch/choral concerts, chmbr music or recitals performed each evening.

Perth Festival of the Arts 3-5 High St, Perth. t: 01577 862420 f: 01577 864519 e: info@perthfestival.co.uk w: www.perthfestival.co.uk Contact Sandra Ralston, admin. Annual arts festival inc classical, opera, jazz, rock, folk, theatre and dance. Venues inc Perth Concert Hall, Perth Theatre and St John's Kirk.

Petersfield Musical Festival Fenns, Reservoir Lane, Petersfield. t: 01730 263539 e: philip._young@virgin.net w: www.petersfieldmusicalfestival.org.uk Contact Philip Young, chair. Choral, orch, youth orch concerts, soloists.

Petworth Festival 151 Whites Green Lodge, Lurgashall, Petworth. t: 01798 343055 e: info@petworthfestival.org.uk w: www.petworthfestival.org.uk Contact Kate Wardle, fin & admin. Arts festival inc chmbr music, jazz, speech, drama and art among other things.

Plaxtol Music Festival PO Box 308, Sevenoaks. t: 01732 811036, also fax e: mcarboni@carbonimedia.com w: www.plaxtolfestival.co.uk Classical chmbr and jazz concerts held in Plaxtol Church and surrounding venues every 2 yrs.

Presteigne Festival of Music and the Arts PO Box 30, Presteigne, Powys. t: 01544 267800 e: georgevass@presteignefestival.com w: www.presteignefestival.com Contact George Vass, artistic dir; Alison Porter, admin; Annie Nethercott, gen mgr. Highly popular festival of music and the arts specialising in the perf of contemporary music, with a strong reputation for innovative and individual programming.

Proms at St Jude's St Jude-on-the-Hill, Central Sq, London. t: 020 8455 8687 f: 020 8458 3143 e: y.

Tunbridge Wells
International Young Concert Artists
Competition

17th Competition
15th to 18th July 2010
(closing date for entries 28th February 2010)
Three Sections: Piano, Strings or Wind
Details from
The Entries Coordinator
TWIYCA Competition Office
PO Box 10
Tunbridge Wells North
TN2 5QZ
United Kingdom

The Tunbridge Wells International Young Concert Artists Competition is a Registered Charity

THE JOHN KERR AWARD FOR ENGLISH SONG

For the promotion of the English Song Repertoire 1600-1900

First Prize £2000 + recital at Finchcocks
Second Prize £1000
Accompanist Prize £500

The next Final of this bi-annual award will be held on 3rd October 2010
at Finchcocks Keyboard Museum, Kent

Closing entry date: 12th July 2010

Participants must be aged between 18 and 35
at the date of the Final.

Further details, rules and application forms may be obtained by downloading
from our website **www.johnkerraward.org.uk** or by contacting **Maureen Lyle**
tel: **01892 530049**, email **maureen.lyle@googlemail.com**

The John Kerr Award Trust is a registered charity

baker@ukonline.co.uk w: www.promsatstjudes.org. uk Contact John Wheeler, chair of proms organising committee; David Harris, mktg & press offr; Yvonne Baker, gen info. Mainly classical concerts, covering orch, choral, chmbr and recitals. Also jazz; lunchtime concerts devoted to young talented musicians.

The Regis School of Music Summer Festival 46 Sudley Rd, Bognor Regis. t: 01243 866462 e: recital@tiscali.co.uk w: www.regisschoolofmusic. co.uk Contact Alexander Levtov, artistic dir; Nina Levtov, admin. International soloists and chmbr music perfs. Competition for amateur musicians at the Recital Hall of the Regis School of Music.

Ripon International Festival Festival Office, Holly Howe, Copt Hewick, Ripon. t: 01765 605508 e: info@riponinternationalfestival.com w: www. riponinternationalfesival.com Contact Janusz Piotrowicz, artistic dir. Symphony, choral, chmbr, world music, drama, puppetry.

RNCM Chamber Music Festival 2009 RNCM, 124 Oxford Rd, Manchester. t: 07733 091771 f: 0161 273 7611 e: jane.thompson@btconnect. com w: www.rncm.ac.uk Contact Alasdair Tait, artistic dir; Jane Thompson, admin. Chmbr music: Vienna - Schubert to Schoenberg. Recitals, m/ classes, lectures, children's project, trade and inst makers' exhibition.

RNCM Manchester International Cello Festival t: 01625 571091 f: 01625 571092 e: info@ cellofestival.co.uk w: www.cellofestival.co.uk

Rotherham Open Arts Festival c/o Community Arts Office, Central Library, Walker Place, Rotherham. t: 01709 823660 e: sean.rourke@ rotherham.gov.uk w: www.rotherhamculture.org Contact Sean Rourke, dir; Claire Saddlington, festival admin. Featuring all perf arts in a Spiegeltent with emphasis on music: classical, world, folk, jazz and blues.

Royal Tunbridge Wells International Music Festival Ockhams, Edenbridge. t: 01732 863630 e: info@tunbridgewellsfestival.co.uk w: www. tunbridgewellsfestival.co.uk

Rye Arts Festival PO Box 33, Rye. t: 01797 224442 w: www.ryeartsfestival.co.uk

Ryedale Festival Memorial Hall, Potter Hill, Pickering. t: 01751 475888 e: rftoffice@aol.com w: www.ryedalefestival.co.uk Contact Justin Doyle, artistic dir. Classical music festival held in various venues within Ryedale, N Yorks.

Sacconi Chamber Music Festival 49 Queen's Gate Terrace, London. e: festival@sacconi.com w: www.sacconi.com/festival Contact Ewa Bogusz-Moore. Chmbr music from England and France.

Saddleworth Festival of the Arts Civic Hall, Lee St, Uppermill, Oldham. t: 01457 874296 e: info@ saddleworthfestival.org.uk w: www.saddleworth festival.org.uk Contact Ken Deighton. Held every 4 yrs.

Salisbury International Arts Festival 87 Crane St, Salisbury. t: 01722 332241 f: 01722 410552 e: info@salisburyfestival.co.uk w: www.salisbury festival.co.uk Contact Caroline Peacock, festival mgr; Maria Bota, festival dir. Multi-arts festival across the Salisbury area in venues from Salisbury Cathedral to Salisbury Arts Centre, churches, village halls and outdoor spaces, inc classical and contemporary concerts, literature, theatre and dance, community projects and street art.

Shaldon Festival Greenbank, Higher Ringmore Rd, Shaldon, Teignmouth. t: 01626 873492 e: shaldonfestival@aol.com w: www.shaldonfestival. co.uk Contact MC Watson, sec.

Shipley Arts Festival c/o The Plat, Thakeham Rd, Coolham. t: 01403 741685 e: shipleyfestival@ bernardimusicgroup.com w: www.bernardimusic group.com Contact Andrew Bernardi, artistic dir; Anne Clarke, art exhibition dir. International music and arts festival serving the community of W Sussex. Patrons: RT Hon Francis Maude MP, Gavin Henderson CBE, Mark Burrell Esq.

Sidmouth FolkWeek Tourist Information Centre, Ham Lane, Sidmouth. t: 01395 578627 e: info@ sidmouthfolkweek.co.uk w: www.sidmouthfolkweek. co.uk The best of folk music, dance and song and more besides in E Devon.

Snape Proms Aldeburgh Music, Snape Maltings Concert Hall, Snape, Saxmundham. t: 01728 687100 f: 01728 687120 e: enquiries@ aldeburgh.co.uk w: www.aldeburgh.co.uk Contact Hettie Hope, artistic admin; Marc Ernesti, head of mktg & media. Offers everything from jazz, classical, world and folk music to comedy and poetry, all in the world-famous Snape Maltings Concert Hall.

Sonorities Festival of Contemporary Music School of Music, Queen's University, Belfast. t: 028 9097 4829 f: 028 9033 5053 e: sonorities@qub. ac.uk w: www.sonorities.org.uk Contact Michael Alcorn. Established festivla of new music showcasing the highest quality international artists across areas such as composition, improvisation, installation and audio-visual.

sound c/o Woodend Barn Arts Centre, Banchory, AB31 5QA. *t*: 01330 825431 *e*: info@sound-scotland.co.uk *w*: www.sound-scotland.co.uk *Contact* Fiona Robertson, festival co-ord. NE Scotland's festival of new music.

Sounds New 127 Shalmsford St, Chartham, Cantebury. *t*: 01227 731818 *e*: info@soundsnew. org.uk *w*: www.soundsnew.org.uk Festival of contemporary music.

Soundwaves Festival 21 Preston Drove, Brighton. *e*: info@soundwaves-festival.org.uk *w*: www. soundwaves-festival.org.uk Festival of new music in Brighton.

Southern Cathedrals Festival Dept of Liturgy and Music, Salisbury Cathedral, 33 The Close, Salisbury. *t*: 01722 555148 *f*: 01722 555117 *e*: s.flanagan@ salcath.co.uk *w*: www.southerncathedralsfestival. org.uk *Contact* David Halls, artistic dir. Features sacred music in the English choral trad, sung by the cathedral choirs of Chichester, Salisbury and Winchester.

Spitalfields Music 61 Brushfield St, London. *t*: 020 7377 0287 *f*: 020 7247 0494 *e*: info@ spitalfieldsmusic.org.uk *w*: www.spitalfieldsmusic. org.uk *Contact* Diana Burrell, artistic dir; Abigail Pogson, exec dir. Classical and new music festival with year-round educ & community programme.

Spring Sounds Orchestra of the Swan, Civic Hall, 14 Rother St, Stratford-upon-Avon. *t*: 01789 267567 *e*: info@springsounds.co.uk *w*: www. springsounds.co.uk Festival featuring Orchestra of the Swan and various acclaimed soloists.

St Cuthbert's Music Festival *t*: 01749 672611 *e*: portpubs@blueyonder.co.uk *w*: www. st.cuthbertswells.co.uk *Contact* Terry Delaney. Annual event at the Church of St Cuthbert, Wells. Lunchtime and evening events covering wide range of musical tastes, with performers ranging form soloists to well-known orchs.

St Davids Cathedral Festival St Davids Cathedral /Gwyl Eglwys Gadeiriol Tyddewi, Deanery Office, St Davids. *t*: 01437 720057 *f*: 01437 721885 *e*: cathedralfestival@onetel.com *w*: www. stdavidscathedral.org.uk *Contact* Katherine Pearce, admin; Alexander Mason, artistic dir.

St Endellion Festival c/o Glebe Farmhouse, St Endellion, Port Isaac. *e*: sally@donegani.com; trevilley@tiscali.co.uk; spicerannie@aol.com *w*: www.endellion.org.uk *Contact* Sally Donegani, artistic admin; Patrick Gale, chair; Annie Spice, PR/ mailing lists. The festival draws on a mixture of professionals and professional-standard amateurs to mount a sequence of opera, orch, choral and chmbr concerts and church services. Most concerts given in ancient church of St Endellion, with one in Truro Cathedral. Participation is by invitiation (send CVs to Sally Donegani). Non-performing volunteers welcome (contact Patrick Gale). Shorter festival each easter.

St Magnus Festival 60 Victoria St, Kirkwall, Orkney. *t*: 01856 871445 *f*: 01856 871170 *e*: info@stmagnusfestival.com *w*: www.stmagnus festival.com *Contact* Glenys Hughes, dir; Angela Henderson, admin. Orkney's midsummer celebration of the arts: music, theatre, visual arts, literature, community events, excursions, Festival Club, Orkney Conducting Course and St Magnus Composers' Course.

Stour Music 2 Rural Terrace, Wye, nr Ashford. *t*: 01233 812267 *e*: mark.deller@virgin.net *w*: www.stourmusic.org.uk *Contact* Mark Deller, festival dir. Festival of early music.

Stratford on Avon Music Festival *t*: 01274 858249 *f*: 01271 858375 *e*: eucorch1@aol.com *w*: www.stratfordmusicfestival.com *Contact* Ambrose Miller.

Stroud and District Arts Festival 2 Bridge St, Cainscross, Stroud. *t*: 01453 750009 *e*: whisper andshout@tiscali.co.uk *w*: www.stroudartsfestival. org *Contact* Fred Ward, chair. Local organisations put on events they would not otherwise attempt. Applications welcome, outlining and costing proposed event for 2009 festival.

Suffolk Villages Festival 119 Maldon Rd, Colchester. *t*: 01206 366603 *f*: 01206 543417 *e*: info@suffolkvillagesfestival.com *w*: www. suffolkvillagesfestival.com *Contact* Peter Holman, artistic dir; Louise Jameson, admin. Early music.

Summer Music - Hallé Promenade Concerts Hallé Concerts Society, The Bridgewater Hall, Manchester. *t*: 0161 237 7000 *f*: 0161 237 7029 *e*: info@halle.co.uk *w*: www.halle.co.uk *Contact* Sir Mark Elder CBE, mus dir; John Summers, chief exec.

Sunbury and Shepperton Arts Festival Riverside Arts Centre, 59 Thames St, Sunbury-on-Thames. *w*: www.riversidearts.co.uk

Swaledale Festival Hudson House, Reeth,

Richmond. *t:* 01748 880018 *f:* 01748 880028 *e:* enquiries@swaledale-festival.org.uk *w:* www.swaledale-festival.org.uk *Contact* Harriet Smithson, admin. Eclectic mix of classical, jazz, folk, world and brass along with arts, poetry and country walks. Tradition of commissioning new works.

Swanage Jazz Festival 2 Alexandra Terrace, Swanage. *t:* 01929 425371 *e:* fredlindop@tiscali.co.uk *Contact* Fred Lindop, artistic dir. Many bands from across the jazz spectrum, inc established names and new talents.

Swansea Festival of Music and the Arts 9 Gabalfa Rd, Sketty, Swansea. *t:* 01792 411570, also fax *e:* admin@swanseafestival.org *w:* www.swanseafestival.org *Contact* Susan Croall, admin; Huw Tregelles Williams, chair.

Symposium for Young String Quartets 8 Woodlands Rd, Romford. *t:* 01708 761423, also fax *e:* info@playquartet.com *w:* www.playquartet.com *Contact* Ruth Wheal, gen mgr. Various diverse events celebrating the art of the string quartet.

Tenby Arts Festival 24 Penally Heights, Penally, Tenby. *t:* 01834 845341 *w:* www.tenbyartsfest.co.uk *Contact* Diana Lunn, sec. Programme available summer 2009.

Tetbury Music Festival PO Box 52, Tetbury. *t:* 01453 833708 *e:* info@tetburymusicfestival.org.uk *w:* www.tetburymusicfestival.org.uk *Contact* Elise Smith, Graham Kean, co-dirs; Steven Isserlis, admin; Sarah Priday, admin; Steven Isserlis, artistic adviser. Annual classical music festival.

Thaxted Festival Clarance House, Thaxted. *t:* 01371 831421, also fax *e:* thaxtedfestival@btconnect.com *w:* www.thaxtedfestival.org.uk *Contact* Gareth Stainer, artistic dir; Ann Pickhaver, admin. Classical music, opera and jazz.

Three Choirs Festival 7c College Green, Gloucester. *t:* 01452 529819 *f:* 01452 502854 *e:* info@3choirs.org *w:* www.3choirs.org *Contact* Geraint Bowen, artistic dir, Hereford; Adrian Partington, artistic dir, Gloucester; Adrian Lucas, artistic dir, Worcester; Paul Hedley, gen mgr. Oldest non-competitive festival in Europe; cycles round the 3 cathedral cities of Hereford, Gloucester and Worcester in rotation. Comprises nightly choral and orch music in one of the cathedrals, alongside a full programme of chmbr mus.

Tilford Bach Festival Fairlawne, Kiln Way, Grayshott, Hindhead. *t:* 01428 713338 *w:* www.tilford-bach.org.uk *Contact* Laurence Cummings, Adrian Butterfield, mus dirs; Sheila Austin, hon sec. At Farnham Castle and All Saints Church, Tilford.

Towersey Village Festival Mrs Casey Music, PO Box 296, Matlock. *t:* 01629 827017 *f:* 01629 821874 *e:* info@towerseyfestival.com *w:* www.towerseyfestival.com Relaxed, family-friendly festival; eclectic mix of concerts, w/shops, dances and dedicated youth and children's programmes.

Tudeley Festival Postern Park Oast, Tonbridge. *t:* 01732 773322 *f:* 01732 773344 *e:* tudeleyfestival@aol.com *w:* www.tudeleyfestival.org.uk *Contact* Stephen Coles, artistic dir.

Two Moors Festival Barkham, Sandyway, Exmoor, South Molton, Devon. *t:* 01643 831370, also fax *e:* enquiries@thetwomoorsfestival.com *w:* www.thetwomoorsfestival.com *Contact* Penny Adie MBE, artistic dir; Jon Adie, chief exec.

UK Songwriting Festival Bath Spa University, Newton Park, Newton St Loe, Bath. *t:* 01225 875522 *f:* 01225 875495 *e:* e.ginn@bathspa.ac.uk *w:* www.uksongwritingfestival.com *Contact* Joe Bennett, artistic dir; Emmanuelle Ginn, admin. Opportunity to share enthusiasm for songwriting with other songwriters; tutors available; chance to record in state-of-the-art recording studio.

Ulverston International Music Festival The Box Office, Coronation Hall, County Sq, Ulverston. *t:* 0845 658 8982 *e:* ulverstonmusicfestival@googlemail.com *w:* www.ulverstonmusicfestival.co.uk *Contact* Rowena Gibbons, admin. Internationally renowned musicians perform in Ulverston and surrounding area. Also autumn and winter concerts, plus educ activity programme.

Upton Jazz Festival Upton Jazz Association Ltd, 18 Riverside Close, Upton-upon-Severn. *t:* 01684 593254, also fax *e:* info@uptonjazz.co.uk *w:* www.uptonjazz.co.uk *Contact* Deirdre Thompson. International jazz festival.

Vale of Glamorgan Festival of Music Festival Office, 20 Orchard St, Llandovery, Carms. *t:* 01550 721565 *e:* valeofglamorgan.festival@virgin.net *w:* www.valeofglamorganfestival.org *Contact* John Metcalf, artistic dir; Deborah Keyser, admin. Annual festival of living composers held at venues in and around the Vale of Glamorgan.

Voices in Paisley 21 Forbes Place, Paisley. *t:* 0141 849 1721 *e:* info@paisleyfestivalcompany.com *w:* www.paisleyfestivalcompany.com Autumn festival incorporating Paisley Choral Festival and Fringe Voices! The festival brings professional and amateur, local, national and international choirs plus performers of vocal harmony in non-choral styles to 'Scotland's choir town'.

Winchester Festival Winchester Festival Ltd, The Cathedral Office, 1 The Close, Winchester. *t:* 01962 857240 *f:* 01962 857201 *e:* winchesterfestival@ winchester-cathedral.org.uk *w:* www.winchester festival.co.uk *Contact* Carol Butler.

Windsor Festival 3 Park St, Windsor. *t:* 01753 714364 *f:* 01753 866845 *e:* info@windsorfestival. com *w:* www.windsorfestival.com *Contact* Martin Denny, festival dir. Over 80 events celebrating music, literature and local heritage. International and local performers and events opportunities for children and families.

Wirksworth Festival Festival Office, Church Walk, Wirksworth. *t:* 01629 824003 *e:* info@wirksworth festival.co.uk *w:* www.wirksworthfestival.co.uk *Contact* Janette Hockley-Webster, operations mgr.

Wooburn Festival Sunrise, Harvest Hill, Bourne End. *t:* 01628 530492 *e:* briandiana@talktalk.net *w:* www.wooburn.com *Contact* Brian Johnson, chair.

Wyastone Summer Series Wyastone Leys, Monmouth. *t:* 01600 891090 *f:* 01600 891052 *e:* concerts@wyastone.co.uk *w:* www.wyastone. co.uk/wyastone *Contact* William Boughton, artistic dir. Biennial series of 12 concerts staged in the Wyastone Concert Hall on the banks of the River Wye outside Monmouth.

Wycombe Arts Festival *t:* 01494 528226 *f:* 01464 512000 *e:* johnw.beaumont@virgin.net *w:* www.wycombeartsfestival.org

York Early Music Christmas Festival The National Centre for Early Music, St Margaret's Church, Walmgate, York. *t:* 01904 632220 *f:* 01904 612631 *e:* info@ncem.co.uk *w:* www.ncem.co.uk *Contact* Delma Tomlin, admin dir.

York Early Music Festival The National Centre for Early Music, St Margaret's Church, Walmgate, York. *t:* 01904 632220 *f:* 01904 612631 *e:* info@ ncem.co.uk *w:* www.ncem.co.uk *Contact* Delma Tomlin, admin dir; John Bryan, artistic adviser; Robert Hollingworth, artistic advisor

IRELAND

CORK

City in the south of the country linked to the coast by river Lee. The port part of city is located in one of the world's largest natural harbours. Ireland's tallest building (the Elysian, a modern design) is in the city; majority of architecture dates from 19th century however.

🎼 Musical life

Cork Opera House stages a range of productions (opera only small part of overall repertoire); opera also at Everyman Palace. Music at Triskel Arts Centre tends to be traditional Irish, jazz, pop etc rather than classical.

🏛 Other cultural information

Art gallery at University College Cork as well as municipal gallery. Everyman Palace the main theatre venue, Triskel Arts Centre has range of performance and visual arts; Cork Arts Theatre is new venue for small-scale theatre productions (100-seat auditorium); Granary focuses on contemporary and experimental performance.

🎭 Festivals and events

Long established annual choral festival in Apr-May. Jazz festival in Oct; Midsummer Festival a multi-arts and entertainment event. West Cork Music in Jun has international classical musicians, not in city but in Bantry (about 50km along coast); East Cork Early Music Festival just outside city in nearby Midleton.

ℹ Tourist information

www.cometocork.com; tel +353 214255100

CIT CORK SCHOOL OF MUSIC

Union Quay, Cork.
t: +353 21 480 7300 f: +353 21 454 7601
e: bmus@cit.ie w: www.cit.ie
Contact Gabriela Mayer (international enquiries). Courses Bachelor of music, master of arts (performance, composition). Application requirements School leaving certificate or equivalent; audition. Term dates Sep-Jun. Application deadline 15 Jan (BMus); 15 May (MA or Erasmus). Fees EUR 3085 (BMus); EUR 3293 (MA). Erasmus students pay fees at home institution. Exchange details Exchange partnerships with conservatoires in Austria, Finland, Germany, Romania, Italy. No of students 117 students.

A new, purpose-built home for the CSM provides 13,000m² of state-of-the-art facilities and includes a library, 60 studios (equipped with new Steinway grand pianos), a large auditorium, a drama theatre, recording studio, an electronic music studio, an Audiolab, a MusicITlab, and a postgraduate centre. CSM is Ireland's largest conservatory of music and drama and its staff includes many performers of national and international standing.

IRELAND

DUBLIN

Irish capital on the river Liffey where it meets the Irish Sea on the east of the country. Main period of historical development was in 17th/18th century period of prosperity; architecture of the city strongly reflects this period – distinctive riverside Custom House is a good example. Also significant location in the uprisings eventually leading to independence of Republic of Ireland from British rule. City is popular among students (3 universities; several other institutions) and attracts visitors from around the world, eg to the nightlife of the Temple Bar area.

♪ Musical life

Gaiety Theatre for opera (base for Opera Ireland) as well as musicals; another Dublin-based company is Opera Theatre Company (company tours throughout the country). National Concert Hall is base for National Symphony Orchestra of Ireland, orchestra managed by RTÉ broadcaster, as is RTÉ Concert Orchestra and Vanburgh Quartet. RDS Concert Hall has classical and rock concerts. Traditional music performed widely in pubs and other venues across the city.

▥ Other cultural information

One of world's most renowned literary cities, counting Joyce, Beckett, Wilde, Yeats, George Bernard Shaw and Swift among its prominent figures. James Joyce Centre promotes events about the author; Shaw Birthplace museum. Theatre therefore a major artform: Abbey Theatre is national theatre and most famous; theatre spaces at The Helix arts centre. Project Arts Centre focused on contemporary performance and visual arts

Festivals and events

Importance of literature reflected in existence of Dublin Theatre Festival and Fringe Festival (both Sep), and Dublin Writers' Festival (early Jun); choir and organ festival in Jun (triennial, next 2011), also triennial piano competition (May, next 2009). Unique event is Bloomsday, every 16 Jun, the day in which Joyce's *Ulysses* takes place, when episodes from the novel are recreated. St Patrick's Day (17 Mar) a big day of national celebration repeated worldwide.

ℹ Tourist information

www.visitdublin.com; tel: 1850 230 330 (from Ireland) / 0800 039 7000 (from UK) / +353 66 979 2083 (from rest of world).

DIT CONSERVATORY OF MUSIC AND DRAMA

163-167 Rathmines Rd, Dublin 6.
t: +353 1 402 3513 *f:* +353 1 402 3512
e: international@dit.ie *w:* www.dit.ie
Contact Ann Flynn, international student officer. *Courses* Bachelor of music, bachelor in music education, foundation certificate in music (1 year); also bachelor of arts in drama (performance). Postgrad: master of music (performance), postgraduate diploma in music (performance), MPhil and PhD by research and compostion. Also Junior Conservatory, part time instrumental and vocal tuition. *Application requirements* See website for details. *Term dates* Sep 2009-Jun 2010 *Application deadline* 1 Feb (EU applicants apply through Central Applications Office); Apr (non-EU applicants apply through DIT International Office). *Fees* EU applicants who are first time undergrads and resident in EU state for at least 3 of the preceding 5 years are not normally required to pay tuition fees for bachelor of music, bachelor in music education and bachelor of arts in drama (performance). For current information on fees, please see website. *Accommodation* Accommodation office produces list of available living accommodation. *No of students* Over 200 full time undergrad/postgrad students.

ROYAL IRISH ACADEMY OF MUSIC

36-38 Westland Row, Dublin 2.
t: +353 1 6764412 *f:* +353 1 6622798
e: info@riam.ie *w:* www.riam.ie
Courses BA and master in music performance, diploma in music (1 year), bachelor in music education, doctorate of music in perfomance; new BA in composition. *Music facilities* Various ensembles: symphony and chamber orchestras; jazz ensemble, wind ensembles, percussion ensemble; choral groups.

UK & IRELAND

IRELAND

MUSIC FESTIVALS

Cork International Choral Festival Civic Trust House, 50 Pope's Quay, Cork. *t:* +353 21 4215125 *f:* +323 21 4215192 *e:* info@corkchoral.ie *w:* www.corkchoral.ie *Contact* John Fitzpatrick, festival director. World class festival celebrating the best of choral and vocal music. Programme includes prestigious international and national competitions, gala and fringe concerts, public performances, and an education programme.

The East Cork Early Music Festival 95 Main St, Midleton, County Cork. *t:* +353 21 463 6761 *e:* info@eastcorkearlymusic.ie *w:* www. eastcorkearlymusic.ie *Contact* Deirdre O'Tuama, festival mgr.

Galway Early Music Festival Caherfurvaus, Craughwell, Co Galway. *t:* +353 87 930 5506 *e:* info@galwayearlymusic.com *w:* www. galwayearlymusic.com *Contact* Maura o Cróinin, chair; Natalie Surina, PR. Medieval, renaissance and baroque music and dance. Imaginative programming in the medieval city of Galway includes concerts, w/shops and free public perfs. 2009 theme: 'Islands and the waters between'.

Kilkenny Arts Festival 9-10 Abbey Business Centre, Abbey St, Kilkenny. *t:* +353 56 776 3663 *f:* +353 56 775 1704 *e:* info@kilkennyarts.ie *w:* www.kilkennyarts.ie *Contact* Aine Dennehy, interim administrator. Multi-arts festival covering classical, jazz, contemporary and traditional music, visual arts, literature, theatre and children's events.

Pipeworks St Catherine's Church, Thomas St, Dublin 8. *t:* +353 85 786 8860 *e:* adminpipeworks@ gmail.com *w:* www.pipeworksfestival.com Triennial festival featuring organ-playing competition.

Quiet Music Festival *w:* www.quietmusicensemble. com *Contact* John Godfrey, mus & artistic dir; Sarah O'Halloran, artistic dir & mgt. Deep listening retreat, new music, improvisation, film, dance.

Shannon International Music Festival *t:* +353 61 213 130 *e:* ico@ul.ie *w:* www.irishchamber orchestra.com *Contact* Boris Hunka.

St Patrick's Spring Fest Limerick City Festival Office, 3rd Floor, 78 O'Connell St, Limerick. *t:* +353 61 404 335 *f:* +353 61 400355 *w:* www.limerick springfest.com *Contact* Sarah Lynch, festival director; Fintan Breen, participant co-ordinator. Includes marching band competition, St Patrick's Day parade, Pery Square fair and ancillary events.

West Cork Chamber Music Festival West Cork Music, 13 Glengarriff Rd, Bantry, Co Cork. *t:* +353 27 52788 *f:* +353 27 52797 *e:* westcorkmusic@ eircom.net *w:* www.westcorkmusic.ie *Contact* Grace O'Mahony, box office/finance managgr; Sara O'Donovan, PR manager

Wexford Festival Opera 49 North Main St, Wexford. *t:* +353 53 91224009 *f:* +353 53 9124289 *e:* info@wexfordopera.com *w:* www. wexfordopera.com

Teach Music? Study Music?

This is your ESSENTIAL guide to MUSIC EDUCATION

British

Music Education

Yearbook 2009

£39

Rhinegold Directories

New edition for 2009 – OUT NOW

The British Music Education Yearbook is a mine of knowledge on all aspects of music education.

 Get the inside track with articles from leading experts and practitioners on everything from music scholarships to summer schools.

 'Masterclasses' from leading experts in conducting, accompanying and rehearsing.

 Career advice – whether you want to be a sound engineer or a music journalist we have the right guidance for you.

Extensive and detailed listings include:

- Application details for hundreds of independent school music scholarships

- Profiles of every UK university music department and comparative table for their degrees

- Invaluable information on scholarships, grants and awards available for music study

- Contact details for hundreds of music retailers, instrument manufacturers, local music services and much more!

To order call +44 (0)20 7333 1720 or visit **www.rhinegold.co.uk**

EUROPE

The European Association of Conservatoires (AEC) – supporting student mobility worldwide

Association Européenne
des Conservatoires,
Académies de Musique
et Musikhochschulen (AEC)

As the music sector is becoming even more international than before, mobility is taking a bigger role in musicians' lives. Studying abroad within or in Europe benefits a music student as they will function in a different social atmosphere and musical environment and give them the opportunity to gain more insight into the international music field. It also offers young musicians the possibility to gain flexibility that is required in the professional world of music. This way, young musicians can also develop their network internationally and make professional contacts.

However, changing countries for the whole study or a study exchange period can sometimes be very challenging. In Europe, there are many differences between national systems for higher music education. Starting with the different use of terminology (conservatoire, conservatory, school of music, music academy, Musikhochschule, and music university), it is already confusing for music students to get an overview of the situation in the European context. Even if the music student chooses the conservatoire or music academy of their choice or to go on an exchange, there are various issues to consider, such as grants, the recognition of studies, visa procedures and working permits. One could find this vast amount of information from different websites or resources, yet one European association uses its expertise in professional music training and its wide European and international network to make this information available as one concentrated source to music students, teachers and conservatoire management.

The European Association of Conservatoires (AEC) was established in 1953 as a cultural and educational network and it currently represents almost 300 institutions for higher music education worldwide (www.aecinfo.org). It aims to stimulate and support international collaboration between member institutions and to realise international project about subjects relevant to professional music training. One of these projects is the 'DoReMiFaSOCRATES' project, aimed at the development of an informational website (www.doremifasocrates.org) for students, teachers and the general public on music activities in the cooperation programmes of the EU. The website is updated regularly and contains a vast amount of information about European cooperation activities in the field of higher music education. Furthermore it offers information to music students as well as teachers on various topics such as recognition of studies, and practical details regarding the Erasmus exchange programmes. A section of the website is dedicated specifically to music students, including a weblog by music students currently on exchange and personal stories by students based on their experiences as exchange students.

Another website hosted by the AEC is the 'Study Music in Europe' website (www.studymusicineurope.org) which is specifically aimed at students outside Europe interested in studying music in Europe. This website is available in five languages (English, French, Spanish, Portuguese and Chinese) and focuses on providing concrete information to music students on studying in European conservatoires and music academies. 'Study Music in Europe' contains access to websites of higher music education institutions and information on national higher education system. It also offers practical information that music students need to take into consideration.

Apart from hosting these websites, the AEC organises many meetings each year: an annual congress, where conservatoire leaders from member institutions come together to discuss issues relevant to the higher music education sector and to present projects or works, and an annual meeting for international relations coordinators where the focus is on international cooperation and the exchanges of students and teachers. Recently, AEC also started two topic specific platforms: the Pop & Jazz Platform and the Early Music Platform to address the needs of these sub-sectors. AEC is also pro-active in maintaining and creating a broad network of relations with the European institutions (European Parliament, European Commission and Council of Ministers), national governments, and institutions and networks in the field of music and education at national, European and international levels. In order to make the voice of the sector heard, AEC publishes policy papers and recommendations on a regular basis dealing with the latest European developments in the fields of education (www.bologna-and-music.org) and culture. In addition, the AEC has been the recipient of various EU grants to run European projects in the field of higher music education, including the Erasmus Network for Music 'Polifonia' (www.polifonia-tn.org), which is the largest European project on higher music education to date.

Crossing Europe to study – An introduction to Erasmus

For those interested in travelling abroad to study, there are three principal ways of doing so. The first is to apply directly to institutions that catch your eye, following whatever degree programme, diploma or other qualification is appropriate. This will mean several years' study abroad, a daunting prospect for some, one which may not be suitable for every subject – going to France to study French literature is one thing; going to study history may or may not be.

Another is to take advantage of exchange partnerships set up between individual institutions. If you are considering travelling abroad as part of your course, it is worth asking the conservatoires or colleges you are interested in whether they have such partnerships and if so, with whom.

In order to give a greater number of students the opportunity to travel abroad within Europe, the European Union set up the Erasmus scheme, the third method. Erasmus stands for European Region Action Scheme for the Mobility of University Students (it is also the name of a Dutch renaissance theologian). It is one of several educational programmes that fall under the umbrella of the EU's 'Lifelong Learning Programme 2007-2013'; others focus or have focused on activity in schools, adult education, vocational training and so on. Erasmus itself has a number of aims as well as increasing the number of exchanges and improving the quality of the experience for those undertaking them, but it is the individual students who are the obvious beneficiaries.

Under the scheme, students and teachers at one of the 2200 or so universities across the 30+ participating countries who are also citizens of one of those countries can take advantage of the opportunity to spend from three months to one academic year at a European university. This kind of year abroad system has been long part of the modern language student's higher education experience, and for obvious reasons – it is surely one of the best ways to learn a foreign language, and students can pick up much about a culture through exposure to daily life there. However, for many of these students the year abroad counts little directly to their final degree results, rather like sandwich years spent working in industry for students more generally.

As with institution-to-institution exchange schemes, conservatoires and universities will have established Erasmus partners (so again, it is worth checking with whom). Although this may appear restrictive, it does mean that the two colleges in question will have developed a relationship, making it less likely that your stay there will be affected by basic lack of understanding between the colleges, or a failure of expectation.

But the real advantage for Erasmus students is that the marks they earn on any courses they take while on exchange are recognised as part of their home degree course. There is another advantage, however: students are not required to pay tuition fees at the institution they are travelling to. This gives Erasmus students an advantage over those applying direct, particularly when travelling to a country with a policy of levying substantial tuition fees. Other financial help is available too. Once offered an Erasmus place, students can apply for an Erasmus grant through the institution they are visiting; this aims to help with living costs, although it is unlikely to be sufficient to cover all living costs.

THE BOLOGNA PROCESS

If you have already started making enquiries about travelling to study within Europe, you will probably have come across the term 'Bologna Process'. Nothing to do with making ragù, the term refers to the long-term aim of harmonising educational standards across the continent, agreed at a meeting in 1999 in the Italian city. Although not an EU initiative in the same way that Erasmus is, its goals are similar: promoting ease of movement between European countries; promoting the European education system more widely; broadening the European knowledge-base.

The principal way in which this aim is being worked towards is the European Credit Transfer and Accumulation System (ECTS). Because different countries have different educational traditions concerning length of degree course, what qualifications are required, course content and how students' knowledge is tested, a mechanism for recognising equivalences was needed. In the system that was chosen, ECTS credits are based on the workload students will undertake to fulfil course requirements. Each year of higher education study amounts to 60 ECTS credits (with 1 credit amounting to 25-30 hours' work).

Since this system is linked to time taken to complete studies, it has also been necessary to draw degree levels closer together. The typical pattern adopted is a 3-cycle system with a 3-year (180 ECTS) 1st cycle equivalent to a bachelors degree; 2-year (120 ECTS) 2nd cycle masters equivalent; 3-year (180 ECTS) doctorate. (Some Bologna-compliant institutions prefer a 4-year bachelors plus 1-year masters.)

That is not to say that the system has been adopted without difficulties. An obvious problem is the insistence that credits in one programme are transferable to another. Your proficiency in literature does not make you a concert-standard pianist, for example, so institutions are necessarily able to use discretion in who they accept. Some countries will be Bologna-compliant in certain areas but not in others; others adopted the proposals quickly, others are still in the process of taking them on board (the aim is for all to conform by 2010).

That said, the process was intended as a framework rather than an absolute rigid structure, and for most students, certainly music students looking to advance their training towards professional levels, much of this is immaterial. Conservatoires in particular are keen to promote themselves internationally, and the more cross-border movement there is, the more they will be helped in achieving this aim.

The following websites are useful for students wanting to find out more:
European Commission Education & Training Detailed website covering education in the EU, including summary of Erasmus and other programmes
http://ec.europa.eu/education
The AEC Bologna Declaration and Music Resource run by Association of European Conservatoires (AEC)
www.bologna-and-music.org
IRIS – Integrated Reporting for International Students Provides information about Erasmus institutions
http://iris.siu.no

Bologna Process signatories – the European Higher Education Area
Albania, Andorra, Armenia, Austria, Azerbaijan, Belgium, Bosnia & Herzegovina, Bulgaria, Croatia, Cyprus, Czech Republic, Denmark, Estonia, Finland, France, Georgia, Germany, Greece, Hungary, Iceland, Ireland, Italy, Latvia, Liechtenstein, Lithuania, Luxembourg, Malta, Moldova, Montenegro, the Netherlands, Norway, Poland, Portugal, Republic of Macedonia, Romania, Russia, Serbian, Slovakia, Slovenia, Spain, Sweden, Switzerland, Turkey, UK, Ukraine

From ancient Greece to 19th century period performances via medieval, renaissance and the baroque

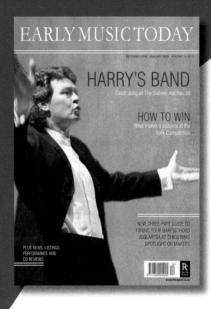

Read interviews with leading conductors, performers and ensembles

Keep up to date with the latest early music news

Receive practical advice from buying a new instrument to managing an ensemble

Find out more about the best new CDs and books

PLUS **Masterclasses, concerts and events in The List**

Austria and Germany

NOTIZ

Austria and Germany

Many would say that Austria and Germany the two countries most closely associated with the classical music tradition over the longest time. This is reflected in the sheer number of institutions dedicated to professional music training there. That is not to mention the number of professional opportunities open to qualified music graduates compared with many other countries.

Many German and Austrian cities have particular associations with composers or musical movements: Salzburg and Mozart, Brahms and Vienna and so on. These connections undoubtedly enhance the musical experience of those studying, living and working there. However, thanks to the number of institutions waiting to welcome students from around the world, there are opportunities to discover many less well-known locations offering a different quality of life, or specific leisure activities.

AUSTRIA

Two types of institution are listed here: state-funded music university and 'Privatuniversität' (private university; actually funded at a municipal level), each offering bachelors and masters degrees following the Bologna system of equivalences. All follow the national 2-semester system, with institutions responsible for setting their own academic calendar within that. Curriculum is also determined by each institution.

In common with many countries, Austria operates a 3-cycle system: bachelor (3 or 4 years depending on the institution), magister (masters) and doktor (doctorate). ECTS credits are awarded at 60 per year of study in the first 2 cycles.

International students can get help finding accommodation in halls of residence across Austria via ÖAD Housing (www.housing.oead.at), with a range of accommodation available. This service is not open to Austrian students. You will, however, have to pay rent and living expenses, but conservatoires may offer grants and scholarships to help, and there are also various foundations and grant-awarding organisations which may be able to help. These will vary from place to place however; contact the international office at the institution you are interested in to find out more, or check websites.

GERMANY

Primarily, professional music training in Germany is through one of its 24 'Staatlichen Musikhochschule' (literally, state music high schools). Each of Germany's states administers one or more such institution; thanks to the government structure of the country, in which each state is an autonomous administrative area linked to the others through a federal apparatus, education systems (and hence the way conservatoires are run) differ from state to state.

Although the Hochschule are equivalent in status to universities, performance students, unlike their counterparts in Austria, do not have the opportunity for doctoral study (although this is under review) — studies at postgrad level conclude with the Konzertexamen. However, and this is where Hochschule differ from universities, undergraduate studies have traditionally lasted 5 years (10 semesters); this situation is changing only gradually. And music graduates usually receive a 'Diplom' rather than a bachelors degree (German law requires that bachelors degrees are completed early enough to allow a masters to be finished in 5 years).

Deutscher Acakadmischer Austausch Dienst (German Academic Exchange Service; www.daad.de) website has comprehensive information for overseas students wishing to study in Germany.

AUSTRIA

GRAZ

Significant student population (6 universities attracting 36,000 from around 100 countries). City has a distinctive Austrian architectural style blending characteristic Austrian gothic and baroque with Balkan and Italian-influenced buildings. Situated in south-facing basin in the shelter of the Alps, giving a more Mediterranean climate than other Austrian towns.

♪ Musical life

Home to Grazer Oper opera company, performing a season of opera at its own baroque opera house; also home to Grazer Philharmonische, which doubles as the opera orchestra. Visiting orchestras at late 19th century Stefaniensaal.

🏛 Other cultural information

Modern Helmut-List-Halle stages broad range of popular and contemporary performances from modern dance to rock. Large number of museums and galleries, including modern art gallery, natural history museum, city museum, gallery of old art, as well as more unusual exhibitions such as the Hans Gross Criminological Museum and the Hanns Schell Collection of locks and keys.

🎪 Festivals and events

Annual Styriarte music festival (named after Styria, the region where Graz is located) in Jun and Jul

ℹ Tourist information

www.graztourism.at; info@graztourismus.at; tel +43 316 8075 0

KUNSTUNIVERSITÄT GRAZ (KUG) (UNIVERSITY OF MUSIC AND PERFORMING ARTS GRAZ)

Palais Meran, Leonhardstr 15, A-8010 Graz.
t: +43 316 389 1100; +43 316 389 1160 (international relations) f: +43 316 389 1101
e: info@kug.ac.at w: www.kug.ac.at
Contact Irene Hofmann-Wellenhof, head of dept of international relations. Courses Bachelors, masters and doctoral study programmes in audio engineering, catholic & protestant church music, conducting, composition & music theory, instrumental studies (accordion, bass tuba, chamber music for strings & pianists, clarinet, double bass, early music recorder, early music harpsichord, early music viola da gamba,

bassoon, flute, french horn, guitar, harp, oboe, organ, percussion instruments, piano, piano vocal accompaniment, saxophone, trombone, trumpet, viola, violin, violoncello), jazz (various instruments & voice), music education (voice & instruments), voice, musicology. Non-degree students also admitted at discretion of intended professor. Also, study programmes in stage design and performing arts/drama. *Application requirements* Min age 17 (15 for instrumentalists). Entrance exam (audition, theory & aural test); certain courses require university entrance qualifications equivalent to Austrian 'Matura'. Details of requirements for Erasmus students available on website. *Term dates* Early Oct -late Jan (winter semester); early Mar-late Jun (summer semester). *Application deadline* Full schedule of application dates and deadlines on website. *Fees* None, or EUR 363.63 per semester, depending on course. For further information on fees, see education ministry website: www.bmwf.gv.at/submenue/studienbeitraege *Scholarships* See website for details. *Exchange details* Erasmus, Ceepus and exchange agreements worldwide. *Language requirements* German. *Music facilities* Library facilities: 190,000 volumes incl books, journals, sheet music, records, tapes and other media. *Accommodation* International students eligible for housing in halls of residence (dependent on space) via ÖAD organisation: www.housing.oead.at *No of students* 2287 students in total, 982 from overseas.

LINZ

A city with a largely industrial background and lacking the characteristic 'fairytale' architectural style, but it has taken advantage of its location on the Danube to become a thriving, culturally active place. One the European Cities of Culture in 2009.

♪ Musical life

Anton Bruckner born just outside the city, hence the riverside Brucknerhaus concert hall (actually 3 separate concert spaces), home to the Bruckner Orchester. As well as its own concerts, the orchestra provides accompaniment for the town's opera company.

🏛 Other cultural information

Very active cultural life, with its own modern art gallery (the Lentos, also near the Danube), and the

EUROPE

Kulturmeile ('culture mile') riverside park with various culture venues and occasional open-air events. Theatre spaces at regional Landestheater Linz and the drama company based there.

Festivals and events
Annual Brucknerfest in September and October, a fairly traditional music festival complemented by the international Ars Electronica fair, celebrating its 30th anniversary in 2009. Brucknerfest is preceded by the 3-day Pflasterspektakel, a festival of street art.

Tourist information
www.linz.at; tourist.info@linz.at; tel +43 732/7070-2009

ANTON BRUCKNER PRIVATUNIVERSITÄT FÜR MUSIK, SCHAUSPIEL UND TANZ
Wildbergstr 18, A-4040 Linz.
t: +43 732 70 1000 0 *f:* +43 732 70 1000 30
e: international@bruckneruni.at *w:* www. bruckneruni.at
Contact Gregor Unterkofler, rectorat. *Courses* 300 courses offered in music, dance and drama. *Application requirements* Entrance exam. *Term dates* 14 Sep-21 Feb (winter term); 22 Feb-3 Jul (summer term). *Application deadline* End Jun. *Fees* EUR 100 per term. *Exchange details* 20 international partners across Europe. *No of students* 840 students, inc 280 from overseas.

SALZBURG
A Unesco world heritage site, place of pilgrimage for Mozart-lovers, and one of Europe's premier cultural tourist destinations, famed for its baroque architecture and overlooked by its hilltop castle, its population of just over 210,000 more than doubles during holiday times as visitors arrive from around the world.

Musical life
Camerata Salzburg is the city's high quality chamber orchestra, and Mozarteum Orchester, its busy regional symphony orchestra. Salzburg's profile makes it an attractive destination for touring performers, especially amateur, youth and student choirs and orchestras, with many concerts in its host of churches. Opera comes via the Salzburger Landestheater.

Other cultural information
Landestheater is the biggest theatre venue in the city, and home also to a theatre company. History of the city told in the Carolino Augusteum museum and its five branches across the city; Mozarts Geburtshaus (birthplace) and Mozarts Wohnhaus (residence, actually a reconstruction) both house museums. These are run by the Internationale Stiftung Mozarteum (International Mozart Foundation), an organisation promoting knowledge of Mozart and his work based in Salzburg.

Festivals and events
Salzburger Festspiele festival during the summer is one of the world's foremost classical music events. Sister festival, Salzburger Osterfestspiele, during the spring, with annual opera performance by Berliner Philharmoniker.

Tourist information
www2.salzburg.info; tourist@salzburg.info; +43 662 88 98 7 0

UNIVERSITÄT MOZARTEUM SALZBURG
Mirabellplatz 1, A-5020 Salzburg.
t: +43 662 6198; +43 662 6198 2230 (foreign relations) *f:* +43 662 6198 3033 *e:* ilse.kainz@ moz.ac.at *w:* www.moz.ac.at
Contact Ilse Kainz, foreign relations manager *Courses* Over 40 artistic and education courses in music, performing and visual arts. International exchange of lecturers and students. *Application requirements* See website for details of entrance requirements. *Term dates* 1 Oct-1 Mar (winter semester); 2 March-30 September (summer semester). *Application deadline* 30 April 2009. *Scholarships* Various scholarships available. *No of students* 1600 students, inc 60 from overseas.

VIENNA
City with a particularly strong musical and intellectual influence, beginning in particular with the music of Haydn, Mozart and Beethoven, but also including the likes of the Second Viennese School in music and the Third Viennese School in psychology. Viennese literature closely identified with the coffee-house culture of the late 19th and early 20th centuries, a culture which still survives today in many ornate or idiomatically designed rooms. Today's combination of more modern

EUROPE

83

attractions, including a diverse and vibrant nightlife, with its historical setting is gives the city an atmosphere of its own.

♪ Musical life

The Wiener Philharmoniker play at the Musikverein whose main hall (nicknamed the Goldener Saal), is as famed for its acoustics as the orchestra is for its quality. Plenty of opera, with the Wiener Staatsoper, Volksoper Wien, Theater an der Wien (which leans towards musicals), and Wiener Kammeroper all promoting full seasons. Also home to one of the world's renowned contemporary music groups, Klangforum Wien. Operetta and concerts of Viennese music typified by the Strauss family abound; Viennese balls are a firm feature of city life, not restricted to tourists.

Other cultural information

City's tradition of intellectual enquiry has left a legacy of theatre, both traditional and contemporary. Several museums and galleries can be found at the Museumsquartier (museum quarter), including the Ludwig Foundation museum of modern art and the Leopold Museum.

Festivals and events

Wiener Festwochen is the main annual arts festival; has a classical music component based at the Wiener Konzerthaus. This is also the venue for the autumn Wien Modern festival of modern music.

ⅰ Tourist information

www.vienna.info; info@wien.info

KONSERVATORIUM WIEN PRIVATUNIVERSITÄT

Johannesgasse 4a, A-1010 Wien.
t: +43 1 512 77 47 89364 (international study programme) *e:* office@konswien.at; studieninfo@konswien.at (international study programme *w:* www.konservatorium-wien.ac.at
Contact Peter Koenigseder, international study programme manager *Courses* Bachelors and masters programmes in music and dramatic arts. General training plus majors in jazz, early music, music theatre, drama and dance, and music education. *Fees* EUR 220 (Austrian and EU nationals) *No of students* Approx 850 students, 40% from overseas.

UNIVERSITÄT FÜR MUSIK UND DARSTELLENDE KUNST WIEN (UNIVERSITY FOR MUSIC AND PERFORMING ARTS VIENNA)

Anton-von-Webern-Platz 1, A-1030 Wien.
t: +43 1 71155; +43 1 71155 *f:* +43 1 71155 199 *e:* aausseninstitut@mdw.ac.at *w:* www.mdw.ac.at
Courses Degree programmes and continuing education courses. *Application requirements* Entrance examination. *Term dates* 1 Oct -31 Jan (winter semester); 2 Mar-30 Jun (summer semester). *Application deadline* May (undergraduate courses); end April (masterstudies programme). *Fees* None (Austrian, EU, EEA and Swiss nationals); EUR 363.36 per semester (others). *Scholarships* Various scholarships available to foreign students registered at the university who have excellent grades and demonstration of need; see website for details. Applications accepted between Feb and Mar. *Exchange details* Various exchange programmes, including Erasmus/LLP and programmes with individual institutions worldwide. *Language requirements* Acceptable level of German proficiency required, assessed by Goethe Institute test. Language courses offered. *Accommodation* See website for details of accommodation agencies. Austrian Exchange Service (ÖAD) can assist in finding dormitory rooms for exchange students.

MUSIC FESTIVALS

34th International Music Festival Lothringerstr 20, A-1030 Wien. *t:* +43 1 242 00 100 *w:* www.konzerthaus.at Part of Wiener Festwochen.

Allegro Vivo International Chamber Music Festival Austria and Summer Academy, Wiener Str 2, A-3580 Horn. *t:* +43 2982 4319 *f:* +43 2982 4314 *e:* office@allegro-vivo.at *w:* www.allegro-vivo.at *Contact* Robert Berger, admin director. Early, baroque, classic Viennese, romantic, contemporary music. Concerts, summer academy.

Austro-Hungarian Music Festival Martin Randall Music Management, Voysey House, Barley Mow Passage, London. *t:* +44 20 8742 3355 *f:* +44 20 8742 7766 *e:* info@martinrandall.co.uk *w:* www.martinrandall.com Annual. Concerts in abbeys, palaces and country homes beside or within easy reach of the Danube, with leading local ensembles and soloists.

Bregenz Festival Platz der Wiener Symphoniker 1,

EUROPE

AUSTRIA

A-6900 Bregenz. *t:* +43 5574 407 6 *f:* +43 5574 407 400 *e:* info@bregenzerfestspiele.com *w:* www. bregenzerfestspiele.com Aida on floating stage.

Bruckner Festival Linz Linzer Veranstaltungs-gesellschaft mbH, Brucknerhaus Linz, Untere Donaulände 7, A-4010 Linz. *t:* +43 7327 76120 *f:* +43 7327 7612 2069 *e:* marketing@liva.co.at *w:* www.brucknerhaus.at Music festival with classical and modern music and a wide range of different musical events including orchestral concerts, opera, chamber music and dance.

Chopin Festival of the International Chopin Society in Vienna at Chartehouse Gaming Biberstr 4, A-1010 Wien. *t:* +43 1512 2374 *f:* +43 1512 237475 *e:* office@chopin.at *Contact* Theodor Kanitzer, director; Doris Tarlowski, general secretary. Orchestral, choral, chamber and symphonic music, recitals.

Franz Liszt Festival Raiding Festival Office, Schloss Esterhazy, A-7000 Eisenstadt. *t:* +43 2682 61866 *f:* +43 2682 61805 *e:* office@franz-liszt. at *w:* www.lisztfestival.at *Contact* Walter Reicher, artistic director; Thomas Mersich, marketing director. Annual festival in the new concert hall at Liszt's birthplace in Raiding.

Haydn Festival - Eisenstadt Festival Office, Schloss Esterhazy, A-7000 Eisenstadt. *t:* +43 2682 61866 *f:* +43 2682 61805 *e:* office@ haydnfestival.at *w:* www.haydnfestival.at *Contact* Walter Reicher, artistic dir; Thomas Mersich, marketing director. Annual festival at the Esterhazy Palace. Orchestras, chamber ensembles, vocal recitals, masses and oratorio. Focusing on Joseph Haydn, with references to other composers.

Innsbruck Festival of Early Music Herzog-Friedrich-Str 21/1, A-6020 Innsbruck. *t:* +43 512 571032 *f:* +43 512 563142 *e:* info@altemusik. at Annual event featuring baroque music (2 operas, 25 concerts) played on period instruments at historic sites.

Internationale Sommerakademie Universität Mozarteum Mirabellplatz 1, A-5020 Salzburg. *t:* +43 662 6198 4500 *f:* +43 662 6198 4509 *e:* summer.academy@moz.ac.at *w:* www.moz.ac.at *Contact* Michaela Bartsch M/classes for voice and most instruments, classical music.

Mozart Week Mozart-Wohnhaus, Theatergasse 2, A-5024 Salzburg. *t:* +43 662 87 31 54 *f:* +43 662 87 44 54 *e:* tickets@mozarteum.at *w:* www. mozarteum.at

Musik-Festival Grafenegg Grafenegg Kulturbetriebsgesellschaft.mbh, Kulturbezirk 2, A-3109 St Poelten. *t:* +43 2742 908070 *f:* +44 2742 908071 *e:* office@tonkuenstler.at *w:* www. grafenegg.at *Contact* Johannes Neubert, manager; Antonia Schmidt-Chiari, festival office; Julia Ormetsmüller, media. International artists in both orchestral concerts and recitals; annual composer-in-residence. Concerts take place in newly built open air auditorium and concert hall.

Musikprotokoll ORF-Steiemark, Marburger Str 20, A-8042 Graz. *t:* +43 316 47 028227 *f:* +43 316 47 028253 *e:* musikprotokoll@orf.at *w:* http:// oe1.orf.at/musikprotokoll Contemporary music.

Musiktage Mondsee Postfach 3, A-5310 Mondsee. *t:* +43 6232 3544, also fax *e:* karten@musiktage-mondsee.at *w:* www.musiktage-mondsee.at Chamber music with international artists.

Opernfestspiele St Margarethen Kirchengasse 20, A-7062 Sankt Margarethen in Burgenland. *t:* +43 2622 82605 *f:* +43 2622 82613.

Osterfestspiele Salzburg Herbert-von-Karajan-Platz 9, A-5020 Salzburg. *t:* +43 662 8045 361 *f:* +43 662 8045 790 *w:* www.osterfestspiele-salzburg.at Sister festival to main Salzburger Festspiele in August.

Salzburger Festspiele Hofstallgasse 1, A-5020 Salzburg. *t:* +43 662 8045 500 *f:* +43 662 8045 555 *e:* presse@salzburgfestival.at *w:* www. salzburgfestival.at *Contact* Jürgen Flimm, artistic director; Helga Rabl-Stadler, president; Ulla Kalchmair, press officer. Opera, plays and concerts of the highest artistic standards. Over 200 performances, 12 venues; eminent opera performers, the best singers, performers and actors worldwide.

Schubertiade Schwarzenberg Villa Rosenthal, Schweizer Str 1, A-6845 Hohenems, Postfach 100. *t:* +43 5576 72091 *f:* +43 5576 75450 *e:* info@ schubertiade.at *w:* www.schubertiade.at

Styriarte/Summer Music Festival in Styria Palais Attems, Sackstr 17, A-8010 Graz. *t:* +43 316 8 12941 *f:* +43 316 825 00015 *e:* tickets@styriarte. com *w:* www.styriarte.com Classical and baroque music, chamber and orchestral music, operas, children's orchestra.

Tiroler Festspiele Erl Adamgasse 1, A-6020 Innsbruck. *t:* +43 512 57 88 88 *f:* +43 512 56 09 98 *e:* info@tiroler-festspiele.at *w:* www.tiroler-festspiele.at *Contact* Hans Peter Haselsteiner,

EUROPE

president; Gustav Kuhn, president & festival director; Andreas Leisner, second director; Maria-Theresia Müller, financial & admin director. Classical music, opera.

Wien Modern PO Box 140, Lothringerstr 20, A-1037 Wien. *t:* +43 12 4200 *f:* +43 12 4200 111 *e:* polzer@wienmodern.at 20th C music. Interdisciplinary festival.

BERLIN

German capital since reunification in 1990, a major international centre. As the point where eastern and western Europe met, it has a unique history, one leaving a city whose architecture, outlook and cultural activities are a diverse blend of old and new.

♪ Musical life

Berliner Philharmoniker is one of world's most prestigious orchestras and although concerts are well subscribed, it is usually possible to get tickets for concerts. Many others besides: Konzerthausorchester Berlin (formerly the Berliner Sinfonieorchester), Deutsches Symphonie-Orchester, Rundfunk Sinfonieorchester Berlin. Many international orchestras tour here. Similarly well provided with opera, with 3 main companies falling under the umbrella of the Stiftung Oper Berlin: Deutsche Oper Berlin, Staatsoper Unter den Linden, and Komische Oper. Modern music – techno, dance, jazz, experimental etc – also strong feature of Berlin nightlife.

🏛 Other cultural information

As with music, various traditional activities (museums, theatres and such like), but noted for adventurous activities in art and performance art. Hosts numerous street carnivals and festivals such as the annual Carnival of Cultures, although the famed Loveparade has had to move elsewhere.

🎭 Festivals and events

Berliner Festspiele organisation runs several annual music events: MaerzMusik (Mar) concentrates on contemporary music; musikfest berlin (Sep) is major international music festival, featuring Berliner Philharmoniker; Jazz Fest Berlin runs in Nov, as does the young musicians' festival Treffen Junge Musik-Szene. Other events also: Inventionen is another modern music event; Berliner Tage für Alte Musik is an autumn early music festival. Berlin hosts one of the world's major film festivals (known as the Berlinale) in Feb.

ⓘ Tourist information

www.berlin-tourist-information.de; information@btm.de. tel: +49 30 26 47 48 0;

HOCHSCHULE FÜR MUSIK 'HANNS EISLER' BERLIN

Charlottenstr 55, D-10117 Berlin.
t: +49 30 688305 700; +49 30 688305 831 (international realtions) f: +49 30 688305 701; +49 30 688305 730 (international relations) e: schmidt_ute@hfm.in-berlin.de w: www.hfm-berlin.de

Contact Ute Schmidt, international relations. Courses Courses from undergraduate to Diplom level: wind and string instruments, voice, piano, composition, coaching, music theory (harmony), percussion, conducting (orchestral, choral), music theatre direction, harp, guitar, jazz (instrumental and vocal). Application requirements Secondary school qualifications (Abitur) or outstanding musical talent; German language test certificate (TestDaF Level 4); audition for main study. Term dates Oct-Feb (winter semester); Apr-mid Jul (summer semester). Application deadline 15 Apr. Fees No tuition fees; small admin fees (approx EUR 250 per semester). Exchange details UK exchange partner: Royal Academy of Music; also partnerships with 37 European and 3 North American institutions. Music facilities Various ensembles including symphony and chamber orchestras, contemporary music ensemble, chorus, symphonic wind orchestra. No of students 242 national, 329 international students.

UNIVERSITÄT DER KÜNSTE BERLIN

Fakultät Musik, Einsteinufer 43-53, D-10587 Berlin.
t: +49 30 3185 2320; +49 30 3185 2196 (foreign student office) f: +49 30 3185 2687; +49 30 3185 2727 (foreign student office) e: aaa@udk-berlin.de (foreign student office) w: www.udk-berlin.de

Contact Ursula Stephan-Rechenmacher, foreign student office. Courses Diplom study courses: artistic training (instrumental or conducting), composition, church music, sound engineering, jazz; pedagogical education (including jazz); musicology and music education (doctoral), and artistic training (choral conducting) available at further level. Exchange details Partnerships with approx 120 foreign institutions. Music facilities University theatre, 2 big concert halls; also studios, rehearsal rooms, library. No of students Approx 130 students from partner institutions around the world.

GERMANY

BREMEN

Town of about half a million people in northern Germany, linked by the river Weser to its port of Bremerhaven based round a medieval old town and market square with its 13th century cathedral and Dutch Renaissance influenced town hall. Location of a statue of the Musicians of Bremen, a tale by the Brothers Grimm, in which Bremen is the intended destination of three mistreated animals in search of a better life.

🎼 Musical life

Main orchestra is Bremer Philharmoniker, gives monthly concerts plus chamber music performances from smaller ensembles drawn from its ranks.

🏛 Other cultural information

Particular maritime theme to town due to its nautical links – there is a maritime museum and even a theatre ship. Contemporary art museum

🎭 Festivals and events

Annual music festival in Aug/Sep, plus triennial international contemporary dance festival, Tanz Bremen. Free Samba carnival in February. The Freimarkt is an annual civic fair, claimed to be the oldest in Germany.

ℹ️ Tourist information

www.bremen-tourism.de; btz@bremen-tourism.de; tel +49 1805 10 10 30

HOCHSCHULE FÜR KÜNSTE BREMEN

Am Speicher XI 8, D-28217 Bremen.
t: +49 4 21 95 95 10 00 *f:* +49 4 21 95 9520 00 *w:* www.hfk-bremen.de
Contact Birgit Harte, international contact. *Courses* Instrumental and vocal courses, plus church music, jazz, music education. 4-semester postgrad concert performance degree. Current diploma courses to be replaced by modular bachelors and masters courses, beginning 2010/11 year. *Music facilities* Range of performance opportunities offered; projects with local orchestras such as Bremer Philharmoniker.

COLOGNE (KÖLN)

Rhineland city, home to one of the world's oldest universities, with links back to ancient Rome. Probably most famous for its cathedral which survived the wartime bombing which destroyed the historic centre; architectural reconstruction in a contrasting postwar style. Echoes of its history do remain, however.

🎼 Musical life

Oper Köln (which runs its own international opera studio) has a relatively varied repertoire. Kölner Philharmonie is the city's major concert hall, with two resident orchestras: WDR Sinfonieorchester Köln and Gürzenich-Orchester Köln, but a varied programme of events including jazz and contemporary music. City has a tradition in baroque music, even if the group that carried its name, Musica Antiqua Köln has now disbanded.

🏛 Other cultural information

Important centre for the art trade, with several trade fairs each year, including Cologne Fine Art, Art.Fair and Art Cologne; art galleries and dealers are plentiful. Among variety of exhibitions, most important museum is surely the Imhoff-Stollwerck Museum of Chocolate! Theatre to suit different tastes, at the Schauspielhaus (where opera also performed) and in more informal cabaret and comedy theatres.

🎭 Festivals and events

Best known event is Carnival, beginning on the same day every year, 11 Nov (the event even has its own museum).

ℹ️ Tourist information

www.koelntourismus.de; tel: +49 221 221 304 00

HOCHSCHULE FÜR MUSIK KÖLN

Dagobertstr, 38, D-50668 Köln.
t: +49 221 912818 0 *f:* +49 221 131204
e: kirstein@mhs-koeln.de *w:* www.mhs-koeln.de
Contact Birgit Kirstein, international affairs. *Courses* Bachelors and masters courses introduced in 2008. Courses in 1st cycle for strings, winds, sax, harp, percussion, accordion, harpsichord, piano, organ, recorder, guitar, mandolin, lute, viola da gamba, opera/concert singing, choral/orchestral conducting, composition (electronic, instrumental), church music, jazz. Masters level for solo instruments, period instruments, new music interpretation, opera singing, lied/recital singing, piano accompaniment, chamber music, electronic composition.

DETMOLD

Small city in northern Germany with a relatively rural setting in the Teutoberg forest (famous as a battlefield in which German tribes resisted Roman advances, establishing the northernmost limit of the Roman empire) and an attractive, largely intact old town.

♪ Musical life

Largely based round the music academy; there is a chamber orchestra in the town, the Detmolder Kammerorchester.

🏛 Other cultural information

Theatres, museums, cabaret and so on; its location and surroundings mean there are various other sport and leisure activities.

🦋 Festivals and events

Biggest events are biennial Strassentheater Festival Detmold (even numbered years), and a summer theatre festival; also a festival of short films in Jun.

ⓘ Tourist information

www.stadtdetmold.de; tourist.info@detmold.de; tel: +49 5231 977 328

HOCHSCHULE FÜR MUSIK DETMOLD

Neustadt 22, D-32756 Detmold.
t: +49 5231 975 773 *f:* +49 5231 975 754
e: info@hfm-detmold.de *w:* www.hfm-detmold.de
Courses Courses for training as composer, orchestral musician, pianist, singer (opera, recital or oratorio), conductor, church musician, music teacher. Additional orchestral training available at Orchesterzentrum in Dortmund. *Fees* EUR 500 per semester, plus EUR 115.07 registration fee. *Music facilities* 10 specially equipped buildings in campus, including concert hall.

DRESDEN

Main city in Saxony, eastern Germany, much of whose historic built environment, legacy of the city's role as a royal residence, was destroyed during World War II. Since then, and particularly since reunification, various restoration projects have got under way, most notably the baroque Frauenkirche.

♪ Musical life

Opera at the magnificent Semperoper, whose orchestra, the Sächsische Staatskapelle also presents a full season of symphony concerts at the house with various international conductors and soloists. Staatsoperette Dresden is one of the few theatres devoted to light music, particularly known for performances of music by Johann Strauss. City is also home to the Dresdner Philharmoniker and its associated choirs such as the Philharmonische Chor. Reputation for choral singing added to by Dresdner Kreuzchor, the boys' choir which sings services at the church of the same name.

🏛 Other cultural information

Several theatres operating under the aegis of the Staatschauspiel Dresden. Several important art collections, with, among others, a gallery dedicated to old masters; a museum (the Grünes Gewölbe) of artefacts, statues, jewellery etc; and the Mathematisch-Physikalischer Salon, a collection of scientific instruments

🦋 Festivals and events

Mainly classical music at the Dresdner Musikfestspiele in May-Jun. Trad jazz at the Dixieland Festival just beforehand; contemporary music at the Dresdner Tage der Zeitgenössischen Musik in October, mostly at the Festspielhaus Hellerau.

ⓘ Tourist information

www.dresden.de; info@dresden-tourist.de; tel: +49 351 49192 100

HOCHSCHULE FÜR MUSIK CARL MARIA VON WEBER DRESDEN

Box 120039, D-01001 Dresden.
t: +49 351 4923 641; +49 351 4923 638 (international relations); +49 351 4923 634 (registrar) *f:* +49 351 4923 604 *e:* rektorat@hfmdd.de; ausland@hfmdd.de (international relations); studsek@hfmdd.de (registrar) *w:* www.hfmdd.de
Contact Gerda Werner, international relations; Sebastian Bauer, head of admission/registrar's office *Courses* Artistic studies in orchestral instruments, voice, piano, conducting, composition, music theory and accompaniment. Also wide range of studies in jazz/rock/pop, music education and musicology. Studies usually 5 years, leading to

equivalent of masters degree; students with bachelor degrees are usually put into 4th year. See website for full breakdown of courses. *Application requirements* Audition in person, entrance exam, suitable proficiency in German. *Term dates* Sep-Feb (winter semester); Mar-Aug (summer semester). *Application deadline* 31 Mar. *Fees* EUR 160 admin fee per semester; tuition fees for postgrad students only (EUR 300 per semester standard rate). *Language requirements* German; no classes offered in foreign languages. Website gives details of institutions in Dresden offering language tuition. *Accommodation* Independent organisation, Studentenwerk Dresden, manages halls of residence. See www.studentenwerk-dresden.de for more information. *No of students* 600 students.

DÜSSELDORF

Busy commercial city in Germany's western region, particularly well-known for its fashion industry. Large overseas population; several educational institutions are based there. Among well-known musical figures from the city is the band Kraftwerk, pioneers in the use of electronic music; Düsseldorf was home to Robert and Clara Schumann towards the end of his life, the Rhine there being the river he made his infamous leap.

♪ Musical life

Two main concert venues: Palais Wittgenstein for smaller concerts and recitals; Tonhalle Düsseldorf for orchestral and larger scale performances – resident orchestra is the Düsseldorfer Symphoniker. This group provides orchestral players for certain performances of the Deutscher Oper am Rhine, based partly in the city, partly in nearby Duisburg. The organisation also runs a ballet company and a youth opera arm.

▥ Other cultural information

Large number of theatres, including town's Schauspielhaus for traditional theatre, Kom(m)ödchen for political satire, Komödie for cabaret and comedy, a puppet theatre, children's theatre and venues devoted to more experimental and avant-garde performance. Several contemporary art galleries. City subsidises 'Art:card' promotions, giving free entry and discounts at various venues

✎ Festivals and events

Altstadtherbst Kulturfestival is annual performing arts event not restricted to music; biennial Robert Schumann festival. Two connected street carnival events in Feb and Nov.

ℹ Tourist information

www.duesseldorf-tourismus.de; info@duesseldorf-tourismus.de; tel: +49 211 17 20 20.

ROBERT SCHUMANN HOCHSCHULE DÜSSELDORF

Fischerstr 110, D-40476 Düsseldorf.
t: +49 211 49 18 0 *f:* +49 211 49 11 618
e: rsh@rsh-duesseldorf.de *w:* www.rsh-duesseldorf.de
Courses Programmes in conducting, church music (evangelical and catholic), composition, orchestrals instrumental music performance, organ, guitar, recorder, music education; musicology (available as accompanying subject, subject on Master's course, or subject of doctorate); also audio and video engineering (in association with University of Applied Sciences, Dusseldorf). Also postgrad courses, doctoral studies. *Application requirements* General higher education entrance diploma; aptitude test for relevant subject. *Term dates* Early Oct-mid Feb (winter term lecture period); early Apr-mid Jul (summer term lecture period). *Application deadline* 31 Mar. *Fees* EUR 500. *Scholarships* None. *Exchange details* Erasmus. *Language requirements* Goethe-Institute certificate B2 in German. *Accommodation* Accommodation available through www.studentenwerk-duesseldorf. de. *No of students* 949.

ESSEN

Ruhr valley city, named European City of Culture on behalf of the Ruhr area for 2010. Traditionally an industrial city not especially thought of as a tourist destination, nonetheless history goes back beyond medieval times, and it boasts an impressive 14th century cathedral. Recent building includes imaginative recycling of industrial buildings for artistic commercial use, such as the converted Zollverein colliery (now a Unesco World Heritage Site).

♪ Musical life

Modern designed Aalto Theater opera house for

EUROPE

opera and orchestral concerts (Philharmonie Essen and visiting orchestras).

Other cultural information

Grillo-Theater staging conventional drama productions; Grugahalle is for larger scale popular entertainment. Museums and galleries include a design museum and poster museum among a handful of the more conventional kind.

Festivals and events

Ruhr Triennale multi-disciplined arts festival in venues in Essen and neighbouring towns and cities during late summer/early autumn.

Tourist information

www.essen.de; touristikzentrale@essen.de; tel: +49 201 8872041

FOLKWANG HOCHSCHULE

Klemensborn 39, D-45239 Essen.
t: +49 201 4903 0 f: +49 201 4903 288
e: info@folkwang-hochschule.de w: www.folkwang-hochschule.de
Courses Instrumental training for different musical instruments (accordion, bassoon, cello, clarinet, double bass, flute, guitar, harp, harpsichord, horn, oboe, organ, percussion, piano, recorder, saxophone, trombone, trumpet, tuba, viola, violin); jazz/performing artist; integrative composition (instrumental composition, electronic composition, jazz composition, pop composition, composition and visualisation); church music; voice (concert performance, lieder, oratorio and music theatre); school music; music pedagogy; musicology in combination with an artistic subject; musicals. Application requirements Entrance exam; sample theory test and application form available from website. Term dates 1 Apr-30 Sep (summer term); 12 Oct-5 Feb (winter term). Application deadline Feb for winter term. Fees EUR 30 application fee; study fees EUR 500 per term Scholarships Scholarships available. Language requirements Certificate A1 for instrument training, jazz/performing artist, composition, voice; Certificate B2 for musicals, school music, music pedagogy, musicology in combination with an artistic subject. Language courses offered by international office; must be completed before semester begins. Music facilities Practice rooms equipped with piano, grand piano, harpsichord; concert hall with concert and practice organ (from 2010). Accommodation Various options inc furnished apartment, flat let, flat share; information about accommodation available from www.studentenwerk.essen-duisberg.de. No of students 800 national, 361 international students.

FRANKFURT

Transport hub with Germany's main airport and the country's largest railway station in the city. Germany's financial centre, reflected in preponderance of modern buildings and its high-rise skyline. Ironically, also home of Institute of Social Research with its history of Marxist enquiry in the so-called Frankfurt School. Frankfurter Allgemeine is one of Germany's best known newspapers. Also location for many trade fairs such as Frankfurt Book Fair and Musikmesse, one of world's major music trade shows.

Musical life

Alte Oper, former opera house reconstructed as a concert hall, with 2 halls (2500 and 700 seats) hosting touring orchestras plus popular shows. One of city's own orchestras, hr sinfonie orchester (actually run by regional radio company Hessische Rundfunk) plays there and elsewhere; Neue Philharmonie Frankfurt, whose repertoire encompasses much crossover work, based at Capitol Theater in nearby Offenbach. Modern design Opern-und Schauspielhaus Frankfurt is base for Oper Frankfurt, a major company with many premieres and new productions.

Other cultural information

City is birthplace of Goethe, and home of the Goethe-Haus. Riverside location well exploited, with various museums along the banks of the Main — Städel Museum is an art gallery there. City has its own modern art gallery.

Festivals and events

Auftakt Festival of contemporary music in autumn; Summer in the City open air festival. Other civic events not specific to classical music, like the summer Museumsuferfest by the river or Opernplatz Festival outside the Alte Oper. Festival of gay cinema, Verzaubert Internationales Queer Filmfestival, every spring.

GERMANY

i Tourist information
www.frankfurt-tourismus.de; info@infofrankfurt.de;
tel: +49 69 212 38800

HOCHSCHULE FÜR MUSIK UND DARSTELLENDE KUNST FRANKFURT AM MAIN

Eschersheimer Landstr 29-39, D-60322 Frankfurt
am Main.
t: +49 69 154007 0; +49 69 154 007 256
(international office) *f:* +49 69 154007 108;
+49 69 154 007 125 (international office)
e: albrecht.eitz@hfmdk-frankfurt.de *w:* www.
hfdmk-frankfurt.de
Term dates Early Oct-mid Feb (winter semester);
early Apr-mid Jul (summer semester). *Application
deadline* 1 Apr 2009. *Fees* None, except EUR 260
social welfare contribution per semester. *Exchange
details* Exchanges available through Erasmus
scheme. *Language requirements* German language
must be proven by one of the following language
certificates: TestDaF level 3, Goethe-Zertifikat B2,
DSH 1, or KMK 1. Other certificates not accepted.
No of students 850.

FREIBURG-IM-BREISGAU

Black Forest city in south-westernmost tip of
Germany, with the warmest climate in the country.
Agreeable old city area with many buildings or
architectural interest like the Gothic minster with its
vertiginous spire or the 16th century Kaufhaus across
the square from it. Longest cable car in Germany
(3600m) runs from the edge of the city; also tram
system throughout. Traditionally an academic city
with several highly regarded institutions.

♪ Musical life

Most prestigious group is Freiburger Barockorchester,
a period instrument group with a repertoire ranging
to early romantics. More general orchestral music
from SWR Baden-Baden und Freiburg
Sinfonieorchester; its concerts in the city are in the
Konzerthaus, a hall with a mixed programming of
classical and popular music, and other entertainment.
Also Philharmonische Orchester Freiburg at the
Theater Freiburg (primarily for opera).

▥ Other cultural information

Theater Freiburg also has programme of drama and
other performing arts. Usual range of museums and
galleries, many reflecting local history and activity.

 Festivals and events
Main music event is Zelt-Musik-Festival, annual
gathering of musicians of various kinds in a nature-
inspired 'tent city'.

i Tourist information
www.freiburg.de; touristik@fwtm.freiburg.de; tel:
+49 761 3881 880

HOCHSCHULE FÜR MUSIK FREIBURG

Schwarzwaldstr 141, D-79102 Freiburg im
Breisgau.
t: +49 761 3 19 15 0 *f:* +49 761 3 19 15 42
e: info@mh-freiburg.de *w:* www.mh-freiburg.de
Courses Bachelors and masters courses, specialist
performer courses, contemporary music, early music,
jazz. *Application requirements* Entrance exam;
requirements vary depending on course level (see
website for full details) *Term dates* Winter and summer
semesters. *Application deadline* 1 May (winter
semester); 1 Dec (summer semester) *Scholarships* 5
annual prizes for instrumentalists and vocalists,
composers, chamber music ensembles and musicologists.
Music facilities 40 practice rooms open 24 hours a
day; 4 concert halls. Performance opportunities at
over 400 public concerts each year.

HAMBURG

Germany's second-largest city with a population
of just under 2 million, and principal port, on the
North Sea. Criss-crossed by many canals and the
many bridges across them (over 2000), city is
architecturally diverse with many modern building
projects under way.

♪ Musical life

Two principal orchestras: Sinfonieorchester des
Norddeutschen Rundfunks is based there but as the
orchestra of the regional radio station also covers
nearby towns of Lübeck, Kiel and Bremen;
Philharmoniker Hamburg (one of the few orchestras
currently with a female music director, Simone Young)
has its own concert season, and also provides
orchestra for Staatsoper Hamburg (opera and
ballet). The opera house has a reputation for new
works. City has a established tradition as destination
for pop and rock bands (the Beatles are especially
associated with venues there), particularly heavy
metal in recent years. New concert hall currently
being built, the Elbphilharmonie, a spectacular ship-

like construction situated in one of Hamburg's docks.

 Other cultural information

Place of pilgrimage for bikers, but has more traditional entertainments including a state-owned theatre and independent theatres – the English Theatre stages English-language performances. City's maritime history contained in Internationales Maritimes Museum Hamburg.

 Festivals and events

No specific classical music events; Festival der Kulturen in Sep is a celebration of world cultures, including national musics.

i Tourist information

www.hamburg-tourism.de; info@hamburg-tourism.de; tel: +49 40 300 51 300.

HOCHSCHULE FÜR MUSIK UND THEATER HAMBURG

Harvestehuder Weg 12, D-20148 Hamburg.
t: +49 40 428482 415 (international relations
f: +49 40 428482 666 (international relations)
e: international@hfmt.hamburg.de *w:* www.hfmt-hamburg.de
Contact Svenja Tiedt, international co-ord. *Courses* Various courses in solo instrumental, composition/theory, multimedia, orchestral conducting, choral conducting, protestant church music, jazz and jazz pedagogy, opera, oratorio; musicology, music education, culture and media management, music therapy. Bachelors and masters courses available as well as Diplom; see website for levels and degrees available, as well as course duration. *Application requirements* See website for details. *Term dates* Oct -Mar (winter); Apr-Sep (summer). *Application deadline* Differs depending on course. *Fees* EUR 375 per term. *Scholarships* Details available from international office *Exchange details* Exchanges run through Erasmus and Freemover schemes. *Language requirements* German; some study programmes available in English. *Accommodation* Help available through international office. *No of students* Approx 850 students.

HANNOVER

Smart northern German city with good transport links. Old town ruined during World War II bombing,

subsequently reconstructed as a 'new old town'. Particularly well-served with places of nature including landscaped gardens, a botanical garden, an award-winning zoo, deerpark, a lake (the Maschsee) not to mention the European Cheese Centre on the outskirts of the city.

 Musical life

Staatsoper Hannover for opera and ballet, has its own orchestra.

Other cultural information

Wealth of museums on a range of topics from contemporary art to the history of the city and its relationship with the British royal family. Many theatres catering for a range of tastes from serious to cabaret and musicals.

Festivals and events

Fête de la Musique in July (celebrated across the world).

i Tourist information

www.hannover-tourismus.de; info@hannover-tourismus.de; tel: +49 511 12345 111.

HOCHSCHULE FÜR MUSIK UND THEATER HANNOVER

Emmichplatz 1, D-30175 Hannover.
t: +49 511 3100 1; +49 511 3100 7272 (international office) *f:* +49 511 3100 7200; +49 511 3100 200 (international office)
e: hmt@hmt-hannover.de; internationaloffice@hmt-hannover.de *w:* www.hmt-hannover.de
Contact Meike Martin, international office *Courses* At undergrad level, students can take traditional Diplom (9 semesters) or the new bachelors degree (6 semesters). Courses in musical performance/artistic training, music teaching, elementary music education, music teaching, voice/professional operatic singing (foundation course), rhythmics, church music, solo performance (postgrad), musicology (doctorate); jazz, rock, pop; also media management. *Application requirements* Admission exam (Jun 2009 tbc) *Term dates* Oct-Feb (winter semester); Apr-Oct (summer semester). *Application deadline* 15 April. *Fees* EUR 500 *Music facilities* Library with over 200,000 items.

GERMANY

KARLSRUHE

Small west German city, close to border with France, based round early 18th century palace, with unusual fan-shaped layout of streets radiating from the palace. Home to several science research institutions

Musical life

Badisches Staatstheater is main music venue for opera (and theatre), with an orchestra (the Badische Staatskapelle) attached to it. Zentrum für Kunst und Medientechnologie Karlsruhe incorporates the Institut für Musik und Akustik, a public-funded organisation combining research and academic activity with an artistic programme; grants made to individuals for residencies.

Other cultural information

Other cultural organisations at the ZKM include museum of modern art, media museum and library, institute for visual media and a film institute.

Festivals and events

Annual Handel festival and free open-air festival in July.

Tourist information

www.karlsruhe-tourism.de; +49 721 37 20 53 83

HOCHSCHULE FÜR MUSIK KARLSRUHE

Postfach 6040, D-76040 Karlsruhe.
t: +49 721 66 29 0; +49 721 66 29 285 (international relations) f: +49 721 66 29 266
e: isabel.eisenmann@hfm-karlsruhe.de w: www. hfm-karlsruhe.de
Contact Isabel Eisenmann, international relations co-ordinator Term dates Oct-Feb (winter semester); Apr-Jul 2010 (summer semester). Accommodation Some accommodation available through Studentenwerk Karlsruhe.

LEIPZIG

City in Saxony (eastern Germany) with a long musical history, particularly associated with Bach; Mendelssohn and Schumann also have strong connections, and it was the birthplace of Wagner. Also has a strong educational tradition, its university being one of the world's oldest, and it is where Goethe studied. It is supposedly he who gave the city its nickname 'little Paris'.

Musical life

Thomaskirche, Bach's church, still has an active and celebrated boys' choir. Gewandhausorchester Leipzig dates back over 200 years with a long line of celebrated principal conductors, and is one of world's most highly regarded. Is the official orchestra of Oper Leipzig, itself an organisation with long history. Bach-Archiv Leipzig is centre for Bach scholarship; also organises concerts and events, and houses a museum dedicated to the composer. Many concert venues around the town.

Other cultural information

Mendelssohn-Haus museum, based in a house he lived in, devoted to the composer. City zoo specialises in primates. Among various civic museums are a coffee museum; Goethe's literary counterpart Schiller has a museum there. Various cabaret and variety theatres, hence its nickname.

Festivals and events

Bachfest Leipzig, a major annual event in June, and biennial Bach Competition, both organised by Bach Archive; international choral festival in Jul. Hosts an annual book fair in Mar, second only to Frankfurt in Germany.

Tourist information

www.leipzig.de; info@ltm-leipzig.de; tel: +49 341 7104 265

HOCHSHULE FÜR MUSIK UND THEATER 'FELIX MENDELSSOHN BARTHOLDY'

Postfach 10 08 09, D-04008 Leipzig.
t: +49 3 41 21 44 55 f: +49 3 41 21 44 503
e: presse@hmt-leipzig.de w: www.hmt-leipzig.de
Contact Birgit Hendrich Courses Artistic and teacher training in all orchestral instruments, voice, piano, coaching, lieder, chamber music with piano, conducting (orchestral or choral), composition, jazz and pop music, musicals, early music, church music, organ; also répétiteur training. Special courses for instruments taken as minors (eg piccolo, sax, contrabassoon). Application requirements Auditions for performance courses, details of repertoire and other requirements available on website; conductors must take piano and piano accompaniment audition; composers submit scores, sit composition and piano exams. Term dates 1 Sep-28 Feb (winter semester); 1 Mar-31 Aug (summer semester). Application

deadline 31 Mar 2009 (for winter semester). *Fees* Vary, depending on course, from free to EUR 253. *Scholarships* None. *Exchange details* UK partner institutions: Birmingham Conservatoire, Royal Academy of Music, Royal Northern College of Music, Royal Welsh College of Music and Drama, Guildhall School of Music and Drama. Also partnerships with over 30 music institutions across Europe. *Music facilities* Advanced students can take audition as stand-in for Gewandhaus or MDR orchestras. *Accommodation* All students entitled to apply for accommodation; information available via www.studentenwerk-leipzig.de *No of students* 584 national students, 290 from overseas.

LÜBECK

Baltic port city, Unesco world heritage site since 1987 thanks to its exceptionally attractive and characteristic gothic brick architecture – its old town, encircled by water, has 1800 listed buildings. Noted as a producer of quality marzipan, and as home of writer Thomas Mann, one of 3 Nobel prize-winners to have lived in the city. Famously, Bach walked from Arnstadt, over 400km away, to Lübeck to meet Buxtehude.

♪ Musical life
Theater Lübeck holds concerts and music theatre (opera and musicals) performances; city is home to Lübecker Philharmoniker. Visiting performances at Lübeckongress (Musik- und Kongresshalle).

🏛 Other cultural information
Each of the 3 Nobel winners is recognised with a museum: Günter Grass-Haus, Willy-Brandt-Haus; Buddenbrookhaus, named after the novel by Thomas Mann celebrates his work and that of his brother Heinrich. Kunsthalle St Annen art gallery (and occasional concerts).

🎭 Festivals and events
Schleswig-Holstein Musik Festival during Jul and Aug for classical music; Duckstein Festival, also in summer, for all-round arts and entertainment.

ℹ Tourist information
www.luebeck-tourism.de

MUSIKHOCHSCHULE LÜBECK
Grosse Petersgrube 21, D-23552 Lübeck.

t: +49 451 1505 0; +49 451 1505 323 (international office) f: +49 451 1505 300; +49 451 150 303 (international office) e: international@mh-luebeck.de w: www.mh-luebeck.de *Contact* Iwona Alexandra Kwiatkowski, international contact. *Courses* Runs Bologna Process compliant bachelor of music (instrumental, vocal, church music, composition, theory); bachelor of arts; advanced courses (instrumental music, composition, opera/concert singing, soloist class, church music); extension courses in chamber music, piano accompaniment, vocal pedagogy. *Application requirements* Entrance audition; for details see website. *Term dates* Oct-Feb (winter term); Apr-Jul (summer term). *Application deadline* 1 Apr (for winter term); 1 Dec (for summer term). *Fees* None; EUR 83.50 student welfare contributions. *Exchange details* Erasmus exchange partnerships with institutions in the UK, Austria, Belgium, Czech Republic, Denmark, Finland, France, Italy, Netherlands, Norway, Poland, Portugal, Spain, Sweden, Switzerland, Turkey; also other partnerships with McNally Smith College (USA) and Xian Conservatory (China). *Language requirements* German language courses available. *Music facilities* Concert halls and practice rooms, sound and media studios, large library; instruments available for loan. Wide number of performance opportunities; several ensembles inlcuding orchestras, choirs, samba project, gamelan, pop groups. *Accommodation* No campus accommodation service; limited number of rooms available through independent student services such as Studentenwerk Schleswig-Holstein. *No of students* 240 national and 226 international students.

MANNHEIM

City in south west Germany. Home of 18th century Mannheim 'school' of composers such as Johann and Carl Stamitz, and the various techniques of orchestration they developed. Streets are laid out in grid pattern, unusual in Germany, leading up to a grand baroque palace, now home to the Universität Mannheim (although parts are still open to the public).

♪ Musical life
Nationaltheater Mannheim houses opera and ballet companies, as well as theatre. Rosengarten congress centre also serves as concert hall for rock and

classical concerts. Stamitz-Orchester Mannheim is one of Europe's oldest amateur/semi-professional orchestras.

🏛 Other cultural information

Kulturmeile Mannheim links the main cultural institutions: the national theatre, Reiss-Engelhorn-Museums (city's history, theatre museum), plantetarium, municipal art gallery.

🎲 Festivals and events

Major film event, the Internationales Filmfestival Mannheim-Heidelberg. Jazz festival.

ℹ Tourist information

www.tourist-mannheim.de; info@tourist-mannheim.de; tel: +49 621 293 8700

STAATLICHEN HOCHSCHULE FÜR MUSIK UND DARSTELLENDE KUNST MANNHEIM

N7, 18, D-68161 Mannheim.
t: +49 6212923511 *f:* +49 621292 2072
e: studienbuero@muho-mannheim.de *w:* www.muho-mannheim.de

Courses Main subjects include orchestral instruments, keyboard instruments, voice (concert and opera), conducting (orchestra and choir); taught in artistic training, music teacher studies, soloist training (postgrad) degree courses. Doctoral studies available in musicology and music pedagogy. Also jazz/popular music studies at degree level. *Application requirements* Full details of requirements for entrance exams available on website; generally, for performers exam will include solo and chamber music, plus sight reading. *Term dates* 1 Oct-31 Mar (winter semester); 1 Apr-30 Sep (summer semester). *Application deadline* 30 Apr (for winter semester); 1 Dec (for summer semester). *Fees* EUR 500 tuition fee, plus EUR 158 admin costs. *Scholarships* Some scholarships and grants available, as well as student loans.

MUNICH (MÜNCHEN)

Bavarian capital, and Germany's third largest city with approaching 1.5 million residents. Characterised by dramatic modern buildings (BMW headquarters, Allianz Arena football stadium, the Olympiapark) but also older architecture on a grand scale such as the Frauenkirche and Theatinerkirche or the Maximilianeum. It is also a city of bold streets, notably its four royal avenues such as the Maximilianstrasse. Major centre for the brewing industry, as well as, coincidentally, higher education institutions.

🎵 Musical life

Home of Bayerische Staatsoper which, with its orchestra the Bayerisches Staatsorchester, performs at the Nationaltheater (as does its associated ballet company); some performances at the Prinzregentheater. Two other orchestras of international importance: Münchner Philharmoniker, based at the Gasteig cultural centre; and, of even greater renown, the Symphonieorchester des Bayerischen Rundfunks, which also appears at the Gasteig centre as well as the former royal palace, the Residenz. 'Munich's smallest opera house', the Pasinger Fabrik, puts on quirky opera and music theatre performances, alongside other performing arts.

🏛 Other cultural information

Huge number of museums; the Jüdisches Museum München is a new addition. Theatre for all, including for children at the Schauburg; Volkstheater focuses on Bavarian writers; contemporary theatre at the art nouveau Kammerspiele; the Deutsches Theater is angled towards the more popular end.

🎲 Festivals and events

Oktoberfest in early autumn is hugely popular. Münchener Biennale (founded by Hans Werner Henze) is a festival of new music theatre, held every 2 years. Olympic park area stages the free Tollwood Festival in the summer, with rock, pop, world music and jazz concerts, plus theatre and other entertainment.

ℹ Tourist information

www.muenchen.de; tourismus@muenchen.de; tel: +49 89 233 96 555

HOCHSCHULE FÜR MUSIK UND THEATRE MÜNCHEN

Arcisstr 12, D-80333 München.
t: +49 89 289 27 450; +49 89 289 27459 (exchange contact) *f:* +49 89 289 27 419
e: verwaltung@musikhochschule-muenchen.de; karin.betz@musikhochschule-muenchen.de
w: www.musikhochschule-muenchen.de

Contact Karin Betz, Socrates/Erasmus co-ordinator. *Application requirements* Evidence of sufficient knowledge of German to follow course of study (not essential, though desirable, for postgrad), see website for details of accepted qualifications. Min age 16, max age depends on year of study. *Fees* EUR 500. *Scholarships* None available. *Exchange details* Exchange partnerships with institutions in Europe, China, Japan, USA. *Accommodation* Approx 181 rooms looked after by Hochschule

MÜNSTER

City in north west Germany, population of 280,000. Has a particular reputation for education, with around 50,000 students enrolled in institutions there, and for quality of life – its environment encompasses elements of rural and town living, and includes Lake Aa. Sometimes referred to as the bicycle capital of Germany, with a wide network of cycle paths, a secure bike parking space and rental schemes.

♪ Musical life
Informal events such as jazz nights predominate. Halle Münsterland is a congress hall promoting some larger scale events, mostly of a popular nature.

🏛 Other cultural information
Museums such as Graphikmuseum Pablo Picasso in old town area. 2 particular areas: Kreativkai for nightlife, theatre, jazz; Kuhviertel is a favourite student hangout.

♻ Festivals and events
Schauraum culture festival in Sep; Hafenfest Münster in Jun for all-round entertainment and sporting events.

ℹ Tourist information
www.muenster.de; info@stadt-muenster.de; tel: +49 2 51 4 92 27 10

MUSIKHOCHSCHULE MÜNSTER
Ludgeriplatz 1, D-48151 Münster.
t: +49 251 83 27410 *f:* +49 251 83 27430
e: info.mhs@uni-muenster.de *w:* www.uni-muenster.de
Courses Bachelor of music and bachelor of arts qualifications.

ROSTOCK

Northern German city, situated on the Warnow river with a link to the nearby Baltic coast in the district of Warnemünde, a picturesque area with 100m of sandy beach. Its university, Universität Rostock, is one of the oldest in Germany, dating back to 1419. Its port location means the city has ferry links to countries around the Baltic.

♪ Musical life
Norddeutscher Philharmonie performs at the Volkstheater Rostock, also a venue for opera, music theatre, ballet and drama. Concerts also take place at the medieval town hall's baroque banqueting hall. Music academy's concerts add to city's cultural calendar.

🏛 Other cultural information
Maritime museum reflects the city's background

♻ Festivals and events
Main music event is annual jazz festival, OstseeJazz in July.

ℹ Tourist information
www.rostock.de; touristinfo@rostock.de

HOCHSCHULE FÜR MUSIK UND THEATER ROSTOCK
Beim St-Katharinenstift 8, D-18055 Rostock.
t: +49 381 5108 0; +49 381 5108 224 (international office) *f:* +49 381 5108 101
e: hmt@hmt-rostock.de; julia.paetow@hmt-rostock.de *w:* www.hmt-rostock.de
Contact Julia Paetow, head of international office. *Courses* Courses for all orchestral instruments, piano, piano chamber music, guitar, orchestral conducting, coaching, composition, music theory, singing, popular music. Also music education and acting. *Application requirements* Entrance exam. *Term dates* 1 Oct-31 Mar (winter semester); *Application deadline* 1 Jan-1 Feb (for summer semester). *Scholarships* Available for highly talented students. *Exchange details* Member of AEC and Association of Baltic Academies of Music. Contacts with music higher education institutions in UK, Belgium, Hungary and Turkey. *Music facilities* Institution is housed in converted monastery. Includes large opera and concert hall and 2 fully equipped theatre stages. Library with facilities for listening to CDs, records, cassettes.

EUROPE

Multimedia studio and recording studio. *No of students* 350 national, 160 overseas students.

SAARBRÜCKEN

City on the river Saar near the border with France with a history that has seen it occasionally become French, just as certain nearby French towns and provinces have been German. Now maintains close cultural and economic links with neighbours in the so-called SarLorLux (Saarland, Lorraine, Luxembourg) region.

♪ Musical life

Two main venues: Saarländisches Staatstheater for opera, concerts and ballet; Sparte4 for more informal, unconventional or experimental performances. City shares one of Germany's newest orchestras, the Deutsche Radio Philharmonie Saarbrücken Kaiserslauten.

⊞ Other cultural information

Riverside modern art gallery has permanent display of German art and puts on special exhibitions; also museum devoted to region's history, a prehistory museum and museum for ecclesiastical art. Theatres of various sizes from the state theatre down to studios such as the Theater im Viertel; also a puppet theatre and a theatre for children.

☻ Festivals and events

30 year old film festival named after Max Ophüls (born in Saarbrücken); festival of French theatre.

ⓘ Tourist information

www.saarbruecken.de; info@kontour.de; +49 681 93809 0

HOCHSCHULE FÜR MUSIK SAAR - UNIVERSITY OF MUSIC

Bismarckstr 1, D-66111 Saarbrücken.
t: +49 681 96731 0 *f:* +49 681 96731 30 *e: i.* kessler@hfm.saarland.de *w:* www.hfm.saarland. de
Courses Basic courses in voice (opera/recital), orchestral instruments, church music, composition, jazz and popular music; postgrad studies in voice (opera/recital), orchestral instruments, orchestral conducting, choral directing, composition, contemporary music, lied duo, chamber music, jazz and popular music, ear training. Bachelors (8

semesters, except for vocal courses where duration is 10) and masters courses (4 additional semesters) available from summer term 2009 *Scholarships* Various subsidiary and stipend programmes, plus competitions for students. *Music facilities* Concert hall with pipe organ. New media rooms for digital sound and music processing; jazz studio. The Hochschule makes use of other facilities in the city for teaching and performing. *No of students* Over 400 students.

STUTTGART

City in south western Germany on the river Neckar, came into importance during 18th and 19th centuries, and its architecture reflects this period. Has significant amount of green space in centre of city, including a botanic gardens. Its location and climate make it one of Germany's main wine-making areas, although city probably best known for its engineering and technology.

♪ Musical life

Strong musical presence in city. Radio-Sinfonieorchester Stuttgart des SWR, with a programme of about 90 concerts per year, based in the city (and is also known for touring abroad). As well as promoting concerts and chamber music events in its own right, the 400 year old Staatsorchester Stuttgart is orchestra for the Staatsoper Stuttgart, and both have their home in the rotunda-shaped Staatstheater; the company also runs a music theatre group performing contemporary works in non-theatrical locations, and a youth opera group. Stuttgarter Philharmoniker is another symphony orchestra; Stuttgarter Kammerorchester a smaller but internationally renowned group with many concerts in the city.

⊞ Other cultural information

Usual range of theatre and museums. Mercedes-Benz museum for motor enthusiasts.

☻ Festivals and events

Musikfest Stuttgart in Sep; ECLAT festival of contemporary music in Feb, as is Stuttgarter Bachwoche.

ⓘ Tourist information

www.stuttgart-tourist.de; info@stuttgart-tourist.de; tel: +49 711 22 28 240

EUROPE

STAATLICHE HOCHSCHULE FÜR MUSIK UND DARSTELLENDE KUNST STUTTGART

Urbanstr 25, D-70182 Stuttgart.
t: +49 711 212 4631 f: +49 711 212 4632
e: rektor@mh-stuttgart.de w: www.mh-stuttgart.de
Courses Artist's diploma (10 semesters) in various areas: strings and plucked instruments, wind instruments, percussion, voice, piano, organ, historical keyboard instruments, composition and music theory, conducting, opera studies, jazz and popular music. Advanced students can follow soloist class courses (4 semesters). Also 8-semester music education courses and church music courses. *Term dates* Early Oct-mid Feb (winter semester); mid Apr-mid Jul (summer semester). *Music facilities* 500-seat concert hall with Rieger organ; chamber music hall (180 seats). Professionally managed theatre, studio for spoken word, electronic music studio, early music studio, recording studio; library with over 100,000 items. More than 200 teaching rooms and 40 oractice rooms (some available 24 hours a day). Average of 450 concerts per year. *No of students* 770 students from over 40 countries.

TROSSINGEN

Very small town in south west corner of Germany, but well known for its musical contribution (it is home to Hohner, probably the world's best known harmonica and accordion company); refers to itself as 'Die Stadt der Musik'.

♪ Musical life

Dominated by harmonicas, accordions and associated instruments, the town hosts harmonica workshops, there is a harmonica museum, and it is home the Hohner-Konservatorium dedicated to the instrument and its uses. As a result, many blues, jazz and folk performances around the town. Visits from regional orchestras for mainstream classical.

ℹ Tourist information

www.trossingen.de; stadt@trossingen.de; tel: +49 7425 25 0

STAATLICHE HOCHSCHULE FÜR MUSIK TROSSINGEN

Schultheiss-Koch-Platz 3, D-78647 Trossingen.
t: +49 7425 94910; +49 7425 9491 17 (international office); +49 7425 949115 (admission/exams) f: +49 7425 949148
e: lenke@mh-trossingen.de
w: www.mhs-trossingen.de
Contact Martina Lenke, admissions & exams office
Courses Bachelor and Masters study, Solistische Ausbildung (soloist training), doctorate. *Application requirements* Audition. *Term dates* 1 Oct-end Feb (winter semester); 1 Apr-end Jul (summer semester). *Application deadline* 15 Apr (winter semester); 15 Nov (summer semester). *Fees* EUR 500 per semester. *Scholarships* DAAD scholarship. *Exchange details* Over 40 Erasmus partners in Europe; also exchange programmes with USA (California and Oregon). *Language requirements* Basic German. *Music facilities* Concert halls, rehearsal rooms, sound studio; also instrument loans. *Accommodation* Student hostel available: hohnerstiftung@gmx.de *No of students* 400 students, inc 190 international students.

WEIMAR

City with strong artistic and intellectual, not to mention political, history. Original home to Bauhaus design school (a new institution in the city has taken its name); associated with Bach and Liszt, Goethe and Schiller and numerous figures from world of art and design.

♪ Musical life

Staatskapelle Weimar linked with the city for over 400 years, counting Bach, Hummel and Liszt among its Kapellmeisters. Now performs, along with theatre, ballet and opera counterparts, at the national theatre building. Liszt museum, run by the music school bearing his name, with exhibition about him.

🏛 Other cultural information

Bauhaus museum houses one of biggest collections of Bauhaus artefacts.

🎏 Festivals and events

Principal festival is Pèlerinages Kunstfest in late summer, primarily art festival but including music, dance and literature. City contributes to Thuringia Bach Festival taking place all over the region in Apr. Yiddish Summer Weimar, Jul, is Germany's main festival of Yiddish music.

ℹ Tourist information

www.weimar.de; tourist-info@weimar.de; +49 3643 745 0

HOCHSCHULE FÜR MUSIK FRANZ LISZT WEIMAR

Postfach 2552, D-99406 Weimar.
t: +49 3643 555 0; +49 3643 555 148
(applications) f: +49 3643 555 147 e: hans-peter.hoffmann@hfm-weimar.de w: www.hfm-weimar.de
Contact Signe Pribbernow, Hans-Peter Hoffmann. Courses Undergraduate and postgraduate courses in music performance; all instruments, singing/opera, church music, conducting, composition, jazz, early music. Also musicology, arts management and school music. Various orchestras and smaller ensembles, choirs and music theatre group. Application requirements Entrance exam or audition. Term dates 1 Oct-19 Feb (winter semester); 1 Apr-9 Jul (summer semester). Application deadline 15 Mar (winter semester); 15 Nov (summer semester). Fees Approx EUR 160 fees per semester, plus study fees. Scholarships Not usually available. Exchange details UK exchange institutions: Guildhall School of Music and Drama, Royal Scottish Academy of Music and Drama. Also about 50 other European partner institutions. Language requirements German language certificate B2 or test during audition. Music facilities Main building houses concert hall, recording studio, studio for electroacoustic music, book and media library. Individual faculties located in several buildings around the city. Accommodation International students eligible for place in student accommodation; single rooms available from EUR 88-287 per month. No of students c 600 national students, c 300 international students.

Welcome to the future of music, welcome to The LISZT SCHOOL of Music.
We are an internationally recognised school of music in the city of Weimar, the cultural heart of Germany. Unparalleled in terms of our fantastic modern facilities and outstanding faculty, we offer students an ideal environment for learning on their path to becoming professional musicians.

WÜRZBURG

Northern Bavarian city just over 100 km upstream from Frankfurt on the river Main. Apart from its many churches in various styles, city's main architectural feature is the Residenz, a spectacularly ornate baroque palace (it is on Unesco's list of world heritage sites) containing halls, chapel, gardens, frescoes and grand staircases. City overlooked by hilltop castle

♫ Musical life

Numerous churches hold concerts, but main concert venues are Congress Centrum Würzburg and s. Oliver Arena for a variety of events; Philharmonisches Orchester Würzburg performs at the Mainfranken Theater, home also to music theatre, ballet and theatre companies.

Festivals and events

Mozartfest in May-Jul; Africa Festival Würzburg is one of Europe's longest-standing and largest festivals of African music and culture. Many other smaller festivals throughout the year.

i Tourist information

www.wuerzburg.de; tourismus@wuerzburg.de; +49 9 31 37 23 35

HOCHSCHULE FÜR MUSIK WÜRZBURG

Hofstallstr 6-8, D-97070 Würzburg.
t: +49 931 32187 0 f: +49 931 32187 2800
e: dirk.braeuer@hfm-wuerzburg.de w: www.hfm-wuerzburg.de
Courses Diplommusikers/Diplommusikerin qualification available in accordion, early/period music, conducting (choir and orchestra), voice, music theatre, guitar, jazz, church music, piano, orchestral

instruments, organ, composition. *Term dates* Begins in Oct. *Application deadline* 31 March. *Fees* EUR 386.60. *Music facilities* 5 concert halls of various sizes (largest seats 799), computer studio with 12 workstations, small studio, recording studio, experimental music studio. Also extensive library. *No of students* 565 students, of whom 145 are from overseas.

MUSIC FESTIVALS

Altstadtherbst Kulturfestival Düsseldorf Bolkerstr 57, D-40213 Düsseldorf. *t:* +49 211 322332 f: +49 211 322203 e: info@altstadtherbst. de *w:* www.altstadtherbst.de Aims to make a new experience out of classical music, bring old and new together, concerts in unfamiliar venues, etc.

Art Point Trombacher Hof, D-55583 Bad Münster. *t:* +494 670 83616 f: +49 670 83653 e: info@artpoint-th.com *w:* www.artpoint-th.com *Contact* Sigune von Osten. Contemporary and traditional music, multicultural, crossover; audiovisual; soundsculptures, light art; poetry and literature.

Bach Festival Leipzig c/o Bach-Archiv Leipzig, Thomaskirchhof 15-16, D-04109 Leipzig. *t:* +49 341 913 7333 f: +49 341 913 7335 e: bachfest@bach-leipzig.de *w:* www.bachfestleipzig.de *Contact* Dettloff Schwerdtfeger, Geschaftsfuehrer. Annual. 2009 theme Bach-Mendelssohn-Reger.

Bachwoche Stuttgart Johann-Sebastian-Bach-Platz, D-70178 Stuttgart. *t:* +49 711 61921 0 f: +49 711 61921 23 e: office@bachakademie. de *w:* www.bachakademie.de Concerts, symposium, masterclasses.

Beethoven Festival Bonn Kurt-Schumacher-Str 3, D-53113 Bonn. *t:* +49 228 201030 f: +49 228 2010322 e: info@beethovenfest.de *w:* www. beethovenfest.de *Contact* Tilman Schloemp, head of artistic management. Annual festival bringing together world-famous artists and young, highly talented musicians to the Rhineland region.

Berliner Tage für Alte Musik Postfach 580411, D-10414 Berlin. *t:* +49 30 447 6082, also fax e: BerlinAlteMusik@t-online.de; ars.musica@knoware.nl *w:* www.berlinaltemusik.com *Contact* Arnold Riesthuis, director. Concerts, instrument market, workshops.

Berlin Jazz Festival Schapenstr 24, D-10719 Berlin. *t:* +49 30 254 89 0 f: +49 30 254 89 111 e: info@berlinerfestspiele.de *w:* www. berlinerfestspiele.de *Contact* Ihno von Hasselt,

production manager; Bianka Goebel, Andrea Duerr, assistants. Established stars of jazz in the same programme as musicians who have led jazz in the direction of electronics, pop, ethnic and new music.

Donaueschinger Musiktage Karlstr 58, D-78166 Donaueschingen. *t:* +49 771 857266 f: +49 771 857263 *w:* www.swr.de New music festival.

Dresden Days of Contemporary Music Europäisches Zentrum der Künste Hellerau, Karl-Liebknecht-Str 56, D-01109 Dresden. *t:* +49 351 26462 0 f: +49 351 26462 23 e: info@kunstforumhellerau.de *w:* www.zeitmusik.de

Dresden Music Festival PO Box 10 04 53, D-01074 Dresden. *t:* +49 351 478 56 0 f: +49 351 478 56 23 *w:* www.musikfestspiele.com

ECLAT - Festival for New Music Stuttgart Musik der Jahrhunderte, Siemenstr 13, D-70469 Stuttgart. *t:* +49 711 629 0510 f: +49 711 629 0516 e: office@mdjstuttgart.de *w:* www.eclat.org Annual. Contemporary music.

European Youth Music Festival Nibelungenstr 8, D-94032 Passau. *t:* +49 851 52575 f: +49 851 71551 e: Ivan.Bakalow@jugend-musik-passau.de *w:* www.jugend-musik-passau.de *Contact* Ivan Bakalow. Annual. Classical music, etc. Artists aged 10-26, singers up to 30 from all European countries.

Festival Alte Musik Knechtsteden Ostpreussenallee 5, D-41539 Dormagen. *t:* +49 2133 210992 f: +49 2133 214097 e: altemusik@t-online.de *w:* www.knechtsteden-altemusik.de *Contact* Hermann Max, artistic director. Concerts with music in authentic interpretation (early, baroque, classical and romantic music); vocal and instrumental.

Festival Orff in Andechs Kloster Andechs, Bergstr 2, D-82346 Andechs. *t:* +49 8152 376271 f: +49 8152 376239 e: orff@andechs.de *w:* www.orff-in-andechs.de *Contact* Andrea Scheithe-Erhardt, managing director.

Halle Handel Festival Grosse Nikolaistr 5, D-06108 Halle. *t:* +49 345 5009 0222 f: +49 345 5009 0416 e: haendel@halle.de *w:* www. haendelfestspiele.halle.de *Contact* Hanna John, director. Opera, concerts, oratorio, open-air performances, scientifc conference.

Händel-Festspiele des Bad Staatstheaters *w:* www1.karlsruhe.de

Heidelberg Castle Festival Friedrichstr 5,

D-69117 Heidelberg. *t*: +49 622 158 35020 *f*: +49 622 158 35990 *e*: theater@heidelberg. de *w*: www.schlossfestspiele-heidelberg.de Opera, musicals, plays, concerts.

International Handel Festival Göttingen Hainholzweg 3-5, D-37085 Göttingen. *t*: +49 551 384813 0 *f*: +49 551 384813 10 *e*: info@ haendel-festspiele.de *w*: www.haendel-festspiele. de *Contact* Benedikt Poensgen. Annual. Baroque music festival. Fringe programme, open air concerts.

International May Festival c/o Hessisches Staatstheater Wiesbaden, PO Box 3247, D-65022 Wiesbaden. *t*: +49 611 132264 *f*: +49 611 132244 *e*: intendanz@staatstheater-wiesbaden. de *w*: www.maifestspiele.de *Contact* Manfred Beilharz, artistic director. International performances of opera, drama, ballet, musicals, gala performances, recitals, children's and youth theatre.

Inventionen – Berliner Festival Neuer Musik c/o DAAD, Berliner Künstlerprogramm, Markgrafenstr 37, D-10117 Berlin. *t*: +49 302 022080 *f*: +49 302 041267 *e*: musik.berlin@ daad.de *w*: www.inventionen.de Sound installations, international electroacoustic music, lectures, concerts.

Kissinger Sommer Festival Stadtverwaltung, Rathausplatz 4, D-97688 Bad Kissingen. *t*: +49 971 807 1110 *f*: +49 971 807 1109 *e*: kissingersommer@stadt.badkissingen.de Annual. Symphony concerts, chamber music, Lieder, jazz.

Klosterkonzerte Maulbron Postfach 47, D-75433 Maulbronn. *t*: +49 7043 7734 *f*: +49 7043 10345 *e*: info@klosterkonzerte.de *w*: www.klosterkonzerte. de *Contact* Jürgen Budday, artistic director. Sacred music concerts, chamber music, all kinds of secular music. Held in different rooms of the monastery of Maulbronn as well as open air.

Kronberg Academy Cello Festival Friedrich Ebert Str 6, D-61476 Kronberg. *t*: +49 6173 783378 *f*: +49 6173 783379 *e*: info@kronbergacademy. de *w*: www.kronbergacademy.de

Kronberg Academy Viola Festival Friedrich Ebert Str 6, D-61476 Kronberg. *t*: +49 3176 783378 *f*: +49 6173 783379 *e*: o.laue@kronberg academy.de *w*: www.kronbergacademy.de

Kurt Weill Festival Ebertallee 63, D-06846 Dessau. *t*: +49 340 619595 *f*: +49 340 611907 *e*: weill-zentrum@t-online.de *w*: www.kurt-weill-

fest.de *Contact* Clemens Birnbaum. 2009 theme: round about Weill.

Leipzig International Choral Festival Festival UK Office, Salcombe House, Long St, Sherborne, DT9 3BU, United Kindom. *t*: +44 1935 810810 *f*: +44 1935 815815 *e*: info@leipzigchoralfestival.com *w*: www.leipzigchoralfestival.com *Contact* Caroline Dunn, festival co-ordinator. Annual 4-day festival in Leipzig. Cultural exchange of choral music with choirs from around the world gathering in one of the most musically dedicated cities in Europe.

Ludwigsburg International Festival Festspiele Baden-Württemburg, Marstallstr 5, D-71634 Ludwigsburg. *t*: +49 7141 939636 *f*: +49 7141 939697 *e*: info@schlossfestspiele.de *w*: www. schlossfestspiele.de *Contact* Wulf Konold, artistic director; Markus Kiesel, admin director. Annual. Classical music, opera, modern dance, theatre, jazz, world music, literature.

MaerzMusik Berlin - International Festival of Contemporary Music Berliner Festspiele, Schaperstr 24, D-10719 Berlin. *t*: +49 302 54890 *f*: +49 302 5489114 *e*: maerzmusik@ berlinerfestspiele.de *w*: www.maerzmusik.de *Contact* Matthias Osterwold, artistic director; Ilse Müller, head of organisation Festival of contemporary music. Established artists and emerging talents present programme of premieres, new and commissioned works. Range from orchestral and chamber music to innovative music theatre, experimental and new media.

Mendelssohn-Festtage Gewandhaus zu Leipzig, Augustusplatz 8, D-04109 Leipzig. *t*: +49 341 127 0316 *f*: +49 341 127 0408 *e*: presse@gewand haus.de *w*: www.gewandhaus.de *Contact* Riccardo Chailly, Gewandhauskapellmeister; Andreas Schulz, director.

Moritzburg Festival Maxstr 8, D-01067 Dresden. *t*: +49 351 810 5495 *f*: +49 351 810 5496 *e*: buero@moritzburgfestival.de *w*: www. moritzburgfestival.de *Contact* Jan Vogler, artistic director; Jana Friedrich, Mandy Jarsumbeck, manager. Chamber music in royal settings with internationally renowned artists.15 performances.

Mozartfest Würzburg Oeggstr 2, D-97070 Würzburg. *t*: +49 931 37 23 36 *f*: +49 931 37 39 39 *e*: info@mozartfest-wuerzburg.de *w*: www. mozartfest.de

Münchener Biennale – Internationales Festival für neues Musiktheater Ludwigstr 8, D-80539

München. *t:* +49 89 280 5607 *f:* +49 89 280 5679 *e:* biennale@spielmotor.de *w:* www.muenchenerbiennale.de *Contact* Peter Ruzicka, artistic dir. New music theatre, world premieres; associated orchestral concerts.

Musica Bayreuth Ludwigstr 26, D-95444 Bayreuth. *t:* +49 921 67367, also fax *e:* info@musica-bayreuth.de *w:* www.musica-bayreuth.de *Contact* Viktor Lukas, conductor & organist. Annual. Classical orchestral, choral and chamber music.

Musica Sacra International Arnauer Str 14, D-87616 Marktoberdorf. *t:* +49 83 42 8964033 *f:* +49 83 4240 370 *e:* office@modfestivals.org *w:* www.modfestivals.org *Contact* Dolf Rabus, director; Brigitte Riskowski, business manager. Biennial. Music from the 5 major world religions' choirs, instrumentalists, singers, dancers, combinations of music and other artforms.

Musikfest Berlin Schaperstr 24, D-10719 Berlin. *t:* +49 30 254 89 0 *f:* +49 30 254 89 111 *e:* info@berlinerfestspiele.de *w:* www.berliner festspiele.de Presents new and unknown pieces alongside significant works of traditional symphonic repertoire. Provides forum for artistic innovation by orchestras, ensembles, composers, conductors and soloists of international standing.

Musikfest Bremen Postfach 10 30 63, D-28030 Bremen. *t:* +49 421 33 66 77 *f:* +49 421 33 66 880 *e:* preisler@musikfest-bremen.de *w:* www.musikfest-bremen.de

Musikfest Stuttgart Johann-Sebastian-Bach-Platz, D-70178 Stuttgart. *t:* +49 711 619210 *f:* +49 711 6192123 *w:* www.bachakademie.de; www.festivalensemble.org *Contact* Andreas Keller, managing director; Helmuth Rilling, conductor. Annual. Features Festivalensemble Stuttgart.

Oleg Kagan Music Festival - Tegernseer Tal Musikfest Kreuth e.V Geschäftsstelle, Nördliche Hauptstr 3, D-83708 Kreuth. *t:* +49 8029 1820 *f:* +49 8029 1828 *e:* musikfest@kreuth.de *w:* www.oleg-kagan-musikfest.de Classical and modern chamber music represented by internationally acclaimed artists.

Opernfestspiele Heidenheim Grabenstr 15, D-89522 Heidenheim. *t:* +49 7 321 327 46 10 *f:* +49 7 321 327 46 11 *e:* opernfestspiele@ heidenheim.de *w:* www.opernfestspiele.de *Contact* Marco-Maria Canonica, director/conductor. Open-air opera festival.

Pèlerinages Kunstfest Weimar Am Palais 13, D-99423 Weimar. *t:* +49 3643 81 14 0 *f:* +49 3643 81 14 44 *e:* pelerinages@kunstfest-weimar.de *w:* www.kunstfest-weimar.de

Rheingau Musik Festival Konzertgesellschaft Rheinallee 1, D-65375 Oestrich-Winkel. *t:* +49 6723 91770 *f:* +49 6723 917719 *e:* info@ rheingau-musik-festival.de *w:* www.rheingau-musik-festival.de Classical, jazz and cabaret music.

Rossini in Wildbad Touristik Bad Wildbad GmbH, Postfach 100326, D-75314 Bad Wildbad. *t:* +49 7081 10284 *f:* +49 7081 10290 *e:* touristik@ bad-wildbad.de *w:* www.rossini-in-wildbad.de Belcanto opera festival.

RuhrTriennale Kultur Ruhr GmbH, Leithestr 35, D-45886 Gelsenkirchen. *t:* +49 209 167 1702 *f:* +49 209 167 1710 *e:* am.boegel@kulturruhr.com *w:* www.ruhrtriennale.de *Contact* J Krings, general manager. International mixed discipline festival of arts with venues throughout the Ruhr district.

Schleswig Holstein Music Festival Palais Ranteau, Parade 1, D-23552 Lübeck. *t:* +49 451 389570 *f:* +49 451 3895757 *e:* info@shmf.de *w:* www.shmf.de More than 130 classical music events in the countryside; concerts in churches, barns, mansions, traditional concert halls.

Schumannfest Düsseldorf Bolkerstr 57, D-40213 Düsseldorf. *t:* +49 211 133222 *f:* +49 211 322203 *e:* info@schumannfest-duesseldorf.de *w:* www.schumannfest-duesseldorf.de Biennial festival.

Schwetzinger Festspiele Hans-Bredow-Str, D-76530 Baden-Baden. *t:* +49 7221 929 4990 *f:* +49 7221 929 4995 *e:* schwetzinger-festspiele@ swr.de *w:* www.schwetzinger-festspiele.de *Contact* Bernhard Hermann, director; Peter Stieber, managing director & artistic director, concerts; Georges Delnon, artistic director, opera. Annual. Opera and concerts.

Sommerkonzerte Audi AG, D-85045 Ingolstadt. *t:* +49 841 8931515 *f:* +49 841 8936195 *e:* sommerkonzerte@audi.de *w:* www.sommer konzerte.de Classical, pop, jazz.

Stockstädter Musiktage Berlinerstr 65, D-64589 Stockstadt-am-Rhein. *t:* +49 615 884818, also fax *Contact* Wilhelm Becker, director; Eva Becker, secretary. Recorder music festival on period instruments, recorder masterclasses, concerts, exhibitions.

Tage Alter Musik Regensburg Postfach 100903,

D-93009 Regensburg. *t:* +49 941 8979786 *f:* +49 941 8979836 *e:* TageAlterMusik@t-online.de *w:* www.tagealtermusik-regensburg.de *Contact* Ludwig Hartmann, Stephan Schmid. Early music from Middle Ages to romantic era on period instruments. Also large exhibition of period instruments.

Thüringer Bachwochen Schwanseestr 33, D-66423 Weimar. *t:* +49 3643 77 69 41 *f:* +49 3643 77 69 48 *e:* info@thueringer-bachwochen.de *w:* www.thueringer-bachwochen.de Baroque music festival focusing on Bach.

Yiddish Summer Weimar other music eV, c/o Kulturbüro LaRete, Goetheplatz 3, D-99423 Weimar. *t:* +49 3643 50 66 77 *f:* +49 3643 49 86 04 *e:* yiddish-summer@other-music.net *w:* www.yiddish-summer-weimar.de Festival of Yiddish and Roma music, culture and identity.

France, Italy and Switzerland

France, Italy and Switzerland

Three countries especially popular with visitors, whether due to their reputations for quality of life or their traditions, whether artistic, historic, architectural or gastronomic. All benefit from the fact that their national languages, French, Italian and German (all three in the case of Switzerland, a country divided into regions in each of which one language dominates), being among the more widely taught (along with Spanish).

Although linked geographically, however, their musical cultures are distinctive. Thanks to its international artistic and cultural importance in a 50-year period spanning the late 19th and early 20th centuries, and significant postwar investment in the arts and its infrastructure, France has a strong reputation in both modern and period music. Across Italy, opera and vocal music predominate, with local and/or municipal companies deeply embedded in the cultural life of their regions. Switzerland has an impressive all-round musical culture, testament to the resources allocated to performing arts and, no doubt, the relative wealth of the country.

FRANCE

Music education in France is highly structured. As far as training for performers goes, this is restricted to the two state-run Conservatoires Nationaux Supérieurs de Musique (managed by the culture ministry) and the independent, but state-recognised, Ecole Normale Supérieure de Musique. Although all three offer practical training at various levels of ability, the ENSM has its a course structure and hierarchy different from the CNSMs, and makes its own decisions about the acceptability of external qualifications. Training at the CNSMs falls into a 2-cycle structure, although it is not exactly equivalent to the model prescribed by the Bologna Process.

Music teacher training is, in the main, handled elsewhere at dedicated training schools (Centres de Formation des Enseignants de la Danse et de la Musique) at a few locations across the country. Music education for children and young people does not take place in schools but in the 30-odd Conservatoires Nationaux de Région.

ITALY

Italy has numerous professional music training colleges spread across the country – indeed, there is a national network of pre-college music schools as well whose aim is not specifically to train musicians but to provide a more general music education. And alongside the numerous government-funded conservatoires, there are around 20 Istituti Musicali Pareggiati, funded with a mixture of local and state money. These are usually located in smaller towns, allowing more students access to some form of advanced tuition, with the conservatoires based in the bigger regional cities. In terms of educational structure, conservatoires have in practice adopted the pan-European model of 1st and 2nd cycle ('livello') higher education (triennio followed by biennio), although many offer it alongside the more traditional system in which attendance at conservatoires begins around age 10, continuing until a set number of years (depending on the instrument/discipline) have been completed.

SWITZERLAND

Switzerland is one of the European countries keenest to adopt the Bologna ideals, both by adopting the 3 years bachelors plus 2 years masters course structure, and by centralising responsibility for the administration of institutions – what was a locally run conservatoire becomes a university equivalent Hochschule, Haute Ecole de Musique or Scuola Universitaria di Musica. To gain this level, institutions must meet certain educational standards stipulated by the government, and in general, authorities are conscientious about the issue of quality assurance.

Many students (some 90%) at Swiss institutions go on to masters level, a strong indication that the most advanced professional performance training is concentrated here and that bachelors level education does no more, in career terms, than equip students with skills appropriate for the wider workplace.

LYON

City in the southern French Rhône area at the confluence of Rhône and Saône rivers and dominated by its twin hills: Fourvière with its dramatic basilica, Croix-Rousse with its characteristic narrow streets and passageways. Its historical importance goes back to Roman times (name Lugdunum), and architectural styles of the city reflect development in various eras. Particular reputation for its food and wine culture. Educational centre with large number of institutions based there.

Musical life

Outside the conservatoire, Lyon's 2 main musical performing organisations are Orchestre National de Lyon and Opéra National de Lyon. Opera (which has been led by a number of important music directors recently) performs full programme based at the Nouvel Opéra house, a modernised version of an early 19th century building. Ballet and occasional concerts also put on there; main concert hall the Auditorium de Lyon, home to Orchestre National de Lyon. City is also home to Grame: Centre National de Création Musicale, a facility for contemporary composers either resident or associated with it.

Other cultural information

Museums reflecting Lyon's history include Musée Gallo-Romain archeological museum and a Centre d'Histoire de la Résistance et de la Déportation. Newest museum is Musée des Confluences, situated where the two rivers meet and devoted to connections between science and society. Several theatres in and around city; some city-centre companies are Théâtre des Celestins covers plays from various different eras; Théâtre des Marronniers for interdisciplinary forms; Théâtre les Ateliers also more contemporary, with international visiting companies.

Festivals and events

Musiques en Scène biennial festival based at Grame (even numbered years). City celebrates Fête de la Musique along with the rest of the country. Non-musical events include a festival of lights (dating back over 150 years); biennial contemporary art festival (odd-numbered years); more unusually, a festival of detective fiction.

Tourist information

www.lyon.fr; tel: +33

CONSERVATOIRE NATIONAL SUPÉRIEUR MUSIQUE ET DANSE DE LYON

3 quai Chauveau, CP 120, F-69266 Lyon Cedex 09.

t: +33 4 72 19 26 26 f: +33 4 72 19 26 00 e: email w: www.cnsmd-lyon.fr

Contact Isabelle Replumaz, head of international relations *Courses* Bachelors and masters courses in 2 cycles, 3 years + 2 years. Courses based around 4 core areas: main study (instrument, voice, composition etc), complementary study (chamber music, orchestra etc), cultural studies (eg history of music), associated study (foreign language, practical aspects of being a musician). *Application requirements* Application via website. Students in music dept must be aged 16-30. *Term dates* Beginning Sep-end Jun, in 2 semesters. *Fees* EUR 628 (includes fees, access to mediatheque and student social security contribution). Bursaries available for EU students in case of need, as well as French students. *Music facilities* 110 teaching rooms, 300-seat concert hall with audio-visual recording facilities, orchestral rehearsal room, 120-seat recital room (with organ), choir room, 2 other performance rooms. Annual programme of over 200 concerts. *Accommodation* 73-bed hall of residence. *No of students* 500 students, 15% of whom come from overseas.

PARIS

Needs no introduction as a city, one of the world's most visited capitals. Being relatively small, it is surprisingly easy to get around on foot, although the Cité de la Musique area where the conservatoire is based is not centrally located, but in north east corner.

Musical life

As a musical city, punches a little below its weight in terms of international profile – outside a well-supported mainstream classical music harder to come by. Paris Opéra National de Paris is one exception, with main house the newer building at Bastille with old Opéra Garnier staging most of the ballet and some other opera. Outstanding reputation for contemporary music at IRCAM research facility and via Ensemble Intercontemporain.

EUROPE

FRANCE

Main orchestras are Orchestre de Paris; the two radio orchestras l'Orchestre Philharmonique de Radio-France and l'Orchestre National de France; regional Orchestre National d'Ile de France based nearby but performs in town. Salle Pleyel, Théâtre des Champs-Elysées and Salle Gaveau main concert halls, with Théâtre du Châtelet venue for opera and music theatre as well as recitals. Orchestre des Champs-Elysées for period music (classical/romantic), an area where Paris (and France) do have excellent reputation – Les Arts Florissants based there, for instance.

🏛 Other cultural information

Large range of all-round cultural activity, particularly art, theatre, cinema and literatre; becoming increasingly diverse with more cultures from France's colonial past gaining some representation (Paris has become a centre for world music recording). A number of popular museums and galleries plus many more of a more specialist nature.

🎭 Festivals and events

Fête de la Musique street festival in June is most popular music event across the city, with many different styles feature. Otherwise cultural events tend to be more local (many arrondissements (districts) have their own local festivals), or run by particular institutions and vary from year to year.

ℹ Tourist information

www.parisinfo.com; agenda@parisinfo.com; tel: +33 8 92 68 30 00

LE CONSERVATOIRE DE PARIS

209 av Jean-Jaurès, F-75019 Paris.
t: +33 1 40 40 45 45; +33 1 40 40 45 79 (international exchanges). e: scolarite@cnsmdp. fr; gamussen@cnsmdp.fr w: www.cnsmdp.fr
Contact Gretchen Amussen, Ania Sergueeva, international exchanges. Courses Classes in 7 departments: classical and contemporary instruments; early music; musicology & analysis; vocal disciplines; writing, composition and orchestral conducting; jazz and improvised music; pedagogy and teacher training. Application requirements Entry by audition; request for application form via website. Term dates Mid Sep-end Jun; various holiday breaks. Fees EUR 400 plus EUR 189 social

security payment. Scholarships Scholarships available to French and EU students from Ministry of Culture and Communication; also some private grants (see website for conditions). Exchange details UK exchange partner institutions: Birmingham Conservatoire, Guildhall School of Music, Royal College of Music, Royal Academy of Music. Also partnerships with institutions in Europe and USA Accommodation Various housing possibilities available through Affaires Scolaires dept, including halls of residence, studios, university residences. Students seeking accommodation must have guarantor undertaking to pay rent if student tenant is unable.

ECOLE NORMALE DE MUSIQUE DE PARIS

114bis blvd Malesherbes, F-75017 Paris.
t: +33 1 47 63 85 72 f: +33 1 47 63 50 42
e: info@ecolenormalecortot.com; admission@ ecolenormalecortot.com w: www. ecolenormalecortot.com
Courses Instrument and voice classes, complementary classes, ensemble classes, theory and composition classes, orchestral conducting classes. Application requirements Application to include letter of motivation, music CV, full personal details, tape/ CD/MD recording, EUR 340 admin fee, 2 photos. If accepted, an audition will determine your level of entry, teachers and obligatory classes. All complementary subjects required for the instrumental or vocal degree must have been passed, or equivalent foreign certificates granted. Term dates 1 Oct-30 Jun. Application deadline 15 Dec. Fees Vary depending on level and class; see website for details. Scholarships Part and full scholarships available; can be applied for when students receive certificate of pre-registration. Accommodation Accommodation available through student services CROUS or Les Foyers: Union Nationale des Maisons d'Etudiants. Website gives details of other student accommodation in Paris. No of students 1100 students, of whom 750 international.

MUSIC FESTIVALS

Besançon International Music Festival 3 bis rue Léonel de Moustier, F-25000 Besançon. t: +33 3 81 25 05 85 f: +33 3 81 81 52 15 e: contact@festival-besancon.com w: www.festival-besancon.com
Biennale Musiques en Scène BP 1185, 9 rue du Garet, F-69202 Lyon Cedex 01. t: +33 4 72 07

37 00 f: +33 4 72 7 37 01 e: email w: www. grame.fr Contact James Giroudon, artistic director; Peter Eötvös, guest director. Biennial. Interdisciplinary showcase for musical creation.

Colmar International Festival 8 rue Kleiber, F-68000 Colmar. t: +33 89 20 68 97 f: +33 89 41 34 13 e: infofestival@ot-colmar.fr w: www. festival-colmar.com Contact Vladimir Spivakov, artistic dir; Hubert Niess, director. Tribute to Sviatoslav Richter.

Festival de l'Epau Centre Culturel de la Sarthe, Hôtel du Département, 40 rue Joinville, F-72072 Le Mans Cedex 9. t: +33 2 43 54 73 45 f: +33 2 43 54 71 02 e: culture@sarthe.com w: www. epau.org Classical music, symphonic and chamber.

Festival de La Chaise-Dieu PO Box 150, F-43004 Le Puy-en-Velay. t: +33 4 71 09 48 28 f: +33 4 71 09 55 58 e: festival@chaise-dieu.com w: www. chaise-dieu.com Baroque, classical, romantic, contemporary, symphonic, sacred and spiritual music.

Festival de Saintes Abbaye aux Dames, 11 place de l'Abbaye, BP 125, F-17104 Saintes Cedex. t: +33 5 46 97 48 30 f: +33 5 46 97 48 40 e: info@ abbayeauxdames.org; bernheim@abbayeauxdames. org w: www.abbayeauxdames.org Contact Odile Pradem-Faure, director; Stephan Maciejewski, artistic director; Pascale Bernheim, PR.

Festival International d'Art Lyrique d'Aix en Provence et Académie Européenne de Musique Palais de l'Ancien Archevêché, F-13100 Aix-en-Provence. t: +33 4 42 17 34 00 f: +33 4 42 96 12 61 e: direction.artistique@festival-aix.com w: www.festival-aix.com Opera, chamber music concerts, recitals, public rehearsals, masterclasses.

Festival International de Musique d'Uzerche c/o Erin Arts Centre, Victoria Square, Port Erin, Isle of Man, United Kingdom. t: +44 1624 835858 f: +44 1624 836658 e: information@erinartscentre.com w: www.erinartscentre.com Contact John Bethell MBE, festival director. Chamber, opera, choral and brass band music, held in the Abbatiale Saint Pierre.

Heures Musicales de l'Abbaye de Lessay. t: +33 2 33 45 14 34 f: +33 2 33 45 77 17 e: concertsheuresmusicales@canton-lessay.com w: www.francefestivals.com/lessay Contact contact 14 concerts, with leading artists and music from the Renaissance to the 20th century.

International Celtic Harp Festival of Dinan La Galerie, F-22490 Plouer. t: +33 2 96 86 84 94, also fax e: contact@maisondelaharpe.org Contact Elisabeth Affolter, director; Myrdhin, artistic director. 23 concerts, workshops, harp exhibition.

Latour de France International Festival of Music and the Arts c/o Mananan Festival Office, Erin Arts Centre, Port Erin, Isle of Man, United Kingdom. t: +44 1624 835858 f: +44 1624 836658 e: information@erinartscentre.com; latourfestival@ orange.fr w: www.erinartscentre.com Contact John Bethell MBE, director. Festival near Perpignan/ Estagel, S of France.

Les Azuriales Opera Festival Villa Serpolette, 46 blvd du Mont Boron, F-06300 Nice. t: +33 4 9356 5141 f: +33 4 9326 5368 e: sarah.holford@ thomasmiller.com w: www.azurialopera.com Contact Sarah Holford, president; Mark Holford, director of development; Bryan Evans MBE, music director. Intimate festival distinguished by the audience's proximity to the performance. Takes place in the Villa Ephrussi de Rothschild on Cap Ferrat, with post-performance dinner in the world-renowned gardens.

Musica International Festival of Contemporary Music 1 place Dauphine, F-67065 Strasbourg. t: +33 3 88 23 46 46 f: +33 3 88 23 46 47 e: info@festival-musica.org w: www.festival-musica. org Contact contact Annual. Contemporary music; concerts, operas, music theatre, dance, films, seminars.

Musique-Cordiale 39 Minster Rd, London, United Kingdom. t: +44 20 7794 0494 e: info@musique-cordiale.com w: www.musique-cordiale.com Contact Pippa Pawlik, festival dir. Annual festival of choral/ opera and chamber music in the S of France, between Nice and Aix-en-Provence.

Orpheus and Bacchus Festival Le Faure, F-33890 Gensac. t: +44 78 08 72 77 35 f: +49 30 2759 4174 e: ian@orpheusandbacchus.com w: www. orpheusandbacchus.com Contact Ian Christians, director. Residential, chamber music and concerto transcriptions for chamber ensemble.

Piano aux Jacobins 9 rue Tripière, F-31000 Toulouse. t: +33 5 61 22 40 05 f: +33 5 61 29 80 46 e: contact@pianojacobins.com w: www. pianojacobins.com Contact Catherine D'Argoubet, artistic director. Annual. Classical and contemporary music, piano festival.

Strasbourg Music Festival 9 avenue de la Liberté, F-67000 Strasbourg. t: +33 3 88 15 29 29 f: +33

EUROPE

FRANCE

3 88 24 0316 e: hlorg@wanadoo.fr w: www.
festival-strasbourg.com Contact Harry Lapp,
general manager. Concerts, operas, recitals, jazz.
Also international singing competition (president of
the jury: Barbara Hendricks)

**Synthèse - Festival International de Musiques
et Créations Electroniques** Institut International
de Musique Electroacoustique de Bourges, F-18001
Bourges. t: +33 2 48 20 41 87 f: +33 2 48 20
45 51 e: administration@ime-bourges.org w: www.
imeb.net Annual. Electroacoustic music.

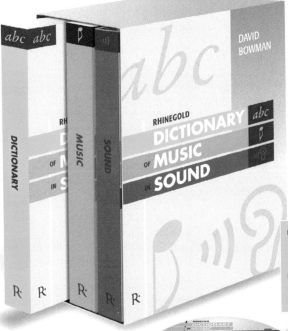

BOLOGNA

Northern Italian city founded around 2500 years ago, but which gained importance during 11th century in particular when its university – the first in the world – was established (city attracts numerous students today) Its architecture still has a strong medieval and renaissance feel to it in general, but also has a distinctive architectural feature not only in the terracotta colour of its rooftops but in its numerous covered walkways (the longest 'portico' comprises over 650 arches and stretches to 3500m). Along with other Italian cities, it has a lingering influence in the kitchen – 'Bolognaise', as in the tomato sauce, is the adjective from Bologna.

♪ Musical life

Teatreo Comunale di Bologna the main centre for classical music, housing city's opera house and orchestra; orchestra gives a varied concert season as well as accompanying opera and ballet. Oratorio di San Rocco a smaller venue with chamber music and recitals. Various music associations based in the city, such as Musicaper, organising concerts and events promoting musical activity.

▥ Other cultural information

City is home to music museum and library. National picture gallery has variety of old paintings (up to 18th century); also modern art gallery. Numerous smaller museums and gallery, including some at the university. Various theatre venues such as Arena del Sole and Teatro delle Moline.

◌ Festivals and events

Bologna Festival more a concert series running Mar-Oct, but does feature international soloists and conductors. Film festival in Jul.

i Tourist information

www.comune.bologna.it

CONSERVATORIO DI MUSICA 'GB MARTINI'

piazza Rossini, 2, I-40126, Bologna.
t: +39 051 221483 f: +39 051 223168
e: segretaria@conservatorio-bologna.com
w: www.conservatorio-bologna.com
Courses 3-year 1st cycle and 2-year 2nd cycle courses in orchestral instruments, guitar, composition, conducting, harpsichord jazz, multimedia music,

electronic music, piano, singing. *Application deadline* 30 Apr.

CATANIA

Sicilian city at the foot of Mount Etna, part of which has been designated a Unesco world heritage site. Enormous number of churches and religious institutions, in baroque and earlier styles.

♪ Musical life

Birthplace of Bellini, hence his presence is relatively strong – the city's opera house is named after him, though repertoire by no means restricted to his music. The house also presents concerts by its resident orchestra and chorus as well as visiting artists. A second venue is the Teatro Sangiorgi, originally an opera house but now renovated and turned over to more general musical use.

▥ Other cultural information

Numerous theatres presenting different styles of work. Sites relating to Greek and Roman history, including 2 amphitheatres, though series of eruptions of Mt Etna have buried much early sites. Hilltop Ursino Castle houses a museum. Street markets for food: fish market is well known.

◌ Festivals and events

Festival celebrating patron saint Sant'Agata in February

i Tourist information

www.apt.catania.it; apt@apt.catania.it; tel: +39 095 7306211

ISTITUTO MUSICALE VINCENZO BELLINI CATANIA

Via Istituto Sacro Cuore, 3, I-95125 Catania.
t: +39 095 7194400; +39 095 7194440
(Erasmus office) f: +39 095 502782
e: erasmus@istitutobellini.it w: www.istitutobellini.it

COMO

City in north of Italy on the shore of the lake of the same name.

♪ Musical life

Teatro Sociale has recitals, opera, dance as well as plays.

Festivals and events
Autumn music festival.

Tourist information
www.lakecomo.it; lakecomo@tin.it

CONSERVATORIO DI MUSICA G VERDI - COMO
Via Cadorna 4, I-22100 Como.
t: +39 031 279827 *w:* www.conservatoriocomo.it
Courses Course outlines depend on which of 7 areas of study degree falls into: singing; 'maestro al cembalo; choral music and choral direction; organ and organ composition; piano; strings, harp, guitar, wind and brass instruments; compostion, electronic music, jazz, percussion. Certain modules are obligatory and common to more than one study area. Biennio (2nd cycle) courses in: singing, guitar, harpsichord, composition, technology; choral music/direction; electronic music and sound technology; chamber music; piano; bowed instruments; wind and brass instruments; percussion. *Application requirements* Applicants tested on ability on chosen instrument/voice; good general musical knowledge, plus secondary school education. *Language requirements* Italian.

COSENZA
Small city located towards the south west tip of Italy in the Calabria region.

Musical life
Teatro Rendano is only major performance venue in the town, but for theatre as well as opera. Otherwise most musical performance based at the consevatoire.

Other cultural information
Teatro Morelli for popular music and entertainment.

Festivals and events
Main arts event is Festival delle Invasioni (the name reflects the town's repeated occupation, by the Visigoths, the Spanish etc). Hosts an annual jazz festival, and a celebration of chocolate.

CONSERVATORIO DI MUSICA S GIACOMANTONIO
Via Portapiana, I-87100 Cosenza.

t: +39 098476627 *f:* +39 098429224 *w:* www.conservatoriodicosenza.it
Courses 1st and 2nd cycle studies in all orchestral instruments, plus new technology, period instruments, band direction, vocal music, choral music/direction, jazz, guitar. At 2nd level, can add choice of harpsichord, recorder, electronic music, chamber music.

CUNEO
Small city in northern Italy's Alpine region. Good rural links to mountains, vineyard areas, the Argentera national park and Valdieri hot springs.

Musical life
Teatro Toselli holds a small series of concerts each year, alongside theatre and cinema.

Other cultural information
Gastronomy in the Piedmontese tradition, with various food and produce fairs in the region.

Tourist information
www.comune.cuneo.it; turismoacuneo@comune.cuneo.it; tel: +39 0171 693258

CONSERVATORIO DI MUSICA 'GIORGIO GHEDINI'
via Roma 19, I-12100 Cuneo.
t: +39 0171 693 148 *f:* +39 0171 699 181
e: cons.amministrativa@tiscali.it *w:* http://web.tiscali.it/conservatorioghedini
Courses Main courses for harp, singing, guitar, woodwind, strings, brass, music teaching, choral music and choral direction, electronic music, organ and organ composition, piano, percussion. Various complementary courses, including general music culture, musical aesthetics, poetic/dramatic literature, score-reading, chamber music, music history, theory/solfege.

FLORENCE (FIRENZE)
Main city in Tuscany famed for its architecture, legacy of its importance during the renaissance, and a Unesco world heritage site. Consequently, one of the most popular tourist destinations in Italy. Most distinctive landmark is the domed cathedral Santa Maria del Fiore, with its façade and bell tower; Ponte Vecchio over the city's river (the Arno) is noted for the shops on it, many of which are built out over the river. City's name also known in culinary

circles, most notably as kind of steak (Bistecca alla Fiorentina). Significant in terms of music history, being the birthplace of opera in the form of early experiments in blending music and drama.

𝄞 Musical life
Teatro del Maggio Musicale Fiorentino opera house and concert hall, home to opera company and orchestra named after it; together with a smaller 600-seat Piccolo Teatro it makes up the Teatro Comunale. Orchestra della Toscana based in the city, but performs widely across region; Orchestra da Camera Fiorentina and Florence Symphonietta are 2 smaller orchestras. Amici della Musica arranges concerts featuring international performers in Teatro della Pergola; also other concert promoters and series, and various churches and other venues round the city put on one-off concerts.

🏛 Other cultural information
Uffizi gallery is one of world's important galleries, and most visited, thanks to its collection of renaissance masterpieces; other examples of art of the period can be found throughout city in churches and other galleries. Teatro Puccini, contrary to what its name suggests, is a venue for plays.

🎭 Festivals and events
Maggio Musicale festival, which gave its name to the main concert venue, one of the more prestigious European music festival events, running late Apr-Jun. Tango festival in early spring.

ℹ Tourist information
www.firenzeturismo.it; tel: +39 055 23320

CONSERVATORIO STATALE DI MUSICA L CHERUBINI
Piazza Belle Arti, 2, I-50122 Firenze.
w: www.conservatorio.firenze.it
Courses New 2-cycle system and traditional Licenze system run parallel. 1st cycle triennio and 2nd cycle biennio in singing, orchestral instruments, composition, harpsichord, recorder, music and new technology, chamber music, choral music/choral music direction, chamber music, jazz, organ, piano accompaniment, percussion, viola da gamba. 1st cycle students take options in several core areas: insturmental/vocal training; music theory, history and culture; music technology; ensembles; composition.

GENOA (GENOVA)
Port city in far north west of Italy, birthplace of Christopher Columbus and Nicolo Paganini. Old harbour area modernised and redeveloped by Genoese architect Renzo Piano (designer of Pompidou Centre) giving a new flavour to city; main centre is Piazza de Ferrari (location of opera house). Some major educational establishments besides conservatoire, notably the university; also base for Istituto Italiano di Tecnologia research institute.

𝄞 Musical life
Teatro Carlo Felice is main opera house and concert hall, with full opera season plus many concerts. Also ballet. Teatro Gustavo Modena is another multipurpose venue, presenting concerts and theatre.

🏛 Other cultural information
Numerous museums, galleries and exhibitions both in and around the city. Museo d'Arte Orientale Edoardo Chiossone is a major collection of Japanese arts and artefacts; a museum of world cultures reflects city's past as an international port, as does Galata maritime museum. Another important historical role was in Italy's path to reunification, documented in the Istituto Mazziniano.

🎭 Festivals and events
Mediterranean Music Festival, every year in Jun and Jul, presents range of world music not limited to the Mediterranean area. Also a popular Festival of Science during autumn.

ℹ Tourist information
www.turismo.comune.genova.it

CONSERVATORIO STATALE DI MUSICA 'NICCOLO PAGANINI' - GENOVA
via Albaro 38, I-16145 Genova.
t: +34 010 3620747 f: +34 010 3620819
e: info@conservatoriopaganini.org; erasmus@conservatoriopaganini.org
w: www.conservatoriopaganini.org
Contact Patrizia Conti, director; Maurizio Tarrini (international enquiries). Courses 1st level 'undergraduate' (3 yrs), 2nd level 'postgraduate' (2 yrs): all musical instruments, singing, composition, jazz, electronic music, didactics. Application

requirements High level of ability on chosen instrument (or voice/composition), tested by admission recital; secondary school-leaving diploma. *Term dates* 1 Nov-mid June. *Application deadline* 1-30 Apr (EU students); non-EU students, check http://www.miur.it/0004Alta_F/0029Studen/0716Studen/index_cf4.htm *Fees* EUR 350-1200. *Scholarships* Scholarships available. *Exchange details* Exchange partnerships with institutions in the Mediterranean (network Ecume and others). *Language requirements* Basic knowledge of Italian (at least level A2 of Common European Framework for Languages). *Music facilities* desc3 *Accommodation* Information and advice on accommodation available on www.arssu.it. *No of students* Approx 600, of whom 6% from overseas.

L'AQUILA

Medieval central Italian town in the Apeninnine mountain area with a walled centre. Capital of remote Abruzzo region, a picturesque, largely mountainous area (depicted in the first movement of Berlioz's *Harold in Italy*) that stretches down to the east coast. City well placed for excursions into the area.

♪ Musical life
Home to Istituzione Sinfonica Abruzzese, the region's state orchestra (about 4 concerts per month) and concert organisation, performing most of its concerts at the baroque Teatro San Filippo. Chamber ensemble I Solisti Aquilani takes its name from the town and performs widely around the world. Auditorium Nino Carloni another music venue. Soc Aquilana dei Concerti 'B Barattelli' promotes subscription concerts throughout the year; similar organisations in other towns in the Abruzzi region.

▥ Other cultural information
As well as Teatro San Filippo, Teatro Comunale de L'Aquila has range of productions. Hilltop castle houses the museum of the region. As well as conservatoire, the town is home to a fine arts academy.

⚲ Festivals and events
Festival of Argentinian tango in July; also short film festival in October, attracts productions from over 30 countries each year.

ℹ Tourist information
www.comune.laquila.it

CONSERVATORIO DI MUSICA 'ALFREDO CASELLA' L'AQUILA
Via Gaglioffi 18, I-67100 L'Aquila.
t: +39 086222122 *f:* +39 086262325
e: studenti@conservatoriocasella.it; erasmus@conservatoriocasella.it
w: www.conservatoriocasella.it
Contact A Lopes Ferreira, Erasmus contact. *Courses* Principal study: orchestral instruments, harpsichord, composition, mandolin, choral conducting, jazz, organ, sax; complementary courses in various areas including general musical culture, literatur courses, theory and solfeggio, piano accompaniment, string quartet, music history and aesthetics. Triennio and biennio system currently being trialled. *Exchange details* Exchange partnerships with institutions in Austria, Denmark, Estonia, Germany, Poland, Portugal, Romania, Slovakia, Spain, Switzerland

LECCE
Town located towards the southernmost point of Italy's heel famed for its baroque architecture.

♪ Musical life
Opera house the Teatro Paisiello, named after the composer Giovanni Paisiello. Small symphony orchestra, comes from 'Tito Schipa' de Lecce foundation

ℹ Tourist information
www.turismo.provincia.le.it

CONSERVATORIO DI MUSICA 'TITO SCHIPA'
Instituzione di Alta Cultura, Via V Ciardo 2, I-73100 Lecce.
t: +39 0832344266 7 *f:* +39 0832340951
e: segretaria@conservatoriolecce.it *w:* www.conservatoriolecce.it
Courses Bachelors level courses in all orchestral instruments, plus early music.

LIVORNO
West Italian coastal city, some of whose characteristic renaissance architecture (canals, bridges, narrow streets, squares and numerous churches and religious buildings) survived World War II damage. In previous centuries contained a

noted Jewish settlement (a community into which the painter Modigliani was born)

🎼 Musical life

Museo Mascagnano celebrates life and work of Mascagni who was born there; the composer is also the subject of the 'Progetto Mascagni' run via the Fondazione Teatro Goldoni. Restored in 2004, this serves as main opera house of the city, with a short annual season, as well as concert hall, theatre and entertainment venue. Several choirs rehearse and perform in the city.

🏛 Other cultural information

Yeshiva Marini museum focuses on Jewish influence in city's past. Summer programme of performing arts events.

ℹ Tourist information

www.comune.livorno.it; turismo@comune.livorno.it; tel: +39 0586 820454

ISTITUTO SUPERIORE DI STUDI MUSICALI 'PIETRO MASCAGNI'

Palazzo della Gherardesca, Via G Galilei 40, I-57122 Livorno.
t: +39 0586 403724 *f:* +39 0586 426089
e: segreteria@istitutomascagni.it *w:* www.istitutomascagni.it
Contact Gabriele Micheli, Erasmus & international co-ord. *Courses* Bachelor and doctorate in performance (also lower levels) in voice, guitar, cello, clarinet, composition, double bass, french horn, bassoon, flute, oboe, percussion, piano, sax, trumpet, viola, violin, *Application requirements* High school degree and audition. *Term dates* 15 Oct-30 Sep. *Application deadline* 1 Apr-30 Sep. *Fees* EUR 76, EUR 1200, EUR 1800, depending on levels. *Scholarships* Number of scholarships available for each study level. *Exchange details* Programmes available through Erasmus. *Language requirements* Italian or English. *Music facilities* Study rooms, recording studio, concert hall, library. *No of students* 500.

MILAN

Italy's second city, in the north of the country, famous for its fashion industry, as a global financial centre and for its 2 rival football clubs (both of whom share the famous San Siro stadium). Also attracts students from around the world to higher education institutions covering a wide range of specialisms as well as the 2 more general universities. Well connected by road and rail (the city holds 5 railway stations) to other parts of Italy, and Europe to the north and west. Most famous architectural site the Duomo, the city's spectacular Gothic cathedral, dating back to the 14th century.

🎼 Musical life

Most celebrated for La Scala, its world-renowned opera house, where the most important conductors and singers brave a vocal audience of opera-lovers. Unlike many opera houses, its orchestra has a strong reputation in its own right, touring internationally as well as giving a year-long concert series at its home. City's other main orchestra is named laVerdi and gives concerts in the Auditorium de Milano; I Pomeriggi Musicali is a chamber orchestra performing at the Teatro dal Verme. Teatro degli Arcimboldi for musical theatre.

🏛 Other cultural information

Vast range of museums, including one at La Scala and a museum of musical instruments. 2 big modern art galleries, Padiglione Arte Contemporanea and Civico Museo Arte Contemporanea; other institutions (including art in churches) cover earlier eras. Despite its name, Piccolo Teatro di Milano is a major company producing work over a range of genres.

🎶 Festivals and events

MITO Settembre Musica festival in collaboration with the city of Turin and other smaller towns in the region. Also annual film and jazz festivals.

ℹ Tourist information

www.turismo.comune.milano.it

CONSERVATORIO DI MUSICA 'G VERDI' DI MILANO

Via Conservatorio 12, I-20122 Milano.
t: +39 027 62110216; +39 027 62110221 (international relations) *f:* +39 027 6020259
e: p.rimoldi@consmilano.it; erasmus@consmilano.it *w:* www.consmilano.it
Contact Paolo Rimoldi, head of international relations; Roberto de Thierry, assistant Erasmus/international relations. *Courses* Majors in harp,

singing, guitar and lute, clarinet, harpsichord, composition, double bass, horn, teaching methods, conducting (choral, orchestral or band), bassoon, accordion, flute, recorder and transverse flute, vocal chamber music, musicology, oboe, organ, percussion, piano, saxophone, sound technology, trumpet, trombone, tuba, viola, viola da gamba, violin, cello. Complementary subjects: harmony, scenic art, 'Letterature poetica e dramatica' (music lyrics), score-reading, chamber music, string quartet, theory and analysis, history of music, aesthetics. *Application requirements* High school diploma, audition. *Term dates* Nov-mid June(official academic year); tuition Oct-end Jun. *Application deadline* 1 Apr-31 Jul (regular students); Erasmus students, see website. *Fees* Bachelors: EUR 400, plus registration and government tax; masters: EUR 800, plus registration and government tax; registration tax in 1st year only. *Scholarships* For regular students only (ie not Erasmus): scholarships for opera singers, chamber music, composition, wind ensembles, piano and chamber music, chamber and vocal music, wind instruments, string instruments, piano, string quartet. *Exchange details* UK partner instituion: Guildhall School of Music and Drama. Partnerships with other institutions in Austria, Estonia, Finland, France, Germany, Iceland, Ireland, Latvia, Lithuania, Netherland, Poland, Romania, Spain, Switzerland. *No of students* Approx 1300, of whom approx 300 from overseas.

NAPLES (NAPOLI)

Ancient city (it is close to Pompeii and Herculaneum, destroyed by the still active Mount Vesuvius) in the bay bearing its name on the Mediterranean coast, but characterised today by architecture from the medieval to baroque periods. Home to one of world's oldest universities, the Frederick II university, and one of Italy's most important (around 100,000 students). One of most famous products connected with the city is the original tomato pizza (the recipe for Neapolitan pizza is now protected by law).

Musical life

By tradition, city strongly associated with music, and not only opera. In singing, Neapolitan song is a characteristic form of popular music, and singing itself has strong place in popular culture generally (Caruso was from the city). Strong association also with development of the guitar. Teatro San Carlo is main opera house, but also runs a concert programme with performances by house and visiting orchestras. Smaller scale concerts at Teatro delle Palme, plus occasional venues around city. Centro di Musica Antica dedicated to research into and presentation of Neapolitan baroque music.

Other cultural information

Teatro Bellini is mixture of more popular musicals and drama productions. Roman artefacts at the Museo Archeologico Nazionale di Napoli; 500 years' worth of Italian art at the distinctive Museo di Capodimonte.

Festivals and events

Theatre festival in Jun; film festival also.

Tourist information

www.inaples.it; tel: +39 081 2457475

CONSERVATORIO DI MUSICA SAN PIETRO A MAJELLA - NAPOLI

Via San Pietro a Majella, 35, I-80138 Napoli.
t: +39 081 5644411 *f:* +39 081 5644415
e: conservatorio_di_napoli@sanpietromajella.it
w: www.sanpietromajella.it
Courses Principal and secondary/complementary study courses (eg literature, ensemble playing, harmony, music history and aesthetics etc). *Application requirements* Admission exam. *Application deadline* 1-30 Apr.

PADUA (PADOVA)

Northern Italian city, not far from Venice, home to numerous medieval and renaissance palaces and churches, including the Cappella degla Scrovegni with its early 14th century Giotto frescoes. City characterised by mix of open spaces such as Prato della Valle near the Santa Giustina basilica and denser streets; historically surrounded by walls, still in evidence in certain areas. Home to one of the oldest universities and which founded the world's oldest botanical gardens, still extant today.

Musical life

Home to Orchestra di Padova e del Veneto, a well-regarded orchestra collaborating with international performers in concerts at the Teatro Verdi or at the conservatoire, as well as further afield in the region. Amici della Musica a concert promoting organisation inviting performers from locally and internationally.

 Festivals and events

Annual Festival Internazionale 'G Tartini' in spring and early summer spreads beyond Padua to the region as a whole

Tourist information

www.turismopadova.it; info@turismopadova.it; +39 049 8767927

CONSERVATORIO STATALE DI MUSICA 'CESARE POLLINI' - PADOVA

Via Eremitani 18, I-35121 Padova PD.
t: tel *f:* fax *e:* resp.socrates-erasmus@conservatorio pollini.it *w:* www.conservatoriopollini.it
Courses Most courses use traditional system of inferiore/medio/superiore studies; some experimental courses available in new form: music and disability, ethnomusicology, composition, recording studio technique. 2nd cycle courses available for bowed or string instruments, wind and brass, piano, vocal ensemble, organ/choirmaster.

PALERMO

Principal city on Sicily whose architecture and overall appearance attests to a history in which different cultural influences have taken hold

Musical life

Teatro Massimo lives up to its name, being built in a monumental neoclassical style and seating well over 3000 for opera and ballet performances and a small selection of concerts by resident orchestra. Late 19th century Teatro Politeama Garibaldi is home for Orchestra Sinfonica Siciliana.

Tourist information

www.palermotourism.com; info@palermotourism.com

CONSERVATORIO DE MUSICA VINCENZO BELLINI

Via Squarcialupo 45, I-90133 Palermo.
t: +39 091 580921 *f:* fax *e:* info@conservatorio bellini.it; erasmus@conservatoriobellini.it
w: www.conservatoriobellini.it
Music facilities 2 concert halls: Sala Scarlatti and Sala Sollima. Various ensembles including symphony and chamber orchestras, new music ensemble. opera chorus. Conservatoire has collection of historic instruments.

PARMA

Northern Italian city, famous as location 11th century university (one of the world's first) and as centre for a particular cured ham, but also with a strong cultural tradition. Several parks and gardens, including a botanic garden, add to the city's relaxed atmosphere.

Musical life

Teatro Regio is well known opera house, although produces only a few (3 or 4) operas per year; various orchestral concerts put on; also Auditorium Paganini in the Barilla Center for more concerts. Other concert events around the city, such as Sunday morning concerts at the Palazzo Marchi; Controtempi series of contemporary music events

Other cultural information

Palazzo della Pilotta is a 16th century palace now used as a cultural centre housing museums, an art gallery, library and theatre (Teatro Farnese). Museums with musical theme include the Casa della Musica (exhibitions plus courses in music appreciation etc), a Toscanini museum and the Casa del Suono (historic recording equipment); the Mondo Piccolo museum, however, is not dedicated to flutes but the work of humourist Giovannni Guareschi.

Festivals and events

Festival Verdi at the Teatro Regio every October featuring productions of Verdi operas plus concerts. Teatro Festival Parma is a theatre festival with elements from other art forms.

Tourist information

http://turismo.comune.parma.it; turismo@comune.parma.it; tel: +39 0521218707

CONSERVATORIO DI MUSICA ARRIGO BOITO DI PARMA

Via del Conservatorio 27/A, I-43100 Parma.
t: +39 0521 381911 *f:* +39 0521 200398
e: direttore.amministrativo@conservatorio.pr.it
w: www.conservatorio.pr.it
Courses 1st and 2nd cycle studies; also diplomi di specializzazione and traditional style courses.

Courses have both optional and obligatory elements.

PERUGIA

Central Italian city, whose built environment fully reflects its medieval history and the various changes in architectural style along the way. Enormous number of churches, palaces, fountains, squares, gates and other constructions associated with the 'typical' Italian town. University dates back to 13th century; city is still popular with students now, with a fine arts academy and a university specifically for overseas students to learn Italian language and culture as well as conservatoire.

♪ Musical life

Fondazione Perugia Musica Classica promotes a concert series and other projects throughout the year. Teatro Morlacchi is main venue for concerts, but others held in various churches such as the San Pietro basilica. Unusually for an Italian city, there is no opera house.

⛫ Other cultural information

Teatro Stabile dell'Umbria theatre company performs at Teatro Morlacchi as well as in other towns in the region. Range of museums and galleries.

🦢 Festivals and events

For classical music, the Sagra Musicale Umbria takes place in Sep each year, spreading across the Umbria region. Also exhibition of musical instruments during same month. Umbria Jazz festival, in July, is one of world's biggest. In Oct, one of Perugia's main products celebrated during an international chocolate festival.

ℹ Tourist information

http://turismo.comune.perugia.it; info@comune.perugia.it; tel: +39 075 5772805-2834

CONSERVATORIO DI MUSICA DI PERUGIA

Piazza Mariotti 2, I-06100 Perugia.
t: +39 075 57 33 844 *f:* +39 075 57 36 943
e: direttore@conservatorioperugia.it *w:* www.conservatorioperugia.it
Contact Nancy Greene, international co-ord. *Term dates* Nov-Jun. *Application deadline* Jul. *Exchange details* Erasmus. Also exchange partnerships with

Royal Academy of Music, Trinity College of Music (UK) and institutions in several countries inc Belgium, Bulgaria, Denmark, Estonia, Finland, Slovakia, Sweden.

PESCARA

City and seaside resort on the Adriatic coast, with long sandy beaches. Developed largely post-war therefore without the historical atmosphere of other Italian cities. Birthplace of Mussolini-supporting poet, Gabriele D'Annunzio (the conservatoire is named after his mother).

⛫ Other cultural information

Small selection of museums and galleries, such as the Museo d'Arte Moderna.

🦢 Festivals and events

Annual summer jazz festival; also open-air theatre festival in August.

ℹ Tourist information

www.regione.abruzzo.it/turismo; +39 085 421 9981

CONSERVATORIO STATALE DI MUSICA 'G ROSSINI' - PESARO

Piazza Olivieri 5, I-61100 Pesaro.
t: +39 072133671 *f:* +39 072135295
e: segretaria@conservatoriorossini.it *w:* www.conservatoriorossini.it
Courses Operates traditional system and experimental triennio/biennio system in parallel. *Application deadline* 14 Apr-24 May. *Music facilities* Auditorium Pedrotti is conservatoire's own concert hall. Various performance opportunities, including ensembles (symphony orchestra, wind orchestra, jazz group, Gregorian choir, flute ensemble)

CONSERVATORIO LUISA D'ANNUNZIO

Viale Leopoldo Muzii 5, I-65123 Pescara.
t: +39 085 4219950 *f:* +39 085 4214341
e: info@conservatorioluisadannunzio.it *w:* www.conservatorioluisadannunzio.it

ROME

Italy's capital, major European destination for tourists and other visitors. Vast number of major buildings and architectural features from ancient

Rome (Colosseum, Circus Maximus, Pantheon etc), but also from medieval, renaissance and baroque eras. 'Home' to pope's redsidence (and hence place of pilgrimage) the Vatican City, in fact a sovereign state in its own right.

♪ Musical life
Parco della Musica is a Renzo Piano-designed complex dedicated to music; contains 3 concert halls and open-air auditorium as well as the city's conservatoire. Substantial classical programme, but not limited to classical, and other art forms are incorporated (drama, film, exhibitions etc). Main opera based at the Teatro dell'Opera di Roma; the Opera di Roma has its own orchestra, also plays for ballet. Large number of open-air concerts during summer months; city's many churches hold concerts and opera performances.

🏛 Other cultural information
Home of Italian cinema, Cinecittà, is in Rome, the city being an iconic film landscape due to the number of well-known sights like the Trevi Fountain and Piazza San Pietro. Several museums devoted to Rome's history. English-language theatre at the English Theatre of Rome

🎭 Festivals and events
Large number of festival events throughout the year, such as Romaeuropa. Summer opera and music events at the Caracalla thermal baths.

i Tourist information
www.romaturismo.it; turismo@comune.roma.it

CONSERVATORIO DI MUSICA SANTA CECILIA
Via dei Greci, 18, I-00187 Roma.
t: +39 06 36096721 *f:* +39 06 36001800
e: segretaria@conservatoriosantacecilia.it
w: www.conservatoriosantacecilia.it
Courses Courses in piano accompaniment, harp, opera singing, guitar, harpsichord, composition, double bass, clarinet, french horn, orchestral conducting, flute, bassoon, jazz accordion, lute, harpsichord direction, choral music and choral conducting, chamber music, electronic music, vocal chamber music, musicology, music education, organ and organ composition, oboe, piano, band orchestration, percussion, saxophone, trumpet,

trombone, tuba, violin, viola, cello, viola da gamba. *Application requirements* Admission exam; preliminary Italian exam for overseas students. High school diploma for 3-year degree course; for the 2nd level degree, high school diploma plus conservatory diploma/university degree. *Term dates* 1 Nov-31 Oct. *Application deadline* Applications for admission 1-30 Apr; for university courses, 1 Jul-9 Aug. *Fees* EUR 175-950, depending on course, plus EUR 150 government tax; EUR 95 for entrance exam. *Scholarships* Details of scholarships, awarded based on musical merit, available on request. *Exchange details* UK exchange partner institutions: City University London, Trinity College of Music, University of Bristol. Other partnerships with institutions (conservatoires and universities) in Austria, Czech Republic, Denmark, Estonia, France, Germany, Greece, Latvia, Malta, Poland, Portugal, Romania, Slovakia, Spain, Switzerland, Turkey *No of students* Over 1500 students in total.

SALERNO
Southern Italian town on the Amalfi coast on the west of the country (it has a long seafront promenade that makes the most of its seaside location). Town with its historic centre based at the foot of hills which overlook it and there are spectacular views of it from them and surrounding areas – eg from the hilltop Castello d'Arechi. Numerous old churches, many decorated with typical artwork and ornamentation; Cattedrale di Salerno has a spectacular interior.

♪ Musical life
The Teatro Municipale Giuseppe Verdi hosts a relatively substantial season, also incorporating concerts by its orchestra the Orchestra Filarmonica Salernitana 'Giuseppe Verdi' (which tours and gives concerts elsewhere) and visiting artists.

🎭 Festivals and events
Festival di Musica Antica runs from Nov-Dec. Also an international film festival in Nov.

i Tourist information
www.turismosalerno.it; info@turismosalerno.it

CONSERVATORIO DI MUSICA 'G MARTUCCI' SALERNO

Via S De Renzi 62, I-84100 Salerno.
t: +39 089241086; +39 089231977 *f:* +39 0892582440 *e:* international@consalerno.com; protocollo@consalerno.com *w:* www.consalerno.com
Contact Francesco De Mattia, dir; Francesco Paolone, international relations co-ord. *Courses* 3 year undergrad degrees with many courses in all orch instruments, plus conducting (inc choral), composition, early music, electronic music, guitar, band instrumentation, jazz and improvisation, multimedia music, musicology (inc pedagogy and management), piano, saxophone, sound technician. 2 year masters in interpretation/composition, technology, teaching. *Term dates* 15 Sep-15 Jun. *Application deadline* 1-30 Apr; no fixed deadline for Erasmus international students. *Fees* Bachelors: EUR 56 enrolment fee; EUR 500 (conducting), EUR 350 (band instrumentation, singing, jazz, improvisation, non-classical music), EUR 200 (other). Masters: EUR 56 enrolment fee; EUR 850 (choir conducting), EUR 600 (other). *Scholarships* Ravello Prize annual grant for best student of the year. *Exchange details* Erasmus exchanges for students with placements on orchestral and conducting courses. Exchange partnerships with institutions in Austria, Belgium, France, Germany, Ireland, Netherlands, Spain, Switzerland. *Language requirements* Italian or English. Special arrangement with Salerno University for Italian language, culture and other courses for international students. *Music facilities* Town facilities used by students, inc Casino Sociale and Teatro delle Arte; recording studio for sound technicians. Some students engaged by Teatro Municipale Giuseppe Verdi opera house in chorus and orch and as accompanists/repetiteurs. *Accommodation* Special arrangements with Ave Gratia Plena hostel in Salerno; AEGEE Salerno helps students find accommodation. *No of students* 1500.

TURIN (TORINO)

Busy city in the Piedmont region of northern Italy with a population of over 2 million and a strong industrial heritage that continues today (motor vehicles and aerospace industries in particular). As Italy's third city, has added a contemporary feel to the baroque and other historical architecture.

♪ Musical life

Comparatively well served orchestrally: Orchestra Filarmonica di Torino is city orchestra, giving concerts in conservatoire concert hall; Orchestra Sinfonica Nazionale della RAI is national radio orchestra and has its own concert hall, the Auditorium RAI. 2-theatre Teatro Regio Torino is home to eponymous opera company; performs full season on stage, plus a smaller 6-month evening concert season and other ancillary concert events. Other concerts in the city include those organised by Lingotto Musica and Unione Musicale, both concert promoting organisations. Teatro Alfa for operetta.

🏛 Other cultural information

Numerous theatres and museums. The latter include weapons museum, museum of typography, national gallery of cinema and new gallery of Asian art as well as more usual art galleries and local history museums. Major theatres include Teatro Stabile Torino (new work and adaptations); more specialist venues too, such as Teatro Gianduja (puppets).

🎭 Festivals and events

Various Festivals and events covering a range of art forms. In music, Festival Internazionale di Musica Antica e Contemporanea run by Ensemble Antidogme in Jun is series of varied concert programmes; city hosts a major music festival in Sep in association with city of Milan. Dance also well represented in festivals, such as Torinodanza. International book fair and film festival.

ℹ Tourist information

www.turismotorino.org; info.torino@turismotorino.org; +39 011 535181.

CONSERVATORIO STATALE DI MUSICA 'GIUSEPPE VERDI'

Via Mazzini 11, I-10123 Torino.
t: +39 011888470 *f:* +39 011885165
e: trimarchi@conservatoriotorino.eu; paolotarallo@tin.it; m.mclara@tin.it; direzione@conservatoriotorino.eu
w: www.conservatorio-torino.eu
Contact Paolo Tarallo, Erasmus; Mariaclara Monetti, international co-ord; Marialuisa Pacciani, dir. *Courses* Diplomas at first and second level: piano, percussion, organ and organ improvisation,

orchestral instruments, saxophone, transverse flute, baroque oboe, harpsichord and historical keyboards, baroque violin, viola da gamba, composition, choral music and conducting, band orchestration, jazz, electronic music, lyric singing, vocal ensemble. Available at 2nd level only: orchestral conducting, pre-polyphony, opera direction & technical theatre. *Application requirements* Applicants assessed on musical ability, musical knowledge (theory and history), and knowledge of Italian language; selection exam during summer. *Term dates* Nov-Jun. *Application deadline* 10 Jun. *Fees* EUR 600-800 depending on level. *Exchange details* UK exchange partner institution: Royal Welsh College of Music and Drama. Also partnerships with institutions in Austria, Estonia, France, Germany, Netherlands, Norway, Poland, Spain, Turkey, also with University of Seoul. *Language requirements* Italian, French or English. *Accommodation* Accommodation in university college or private flats. *No of students* Approx 900.

TRENTO

Town in a mountain region of the far north of Italy. Its particular history – for part of the 19th century the town was under Austrian ownership as part of the Hapsburg Empire – the built environment demonstrates both Italian and Austrian influences.

Musical life

Societa Filarmonica Trento organises events at the Sala dei Concerti. Centro Servizi Culturali Santa Chiara is a more general performing arts centre, including concerts in its programme. No major symphony orchestra, but, along with Bolzano, the town is home to the Orchestra Haydn chamber orchestra.

Other cultural information

Teatro San Marco and other venues at the Santa Chiara cultural centre stage theatre, dance and other performances.

Festivals and events

Annual jazz festival. Mountainfilm Festival a distinctive festival showing films about mountains, exploration and related subjects, plus other events. Autumn harvest festival shows off produce from the region.

Tourist information

www.apt.trento.it; informazioni@apt.trento.it; tel: +39 0461 216000

CONSERVATORIO DI MUSICA 'FA BONPORTI' TRENTO

Gallerie dei Legionari 5, I-38100 Trento.
t: +39 0461 261673 *f:* +39 0461 263888
e: direttore@conservatorio.tn.it
w: www.conservatorio.tn.it
Contact Antonella Costa *Courses* 23 3-year courses (level 1), 28 2-year courses (level 2); also masters course and course for specialists. *Application requirements* Entrance exam and appropriate prior qualifications. *Term dates* Early Nov-end Oct. *Application deadline* 1 Jul-30 Aug. *Fees* EUR 400 (level 1), EUR 650 (level 2), EUR 1300 (masters), EUR 1500 (specialism) *Scholarships* Contact university. *Exchange details* Partner institutions in Austria, Belgium, Finland, Germany, Hungary, Spain, Turkey. *Language requirements* Italian or English. *Music facilities* Practice rooms can be booked in early morning or late afternoon (3 days a week until 10pm). *Accommodation* Accommodation available through Opera Universitaria (www.operauni.tn.it) which manages a network of accommodation, canteens, leisure services, sport and cultural activities. Accommodation prices from EUR 160 per month (depending on type). *No of students* 750 students in total.

TRIESTE

North eastern Italian port on the east side of the Adriatic whose location has given it a unique flavour. It was part of the Austrian empire until the 1920s; there is a strong influence from Slovenia, whose border surrounds the city on 2 sides, and whose language is spoken in some quarters; Churchill pinpointed the city as the southernmost end of the iron curtain – prior to that it attracted cultural tourists from all over Europe. City maintains a 'Mitteleuropa' feel in line with the likes of Austrian, Czech and Hungarian capitals. Also a traditional wine-making region.

Musical life

Teatro Lirico Giuseppe Verdi, with its opera company, orchestra, chorus and ballet company, is the main music venue; the Sala Tripcovich, part of the same theatre foundation but located elsewhere, provides another venue for the city.

Other cultural information

Teatre Stabile del Friuli-Venezia Giulia – Il Rossetti, with its distinctive ceiling decorated with twinkling stars, stages both drama and musical theatre. Reflecting geography, there is Slovenian-language theatre, with performances surtitled in Italian.

Festivals and events

2 music festivals in particular, at opposite ends of scale: operetta festival at the Teatro Verdi during the summer; in November, Trieste Prima is a contemporary music gathering.

Tourist information

www.turismofvg.it; info@turismo.fvg.it; tel: +39 432 815111

CONSERVATORIO DI MUSICA GIUSEPPE TARTINI TRIESTE

Via Ghega 12, I-34134 Trieste.
t: +39 040 6724911 f: +39 040 370265
e: triennio@conservatorio.trieste.it; erasmus@conservatorio.trieste.it w: www.conservatorio.trieste.it
Courses Courses in all classical instruments, electronic music, jazz. Application requirements Italian high school diploma (contact Italian embassy for equivalents). Term dates Nov -Jun. Application deadline 15 Jul. Fees Approx EUR 500 pa. Exchange details All European countries. No of students Approx 600 students.

UDINE

City in north east Italy.

Musical life

City has a modern theatre and concert hall presenting concerts from visiting artists as well as local Orchestra Sinfonica del Friuli Venezia Giulia based in the city (but performs across the region), opera (some from nearby Trieste company), musicals, dance and other kinds of entertainment.

Festivals and events

Mittelfest is an arts festival in July that which includes music (its name alludes to the term 'Mitteleuropa' often used to describe cities in the area). Far East Film Festival is a major event of its kind.

Tourist information

www.udine-turismo.it; info@udine-turismo.it; tel: +39 0432 295972

CONSERVATORIO STATALE DI MUSICA JACOPO TOMADINI - UDINE

Piazza 1° Maggio 29, I-33100 Udine.
t: +39 0432 502755 f: +39 0432 510740
e: erasmus@conservatorio.udine.it; coranglais58@hotmail.com w: www.conservatorio.udine.it
Contact Sandro Caldini. Courses Bachelor and masters courses for strings, woodwind, brass, piano, organ, harpsichord, percussion, harp, guitar, singing, chamber music for singers, composition, wind band composition, choral music. Special courses in baroque oboe and cor anglais. Application requirements Admission exam. Term dates 1 Nov-31 Oct. Application deadline 30 Apr. Fees EUR 400 (bachelor); EUR 600 (masters); EUR 400 (special courses). Scholarships Scholarships available. Exchange details Exchange partnerships with institutions in Austria, Estonia, Germany, Latvia, Lithuania, Norway, Spain. Language requirements Italian, English or German. Music facilities Vivaldi Hall, Monteverdi Hall, concert hall. Accommodation Contact Prof Sandro Caldini for details of accommodation available. No of students 600 national students and 15 from overseas.

VENICE

One of the world's foremost destinations for visitors, with its unique lagoon location on the Adriatic coast providing its signature network of canals (the city is exclusively negotiated on foot or by some form of river transport – vaporetto, gondola or other kind of boat – or on foot). Famous for many other things besides, from its glass-making to its bridges, palaces and squares. The largest of these, the Piazza San Marco is one of the world's best known gathering places.

Musical life

La Fenice, an opera house of international repute with a habit of living up to its name, 'phoenix' – twice the current building has been damaged by fire and rebuilt, most recently in 1996 (it reopened in 2003). A second venue, run by Fenice foundation, is Teatro Malibran, another opera house. As well as opera, the theatres host chamber concerts, perhaps arranged by the Societa Veneziana di Concerti, and orchestral concerts by its own orchestra.

🏛 Other cultural information
No shortage of historical interest; beyond the architecture and location of the place, there are extensive museums and galleries. City gave its name to a school of painting from the mid-15th century on, Titian foremost among them but Tintoretto and Bellini are 2 others whose work is also very evident in Venice.

🔍 Festivals and events
The Venice Biennale is one of the top art events in the world, and an international contemporary music festival, Biennale Musica (actually an annual event), runs alongside it. There are also events dedicated to theatre, cinema and architecture.

ℹ Tourist information
www.turismovenezia.it; info@turismovenezia.it; +39 0415298711

CONSERVATORIO DI MUSICA 'BENEDETTO MARCELLO' DI VENEZIA
Palazzo Pisani, San Marco 2810, I-30124 Venezia.
t: +39 041 522 56 04 *f:* +39 041 523 92 68
w: www.conseve.it

VERONA
Historical northern Italian city and Unesco world heritage site with a number of buildings and monuments surviving from ancient Roman times such as its amphitheatre, still in use today (though not for gladiatorial competitions). City's historic architectural character added to by large number of medieval Romanesque buildings such as the Basilica di San Zeno. Its attractiveness to visitors increased by proximity of Lake Garda.

🎼 Musical life
Teatro Filarmonico holds a series of concerts from Oct to May, similarly opera and ballet. Concert society Amici della Musica di Verona runs substantial concert season of mostly chamber music and recitals in churches; Accademia Filarmonica di Verona another musical organisation, promoting concerts at its premises like the Sala Maffeiana.

🏛 Other cultural information
Teatro Nuovo is the main theatre, focusing on classics but with other spaces hosting comedy and other entertainment. Variety of museums and exhibitions.

🔍 Festivals and events
Major opera festival at the arena throughout the summer attracts many spectators from around the world. Also choral festival/competition. The Settembre dell'Accademia is a short season of concerts by prestigious visiting orchestras, arranged by the Accademia.

ℹ Tourist information
www.tourism.verona.it; iatverona@provincia.vr.it; +39 045 8068680

CONSERVATORIO STATALE DI MUSICA EVARISTO FELICE DALL'ABACO
Via Abramo Massalongo 2, I-37121 Verona.
t: +34 045 8002814 045 *f:* +34 045 8009018
e: abaco@conservatorioverona.it; internazionale@conservatorioverona.it
w: www.conservatorioverona.it
Contact Hugh Ward-Perkins, international relations & Erasmus co-ordinator. *Courses* Traditional and experimental triennio/biennio systems run in parallel. Triennio available in orchestral instruments, composition, singing, viola da gamba, harpsichord, lute. Taught via 4 core modules: principal and complementary study; common subjects (harmony, analysis etc); other ancillary subjects (eg psychology of music); other options (eg languages). After biennio, also various specialist courses: music therapy; chamber music with piano; early music. *Application requirements* Admission exams in Jun; CD/DVD recordings accepted in some circumstances. *Application deadline* 30 April. Non-EU students must apply through Italian embassy in home country. *Fees* Approx EUR 540 (1st cycle); approx EUR 800 (2nd cycle and specialist courses). *Exchange details* UK Erasmus partner institutions: Royal Welsh College of Music and Drama, University of Leeds School of Music, Royal Northern College of Music, Royal Scottish Academy of Music and Drama. *Music facilities* 150-seat auditorium, chamber music rooms. Concerts also arranged in churches in and around Verona; there are several regular series. *No of students* Approx 150 higher education students

VICENZA

City in northen Italy not far from Venice. Closely associated with 16th century architect Palladio; the connection has led to city being listed as Unesco world heritage site.

i Tourist information

www.comune.vicenza.it; assturismo@comune.vicenza.it; tel: +39 444 222 169.

CONSERVATORIO DI MUSICA DI VICENZA 'ARRIGO PEDROLLO'

Contra San Domenico 33, I-36100 Vicenza. *t*: +39 0444 507551 *f*: +39 0444 302 706 *e*: direttoreamministrativo@consvi.it; relazioniinternazionali@consvi.org *w*: www.consvi.org

Contact Franca Moretto, Terrell Stone (international enquiries). *Courses* 1st and 2nd level diploma courses following international credit system. Courses in orchestral instruments (baroque, classical and modern), harpsichord, lute, sax, viola da gamba; also courses in Indian instruments (sitar, tabla) at 1st level. At 2nd level can also take liturgical music, piano accompaniment *Application requirements* Admission exam, testing musical ability, language test, musical knowledge test. *Term dates* Mid Oct -end Jun. *Application deadline* 10 June. *Fees* EUR 600 pa (1st level); EUR 800 pa (2nd level). *Scholarships* Limited number of scholarships offered by local, regional and national entities for conservatory students. *Exchange details* Exchange partnerships with over 10 institutions. *Language requirements* Italian. *No of students* 684 students, of which 31 from overseas.

MUSIC FESTIVALS

Festival della Valle d'Itria Centro Artistico Musicale Paolo Grassi, Palazzo Ducale, I-74015 Martina Franca. *t*: +39 080 4805100 *f*: +39 080 4805120 *e*: festivaldellavalleditria@tin.it *w*: www.festivaldellavalleditria.it

Festival Internazionale di Danza e Musica Antica Via Romagna 11, I-20031 Cesano Maderno (MI). *t*: +39 0362 54 95 80, also fax *e*: ass.mus.humorallegro@libero.it *w*: www.humorallegro.com

Festival Internazionale di Musica e Arte Sacra Via Paolo VI n 29 (Piazza S Pietro), I-00193 Roma. *t*: +39 06 6869187 *f*: +39 06 6873300

e: festival@promusicaeartesacra.it *w*: www.festivalmusicaeartesacra.it *Contact* Ruth Prucker, secretary. Sacred music concerts in the Roman papal basilicas, fundraising concerts for the support of the conservation and restoration of sacred art treasures. Concerts are for supporters of the Foundation; see website for details.

Festival Musica Antica a Magnano Via Roma 43, I-13887 Magnano (BI). *t*: +39 015 67 93 69; +39 015 67 91 76 *e*: info@MusicaAnticaMagnano.com *w*: www.MusicaAnticaMagnano.com *Contact* Bernard Brauchi, pres.

Festival Organistico Internazionale Citta di Treviso Palazzo Umanesimo Latino, Riviera Garibaldi 13, I-31100 Treviso. *t*: +39 0422 545895 *f*: +39 0422 513526 *e*: festorganisticotv@tin.it *w*: www.organidimarca.it *Contact* contact International Organ Academy with seminars, lectures, cultural exchanges and masterclasses with international teachers.

Festival Pianistico Internazionale 'Arturo Benedetti Michelangeli' di Brescia e Bergamo c/o Teatro Grande, Via Paganora 19/A, I-25121 Brescia. *t*: +39 030 293022 *f*: +39 030 2400771 *e*: info@festivalmichelangeli.it *w*: www.festivalmichelangeli.it Annual. Classical piano.

Festival Pontino Via Varsavia 31, I-04100 Latina. *t*: +39 07 7360 5551 *f*: +39 07 7362 8498 *e*: campus.musica@panservice.it *w*: www.campusmusica.it *Contact* Riccardo Cerocchi, manager. Classical and contemporary, including premieres.

Festival Puccini c/o Fondazione Festival Pucciniano, 4 Torre del Lago Puccini, I-55048. *t*: +39 0584 350567 *f*: +39 0584 341657 *e*: info@puccinifestival.it *w*: www.puccinifestival.it *Contact* contact Opera, concerts, lyric music.

Festival Spaziomusica Associazione Spaziomusica, Via Liguria 60, I-09127 Cagliari. *t*: +39 070 400844, also fax *e*: info@festivalspaziomusica.it *w*: www.festivalspaziomusica.it *Contact* Marcello Pusceddu, artistic director & president. Contemporary music.

Grandezze & Meraviglie, Festival Musicale e Estense Via S Michele 40/42, I-41100 Modena. *t*: +39 059 214 333, also fax *f*: fax *e*: festival@grandezzemeraviglie.it *w*: www.grandezzemeraviglie.it *Contact* Enrico Bellei, dir.

Incontri Europei con la Musica Associazione Musica Aperta, Via Borgo Palazzo 31, I-24125 Bergamo. *t*: +39 035 242287, also fax *e*: mabg@

unibg.it *w:* www.unibg.it/mabg *Contact* Pieralberto
Cattaneo. Classical, modern and contemporary
chamber music.

International Choir Festival: Orlando di Lasso
Associazione Internazionale Amici della Musica
Sacra, Via Paolo VI, 29, I-00193 Roma. *t:* +39 06
68 805816 *f:* +39 06 68 210889 *e:* info@aiams.
it *w:* www.amicimusicasacra.com

Rassegna di Nuova Musica CP 92, I-62100
Macerata. *t:* +39 07 3326 1334 *f:* +39 07 3326
1499 *e:* info@sferisterio.it *w:* www.rassegna
dinuovamusica.it

Ravenna Festival Via Dante 1, I-48100 Ravenna.
t: +39 0544 249211 *f:* +39 0544 36303 *e:* info@
ravennafestival.org *w:* www.ravennafestival.org

Rossini Opera Festival Via Rossini 24, I-61100
Pesaro. *t:* +39 07 213 800201 *f:* +39 07 213
800220 *e:* rof@rossinioperafestival.it Annual.
Rossini's operas, concerts.

Settimana Musicale Senese Fondazione
Accademia Musicale Chigiana, 89 Via di Citta,
I-53100 Siena. *t:* +39 05 772 2091 *f:* +39 05
772 88124 *e:* stampa@chigiana.it *w:* www.
chigiana.it *Contact* Guido Burchi, musicological
consultant. Ancient instrumental music of the Italian
baroque tradition.

**Settimane Musicali di Stresa e del Lago
Maggiore - Festival Internazionale** Via Carducci
38, I-28838 Stresa (VB). *t:* +39 03 233 1095
f: +39 03 233 3006 *e:* info@settimanemusicali.
net *w:* www.settimanemusicali.net Orchestras,
recitals and performances by young winners of
international music competitions; exhibitions.

**Settimane Musicali Meranesi-Meraner
Musikwochen** Corso Liberta 45, I-39012 Merano.
t: +39 0473 212520 *f:* +39 0473 239043
e: info@meranofestival.com *w:* www.meranofestival.
com Annual. Symphony orchestras and chamber
music.

Torino Settembre Musica Citta di Torino, Divisione
Servizi Culturali, Via S Francesco da Paola 3,
I-10123 Torino. *t:* +39 011 442 4715 *f:* +39 011
443 4427 *e:* settembre.musica@comune.torino.it

Verona Festival Piazza Bra 28, I-37121 Verona.
t: +39 045 800 5151 *f:* +39 045 801 3287
e: ticket@arena.it *w:* www.arena.it

NOTES / APPUNTI / NOTIZ

BASEL (BASLE)

German-speaking city, at junction of borders with Germany and France. Although not EU nor European Economic Area, member, it maintains various treaties with the rest of Europe. Architecture is mix of old and new, with several buildings from prominent modern architects. City's university is oldest in Switzerland.

♪ Musical life

Number of orchestras have their home in the town. Most prominent is Sinfonie Orchester Basel, with main venue the Stadtcasino Basel's music room but also at Theater Basel (venue for opera also); Collegium Musicum Basel another symphony orchestra. Basel Sinfonietta is an orchestra with a substantial but not exclusively contemporary music programme; Kammerorchester Basel is slightly smaller in size, and both perform concerts across the country. Also choirs such as Basler Bach-Chor and Gesangverein and strong chamber music presence. Many concerts promoted through city's music organisation, the Allgemeine Musikgesellschaft; Kammermusik.org another promoting organisation. Gare du Nord is unusual venue for new music, a converted railway station; Musical Theater Basel for lighter entertainment.

🏛 Other cultural information

Large number of museums and galleries, from modern art and local history to more specialist (there's a cartoon museum, design museum and doll's house museum, for example). Theatre and other performing arts in abundance covering many genres: traditional, avant-garde, satirical, cabaret genres. Range on offer reflects city's reputation as Swiss capital of culture.

🎭 Festivals and events

International festival of chamber music in city museums during Apr. Also annual jazz and Irish folk festivals, and dance festival in Sep.

ℹ Tourist information

www.basel.com; info@basel.com; tel: +41 61 268 68 68

MUSIK-AKADEMIE DER STADT BASEL HOCHSCHULE FÜR MUSIK

Leonhardsstr 6, Postfach, CH-4003 Basel.
t: +41 61 264 57 57 *f:* +41 61 264 57 13
e: hsm@mab-bs.ch *w:* www.mab-bs.ch
Courses BA in music, BA in music and movement; MA in music pedagogy, MA in music performance; MA in specialist music performance; MA in composition and theory. *Application deadline* End Feb, except for MA in specialist contemporary music performance (20 Mar).

BERN (BERNE)

Swiss capital, though not the largest, and officially German-speaking. Largely medieval city centre, located in a crook of River Aare, is a Unesco world heritage site

♪ Musical life

Camerata Bern is small flexible chamber group; Berner Kammerorchester another small orchestra with a particular reputation for commissioning and performing new works. Berner Symphonie Orchester older ensemble, based at Kultur-Casino Bern; also provide accompaniment for season of opera at Stadttheater Bern.

🏛 Other cultural information

Plays at Stadttheater, with smaller venues adding range to drama performance. Numerous cellar theatres staging more experimental work, comedy or puppet shows. Various museums: Zentrum Paul Klee is world's largest collection of the artist's work, but is also a wider cultural centre, housing a 300-seat concert auditorium and theatre space. Einstein's work in the city where he lived while working on special theory of relativity recognised in renovated Einstein-Haus.

🎭 Festivals and events

One of more unusual events is an annual festival of busking. There is a noted jazz festival every spring.

ℹ Tourist information

www.berninfo.com; info@berninfo.com; tel: +41 31 328 12 12

HOCHSCHULE DER KÜNSTE BERN

Papiermühlestr 13a, CH-3014 Bern.
t: +41 31 634 93 93 *f:* +41 31 634 91 71
e: musik@hkb.bfh.ch *w:* www.hkb.bfh.ch
Courses Undergrad and postgrad courses divided

EUROPE

into 4 areas: classical, jazz, music and media art, eurythmics and music. *Term dates* 14 Sep -15 Jan (autumn semester); 22 Feb-4 Jun (spring semester). *Fees* CHF 719 per semester.

GENEVA (GENÈVE)

French-speaking city Based on the south western end of Lake Geneva. Has an high global profile and international flavour due to presence of numerous international organisations there, such as World Trade Organisation, Red Cross/Crescent, World Health Organisation; this also means a high percentage of population comes from abroad.

♪ Musical life

Busy classical music scene, with numerous performing organisations. Best known is Orchestre de la Suisse Romande based at Victoria Hall but performing throughout the region as well as at main opera house, Grand Théâtre de Genève. L'Orchestre de Chambre de Genève for more reduced repertoire. Various semi-professional and occasional orchestras also. Several concert promoters arranging events at specialist and non-specialist venues. Bâtiment des Forces Motrices is an industrial building converted into an arts venue – concerts include symphonic and chamber events.

🏛 Other cultural information

Other art forms well catered for – dozens of theatres of various sizes in the city, and many more theatre companies. Some societies promote English-language theatre. Particularly thriving contemporary art scene, with the city funding a number of art centres devoted to artistic production. Various museums and exhibitions, some run by the city (and some of which offer free entry), others private concerns.

🎪 Festivals and events

Musiques en Eté festival (Jul-Aug) is all-round music festival including classical, jazz and world music. Mai en Fanfare a series open air performances; similar kind of event in Jun, Fête de la Musique. Contemporary music at Archipel festival in Mar. Large number of non-classical music festivals (eg jazz, flamenco, hip hop) and non-music festivals throughout the year.

ℹ Tourist information

www.geneva-tourism.ch; tel: +41 22 909 70 70

CONSERVATOIRE DE MUSIQUE DE GENÈVE HAUTE ECOLE DE MUSIQUE

12 rue de l'Arquebuse, CH-1211 Genève 11.
t: +41 22 319 60 60; +41 22 319 60 83 (international relations) *f:* +41 22 319 60 62
e: info@hemge.ch *w:* www.hemge.ch
Courses Bachelors and masters courses. For bachelors, students must complete 10 modules in following areas: 3 in principal study (instrument, baroque instrument, singing, composition, Dalcroze movement, school music, or music and musicology; 3 in practical training; 3 in theoretical and cultural aspect; 1 in preparatory class for masters. Masters available in interpretation, composition and theory, specialist interpretation (ie advanced performance), or pedagogy. *Application requirements* No age limit, but priority given to younger students. Applicants assessed on instrumental/vocal ability and general musical knowledge. See website for audition dates. *Application deadline* 15 Mar. *Fees* CHF 80 fee must be sent with application. *Exchange details* UK Erasmus partner institutions: Guildhall School of Music and Drama, Royal Academy of Music, Trinity College of Music, Royal Northern College of Music *Language requirements* Classes in French only. *Accommodation* Conservatoire cannot guarantee to provide accommodation, but students have access to various accommodation services. *No of students* Approx 550 students from around the world.

LAUSANNE

French-speaking city on the north bank of Lake Geneva. Its location gives a spectacular panorama over the lake and mountains nearby. Lake also provides leisure opportunities, the city itself being well-appointed with green spaces adding to its high quality of life.

♪ Musical life

Orchestre de Chambre de Lausanne presents various open and subscription concert series at Salle Métropole; some are chamber concerts using orchestra members. Sinfonietta de Lausanne effectively an advanced training orchestra, giving repertoire and concert experience to young musicians. This includes pit work at city's opera, although OCL is usual accompanist. City is home to one of world's leading choral groups, the Ensemble Vocal de Lausanne, although it is often touring.

Other cultural information

City is home to International Olympic Committee, and there is a unique museum devoted to Olympic history. Otherwise there are various general and specialist interest museums. Art activity across the board, with several art galleries (including one at the city's art school) and sculpture spread throughout city's parks.

Festivals and events

Well supplied with festivals. Lausanne Estivale, city-wide all-round arts festival running throughout the summer; similarly Festival de la Cité (Jul only). City is home to Quatuor Sine Nomine who organise a biennial festival in Jun (odd numbered years). Bach Festival in autumn. Guitar festival in May, jazz festival in Apr, another in autumn; also a festival of improvised classical music in August, and a separate improvised music festival Rue du Nord in Feb. Other main international festival is Festival International de Danse in early autumn.

Tourist information

www.lausanne-tourisme.ch; information@lausanne-tourisme.ch; tel: +41 21 613 73 73

CONSERVATOIRE DE LAUSANNE HAUTE ECOLE DE MUSIQUE

rue de la Grotte 2, CP 5700, CH-1002 Lausanne.
t: +41 21 321 35 20 *f:* +41 21 321 35 25
e: infohem@cdlhem.ch *w:* www.cdlhem.ch
Courses Bachelors and masters courses in classical music and jazz departments. *Application requirements* Instrumental/vocal test, theory exam and interview. School-leaving certificate or similar qualification required. *Term dates* Sep-end Jun. *Application deadline* 31 Mar. *Fees* Vary, see website for details. *Scholarships* Overseas students can apply for grants through Swiss government. See website of the Rectors' Conference of Swiss Universities www.crus.ch/information-programmes for more details. *Exchange details* Partnerships through Erasmus.

LUGANO

Italian speaking city at the very south of the country. Popular tourist destination at a very picturesque location on the shores of the lake with the same name; ideal base for outdoor activities such as Nordic walking, mountain biking or those on the lake.

Musical life

Orchestra della Svizzera Italiana based in the city at the Palazzo dei Congressi. Venue also receives visits from other orchestras and performing organisations.

Other cultural information

Several modern art galleries, including a poster museum and a museum of photography; variety of museums, including unusual ones such as that devoted to history of smuggling in the region

Festivals and events

Lugano festival during spring sees performances from a number of visiting orchestras. Immediately followed by Progetto Martha Argerich throughout Jun, more focused on chamber music and recitals. Various jazz and blues events throughout rest of summer. Summer festival season ends with a weekend celebrating local produce.

Tourist information

www.lugano-tourism.ch; info@lugano-tourism.ch; tel: +41 91 913 32 32

CONSERVATORIO DELLA SVIZZERA ITALIANA

Via Soldino 9, CH-6900 Lugano.
t: +41 91 960 30 40 *f:* +41 91 960 30 41
e: info@conservatorio.ch *w:* www.conservatorio.ch
Contact Ellen Frau, BA and MA course administrator; Marlies Bärtschi, student officer. *Courses* BA in music, BA in music & movement, BA in music (composition & theory); MA in music pedagogy, MA in music performance, MA in specialised music performance, MA in composition and theory. *Application requirements* High school degree (Matura or equivalent); see website for details. *Term dates* Sep-Jan, Feb-Jun. *Application deadline* No later than 15 Apr. *Fees* c EUR 2300 pa. *Scholarships* Contact student office for details. *Exchange details* Exchanges arranged through Erasmus programme. Partnerships with institutions in Denmark, Finland, Germany, Hungary, Italy, Netherlands, Norway, Poland, Spain, Sweden, United Kingdom (Trinity College). *Language requirements* Italian and/or English. *Accommodation*

EUROPE

Contact student office for details. *No of students* More than 60% of students from overseas.

LUCERNE (LUZERN)

Located on Vierwaldstättersee (Lake Lucerne), official language is German. Historic city, with significant medieval presence in city centre (the Kapellbrücke bridge is a restored version of the 14th century original) and well located for tourist

♪ Musical life

Well provided for musically. New Kultur- und Kongresszentrum Luzern built as an all-round performing arts and cultural centre, and provides home for Luzerner Sinfonieorchester. The orchestra gives its own season of concerts, and provides accompaniment at Luzerner Theater for opera and ballet. Lucerne Festival Orchestra is attached to festival, a unique group made up of the foremost chamber musicians and soloist handpicked by Claudio Abbado. Festival also runs a Festival Academy, headed by Pierre Boulez. Festival Strings Luzern another, smaller orchestra, runs its own series of concerts at the KKL independently of the festival. Plans for new flexible performance space under way (construction due to finish in 2013)

▥ Other cultural information

Luzerner Theatre also has programme of drama on stage, plus ancillary events, discussions etc. Another cultural centre, called Boa, stages range of contemporary performance across a number of art forms. City also well provided with museums and galleries, including Richard Wagner Museum. Kulturmagazin available to subscribers to keep up to date with events.

☜ Festivals and events

Lucerne Festival runs for 5 weeks in Aug-Sep attracts major musicians and ensembles; associated events are a week-long easter event and piano festival in Nov, with big name international classical and jazz musicians invited. Various jazz events.

ⓘ Tourist information

www.luzern.org; luzern@luzern.com; tel: +41 41 227 17 17

HOCHSCHULE LUZERN – MUSIK

Zentralestr 18, CH-6003 Luzern.
t: +41 41 226 03 70 *f:* +41 41 226 03 71
e: musik@hslu.ch *w:* www.hslu.ch/musik
Contact Claire Thilo, international office. *Courses* BA (music, church music, music and movement); MA in music with majors in performance/interpretation, orchestra, chamber music, solo performance, contemporary art performance, composition, conducting (orchestral, choral, brass band), music theory, church music, jazz performance; also MA in music pedagogy. *Application requirements* Entrance exam. *Term dates* Sep-Jun. *Application deadline* Beginning Mar. *Fees* CHF 120 application fee; BA/MA/ Diploma studies: CHF 1000 per semester, plus CHF 100 for module exams. *Scholarships* Several available for highly talented students; please contact for details. *Exchange details* Erasmus exchange partnerships with approx 20 music schools across Europe. *Language requirements* C1 in German for BA/MA; MA solo performance possible in English or other languages. *Accommodation* StuWo Luzern runs student accommodation for various institutions in the city: www.stuwo-luzern.ch. *No of students* 502 students in total, of whom 75 from overseas.

NEUCHÂTEL

Small French-speaking lakeside town at the foot of the Jura range in western Switzerland with smart old town and interesting architectural features. Ideal for many outdoor leisure activities with numerous ski resorts nearby.

♪ Musical life

Despite size, the town supports a decent array of music. The Ensemble Symphonique de Neuchâtel is new group formed from merger of the town's symphony and chamber orchestras, and aims to become a firm presence in region's cultural activity.

▥ Other cultural information

Town's cultural centre includes a theatre.

☜ Festivals and events

Biennial choral festival (even-numbered years) is in fact a choral competition.

www.neuchateltourisme.ch; info@ne.ch; tel: +41 32 889 68 90

CONSERVATOIRE DE MUSIQUE NEUCHÂTELOIS
Avenue du Clos-Brochet 30-32, CH-2002 Neuchâtel.
t: +41 32 725 20 53 *f:* +41 32 725 70 24
e: conservatoire.NTEL@ne.ch *w:* www.conservatoire-ne.ch
Courses Bachelors available in various specialisms: instruments, period instruments, jazz (instruments, singing or composition), singing, baroque singing, composition, Dalcroze movement and music, school music. *Application deadline* 30 Apr. *Fees* CHF 900 per semester, plus course and exam fees.

ZÜRICH
The country's most predominant and wealthy city with a major global importance in financial and commercial industries (Swiss stock exchange based there); its wealth helps sustain a busy musical life. Located in German-speaking north of the country at tip of Lake Zürich.

Musical life
Principal orchestra, and one of the oldest, is the busy Tonhalle-Orchester, named after the venue it calls home (it has a main concert hall and smaller space for chamber music); also receives visits from major overseas orchestras. Several other orchestras besides, ranging from Symphonisches Orchester Zürich at larger scale to chamber orchestras like Zürcher Kammerorchester (based at its own 250-seat hall, the ZKO-Haus) and even smaller Camerata Zürich. Contemporary music and performing arts at Kunstraum Walcheturm, where you might hear city-based Ensemble für Neue Musik Zürich. Opera and ballet at Opernhaus Zürich which has own orchestra (it gives concerts in its own right outside the busy opera season).

Other cultural information
For more alternative style of culture, Rote Fabrik promotes various art forms. Kulturmarkt another venue with eclectic all-round programme. Very good range and variety of galleries, especially of modern and contemporary art and design. Theatre provision includes Herzbaracke, a floating variety theatre on Lake Zürich; largest theatre is Schauspielhaus Pfauen, for more conventional range of drama; Theater der Künster aims for a multi-disciplinary approach.

Festivals and events
Month-long Zürcher Festspiele in Jun-Jul features music strongly among theatre and art events. Biennial festival of site-specific performance around the city, Stromereien (odd-numbered years).

www.zuerich.com; information@zuerich.com; tel: +41 44 215 40 00

ZÜRCHER HOCHSCHULE FÜR KUNSTE (ZURICH UNIVERSITY OF THE ARTS)
Florhofgasse 6, CH-8001 Zürich.
t: +41 43 446 20 56 (international office)
f: +41 43 446 51 30 *e:* empfang.florhof@zhdk.ch (music); bettina.ganz@zhdk.ch (international office) *w:* www.zhdk.ch
Contact Bettina Ganz, international affairs co-ord.
Courses Bachelor and masters studies in classical music (solo, opera, orchestra, chamber music, lied-duo, piano chamber music, instrumental pedagogy); jazz pedagogy; pop pedagogy; music and movement; school music; church music (organ, choir); conducting (orchestral, choral); composition (contemporary; electro-acoustic; film, theatre and media); music theory; sound engineering. *Application requirements* See website for full details. *Application deadline* 28 Feb. *No of students* 40% of students from 51 overseas countries.

MUSIC FESTIVAL
ARCHIPEL. Festival des Musiques d'Aujourd'hui
8 rue de la Coulouvrenière, CH-1204 Genève.
t: +41 22 329 42 42 *f:* +41 22 329 68 68
e: festival@archipel.org *w:* www.archipel.org
Contact Marc Texier, director; Jacques Menetrey, admin. Modern/contemporary music, video, dance, installations. Various venues.
Classic Openair Hans Roth-Str 15, CH-4500-Solothurn. *t:* +41 32 6223070 *f:* +41 32 621 6302 *w:* www.classic-openair.ch
Fribourg International Festival of Sacred Music Rue des Alpes 7, CP 540, CH-1701 Fribourg. *t:* +41 26 322 4800 *f:* +41 26 322 8331 *e:* office@fims-fribourg.ch *w:* www.fims-

EUROPE

fribourg.ch Contact Nicole Reveney, administrator. Biennial. 10 concerts of medieval, renaissance, baroque, romantic and contemporary music; 4 concerts of traditional and sacred music. Gregorian chant workshop; masterclass by Marco Beasley: 'A Voce Sola: Recitar Cantando (16th-17th C); lectures. Co-produced by Swiss radion RSR-Espace 2.

Lucerne Festival Hirschmattstr 13, CH-6002 Lucerne. t: +41 41 226 4400 f: +41 41 226 4460 e: info@lucernefestival.ch w: www.lucernefestival. ch Classical music festival with symphony concerts, chamber music, recitals, choral concerts, serenades, musica nova, composer-in-residence.

Lucerne Festival Am Piano. w: http://e.lucerne festival.ch

Menuhin Festival Gstaad Haus des Gastes, Postfach 65, CH-3780 Gstaad. t: +41 33 748 83 38 f: +41 33 748 83 39 e: info@menuhin festivalgstaad.com; desmondcecil@dial.pipex.com w: www.menuhinfestivalgstaad.com Contact Beatrice Frautschi, festival administrator; Desmond Cecil, festival international representative Some 40 concerts in beautiful old churches and festival tent (seating 2000). Chamber music, symphony concerts, contemporary music, violin music. Top artists and young musicians. Theme of 2009: 'Perfection'.

Montreux Choral Festival PO Box 1526, CH-1820 Montreux. t: +41 21 966 55 50 f: +41 21 966 55 69 e: montreuxchoralfestival@bluewin. ch w: www.choralfestival.ch Contact Daniel Schmutz, president. Open to all choirs, offering choice of a free programme and attractive prizes.

SOLsberg Festival t: +41 79 322 14 34 e: info@ solsberg.ch w: www.solsberg.ch Contact Christoph Mueller, artistic director. 6 concerts over 2 weekends.

Verbier Festival 4 rue JJ Rousseau, CH-1800 Vevey. t: +41 21 925 9060; +41 848 771 882 (box office) f: +41 21 925 9068 e: info@ verbierfestival.com w: www.verbierfestival.com Contact Kim Gaynor, managing director. Annual. Summer performing arts academy; over 200 events with internationally renowned artists, including songs, symphonic and chamber music, recitals and masterclasses.

Zurich Festival c/o Opernhaus Zürich, Falkenstr 1, CH-8008 Zürich. t: +41 44 269 90 90 f: +41 44 260 70 25 e: info-office@zuercher-festspiele. ch w: www.zuercher-festspiele.ch

EUROPE

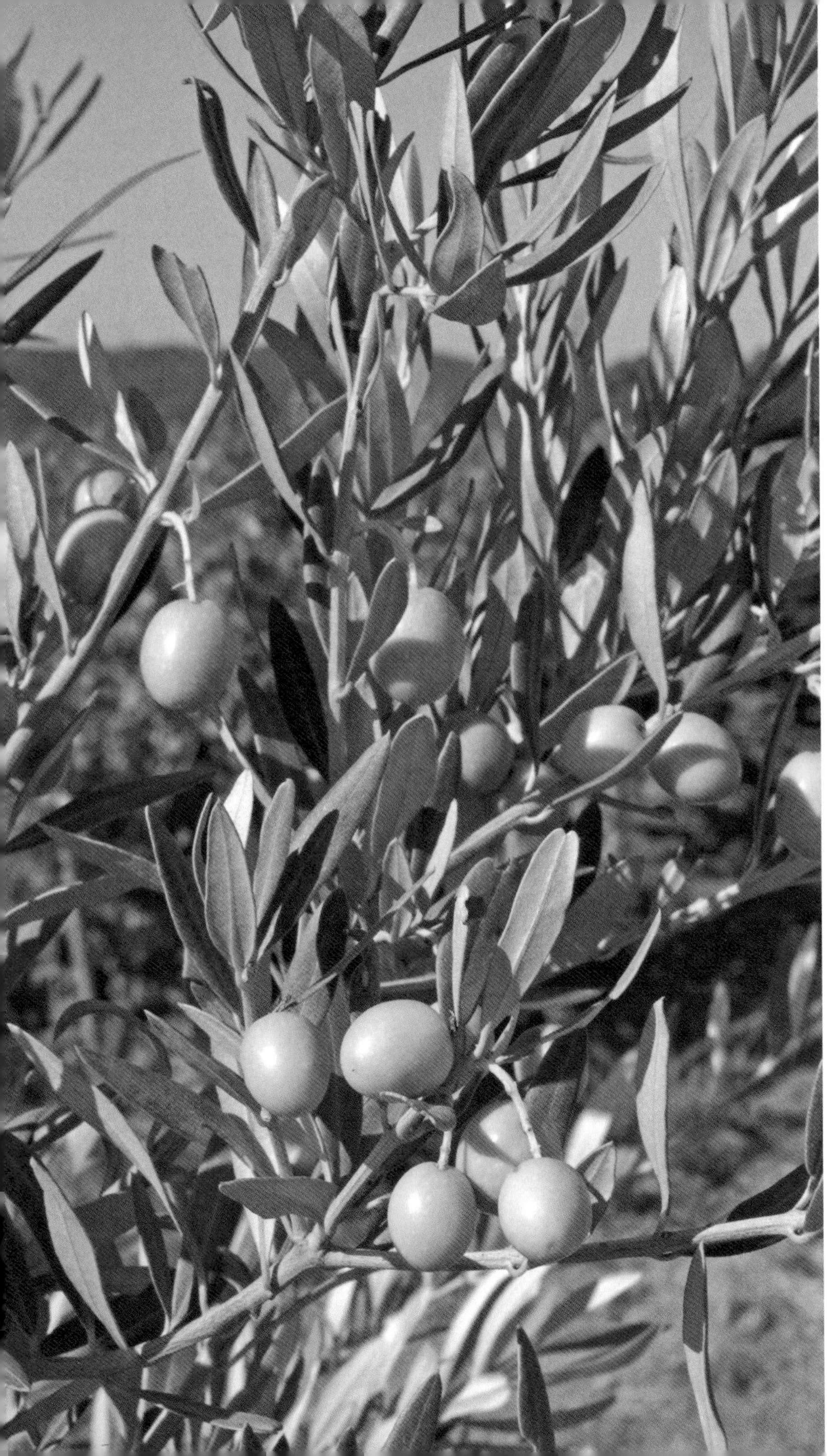

Spain and Portugal

NOTAS

Spain and Portugal

Among orchestral musicians, primarily those starting out their professional career, Portugal and Spain have been useful sources of employment. Not only is there the attractive climate and quality of life in many places, but the increased investment in cultural activities and consequent growth in number of orchestras in Spain over the past 30 years means vacancies arose frequently.

This is not so much the case now, however; although there are still numerous performing organisations (around 50 orchestras across Spain, for example), player lists have consolidated making available positions less numerous. This is where a foot in the door at a conservatoire can help – it is not unusual for local orchestras to offer extras places to advanced students, for example. And if nothing else, a year or so in a more relaxed environment may well put things in perspective if you have to return to less ideal conditions.

SPAIN

Professional music training at higher education level is treated separately from the university system, although it does run parallel to the general education system with elementary, intermediate and superior levels (the latter being where professional training falls). Superior level courses can only be taught by institutions with the correct authority, whether these are private or public. In the main, national students qualify for entry to the courses by successful completion of the intermediate level of music study along with high school qualification, although the rules are not hard and fast.

Currently, conservatoires do not follow the Bologna structure, and they operate a credit system that does not relate to ECTS. In addition, they do not offer masters degrees but a single 4-year qualification (5 years for composition and conducting). Doctoral studies in musicology can be pursued at the end of this period, but only at universities (the superior level qualification gives direct access).

PORTUGAL

Portugal's two public conservatoires are considered part of the polytechnic system (as opposed to the university system). Unlike Spain, the country has been quick to adopt the Bologna process structure, so students spend 4 years studying for the first licenciado and a further 1 for masters qualification. As with Spain, doctoral studies are only available in universities. Funding comes through a combination of state funding and students' fees.

Outside the public conservatoires, music education is available elsewhere; either in private higher education institutions like Lisbon's orchestral academy (funded by student fees with some state assistance), or in universities where music teacher training goes on – professional music teachers cannot qualify at conservatoires. Music education at earlier ages is through a combination of specialised music schools (ages 10-18) or professional music schools (12-18).

BADAJOZ

City in west of Spain near border with Portugal.

CONSERVATORIO SUPERIOR DE MUSICA DE BADAJOZ

Duque de San German 6, E-06071 Badajoz.
t: +34 924 224 935 *f:* +34 924 224 771
w: www.dip-badajoz.es/cultura/conservatorio
Courses Conservatoire divided in 5 departments: harmony, composition and theory; strings, guitar, harp, chamber music, accordeon; choral and vocal; piano; wind, brass and percussion. *Music facilities* Various ensembles: choir, symphony and chamber orchestras, sax group, electroacoustic group, wind band.

BARCELONA

Capital of Catalunya on the Mediterranean coast towards the north east of Spain, located at the foot of a mountain range giving the city a spectacular setting; Montjuïc is a case in point, an area including various gardens. Unique mix of modern architectural styles, whether exotic designs of Gaudí, the Catalan version of art nouveau or more minimal style. The city's attraction to visitors (of which there are many) is enhanced by the presence of long beaches close to the centre, and by its bustling nightlife.

Musical life

Palau de la Música Catalana one of world's most spectacular concert halls, with distinct decorative style both inside (the concert hall itself dominated by stained glass windows) and on exterior. It attracts major artists from all around the world, as well as Catalan performers; there's also a smaller accompanying Petit Palau built in different style. Gran Teatre del Liceu opera house in the busy Rambla area puts on own productions (there's resident chorus and orchestra) and acts as receiving house. Orquestra Simfònica de Barcelona I Nacional de Catalunya is main orchestra; based at new L'Auditori hall which also stages wide range of classical music performed by other groups and individuals. Orquestra de Cadaqués has HQ in Barcelona but is in fact a festival orchestra that gathers for Cadaqués Festival and tours.

Other cultural information

Extensive range of exhibitions, including galleries focusing on Picasso and Miró, on post-war Catalan and Spanish art, Catalan history etc. Large number of theatres.

Festivals and events

Numerous arts festivals throughout the year. Festival de Barcelona Grec (Jun) features flamenco and various other modern music, dance and performance. Sónar music festival, also in Jun, features contemporary mixed media art and music. Early music at the Festival de Música Antiga in Apr, organised by L'Auditori; venue also runs contemporary music event in Mar. More contemporary music at Festival Internacional de Música Experimental.

Tourist information

www.bcn.es

CONSERVATORI LICEU

La Rambla 63, E-08002 Barcelona.
t: +34 93 304 11 11 *f:* +34 93 412 48 87
e: conservatori@conservatori-liceu.es *w:* www.conservatori-liceu.es
Courses Principal studies are classical and contemporary music instruments and singing; composition; orchestral conducting; jazz and modern music instruments (drums, electric bass, double bass, electric guitar, percussion, piano, saxophone, keyboards, trombone, trumpet) voice. Also department of Flamenco. Details of academic programme, including mandatory and optional courses, available on website. Postgrad specialisation includes orchestral conducting, music analysis, composition, music history and aesthetics, musicology, music education. *Application requirements* Admission test: performance of prepared repertoire, musical analysis, sight reading, contemporary music, *Scholarships* All students registered in a course can apply to conservatoire's scholarships programme. *Exchange details* Latin American Collaboration programme (workshops and masterclasses, concerts, scholarship programme).

ESCOLA SUPERIOR DE MUSICA DE CATALUNYA

Edicife L'Auditori, Padilla 155, E-08013 Barcelona.
e: international.relations@esmuc.net *w:* www.esmuc.cat
Contact Oriol Pausa. *Courses* Degrees in classical

music (orchestral and non-orchestral instruments), jazz and modern music, early music, conducting, musicology, sonology, theory and composition; also traditional music. Curriculum consists of core subjects, compulsory specialist subjects and options. School also arranges complementary extra-curricular activity (eg masterclasses, conferences, student concerts, professional development activity etc). *Scholarships* None. *Exchange details* Programmes arranged through Erasmus. *Music facilities* Library with audiovisual facilities and computers with music software; instrument office offering loans and technical advice; study classrooms and rehearsal rooms; audiovisual office. *No of students* Capacity of about 600, with c 150 new students accepted each year.

CORDOBA

City in Andalusia, southern Spain and Unesco heritage site with interesting history combining Spanish, Moorish and even Roman influences. Famous for its unique Mezquita Catedral, a church converted by north African conquerors to a mosque, then back to a church again (with a new Christian building built at its heart) following the Spanish reconquest. City's religious importance emphasised by presence of its 14th century synagogue. Interesting architectural contrasts, from narrow streets of old town to its main square the Plaza de la Corredera, with a more modern area also.

♪ Musical life
City has its own orchestra, Orquesta de Córdoba. Gran Teatro includes music events among its wider programming.

⊞ Other cultural information
Various museums, many of which result from Córdoba's importance historically.

🐚 Festivals and events
Various town events such as its Patio Festival, where houses open up their distinctive courtyards for public to look at. Main music event is the annual guitar festival in Jul.

ⅰ Tourist information
www.turismodecordoba.org; infoave@ turismocordoba.org; tel: +34 902 201 774

CONSERVATORIO SUPERIOR DE MUSICA DE CORDOBA 'RAFAEL OROZCO'
Angel Saavedra 1, E-14003 Cordoba.
t: +34 957379647 *f:* +34 957379653
e: erasmus@csmcordoba.com *w:* www.csmcordoba.com
Contact Monica Marquez Carrasco (international enquiries)

GRANADA

City in the far south of Spain, in Andalusia. Like other places in the region, the history and architecture of the place influenced by various factors, but have left one of Spain's most impressive monuments in the form of the hilltop Alhambra palace. Many other historic locations too. Proximity to Sierra Nevada mountains means visitors attracted during winter for skiing.

♪ Musical life
Centro Cultural Manuel de Falla concert hall and Palacio de Exposiciones (with halls named after Falla and writer García Lorca, both of whom have strong attachment to the city), are main music venues. Teatro Alhambra has varied programme including music. Other venues, such as Teatro Municipal Isabel la Católica, also used occasionally for concerts. City's home orchestra is the busy Orquesta Ciudad de Granada which can also be heard in other nearby cities such as Sevilla.

⊞ Other cultural information
Flamenco a predominant form of expression in the region with many events throughout the year; otherwise numerous cultural events organised by city council.

🐚 Festivals and events
Three-week long Festival of Music and Dance runs from late June in various venues around the city. Festival Internacional de Tango de Granada in spring, and major jazz festival in Nov.

ⅰ Tourist information
www.turgranada.es; tel: +34 958 24 71 46

REAL CONSERVATORIO SUPERIOR DE MUSICA 'VICTORIA EUGENIA' DE GRANADA
Calle San Jeronimo n° 46, E-18001 Granada.
t: +34 958 276 866 *f:* +34 958 276 716

EUROPE

e: info@conservatoriosuperiorgranada.com; internacional@conservatoriosuperiorgranada.com *w:* www.conservatoriosuperiorgranada.com *Contact* Sara Ramos, contact for international enquiries *Courses* Music degrees. *Application requirements* Entrance exam. *Application deadline* 15 May. *Exchange details* Exchanges through Erasmus. *No of students* 350 students.

MADRID

Spanish capital, though not an old city compared with some of the urban centres in the south – made capital only in mid 16th century, supposedly because of its location right in the centre of the country. Famed now for its busy nightlife (a night out begins at 10pm), a legacy of a key moment in recent history known as 'La Movida'. In the euphoria following the death of the dictator Franco, the city became the focus for an explosion of hedonistic activity. Despite busy life there, however, and the large number of things to do, city holds a number of parks and gardens for relaxation – main park is the Retiro, there is also a botanical garden.

Musical life

Various orchestras based in and performing in the city. Orquesta Nacionale de España (which has an associated choir) based at Auditorio Nacional de Música, but gives plenty of concerts elsewhere; Orquesta Sinfónica de RadioTelevisiónEspañola (also with an associated choir) is country's main broadcaster-subsidised orchestra; Orquesta de Cámara Reina Sofia smaller-scale group. Orquesta Sinfónica de Madrid, one of Spain's longest established orchestras, gives a substantial concert series as well as providing accompaniment at the Teatro Real (opera and ballet). Spanish popular music theatre has its own venue at Teatro de la Zarzuela; this is also home of the Orquesta de la Comunidad de Madrid. Many other concert venues, cultural centres and theatres with occasional music performance besides, not to mention jazz clubs, rock venues etc.

Other cultural information

City holds one of the world's finest art collections at the Prado art gallery; Reina Sofia gallery nearby, its collection predominantly of works by modern Spanish artists, especially Picasso. Apart from the big 3 (the other being the Museo Thyssen

Bornemisza), plenty of others to choose from. For many, the chief cultural activity is provided by the Madrid football teams, Real and Atlético.

Festivals and events

Autumn festival of performing arts in Oct-Nov; Conciertos de Semana Sancta is a week of concerts in Madrid churches in the run-up to Easter. Jazz festival in Oct-Nov.

Tourist information

www.esmadrid.com

REAL CONSERVATORIO SUPERIOR DE MUSICA DE MADRID

C/ Doctor Mata 2, E-28012 Madrid.
t: +34 915392901 *f:* +34 915275822
e: infosecre@real-conserv-madrid.es *w:* www.educa.madrid.org/web/csm.realconservatorio.madrid/
Term dates 1 Oct-10 Jun.

MURCIA

City traversed by river Segura in south east of Spain in region of the same name, close to Mediterranean coast. Has a mix of architectural styles – even the cathedral was built over 3 different periods – though has remained relatively undeveloped in past few years compared with other coastal cities not so far away

Musical life

The region has an orchestra, the Orquesta Sinfónica de la Région de Murcia, and concert hall, the Victor Villegas auditorium and congress centre where it gives most of its concerts; hall also receives visting orchestras, chamber music, choral events etc, and non-classical performers.

Other cultural information

Romea Theatre for theatre and dance, also music theatre and flamenco events. A number of city's museums touch on religious themes (eg the Salzillo Museum, or Cathedral Museum), echoing the city's tradition as producer of nativity scenes; art galleries also present, and museum charting city's history. Bullfighting a particular tradition in southern Spanish regions, and Murcia has its own bullring and bullfighting museum.

SPAIN

Festivals and events

Like many Spanish cities, has popular processions during religious festivals. Also Murcia Tres Culturas, a festival of cultural activities focusing on interaction between Islam, Christianity and Judaism. Week-long jazz festival in May

Tourist information

www.murciaciudad.com; promocionturistica@ayto-murcia.es; tel: +34 968 358600.

CONSERVATORIO SUPERIOR DE MUSICA DE MURCIA

Paseo del Malecon 9, E-30004 Murcia.
t: +34 968 29 47 58 *f:* +34 968 29 47 56
e: info@csmmurcia.com; erasmus@csmmurcia.com *w:* www.csmmurcia.com

Application requirements Courses in orchestral instruments, accordion, singing, harpsichord, guitar and flamenco guitar, baroque instruments; also composition, choral and/or orchestral direction, musicology, music education. Courses made up of obligatory modules to give all students a common musical base and optional choices to complement students' specialisms. All instrumental students give recitals as part of course.

OVIEDO

City in north west Spain on the Bay of Biscay with pre-Romanesque architectural style predominant. At centre is an old town whose layout still reflects the city's medieval heritage, and includes striking cathedral.

Musical life

2 orchestras based in the city: Oviedo Filarmonia and regional Orquesta Sinfónica del Principado del Asturias. Both perform at the new Auditorio Príncipe Felipe, a flexible 3-hall venue (the biggest hall seats well over 2000, the chamber hall 400) that is part of a congress centre complex. The Oviedo Filarmonia (one of Spain's newest, founded in 1999) also providing orchestra for opera at the Teatro Campoamor. Opera includes important Zarzuela season. A little confusingly, it is not based at the town's Teatro Filarmonica, the stage being too small for full size orchestra concerts, but musical events do feature as part of its programming. Also Oviedo Filarmonia Youth Orchestra, invites young musicians from different countries. Some music events at the university (advertised on its website).

Other cultural information

Handful of galleries and museums: fine arts museum is largest.

Festivals and events

Jazz festival in Jul. Numerous religious processions, and carnival in Feb.

Tourist information

www.ayto-oviedo.es; oficina.turismo@ayto-oviedo.es

CONSERVATORIO SUPERIOR DE MUSICA EDUARDO MARTINEZ TORNER

Corrada del Obispo S/N, E-33003 Oviedo.
t: +34 985217556 *f:* +34 985203720 *w:* www.consmupa.es

Courses Majors in accordion, composition, guitar, organ, percussion, piano, saxophone, singing, string instruments, brass instruments, woodwind instruments. *Exchange details* Exchange partnerships with institutions in Austria, Belgium, Finland, France, Germany, Iceland, Italy, the Netherlands, Poland, Romania, Slovenia, UK. *Music facilities* Ensembles includes symphony and chamber orchestras, percussion ensemble, sax ensemble, symphonic wind band and various chamber ensembles.

SALAMANCA

City in western Castille y León region of Spain, home to Spain's oldest university (early 13th century); today city is a popular student destination giving it a lively nightlife that contrasts with its quieter daytime character. Old town, with its square and numerous old buildings of varying styles and Plaza Mayor square, is a Unesco world heritage site. Nicknamed the 'golden city' due to the colour its sandstone buildings take as the sun sets.

Musical life

Palacio de Congresos y Exposiciones is main venue. Watch out for 'tuna', songs sung all around the city, typically by students dressed in medieval costume. Also concerts at various cultural centres and theatres.

EUROPE

 145

Other cultural information

Houses a Filmoteca, a cinema which, as well as putting on various film season, allows you to watch your own choice of filmArchive of Spanish Civil War based in the city. Museums include a museum of art nouveau and art deco, and a small fine arts museum, with contemporary art at the Centro Internacional de Arte.

Festivals and events

All-round arts festival, as well as a festival of flamenco, runs in Jun. Contemporary music at Festival SMASH in Oct; also Salamanca Solotech festival of electronic music in same month. Jazz festivals in spring and summer. Festival of religious music during run-up to Easter.

i Tourist information

www.salamanca.es

CONSERVATORIO SUPERIOR DE MUSICA DE SALAMANCA

C/ Lazarillo de Tormes 54-70, E-37005 Salamanca.

t: +34 923 28 21 15 *f:* +34 923 28 28 78 *e:* info@consuperiorsal.com; erasmus@consuperiorsal.com *w:* www.consuperiorsal.com
Courses Courses in the following departments: musicology/ethnomusicology; conducting; composition and music theory; early music; strings; voice, woodwinds; brass and percussion. Full list of courses available on website.

SAN SEBASTIAN

City in Basque region of Spain on north coast on the Bay of Biscay, known as Donostia in Basque. Famed as a beach resort, overlooked by a mountain range, city is made up of several quarters of contrasting character such as the old quarter (as much of the city was destroyed by fire in 1813, this is not so old) with its fishing village and squares

Musical life

Kursaal Conference Centre has 2 concert halls is main classical venue, although programming not limited to classical. Casa de Okendo is another venue, a former stately home. Conciertos de Primavera series of concerts and music performances of various types throughout the city

 Other cultural information

Teatro Victoria Eugenia for plays, but some music events (eg during festival). San Telmo Museum focuses particularly on Basque art; Koldo Mitxelena cultural centre is a multi-purpose hall including exhibition spaces and rooms for other events.

Festivals and events

Quincena Musical is a month-long classical music festival running Aug-Sep; its international piano competition has events open to public (Mar). International jazz and film festivals (Jul and Sep respectively). Basque Week in early Sep celebrates Basque culture and traditions.

i Tourist information

www.donostia.org

MUSIKENE - EUSKAL HERRIKO GOI MAILAKO MUSIKA IKASTEGIA (MUSIKENE - HIGHER SCHOOL OF MUSIC OF THE BASQUE COUNTRY)

Palacio Miramar, Mirakontxa 48, E-20007 San Sebastian.

t: +34 943 316778 *f:* +34 943 316916 *e:* erasmus@musikene.net *w:* www.musikene.net
Courses Higher diploma courses for accordion, orchestral instruments, composition, voice, choral and orchestral conducting, traditional and folk instruments, jazz (various instruments), organ, music education. *Application requirements* Certificate of upper level secondary education, entrance exam *Application deadline* Between beginning Apr and mid May. *Exchange details* Exchanges arranged through Erasmus. UK exchange partner institution: Royal Academy of Music. Also partnerships with 15 other European music institutions.

VALÈNCIA

City on Mediterranean coast in east of Spain (there are beaches within reach of city centre). Range of architectural styles, with narrow winding streets, Gothic cathedral and churches but also numerous buildings in more modern style. Culinary speciality is a particular variety of paella; crowds also drawn in by the annual Tomatina, at which huge quantities of the fruit are thrown throughout the nearby town of Buñol.

🎼 Musical life

Home to recently opened Ciutat de les Arts i de les Ciènces, an enormous complex that includes the Palau de les Arts Reina Sofía; this itself houses 4 performance spaces. Alongside its construction came creation of a brand new orchestra, the Orquestra de la Comunitat Valenciana. Palau de la Música has several concert halls, and is home to the Orquesta de València; several concert series involving international artists run here. A more local musical tradition is for brass bands.

🏛 Other cultural information

As well as music venues, City of Arts and Sciences holds Europe's largest aquarium and a science museum. Other exhibitions throughout the city: modern art institute, fine arts museum, museum of bullfighting etc.

🎷 Festivals and events

Contemporary performing arts festival in Feb. City is host of Operalia (Oct), the opera competition directed by Plácido Domingo. Annual and long-standing brass band festival; several other events spotlighting local traditional music. Las Fallas is a noisy series of celebrations in March featuring giant papier mâché structures, street parties with characteristic firecrackers and firework displays.

ℹ️ Tourist information

www.turisvalencia.es; turisvalencia@turisvalencia.es; tel: +34 963 606 353

CONSERVATORIO SUPERIOR DE MUSICA DE VALENCIA

Cami de Vera 29, E-46022 Valencia.
t: +34 963605316 *f:* +34 963605701
e: info@csmvalencia.es *w:* www.csmvalencia.es

ZARAGOZA

City in Aragon (north east Spain). Its 16th century university attracts over 40,000 students each year, including numerous overseas students. Some of its buildings reflect its past as an Arab-run city, notably the Moorish castle, the Aljafería; but there are also several churches dating back to the 14th century. In fact, there are influences from all kinds of European cultures in the city – city takes its name from Caesar Augustus.

🎼 Musical life

Classical music at the Auditorio de Zaragoza, from visiting orchestras and soloists as well as resident performers Orquesta de Cámara del Auditorio and Coro Amici Musicae; also resident is Al Ayre Español early music ensemble.

🏛 Other cultural information

Teatro Principal Zaragoza for classical theatre. Large collection of tapestries at La Seo cathedral; Museo del Foro an exhibition of life in the city during Roman times. History centre at the San Agustin convent has archaeological findings from throughout city's history.

🎷 Festivals and events

Pilar Festival, with mixture of events from rock and folk music to handicraft fair as well as classical music concerts, takes over the town in Oct. Like many Spanish cities, has a carnival event in Feb. Jazz festival in Nov, folk music and art festival in Sep.

ℹ️ Tourist information

www.zaragoza.es; turismo@zaragoza.es; tel: +34 902 14 2008

CONSERVATORIO SUPERIOR DE MUSICA DE ARAGON

Via Hispanidad 22, E-50009 Zaragoza.
t: +34 976 716980 *f:* +34 976 716981
e: informacion@csma.es; erasmus@csma.es
w: www.consersup.com
Contact Hector Fouce, Erasmus co-ordinator

MUSIC FESTIVALS

Contemporary Music Festival of Valencia – ENSEMS C/ Grabador Esteve 5-1-2a, E-46004 Valencia. *t:* +34 96 316 3723 *f:* +34 96 316 3724 *e:* ensems@ivm.gva.es *w:* www.ivm.gva.es Contemporary music. Conferences, composers, meetings, installations, etc.

Deia Festival Festival Internacional de Deia, Davall es Penya, E-07179 Deia, Mallorca. *t:* +34 971 639178, also fax *e:* patrick@soundpost.org *w:* www.soundpost.org Chamber music only.

Festival de Barcelona Grec Institut de Barcelona, La Rambla 99, E-08002 Barcelona. *t:* +34 93 316 1112 *f:* +34 93 316 1110 *e:* bcnfestival@mail.bcn.es *w:* www.barcelonafestival.com Contact Ricardo Szwarcer, artistic director. Annual.

Contemporary, flamenco and rock music.

Festival de Musica de Calonge Plaza de Castell Medieval 1, E-17251 Calonge (Girona). *t:* +34 97 265 0311 *f:* +34 97 265 0673 *w:* www.festivals calonge.com Orchestral, jazz, flamenco. Summer season of concerts held in the medieval castle of Calonge, followed by autmun/winter season of piano concerts.

Festival de Musica de Canarias Avda de Canarias, 8 Trasera Edf Tucan, E-35002 Las Palmas de Gran Canaria. *t:* +34 928 247 442 *f:* +34 928 276 042 *e:* info.festival@canariasculturaenred. com *w:* www.festivaldecanarias.com *Contact* Juan Mendoza, director; Celia Manrique de Lara, festival secretary. Annual. Classical, symphonic, choral, chamber music concerts and recitals, including premieres of works commissioned by the festival. Located on Gran Canaria, Tenerife and throughout the Canary Islands.

Festival de Musiques Religioses i del Mon Girona Passeig de la Devesa 35, E-17001 Girona. *t:* +34 872 08 07 09 *e:* musiquesreligioses@ ajgirona.org *w:* www.ajuntament.gimusiques religioses *Contact* Victor Garcia de Gomar, David Ibañez, directors.

Festival de Opera de Las Palmas de Gran Canaria Alfredo Kraus Plaza de San Bernardo 8, E-35002 Las Palmas de Gran Canaria. *t:* +34 928 37 01 25 *f:* +34 928 36 93 94 *e:* artistico@ operalaspalmas.org *w:* www.operalaspalmas.org *Contact* Mario Pontiggia, artistic dir.

Festival Internacional de Música Contemporánea de Tres Cantos C/Saturno 23, E-28760 Tres Cantos (Madrid). *t:* +34 918040571, also fax *e:* festivaltc@terra.es *w:* www.festival trescantos.com *Contact* Rosamaría Calle, mgr.

Festival Internacional de Musica de Camara addressall. *e:* chamberartmadrid@yahoo.es *w:* http://personales.ya.com/acamadrid

Granada International Festival of Music and Dance Aptdo Correos 64, E-18080 Granada. *t:* +34 95 827 6200 *f:* +34 958 286 868 *e:* ofi@ granadafestival.org *w:* www.granadafestival.org Annual. Classical music, flamenco, opera, ballet, recitals, workshops, fringe.

International Festival Andres Segovia C/ Fuerte de Navidad 2-6d, E-28004 Madrid. *t:* +34 91 470 2655, also fax *e:* pablocconcejal@hotmail. com *w:* www.pablodelacruz.net *Contact* Pablo de la Cruz, artistic director. Annual international guitar festival. Includes new music, and a new work each year for solo guitar and strings.

International Festival of Contemporary Music Centro para la Difusion de la Musica Contemporanea, Centro de Arte Reina Sofia, Santa Isabel 52, E-28012 Madrid. *t:* +34 91 7741072 *f:* +34 91 7741075 *e:* cdmc@inaem.mcu.es *w:* www.cdmc.mcu.es Contemporary or new music with operas, ballets, chamber music, orchestral, electronic, radio art and multimedia events.

Musica Antigua Aranjuez Cimbalo Producciones SL, C/ Apodaca 9, Bajo derecha, E-28004 Madrid. *t:* +34 91 447 64 00 *f:* +34 91 447 96 99 *e:* cimbalo@cimbalo.es *w:* www.musicaantigua aranjuez.net *Contact* Javier Estrella, director.

Quincena Musical Avd Zurriola 1, E-20002 San Sebastian. *t:* +34 94 300 3170 *f:* +34 94 300 3175 *e:* quincenamusical@donostia.org *w:* www. quincenamusical.com Annual. Opera, ballet, early music, chamber music, contemporary music, symphonic, organ, recitals.

PORTUGAL

LISBON (LISBOA)

Portuguese capital at the river Tagus on Atlantic coast. City has varied history, being successively conquered by Romans, Moors and eventually Portuguese again in 12th century. This history occasionally reflected in general architecture of the city, however following famous earthquake in 1755 (not the only one to have struck the city), major rebuilding took place in more contemporary style; the Alfama quarter is one that survived the disaster. Among various modern architectural structures is the longest bridge in Europe, the Vasco da Gama Bridge across the Tagus.

♪ Musical life

Gulbenkian Foundation is major musical presence (named after the philanthropist Calouste Gulbenkian, well known in other countries for his acts of charity in the cultural field), supporting both an orchestra and choir as well as programming various concert series in the three halls it houses. Other concert venues include Centro Cultural de Belém stages all kinds of performing arts events from opera and classical music (Orquestra Metropolitana de Lisboa is a regular visitor) to theatre and dance. Teatro Nacional de São Carlos is city's opera house, staging full season plus symphony concerts by its house orchestra, the Orquestra Sinfónica Portuguesa (sometimes with the opera chorus). City closely associated with Fado, a unique, melancholy style of singing; there are numerous venues (bars and suchlike) where it can be heard.

🏛 Other cultural information

Modern art gallery at Gulbenkian Foundation; also Museu Calouste Gulbenkian, an exhibition of his private collection. Various museums devoted to Lisbon's and Portugal's history, customs and crafts; unusual museum of royal horse-drawn carriages. City's variety of theatres include a few either for or of interest to children.

🎭 Festivals and events

Alkantara is a biennial performing arts event (even years) that started out as dance-focused but now has a wider scope. Not far outside city is Sintra Music Festival, classical music event running Jun-Jul. Jazz festival in Aug.

ℹ Tourist information

www.visitlisboa.com; atl@visitlisboa.com; tel: +351 210 312 700

ACADEMIA NACIONAL SUPERIOR DE ORQUESTRA

Associação Música-Eudcaçao e Cultura, Travessa da Galé, 36, P-1349-028 Lisboa.
t: +351 21 361 73 20 f: +351 21 362 38 33
e: anso@oml.pt w: www.oml.pt
Courses Bachelors and masters level qualifications for training in orchestral instruments or orchestral conducting. Also degree in piano accompaniment / piano in chamber music. Fees 1st cycle: EUR 2750 (orchestral conducting), EUR 2420 (orchestral instruments), EUR 2530 (piano); 2nd cycle: EUR 2420 (orchestral conducting), EUR 2420 (orchestral instruments), EUR 2530 (piano).

ESCOLA SUPERIOR DE MUSICA DE LISBOA

Rua do Ataide 7A, P-1200 Lisboa.
t: +351 21 3224940 f: +351 21 347 1489
e: esml@esml.ipl.pt w: www.esml.ipl.pt
Contact José João Gomes dos Santos, dir; Cecilia de Almeida Gonçalves, deputy dir/external relations co-ord Courses 1st cycle: music (composition, choral conducting, instruments, voice); community music; musical communication (programming, production & stage techniques, audio & musical technology). 2nd cycle: masters in music. Application requirements 1st cycle: general or musical secondary education, audition and written test. 2nd cycle: a 1st cycle or equivalent qualification. Term dates Sep-Jan; Feb-Jun. Application deadline 2nd cycle: Feb; 1st cycle: May. Further details available on website. Fees 1st cycle: to be decided (EUR 980 per year for 2008-09); 2nd cycle: EUR 1600 per year. Exchange details UK Erasmus partner institution: Guildhall School of Music and Drama, Welsh College of Music and Drama, Dartington College of Arts. Language requirements Portuguese, for attending theoretical lectures. Music facilities Concert halls, electroacoustics studio, open-air auditorium Accommodation Students' residence available. No of students Approx 300 national students.

OPORTO (PORTO)

Portugal's second city, in the north of the country on the Atlantic coast. Its centre, with its baroque and Romanesque architecture, is an Unesco world heritage site. Sometimes nicknamed 'city of bridges' due to the number crossing the river Douro – the Ponte Maria Pla was designed by Gustave Eiffel, and is a clear precursor of the Eiffel Tower in its design. City's pre-eminent role in export of fortified wine to Britain gave the drink port its name; there are numerous port cellars in the city where examples can be tried.

♪ Musical life

Casa da Música, its unusual polyhedric design by Rem Koolhaas, is the prestigious music venue and home for Orquestra Nacional do Porto, a full-size symphony orchestra with interesting range of programming. Three other groups resident there: chorus; a baroque music ensemble; and Remix Ensemble, an internationally renowned contemporary music group. Coliseu do Porto, an art deco concert hall with a varied programme of classical music and other events.

⛪ Other cultural information

Main museums are Soares dos Reis museum (art, ceramics, furniture etc) and Museu de Serralves (modern and contemporary art). City is home to an unusual artistic co-operative with a troubled history, Árvore, a place dedicated to artistic creation and display.

🎭 Festivals and events

Annual cartoon festival running over summer months. Various city festivities such as Festa da São João (Jun) or Queima das Fitas (May) the last hurrah of city's students before exams begin.

ℹ️ Tourist information

www.portoturismo.pt; turismo.central@cm-porto.pt; tel: +351 223 393 472

ESCOLA SUPERIOR DE MUSICA E DAS ARTES DO ESPECTACULO DO PORTO (PORTO SUPERIOR SCHOOL OF MUSIC AND PERFORMING ARTS)

Rua da Alegria 503, P-4000-045 Porto.
t: +351 22 519 37 60 f: +351 22 518 07 74
e: international@esmae-ipp.pt w: www.esmae-ipp.pt
Contact Bruno Pereira. Courses Music courses: instrumental, composition, music production and technology, jazz, early music; also courses in theatre, photography, cinema, audiovisual and multimedia. Application requirements See website for details of application requirements. Application deadline Mar 2009. Exchange details UK exchange partner institutions: Dartington College of Arts, Northumbria University; also partnerships with over 30 other European institutions. No of students 675 national students, 35 from overseas

MUSIC FESTIVALS

Festival do Estoril Galerias Estoril, Rua de Lisboa 5, Lj 12, P-2765-240 Estoril. t: +351 21 468 5199 f: +351 21 468 5607 e: festivaldoestoril@sapo.pt w: www.estorilfestival.net Symphonic, chamber, recitals, master courses, competition, seminars, conferences, composers meeting.

Festival Internacional de Musica da Povoa de Varzim Rua D Maria I - 56, P-4490-538 Povoa de Varzim. t: +351 52 5261 4145 f: +351 52 5261 2548 e: auditorio@cm-pvarzim.pt w: www.cm-pvarzim.pt/go/festivalinternacionalmusica Contact J Marques, director. Medieval, renaissance, baroque, classical, romantic and contemporary music.

Ponte de Lima Festival of Opera and Classical Music Associacao Cultural do Norte Portugal, Quinta de Igreja, Feitosa, P-4990-341 Ponte de Lima. t: +351 258 931 141 f: +351 258 931 143 e: operafaber@simplesnet.com w: www.operalima.com Contact Carole Ludlow, president

Sintra International Choir Festival t: +351 21 916 26 28 e: Sintrachoirfestival@gmail.com w: www.sintrachoirfestival.com

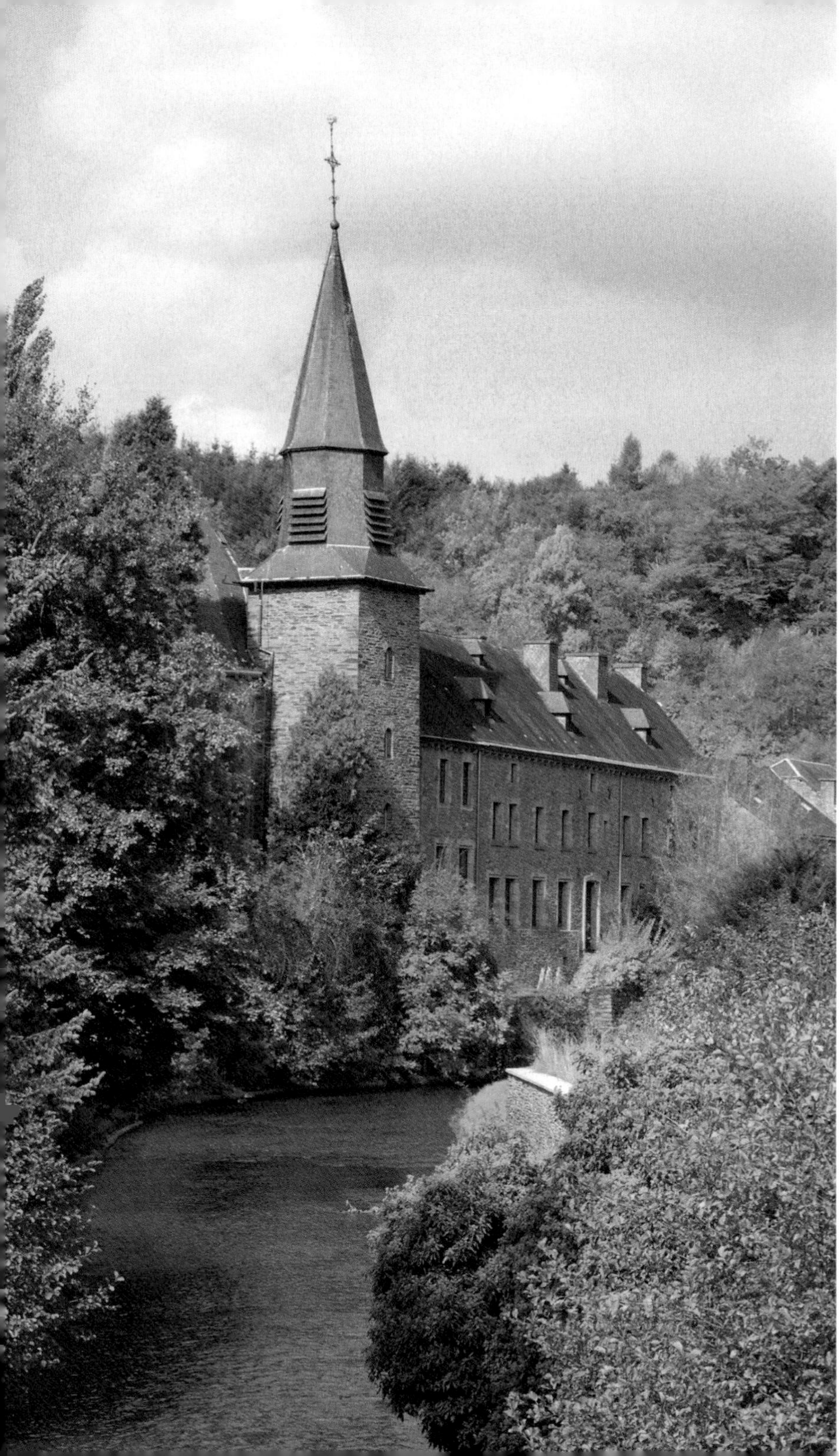

Belgium and the Netherlands

QUEEN ELISABETH COMPETITION

2009 ▸ 2011

BRUSSELS — BELGIUM

VIOLIN 2009 04 ▸ 30/05/2009
MASTER CLASSES, MIM (Musical Instrument Museum)
Boris KUSCHNIR, Gérard POULET, Lewis KAPLAN & Mihaela MARTIN

COMPOSITION 2009 [Age limit: 40]
WORK FOR PIANO AND SYMPHONY ORCHESTRA
JURY: Arie Van Lysebeth (Chairperson), Luca Francesconi, Benoît Mernier,
Kaija Saariaho, Frederik van Rossum...
DEADLINE for submission of applications: **07/11/2009**

PIANO 2010 [Age limit: 27] 02 ▸ 29/05/2010
02 ▸ 08/05/2010 **FIRST ROUND**, Royal Brussels Conservatory
10 ▸ 15/05/2010 **SEMI-FINAL**, Royal Brussels Conservatory
         with the Orchestre Royal de Chambre de Wallonie, dir. Paul GOODWIN
18 ▸ 21/05/2010 **MASTER CLASSES**, MIM (Musical Instrument Museum)
24 ▸ 29/05/2010 **FINAL**, Brussels Centre for Fine Arts (Palais des Beaux-Arts)
         with the National Orchestra of Belgium, dir. Marin ALSOP

SINGING 2011 [Age limit: 30] 05 ▸ 21/05/2011

WWW.QEIMC.BE

QUEEN ELISABETH INTERNATIONAL MUSIC COMPETITION OF BELGIUM
INFO: RUE AUX LAINES 20, B-1000 BRUSSELS (BELGIUM)
TEL : +32 2 213 40 50 - FAX : +32 2 514 32 97 - INFO@QEIMC.BE

Belgium and the Netherlands

Students intending to apply to institutions in Belgium will need to bear in mind the dual-language constitution of the country. Flanders is to the north (it includes the cities of Antwerp, Gent and Leuven) and is Dutch-speaking; the south (the part of the country known as Wallonia and whose main city is Liège) is French-speaking. The anomaly is the capital Brussels (Brussel in Dutch, Bruxelles in French) which lies in the southern part but is officially bilingual, a situation complicated by the fact that increasingly French has come to predominate. For various reasons, such as the relative wealth of the north compared to the south, this is quite a contentious issue in Belgian politics and society, and visitors should be aware of it before arriving. In the Netherlands, English is widely understood (though not universally) in the main cities.

Both countries offer much to the visitor wishing to spend a period of time there. For instance, both countries have long histories with periods of great prosperity and influence and this has left its mark in town planning and architectural styles – think gothic town halls, cobbled streets and market places. Both are well-connected, with Amsterdam airport a major European hub and Brussels one of the homes of the European parliament.

BELGIUM

The situation in Belgium is somewhat complicated for those coming from overseas because of the two cultural systems. Both systems have adopted the Bologna system of 3 (bachelors or 1st cycle) + 2 (masters or 2nd cycle) year levels, although there are slight differences between the systems.

In French-speaking institutions, for instance, students can supplement their studies with a further 60 ECTS credits to gain a 'specialist artist' masters. The curriculum in the French-speaking institutions is to a large extent determined centrally, with all institutions teaching the same courses; only one third of the curriculum is set by the individual conservatoires.

In the Flemish system, degrees are offered by the conservatoires (officially known as Hogescholen, or high schools) in association with universities, and quality assurance is undertaken on the same basis as academic degrees. Institutions are at liberty to design their own courses, although the nature of advanced musical studies in many areas means there are inevitably similarities. The one slightly unusual exception is the Gent-based Orpheus Instituut, a specialist music academy operating at postgraduate level only.

In both Flemish and Walloon/Brussels systems, earning a bachelors automatically qualifies a student to progress to masters level.

THE NETHERLANDS

Bachelors courses in the Netherlands last 4 years, with an additional 2 for masters studies, and institutions have a great deal of flexibility in the modules they can offer – the Utrecht college offers a degree in bell-ringing, for instance. However, they are required to ensure courses are designed in such a way that certain stipulated competencies for that course are met.

Tuition fees for non-EU/ EEA students have been considerably increased for the 2008-2009 academic year, and event students from within the European area now must expect to pay some fees (probably at least EUR 1500, depending on course and location). This is a result of changes in the Dutch government's allocation of its education resources; in the case of non-EU/EEA students, government funding has ceased, forcing Dutch universities and other institutes of higher education to introduce tuition fees.

BELGIUM

EUROPE

ANTWERP (ANTWERPEN)

City in the Dutch-speaking part of Belgium (Flanders) on the river Scheidt at the North Sea, it came into prominence during the 16th century thanks to its success as a trading port, one of the principal cities in Europe at the time. Its wealth at that time has left a legacy in the city's distinctive architecture, such as that around the main square, although there has been modern development around the river and its quays. Now also famous as centre for diamond trade.

♪ Musical life

Large amount of musical performance. Vlaamse Opera performs some of its season at the opera house (other shows are in Gent), its orchestra giving occasional concerts too. Similarly Symfonieorkest Vlaanderen, which has bases in cities around Flanders. A third orchestra, and one of the busiest, is de Filharmonie, performing at de Singel arts centre or the Queen Elizabeth Hall.

ℹ Other cultural information

Significant in fine art due to the style of painting known as the Antwerp School (Rubens, Van Dyck and so on). This is well represented in city's galleries, such as the Rubenshuis, or the Royal Museum of Fine Arts

Festivals and events

Under the umbrella of Flanders Festival-Antwerp is small event, Laus Polyphoniae, in Aug focusing on period music. Larger scale Antwerp Summer Festival features all kinds of music as well as circus, theatre, dance and other performances. City hosts an annual book fair in November. Slightly more unusual is annual Laundry Day, a street party whose name refers to the custom in earlier times of women gossiping while hanging out laundry in the street.

Tourist information

www.antwerpen.be; toerisme@stad.antwerpen.be; tel: +32 3 232 01 03

ARTESIS HOGESCHOOL ANTWERPEN - KONINKLIJK CONSERVATORIUM

Desguinlei 25, B-2018 Antwerpen.
t: +32 3 244 18 00 f: +32 3 238 90 17
e: conservatorium@artesis.be w: www.artesis.be/conservatorium

Contact Wilma Schneider, international relations co-ord; Birgit Soil, head of the student admin. *Courses* Bachelor degrees (180 ECTS) in instrumental studies, vocal studies, theory of music/harmony and counterpoint, jazz and popular music. Masters degrees (120 ECTS) in instrumental studies, vocal studies, conducting, composition, music pedagogy, jazz and popular music. Also postgrad course (1 year, 60 ECTS) specialising as instrumental or vocal concert soloist, in composition, accompaniment, chamber music or orchestra. *Application requirements* Appropriate diploma and artistic entrance exam. Overseas students may be admitted on the basis of a DVD/video recording (not CD). *Term dates* 21 Sep-2 Jul. *Application deadline* Mid May (first session); end Aug/beginning Sep (second session). Exact dates to be confirmed. *Fees* Approx EUR 540; EUR 2250 for postgrad course; EUR 5700 for students outside EEA. All fees to be confirmed May 2009. *Scholarships* None. *Exchange details* No UK exchange partners, but 40 partnerships with various European institutions. *Language requirements* Level A1 for theory of music/harmony. *Music facilities* Library inc scores, reference works, online reference (inc Grove Online) *No of students* 400 national students; about 80 from overseas.

BRUSSELS (BRUSSEL, BRUXELLES)

Belgian capital, and centre for European politics (it holds the headquarters of the European Commission). Although located in the (wealthier) Dutch-speaking part of the country, most residents have French as their first language and it has taken over as lingua franca (!). In fact, both languages have official status. This is, perhaps understandably, a cause of some tension, particularly among the Dutch community. At the centre of the city is one of Europe's most spectacular squares, the medieval Grote Markt / Grand Place, although the city as a whole does not have the historic feel of other Flemish cities.

♪ Musical life

La Monnaie / De Munt is the city's opera house, and apart from the opera orchestra, 2 other main groups based there: National Orchestra of Belgium, performing about 70 concerts a year at Palais des Beaux-Arts / Paleis voor Schone Kunsten, around Belgium and abroad; Brussels Philharmonic is new name for the Flemish Radio Orchestra, and has a new home, the multi-space Flagey building. Orchestra still associated with Flemish Radio Choir. Various concert series run through the year.

Other cultural information
Several museums and galleries; the museum complex Musées Royaux des Beaux Arts / Koninklijke Musea voor Schone Kunsten houses several in one place. Brussels a notable contributor to Art Nouveau, and the home of Art Nouveau architect Victor Horta is open to public. Musical instrument museum (located in a Horta building) is one of most comprehensive in the world.

Festivals and events
Specialist contemporary music festival in spring, Ars Musica. Early music festival at the Grand Sablon church, also in spring. KlaraFestival begins at end of Aug and runs for 2 weeks. Free concerts in all kinds of music styles during Brussels Summer Festival and classical music at Royal Parc festival in Jul; jazz during Jan festival at Théâtre Marni, during weekend in May (Brussels Jazz Marathon) as well as Jul (Brosella Folk and Jazz Festival).

Tourist information
www.brusselsinternational.be; tourism@brusselsinternational.be; +32 2 513 89 40

KONINKLIJK CONSERVATORIUM BRUSSEL
Regentschapsstraat 30, B-1000 Brussel.
t: +32 2 513 45 87 f: +32 2 513 22 53
e: kcb@kcb.be w: www.kcb.be
Courses Bachelors in academic music or professional music training

CONSERVATOIRE ROYAL DE BRUXELLES
Rue de la Régence 30, B-1000 Bruxelles.
t: +32 2 500 87 17 f: +32 2 512 69 79
e: secretariat@conservatoire.be; erasmus@conservatoire.be w: www.conservatoire.be
Courses 2-cycle structure leading to either bachelors or masters. Specialisms in orchestral instruments, period instruments, singing, music theory, jazz. Application requirements By application and audition (timetable of auditions available on website) Term dates 3 terms: mid Sep-late Jan, late Jan-mid May, mid May-mid Sep. Last term includes summer holiday and 2 exam sessions. Full details of mid-term holidays available on website.

KONINKLIJK CONSERVATORIUM BRUSSEL
Koninklijk Conservatorium Brussel,
Regentschapsstraat 30, B-1000 Brussel.
t: +32 2 513 45 87 f: +32 2 513 22 53
e: kcb@kcb.be w: www.kcb.be
Courses Bachelors in academic music or professional music training

GENT (GHENT)
City in the Dutch-speaking part of Belgium with a very distinctive medieval flavour thanks to the predominance of its architecture of the period.

Musical life
Home to one of the world's great vocal ensembles, the Collegium Vocale Gent; also main base for Vlaamse Opera.

Other cultural information
Many museums and galleries. Museum of Fine Arts for old masters, including Flemings like Hieronymus Bosch; also contemporary art gallery, design museum, textile museum, even a museum of psychiatry. Vooruit Arts Centre for contemporary performance.

Festivals and events
Gentse Feesten, 10-day festival of music and theatre including many street events, beginning in July.

Tourist information
www.visitgent.be; visit@gent.be; tel: +32 9 266 56 60

HOGESCHOOL GENT CONSERVATORIUM
Hoogpoort 64, B-9000 Gent.
t: +32 9 225 15 15; +32 9 266 08 01 (foreign relations) f: +32 9 269 20 08 e: cons@hogent.be; katrien.vanacker@hogent.be (foreign relations) w: http://cons.hogent.be
Contact Katrien VanAcker, foreign relations. Courses Majors in performing music (instrumental, vocal; classical, jazz or pop); creative music (composition, music production); music theory/harmony and counterpoint; also instrument making. Post-Masters in orchestral conducting, composition, contemporary music solo performance. Application requirements Entrance exam; details of exam requirements and application form available on website. Music

facilities 2 concert halls (Salle Miry, 504 seats; Salle Mengal, 96 seats); theatre hall, recording studio, library, study facilities

ORPHEUS INSTITUUT

Korte Meer 12, B-9000 Gent.
t: +32 9 330 40 81 *f:* +32 9 330 40 82
e: info@orpheusinstituut.be *w:* www.orpheus instituut.be
Courses Only postgrad studies, all musical styles and trends. Laureate programme, tailor-made to student's artistic choices and personal background; doctoral programme 'docARTES', 2 year curriculum, title awared to musicians who can combine artistic performances at the highest level with systematic theoretical reflection. *Application requirements* For laureate programme, application by portfolio (see website for details of requirements), interview and possible admission exam; for doctoral programme 'docARTES', see www.docartes.be. *Term dates* Duration of study period determined once candidate is accepted for enrolment. *Application deadline* Anytime during year (laureate programme); 1 Oct or 1 Apr (docARTES programme). *Fees* EUR 2500 enrolment fee (laureate and doctoral programmes). *Music facilities* 120 seat concert hall (converted cinema) with Steinway and harpsichord, audiovisual equipment; conference room, study rooms, library, recording studio *No of students* 25 overseas students on doctoral programme.

LEUVEN (LOUVAIN)

Small Flemish city with a large student population (it is the location for the world's oldest Catholic university and a number of other higher education institutions). City includes a number of characteristic northern European gothic buildings, like the towering town hall and St Peter's Church across the square. Considered by many Belgium's beer capital because of close association between brewing and the city.

♪ Musical life
Base for internationally renowned early music group La Petite Bande

▦ Other cultural information
Festivals and events International organ festival in May

ⓘ Tourist information
www.leuven.be; tourism@leuven.be; +32 16 20 30 20

LEMMENSINSTITUUT LEUVEN HOGESCHOOL VOOR WETENSCHAP & KUNST (FACULTY OF MUSIC, PERFORMING ARTS AND EDUCATION)

Herestraat 53, B-3000 Leuven.
t: +32 16 23 39 67 *f:* +32 16 22 24 77
e: info@lemmens.wenk.be *w:* www.lemmens.wenk.be
Contact K Wittevrongel. *Courses* Bachelor and masters in composition, conducting, music education, music therapy, instrumental and vocal music, jazz; also drama. *Application requirements* Admission test or proof of degree equivalence. *Term dates* Sep-Jan; Feb-Jun. *Fees* EUR 25 (EU members); EUR 5700 (non-EU members). *Exchange details* Exchanges arranged through Erasmus; 30 partners in 20 countries. *Music facilities* Free entrance to weekly concerts in the Lemmensinstituut. *Accommodation* 80% of students live in private accommodation; assistance available through University of Leuven housing service. *No of students* 450 students.

MONS (BERGEN)

French-speaking city with picturesque central square and gothic town hall.

ⓘ Tourist information
www.monsregion.be

CONSERVATOIRE ROYAL DE MONS

7 rue de Nimy, B-7000 Mons.
t: +32 6534 7377 *f:* +32 6534 9906 *e:* info@conservatoire-mons.be *w:* www.conservatoire-mons.be
Courses Bachelors (3 years) and masters (2 years) music teaching, theory (with option in composition), keyboard instruments, string instruments, percussion, woodwind and brass instruments, opera, singing, early music (various instruments), electroacoustic/acousmatic music.

NAMUR (NAMEN)

French-speaking city in the south of Belgium.

ⓘ Tourist information
www.namurtourisme.be

INSTITUT SUPERIEUR DE MUSIQUE ET DE PEDAGOGIE

28 rue Juppin, B-5000 Namur.
t: +32 81 73 64 37 *f:* +32 81 73 95 14
e: info@imep.be; erasmus@imep.be *w:* www.imep.be
Contact Christian Croufer, Erasmus exchange admin. *Courses* Institute based in Christian educational tradition. *Application requirements* Entrance exam; application form available online. *Fees* See website for details of course material and inscription fees.

WATERLOO

French-speaking town near Brussels; its location there means many of its residents are from overseas.

ℹ Tourist information

www.waterloo-tourisme.be; info@waterloo-tourisme.be; tel: +32 2 352 09 10

CHAPELLE MUSICAL REINE ELISABETH ASBL

445 Chaussée de Tervuren, B-1410 Waterloo.
t: +32 2 352 01 10 *f:* +32 2 351 10 24
e: info@cmre.be; jmtom@wanadoo.fr *w:* www.cmre.be
Contact Jean-Marie Tomasi, international consultant *Courses* Four areas of study: preparatory class for exceptional young talents aged 8-15 (piano, violin, singing); class for advanced musicians aged 16-22 (piano, violin, singing); 'Master after Master' diploma for students at post-conservatoire level (piano, violin, singing, chamber music); Opera Studio. *Application requirements* Application details and application form available on website. *Music facilities* Library and record collection. *Accommodation* Study bedrooms including pianos.

MUSIC FESTIVALS

Bruges Early Music Festival Concertgebouw, 't Zand 34, B-8000 Brugge. *t:* +32 50 332283 *f:* +32 50 345204 *e:* musica.antiqua@telenet.be *w:* www.festival.be/brugge *Contact* Tomas Bisschop, Hendrik Storme, directors. Competition and exhibition for instrumental and vocal soloists. Lunchtime and evening concerts.

Le Clavecin en Fête *t:* +32 16 48 08 36, also fax *e:* betty.bruylants@cyclone.be *w:* www.amsiduclavecin.be *Contact* Betty Bruylants, artistic direction.

Festival Ars Musica 203/1 Galerie Louise, B-1050 Bruxelles. *t:* +32 2 219 2660 *f:* +32 2 219 8814 *e:* info@arsmusica.be *w:* www.arsmusica.be Annual festival of contemporary music worldwide. Concerts, conferences, masterclasses, multi-disciplinary activities (exhibitions, films), opera.

Festival de Wallonie Rue de l'Armée, Grouchy 20, B-5000 Namur. *t:* +32 81 733781 *f:* +32 81 742503 *e:* info@festivaldewallonie.be *w:* www.festivaldewallonie.be *Contact* Baudouin Muylle, general secretary; Claire Ringlet, artistic secretary.

International Acousmatic Festival: L'Espace du Son Musiques & Recherches, Place de Ransbeck 3, B-1380 Ohain. *t:* +32 23 544368 *f:* +32 2 351 0094 *e:* musiques.recherches@skynet.be *w:* www.musiques-recherches.be 4-day festival, acousmatic music.

Laus Polyphoniae 12 Everdijstraat, B-2000 Antwerp, Belgium. *t:* +32 3 202 46 69 *f:* +32 3 202 46 64 *e:* flanders.festival@stad.antwerpen.be *w:* www.festival.be Festival focusing on historically informed performance.

Les Nuits de Septembre rue des Mineurs 17, B-4000 Liege. *t:* +32 42 236674 *f:* +32 42 221540 *e:* jmlg@jeunessesmusicales.be *w:* www.festivaldewallonie.be *Contact* Jerome Lejeune, director; Nicolas Keutgen, manager. Baroque music.

Zomeropera Alden Biesen Kasteelstr 6, B-3740 Bilzen. *t:* +32 89 79 41 27 *e:* info@zomeropera.be *w:* www.zomeropera.be *Contact* Piet Vanischen, artistic director.

EUROPE

NETHERLANDS

ALKMAAR

City in west of Netherlands, famous in the country for its cheese market (there is even a cheese museum, not to mention a beer museum). Not a large place, but its canals and historic buildings lend it charm.

ℹ Tourist information

www.vvvalkmaar.nl; info@vvvalkmaar.nl; tel: +31 72 5114284

CONSERVATORIUM HOGESCHOOL INHOLLAND ALKMAAR

PO Box 403, NL-1800 AK Alkmaar.
t: +31 72 518 35 55; +31 72 518 34 56 (international office) *f:* +31 72 518 35 54
e: Intoffice.Alkmaar@inholland.nl (international office) *w:* www.inholland.nl
Fees EUR 1565 (Dutch and EU/EEA students); EUR 6500 (non-EU/EEA).

AMSTERDAM

Capital of the Netherlands, though not the seat of government, and a major tourist destination. Historically prominent due to its importance as a trading port in the 17th century, at which time the first of the canals which run around it for which it is now famous were built. Architecturally mixed, with renaissance, baroque, neo-gothic examples, but also more modern style from art nouveau and art deco and after. Ideal for cyclists as the city has a strong culture of cycle riding.

🎼 Musical life

Royal Concertgebouw Orchestra, one of world's best, performs at the hall from which it takes its name. Opera at Muziektheater, a modern building in keeping with surroundings, home to De Nederlandse Opera. Various orchestras provide accompaniment here, including Amsterdam-based Netherlands Philharmonic. Amsterdam Symphony Orchestra also travels to Den Haag and Rotterdam as well as playing at Concertgebouw. Nieuw Ensemble is an Amsterdam-based contemporary music group; Orchestra of the Eighteenth Century a period classical ensemble. Jazz and improvised music have their own specialist venue, the Bimhuis, next to a specialist contemporary music venue, the Muziekgebouw aan 't IJ. Concerts in other venues too, such as Oude Kerk (the city's cathedral), and city is popular destination for touring amateur choirs, youth orchestras etc.

🏛 Other cultural information

City has a Museum Square, with the main Rijksmuseum (Dutch art in particular, especially Rembrandt — there is also a Rembrandt museum elsewhere), the Van Gogh Museum and Stedelijk Museum (modern art, currently closed for renovation, reopening Dec 2009) the main institutions. Away from the square, many pay a visit to Anne Frank's House; many other small museums and exhibitions too. Famous Russian Hermitage museum opening a new branch in the city in summer 2009.

🎭 Festivals and events

Holland Festival (Jun) is largest event in the city, featuring music and opera as part of wider performing arts programme. Aug sees a festival celebrating city's canals, Grachtenfestival, with concerts in various venues, private buildings, restaurants and churches as well as concert halls.

ℹ Tourist information

www.iamsterdam.com; info@atcb.nl; tel: +31 20 2018800

CONSERVATORIUM VAN AMSTERDAM

Oosterdokskade 151, Postbus 78022, NL-1070 LP Amsterdam.
t: +31 20 527 7550 *f:* +31 20 676 1506
e: info@ahk.nl *w:* www. conservatoriumvanamsterdam.nl
Contact Rita Spin, international relations office. *Courses* Bachelors and masters in classical music, bachelors and masters in jazz, bachelors in pop, masters in opera, bachelors in music in education. *Application requirements* Entrance exam consisting of practical part and general part (ear tests, musical knowledge); sample test available on website. For exchange students a recording is sufficient. *Term dates* See website for course dates. *Application deadline* 1 Apr; entrance exam in May/ Jun, early exam in Jan possible. *Fees* EUR 1300-2000, depending on nationality and course. Further details on website. *Exchange details* Exchanges through Erasmus. *Language requirements* English or Dutch. *Music facilities* New conservatory building contains c 100 teaching rooms, 4 concert halls, 60 study rooms, library, internet café, 2 recording

studios with channels to the concert halls. *Accommodation* No campus accommodation; some advice on finding housing is provided *No of students* 50% of student intake from overseas.

ARNHEM

Eastern Dutch city, and location of a notorious World War II battle.

🎼 Musical life

Main performing arts venue is Musis Sacrum Schouwberg, featuring classical music among its wider programme. Het Gelders Orkest performs there, and elsewhere in the region

🏛 Other cultural information

Several museums, like the Arnhem Museum for Modern Art. The Liberation Route reflects the city's part in the end of WWII.

ℹ Tourist information

www.vvvarnhemnijmegen.nl

ARTEZ SCHOOL OF MUSIC

Utrechtsestraat 85, PO Box 49, NL-6800 AA Arnhem.
t: +31 26 35 35 643 *f:* +31 26 35 35 637
e: conservatorium.arnhem@artez.nl *w:* www.artez-conservatorium.nl; www.artez.nl
Contact Thom Koldenhof, dir of Arnhem location. *Courses* Classical music, jazz and pop, music theatre. *Application requirements* Entrance exam and practical test; see website for full details. *Term dates* Aug-Jul. *Application deadline* 1 May. *Fees* EU/EEA: EUR 1805 (full time), EUR 996 (part time); non-EU/EEA: EUR 7763. Loans may be available; see website for more details. *Scholarships* Scholarships for non-European students only. *Exchange details* Exchange partnerships with more than 20 European conservatoires; also with 1 Chinese conservatoire. *Language requirements* Dutch is official language, although some bachelors programmes are bilingual (Dutch/English). Most masters courses in English. Intensive language courses for non-Dutch speakers. *Music facilities* Concert auditoria, studios, mediatheques, variety of workshops for audio-visual productions, graphics, music and sound. *Accommodation* Website gives details of accommodation agencies in each location. *No of students* 900 students; 45% from overseas.

THE HAGUE (DEN HAAG)

City on the North Sea, Seat of Dutch government, home of royal family, but not capital city. Also home to various international political organisations such as International Court of Justice and other judicial institutions. Apart from conservatoire and an applied sciences institute, there is no university so student life not as extensive as elsewhere. Architecture and built environment atypical of the country without prominent canals or narrow streets encountered elsewhere. City has two popular beaches nearby.

🎼 Musical life

The Residentie Orkest is main orchestra, performing at the Anton Philipszaal, next door to specialist dance venue, Lucent Danstheater.

🏛 Other cultural information

City houses substantial collection of art by Piet Mondriaan (Gemeentemuseum); numerous other galleries and museums. Panorama Mesdag an unusual, large 360 degree painting of a late 19th century landscape; Beelden aan Zee is collection of outdoor sculptures. Numerous theatres also, ranging from the classical Royal Theatre to circus and theatre in a converted swimming baths (Theatre de Regentes)

🎊 Festivals and events

Jazz festival in May. Major festival celebrating Indonesian and European culture, the Pasar Malam Besar, reflects the city's and country's role in historical trading with Indonesia (May-Jun).

ℹ Tourist information

www.denhaag.com; tel: +31 900 3403505.

KONINKLIJK CONSERVATORIUM, DEN HAAG (ROYAL CONSERVATOIRE, THE HAGUE)

Juliana van Stolberglaan 1, NL-2595 CA Den Haag.
t: +31 703151515 *f:* +31 703151518
e: e.eijken@admin.koncon.nl *w:* www.koncon.nl
Contact Eugene Eijken, international students adviser *Courses* Bachelor of music and master of music, in classical music, early music, jazz, sonology, art of sound, composition, music pedagogy, opera; also dance (ballet). *Application requirements* See website for full details, including set works for

auditions. *Term dates* 1 Sep-30 Jun. *Application deadline* 1 May. *Fees* EUR 3194. *Exchange details* UK exchange partner institutions: Royal Academy of Music, Trinity College of Music, Royal College of Music, Guildhall School of Music and Drama, Royal Northern College of Music. Approx 50 European exchange partner institutions. *No of students* Approx 800 students, inc c 500 from overseas.

ENSCHEDE

City in east Netherlands near Germany, former mainstay of the Dutch textile industry and undergoing a number of urban renewal projects to help reverse years of decline. Science and technology predominates in city's educational background, but arts academy too.

♪ Musical life
City has its own opera company, Nationale Reisopera. Netherlands Symphony Orchsetra based there. Podium Twente manages concerts at 3 venues — Muziekkwartier, Muziekcentrum and Grote Kerk

🎲 Festivals and events
Festival of Jewish music in Dec; Cross-Linx is a festival focusing on cross-over music in Mar; . International circus festival in Dec.

i Tourist information
www.visitenschede.nl;

ARTEZ SCHOOL OF MUSIC
Van Essengaarde 10, NL-7511 PN Enschede.
t: +31 53 48 28 130 *f:* +31 53 43 01 689
e: conservatorium.enschede@artez.nl *w:* www.artez-conservatorium.nl; www.artez.nl
Contact Juul Diteweg, dir of Enschede location. *Courses* Classical music, jazz & pop, academy of pop music, media music, music therapy, education in music. For more details see under Arnhem.

GRONINGNEN

Small northern Dutch city, with a population that fluctuates depending on academic term dates — it has a large number of students attending the university or fine art academy as well as the music school, and consequently a busy nightlife.

♪ Musical life
Wide variety of music on offer in the city in informal venues. Main formal venues are Martini Plaza (musicals), De Oosterpoort and De Stadsschouwburg (classical, pop, jazz and world music). Has its own orchestra in the shape of Noord Nederlands Orkest, although many of its performances are outside the city in other towns in the region.

🏛 Other cultural information
Groninger Museum a highly regarded contemporary art gallery; also comic museum and graphic museum.

🎲 Festivals and events
Outdoor festival, Noorderzon, in Aug, featuring theatre and range of music.

i Tourist information
http://toerisme.groningen.nl; info@vvvgroningen.nl; tel: +31 900 2023050

PRINCE CLAUS CONSERVATOIRE
Veemarktstraat 76, NL-9724 GA Groningen.
t: +31 50 595 13 01 *f:* +31 50 595 13 99
e: prinsclausconservatorium@org.hanze.nl; j.kruger@pl.hanze.nl (international affairs)
w: www.hanze.nl
Contact Jan-Gerd Kruger, international affairs *Courses* Music BA (jazz, classical, composition, conducting); music education BA; art education MA; music MA (performing, teaching, joint programme). *Application requirements* See website for details. *Term dates* Early Sep-mid Jul. *Application deadline* Sep 2009. *Fees* Approx EUR 1600 per year. *Scholarships* Scholarships available, applications required well before deadline; see website for full details. *Exchange details* UK exchange partners: Guildhall School of Music and Drama, Trinity Laban, University of Salford. 37 other exchange partners in Austria (3), Belgium (1), Czech Republic (2), Denmark (2), Estonia (1), Finland (4), France (1), Germany (6), Iceland (1), Italy (2); USA partners: State University of New York, Purchase College of Music; Long Island University; University of the Arts, Philadelphia. *Language requirements* Dutch or English (TOEFL 5.5). *Music facilities* Fully equipped practice rooms, most with grand pianos; 3 concert venues (40-200 seats); studio factilities. *Accommodation* Overseas students can apply for accommodation for up to 12 months through www.housingoffice.nl. *No of students* 380 students.

MAASTRICHT

Pleasant city straddling the river Meuse in the south of the country almost on the border with Belgium. Historically important as a fortress (some of walls are still present) as well as a trading city, and claims to be oldest city in the Netherlands. Large number of students due to university and other higher education institutes.

Musical life

Opera Zuid a small company putting on a small number of productions each year, using orchestras from elsewhere. Other opera companies also visit from out of town. Home orchestra is Limburgs Symfonie Orkest which performs at Theater aan het Vrijthof, a venue with its own concert series (chamber music, choral music, children's concerts etc).

Other cultural information

Theater an het Vrijthof programme goes beyond music, with theatre and fringe type events.

Festivals and events

Musica Sacra Maastricht, short festival in Sep focusing. Jazz Maastrich festival in Oct.

Tourist information

www.vvv-maastricht.eu

CONSERVATORIUM MAASTRICHT

Bonnefantenstr 15, NL-6211 KL Maastricht.
t: +31 43 3466 680 *f:* +31 43 3466689
e: info.conservatorium@hszuyd.nl *w:* www.conservatoriummaastricht.nl
Courses Bachelors and masters courses in classical music, including composition, orchestral and wind band conducting, opera singing and specialist options; also jazz/pop and music in education courses. *Term dates* See website for up-to-date details. *Language requirements* Dutch or English. *Music facilities* Music library including books and scores. 3 concert halls in 2 buildings; studio equipped with Pro Tools equipment; practice rooms. *No of students* 70% international students from c 48 countries, 30% Dutch.

ROTTERDAM

Dutch city at the Rhine/Meuse delta, the largest port in Europe and second largest city in the country.

Biggest historical development came at the end of the 19th century; consequently, architecture of the city is more modern in feel than elsewhere, including some striking developments like the Erasmus bridge or the Euromast; perhaps most striking are distinctive, lopsided 'Cube Houses' residential accommodation, one of which is open to public.

Musical life

Rotterdam Philharmonic Orchestra is one of most respected in the world. Its home is De Doelen convention centre, a complex with one large and two smaller concert halls (programme not limited to classical music).

Other cultural information

Usual range of museums and galleries, a few reflecting Rotterdam's history (such as the Maritime Museum). Architecture Institute reflects the city's unique culture of modern design; modern art also prominent in city's numerous smaller galleries.

Festivals and events

Festivals feature variety of music: as well as rock and pop, and summer carnival event, North Sea Jazz Festival (Jul) features a wide range of jazz genres. For classical the Gergiev Festival (Valery Gergiev was chief conductor of the Rotterdam Philharmonic) runs for a week from Aug to Sep. Also a film festival at the beginning of the year and international poetry festival in Jun.

Tourist information

www.rotterdam.info; info@rotterdam-store.com; tel: +31 10 271 01 20

CODARTS HOGESCHOOL VOOR DE KUNSTEN

Kruisplein 26, NL-3012 CC Rotterdam.
t: +31 10 2171100 *f:* +31 10 2171101
e: codarts@codarts.nl *w:* www.codarts.nl
Courses Bachelors and masters courses. *Application requirements* Assessment by exam, then aural tests, theory tests, instrumental/vocal tests; conductor tests include practical rehearsal with pianos or wind band. *Fees* Approx EUR 1600 per year for bachelors. EUR 55 application fee. *Scholarships* Some reimbursements available for EU/EES countries under certain circmstances. *Language requirements* Dutch, or English for overseas students.

Music facilities Music auditorium, theatre room, ensemble room, recording studio, 10 dance studios, media libary (over 15,000 items of sheet music), 40 practice/teaching rooms, 16 study cells; instruments include 74 pianos, drum kits and audio sets. *Accommodation* Institution has an agreement with Stadswonen (city housing) to help house 1st year students; foreign students given priority. *No of students* 1200, half of whom come from overseas (from around 60 countries)

UTRECHT

City in centre of Netherlands on the river Rhine with medieval, previously walled, centre exemplified in the Dom tower (part of a planned cathedral which was never completed). City has developed beyond that over past 200 years or so.

♪ Musical life

Muziekcentrum Vredenburg is main concert hall – programming goes beyond classical music. Town is base for the Netherlands Bach Society, although this is a predominantly touring group.

Other cultural information

Several museums on range of topics. Centraal Museum displays art and cultural artefacts from different periods; mechanical musical instrument museum; museum of Australian aboriginal art; even museum dedicated to Utrecht resident and creator of Miffy children's character, Dick Bruna.

Festivals and events

Early Music Festival (Aug-Sep) includes many concerts in churches across Utrecht. Festival aan de Werf is a platform in May for young artists, musicians and other performers to show off new work in indoor and outdoor locations. Netherlands Film Festival takes place in Utrecht (Sep-Oct).

ℹ Tourist information

www.utrechtyourway.nl

UTRECHTS CONSERVATORIUM

Utrecht School of the Arts, Mariaplaats 28, NL-3511 LL Utrecht.
t: +31 30 2314044 *f:* +31 30 2314004
e: info@muziek.hku.nl *w:* www.hku.nl
Courses Bachelor of music and master of music degrees. *Application requirements* Entrance exam

and suitable educational qualifications required; see website for full details. *Term dates* Sep-Aug *Application deadline* 15 Apr. *Fees* 2008-09 fees: EUR 1565 (EU/EEA nationals); EUR 3130 (other); 2009-10 fees to be confirmed. *Scholarships* For more information contact marijke.arnold@muziek. hku.nl *Exchange details* UK exchange partner institutions: Royal Welsh College of Music and Drama, Guildhall School of Music and Drama, Royal College of Music. Also partnerships with over 40 institutions across Europe. *Language requirements* Dutch and English. *Music facilities* Various concert halls, chapel, studio, library, music software/ICT support etc. *Accommodation* Through student service centre *No of students* 600 students in total; 32% of bachelors students, 50% of masters students from overseas.

ZWOLLE

City with population of about 115,000 and whose centre contains various historic buildings, canals etc.

ℹ Tourist information

www.zwolle.nl; +31 900 112 23 75.

ARTEZ SCHOOL OF MUSIC

Aan de Stadsmuur 88, NL-8011 VD Zwolle.
t: +31 38 42 70 500 *f:* +31 38 42 70 565
e: conservatorium.zwolle@artez.nl *w:* www.artez-conservatorium; www.artez.nl
Contact Wim Fiselier, dir of the Zwolle location. *Courses* Classical music, jazz & pop, education in music. For more details see under Arnhem.

MUSIC FESTIVALS

Europa Cantat Haus der Kultur, Weberstr 59a, D-53113 Bonn. *t:* +49 228 912 5663 *f:* +49 228 912 5658 *e:* info@europacantat.org *w:* www. europacantat.org *Contact* Sonja Greiner, secretary general. Triennial singing festival, next in Utrecht.
Holland Festival Early Music Utrecht Organisatie Oude Muziek, PO Box 19267, NL-3501 DG Utrecht. *t:* +31 30 232 9000 *f:* +31 30 232 9001 *e:* info@oudemuziek.nl *w:* www.oudemuziek.nl Annual.
International Chamber Music Festival Utrecht/ Janine Jansen 217 Groot Hertoginnelaan, NL-2517 ES Den Haag. *t:* +31 70 2539 271 *f:* +31 70 3659 021 *e:* info@kamermuziekfestival.

nl *w:* www.kamermuziekfestival.nl *Contact* Marjon Koenekopp, dir. custom2

International Gaudeamus Music Week Music Center the Netherlands, Rokin 111, NL-1012 KN Amsterdam. *t:* +31 20 3446060 *f:* +31 20 6733588 *e:* info@gaudeamus.nl *w:* www.gaudeamus.nl *Contact* Henk Heuvelmans, dir. Annual in Amsterdam. Contemporary music; performances of works by winners of the International Gaudeamus Composers' Competition prize. International selection of approx 40 works in very different musical styles by composers aged 30 and under.

International Organ Festival Haarlem PO Box 1091, NL-1000 BB Haarlem. *t:* +31 20 488 04 79 *f:* +31 2 488 04 78 *e:* organfestivalhaarlem@ klankwerk.nl *w:* www.organfestival.nl Biennial. Various recitals (organ, choir, instrumental).

Orlando Chamber Music Festival Piet Heinkade 5, NL-1019 BR Amsterdam. *t:* +31 20 519 1870 *f:* +31 20 519 1871 *e:* info@orlandofestival.nl *w:* www.orlandofestival.nl *Contact* Arjen Polman, general manager. International chamber music festival.

EUROPE

NOTY

Czech Republic, Hungary and Poland

Czech Republic, Hungary and Poland

There are certain places so imbued with a musical atmosphere that this becomes as much a reason to visit as city's architecture or art gallery. This is especially so in central Europe, and Poland, Hungary and the Czech Republic in particular.

All three countries here have strong musical traditions, each with its own particular flavour. In the Czech Republic, classical music is often associated with Prague. Mozart lived there for a while (there is a 'Prague' symphony; Don Giovanni was written for the Estates Theatre there); its river Vltava, as immortalised by Smetana in Ma Vlast, is a strong symbol of Czech nationhood. But the Czech music is not just an urban phenomenon — it is not hard to see how the emergence of Czech classical music is closely linked with the country's folk music.

The same could be said of Hungary, although the folk influences seem to point more to the future, notably in the work of Kodály and Bartók, two figures who dominate the Hungarian musical imagination. Then there is Poland, whose musical sensibility combines something of the two: the intimacy of Chopin and romantic expression of a Wieniawski on the one hand; uncompromising modernity, more recently, on the other.

CZECH REPUBLIC
Students attending the two university level specialist music institutions will in most cases be the cream of those having passed through one of the lower music schools (lower in terms of students' age and educational level). In the Czech system, these schools are known as 'conservatories' (the higher education institutions are 'academies'); they also offer vocational training courses to those choosing not to follow a performance path.

HUNGARY
Professional training in Hungary is relatively straightforward in that there is only one independent institution providing specialist tuition of this kind, although there are music departments at universities where performance studies are part of the curriculum. Diplomas are awarded after 10 semesters of study, equating to a masters degree under the Bologna Process, with the ECTS grading adopted; indeed the first Bologna-compliant 2-cycle courses have recently been introduced. Music teacher training qualifications are achieved after 8 semesters.

The highest level of training is at the pyramid of a music education system that begins at elementary school, and is much influenced by the work of Zoltan Kodály. Pre-conservatoire training is via 21 secondary music schools, plus the junior department at the Liszt Academy.

POLAND
Poland has been one of the most keen to adopt the 2-cycle system, with all 8 of its conservatoires running degree courses according to the 3+2 scheme; indeed, certain of them also offer a doctoral level 3rd cycle. In addition, all academies are government funded institutions; one outcome of this is that a certain degree of curriculum consistency can be maintained between them — approx one third of conservatoires' curriculum is determined as core, with the remainder left to their discretion. Part of the core training is given over to music teacher training, meaning that conservatoire graduates have some experience in this field as well as in performing.

As with Hungary, music training begins at an early age, with state institutions taking children from the age of 7. However, these are not specifically music schools; rather, they offer general education (graduates of the Music Lyceums, around age 18 or 19, are not obliged to study music at higher education level, but can choose from the full range of degree courses offered).

BRNO

City in Moravian region of south eastern Czech Republic, the country's second largest city, surrounded by forests. Characterised by distinctive central European architectural styles and dominated by city centre cathedral of St Peter and St Paul, although more recent industrial heritage has led to a more functional modern element. Overlooked by hilltop Spilberk castle, now a museum but formerly active as a fort.

♪ Musical life

Brno Philharmonic gives public and subscription concerts at its base, the Besední dům, as well as at the Janáček Theatre in the National Theatre, a venue for opera and ballet also. National Theatre encompasses other buildings too: Mahen Theatre is primarily a venue for drama, but has a smaller associated space, Theatre on the Wall, for chamber music and recitals; Reduta Theatre a mixture of drama, music theatre and opera. Though principally an art gallery of Czech artists, the Wannieck Gallery hosts occasional concerts by the Brno Philharmonic and the Czech Philharmonic Brno choir.

🏛 Other cultural information

Brno Cultural Centre houses a number of small galleries with changing exhibitions; City Museum one of several providing historical information about the city and the region; mechanical musical instruments part of the various exhibitions at the Technical Museum. Other cultural exhibitions include the Museum of Gypsy Culture.

🔍 Festivals and events

Brno International Music Festival is largest music event, running for 3 weeks in autumn. Associated with other spin-offs such as Exposition of New Music (Mar) and easter Festival of Sacred Music. Plenty of other events besides: Spilberk Festival feature Brno Philharmonic in concerts during Aug; musical theatre festival in Jun; also theatre and dance festivals at various points throughout the year.

ℹ Tourist information

www.brno.cz; info@ticbrno.cz; tel: +420 542 211 090

JANACKOVA AKADEMIE MUZICHYCH UMENI V BRNE (JANACEK ACADEMY OF MUSIC AND PERFORMING ARTS)

Faculty of Music, Komenskeho nam 6, CZ-662 15 Brno.
t: +420 542 591 607 *f:* +420 542 591 633
e: konarkova@jamu.cz *w:* http://hf.jamu.cz
Contact Petra Konarkova. *Courses* Bachelor's degree programmes in composition, orchestral/choral conducting, church music, music management, opera direction, voice, orchestral instuments; all available for master's degrees, except church music. Doctoral programmes in interpretation and the theory of interpretation, composition and theory of composition. *Application requirements* CV and copy of academic qualifications. *Application deadline* 15 Dec (BA study), 15 Apr (MA study), 15 Jun (PhD study) *Fees* None for degree programmes; fees charged for lifelong learning programmes. All applicants must pay entrance admission fee. *Exchange details* UK exchange partner institutions: Trinity College of Music, University of Leeds, Royal Welsh College of Music and Drama. Also partnerships with institutions in EU, eastern Europe and far east. Member of ELIA, ENCATC, Prospero. *Language requirements* Czech language exam for non-Czech or Slovak students. Lifelong learning programmes may be taught in English or German. *Music facilities* Library, inc music and students' work, also films; studies and reading rooms. Chamber opera studio, concert hall; various classrooms and practice rooms. Music faculty students may qualify for discounts and free tickets for certain events. *Accommodation* Hall of residence near music faculty building; shared rooms. Applications for accommodation must be received by 15 May. *No of students* 66 overseas students.

PRAGUE (PRAHA)

Czech capital situated on the river Vltava in Bohemian region of the country. City has had a dominant role in central European history, and this is reflected in its magnificent city architecture whether the hilltop castle that envelops St Vitus cathedral in the old town, the Charles Bridge, any number of buildings around Wenceslas Square and throughout the city. As well as having political importance over the years, city also a significant musical city, absorbing musical influences from various surrounding countries. This legacy has made it one of the world's most visited destinations generally, but also among music lovers in particular.

𝄞 Musical life

City has extremely active musical life with numerous orchestras (Czech Philharmonic Orchestra, Prague Symphony Orchestra, Prague Philharmonic Orchestra, Prague Radio Symphony Orchestra, Czech National Symphony Orchestra); opera (Prague National Theatre, Estates Theatre and Prague State Opera); the city is also home to plenty of early music and chamber ensembles. Various concert series either at specific venues or arranged by concert promoters such as EuroArt's chamber music series. City is popular touring destination for choirs, orchestras and chamber groups from all over the world.

🏛 Other cultural information

Various galleries and museums such as the National Gallery and the City Museum; modern culture celebrated also, at Museum of Czech Cubism, the Centre for Modern and Contemporary Art and the Franz Kafka Museum. Unofficial 'ball season' takes over during Jan-Feb at various locations such as the Palace Lucerna.

🎭 Festivals and events

City hosts a number of festivals: Prague Spring Festival in May is one of the most prestigious European festivals but there are also events in summer and autumn. Summer festival of sacred music includes a choir competition. Various festivals of local or traditional music and folklore from Feb Bohemian Carnival to a festival of Roma culture in May.

ℹ Tourist information

www.pis.cz; tourinfo@pis.cz; tel: +420 12 444

AKADEMIE MUZICKYCH UMENI V PRAZE
Malostranske nam 13, CR-118 01 Praha 1. *t:* +420 257 533 618; +420 257 530 698, also fax (international office) *f:* +420 257 530 697 *e:* studijni@hamu.cz; jiri.kucmas@hamu.cz *w:* www.hamu.cz
Contact Ing Lea Motlova, head of student dept; Jiri Kucmas, international office *Courses* 3-year BA, 2-year MA, PhD programme. Study at both levels in orchestral instruments, conducting, opera direction,

organ, harpsichord, guitar, music theory, music direction, music management, sound production, chamber music (some courses not offered every year). Options also available in areas such as music history, music aesthetics, cultural education, languages, as well as teaching courses. PhD programme covers composition and compositional theory, interpretation and interpretational theory, music theory, sound production, music production. *Application requirements* For BA, entrance exams end Jan covering individual specialism, music history and theory, and practical piano. See website for specific details of exam contents (specific for each course). For MA, an outstanding BA degree is required *Application deadline* 30 Nov. *Fees* Kc 599 admin fee *Exchange details* Partners within Erasmus programme. *Music facilities* Music library and sound archive, sound studio for electro-acoustic compositions, acoustic research laboratories; opera studio, contemporary music studio and chamber music room. *No of students* 360 national students and 40 from overseas.

MUSIC FESTIVALS

XX Festival Forfest Czech Rupublic 2009 Artistic Initiative of Kromeriz, Kojetinska 1425, CR-767 01 Kromeriz. *t:* +420 573 341316, also fax *e:* forfest@quick.cz; forfest@seznam.cz *w:* www.forfest.cz *Contact* MgA Zdenka Vaculovicov, artistic director. International festival of contemporary arts with spiritual orientation. Concerts, exhibitions, workshops and lectures with local and foreign artists. Presentation of young composers and creative artists; portraits of well-known artists.

Brno International Music Festival Hybesova 29, CR-602 00 Brno. *t:* +420 543 420 951 *f:* +420 543 420 950 *e:* mhfb@arskoncert.cz *w:* www.mhf-brno.cz *Contact* Lenka Simeckova.

Emmy Destin Music Festival A Barcala 404/38, CR-370 05 Ceske Budejovice. *t:* +420 38 644 4448, also fax *e:* fked@volny.cz *w:* www.festival.ed-cz Operatic, oratorio and chamber music repertoire.

International Jazz Festival Prague Pragokoncert Arts Agency, U Bulhara 3, Praha 1. *t:* +420 224 235 340 *f:* +420 224 234 340 *e:* Letov@pragokoncert.com *Contact* Ivo Letov, artistic director. Jazz, from traditional to modern.

International Jazz Festival Janaček 28 Rijna 124, CR-702 00 Ostrava. *t:* +420 597 489 421 *f:* +420

EUROPE

597 489 422 e: festival@janackuvmaj.cz w: www.janackuvmaj.cz Contact Jaromír Javurek, director.

Mahler-Jihlava International Festival Balbinova 14, CR-120 00 Praha 2. t: +420 224 238 673 f: +420 224 238 619 e: arcodiva@arcodiva.cz w: www.arcodiva.cz Annual. Classical music (chamber, symphonic) festival in Jihlava, southern Czech Republic.

Prague Autumn International Music Festival Poibinicka 20, CR-130 00 Praha 3. t: +420 222 540 484 f: +420 222 540 415 e: festival@ prague autumn.cz w: www.prague autumn.cz Annual classical music festival.

Prague Spring International Music Festival Hellichova 18, CR-118 00 Praha 1. t: +420 257 320 468 f: +420 257 313 725 e: info@festival.cz w: www.festival.cz Classical music festival, also competition.

Smetana's Litomysl Smetanova Litomysl ops, Jiraskova 133, CR-570 01 Litomysl. t: +420 603 801 740 e: helpdesk@smetanaoperafestival.com w: www.smetanaoperafestival.com Contact Ruzena Skrobankova, customer helpdesk; Jan Pikna, festival director; Vojtech Stritesky, festival artistic director. Opera presentation at grand opening, plus more than 20 concert performances at the Unesco-listed Litomysl Renaissance Castle. Official event during Czech EU governance in 2009.

Spilberk Festival Komenského námestí, CR-302 00 Brno. e: info@filharmonie-brno.cz w: www.filharmonie-brno.cz

Summer Festivities of Early Music Melantrichova 971/19, CR-110 00 Prague. t: +420 224 229 462 f: +420 224 233 417 e: info@collegium marianum.cz w: www.collegiummarianum.cz Contact Marketa Semeradova, director; Zaneta Novackova, producer. Festival programmes presented by renowned soloists and ensembles demonstrate variations and connection between European cultures.

HUNGARY

BUDAPEST

Capital of Hungary on the river Danube, originally two towns (Buda and Pest) separated by it. Since the end of the Cold War has become a popular destination for tourists attracted by its distinctive mid-European atmosphere and architecture such as the dramatic riverfront parliament building and the vast hilltop castle area on the opposite bank. Much of this atmosphere is down to city's prominent position in late 19th century Austria-Hungary.

♪ Musical life

State opera house, ornate late 19th century building with stunning interior on city's Andrássy avenue, stages Hungarian State Opera and Ballet companies. Budapest Philharmonic Orchestra is the country's oldest still in operation and gives its concerts at the opera house; other orchestras based in the city include Hungarian National Philharmonic Orchestra, Hungarian Radio Symphony Orchestra; particularly noteworthy is Budapest Festival Orchestra, a group that has high international reputation. Various chamber orchestras and ensembles as well: Franz Liszt Chamber Orchestra is one of the better known.

▥ Other cultural information

Millenáris is a modern cultural centre incorporating theatre, exhibitions and exhibition spaces. Városliget park encompasses a number of attractions, such as botanical gardens, medicinal baths and Vajdahunyad Castle. City has a national gallery and fine arts museum. Unusual among capital cities in being renowned for its thermal baths, with many visitors treating.

☙ Festivals and events

Budapest Spring Festival is country's biggest music event with performers coming from all over the world; performances not limited to classical music. International choir festival runs during easter, centred round a competition. Budafest is summer music festival event with gala performances, opera etc; Autumn Festival has classical music component but features wide range of performing arts and film.

ℹ Tourist information

www.budapestinfo.hu; tel: +36 1 266 0479

LISZT FERENC MUSIC ACADEMY

Liszt Ferenc ter 8, HU-1061 Budapest.
t: +36 1 462 4615 (international studies)
e: international@lfze.hu *w:* www.liszt.hu
Courses 3-year BA and 2-year MA courses in several faculties: piano (inc other keyboard instruments and harp), church music, music education, choral conducting, wind and percussion instruments, chamber music, solo singing and opera, strings, music theory, composition and conducting, musicology. Part time study available also. *Application requirements* Min age 18. Students must have secondary school diploma; MA applicants must have BA or equivalent diploma; entrance exam. Exam held end Jun/beginning Jul in Budapest, except for candidates in Pacific countries who can take test in Japan (Feb or Jul). Exam covers solfege/theory, piano test, audition on main instrument (see website for specified works). MA students must also take test. *Fees* Annual fees vary according to course; for BA, EUR 3793-7773; for MA, EUR 0-7765. EUR 50 application fee; EUR 50 registration fee at beginning of studies. *Language requirements* Hungarian, English or German. *Music facilities* Library, multimedia library, audio-visual studio. *Accommodation* No student housing facilities, but international affairs department can assist in finding rental accommodation.

MUSIC FESTIVALS

Budafest VIP Arts Manager & Production Office, Hajos ut 13-15, H-1065 Budapest. *t:* +36 1 332 4816 *f:* +36 1 302 4290 *e:* viparts@viparts.hu *w:* www.viparts.hu custom2

Budapest Autumn Festival Budapest Festival Center, Szervita ter 5, H-1052 Budapest. *t:* +36 1 486 3322 *f:* +36 1 486 3310 *e:* bof@festival city.hu *w:* www.bof.hu *Contact* Zsofia Zimanyi, managing director; Balazs Kovalik, artistic director. Various music, dance, theatre performances, film screenings, fine art, photography and computer art, orchestra and chamber concerts, composer competition, conferences, world and Hungarian premieres. Features independent and experimental artists, events and ideas.

Budapest Spring Festival Budapest Festival Center, Szervita ter 5, H-1052 Budapest. *t:* +36 1 486 3300 *f:* +36 1 486 3310 *e:* info@festivalcity.hu *w:* www.festivalcity.hu *Contact* Zsofia Zimanyi, director. Opera, orchestral and chamber concerts, dance, jazz, theatre, open-air programmes, folk music.

Esztergom International Guitar Festival Szendrey-Karper Laszlo International Guitar Festival Foundation, PO Box 8, H-2501 Esztergom. *t:* +36 22 460267, also fax *w:* www.guitarfestival.hu Concerts, masterclasses, guitar competition, exhibition of guitars, guitar orchestra.

International Bartók Seminar & Festival Filharmonia Concert Agency, Kazinczy u 24-26, H-1075 Budapest. *t:* +36 1 266 1459 *f:* +36 1 302 4962 *e:* kadar.csilla@hu.inter.net; szell.agnes@hu.inter.net *w:* www.filharmoniabp.hu; www.bartokfestival.hu *Contact* Csilla Kádár, Ágnes Széll, managers. Annual. 20th C, Bartók and contemporary music.

International Choir Festival & Competition Budapest INTERKULTUR, Am Weingarten 3, D-35415 Pohlheim. *t:* +49 6403 956525 *f:* +49 6403 956529 *e:* mail@musica-mundi.com *w:* www.musica-mundi.com

International Kodály Festival POB 188, H-6001 Kecskemet. *t:* +36 76 481 518 *f:* +36 7 632 0160 *e:* office@kodaly.hu *w:* www.kodaly.hu *Contact* Laura Keri, deputy director. Chamber concerts and recitals, exhibitions, introduction of prize-winning young artists. Works of Kodály and contemporary Hungarian music.

Summer on a Chain Bridge Budapest Festival Center, Szervita ter 5, H-1052 Budapest. *t:* +36 1 486 3300 *f:* +36 1 486 3310 *e:* info@festivalcity.hu *w:* www.festivalcity.hu *Contact* Zsófia Zimányi, director. Open air programmes.

EUROPE

BYDGOSZCZ

City towards the north of Poland on Brda and Vistula rivers. Its development began in 15th century and town's architecture encompasses various styles from that time on; today there are various plans to develop and expand the city further. Home to several higher education institutions apart from music academy.

Musical life

Filarmonia Pomorska is home base for Pomeranian Philharmonic Orchestra. Opera Nova is a modern design opera house putting on a range of productions from opera to music theatre and operetta; also orchestral concerts.

Other cultural information

Teatr Polski for all kinds of theatre production, plus a range of music events (concerts, cabaret, pop and traditional music). There is a regional Culture Centre has courses and events in various art forms. Several small art galleries and museums.

Festivals and events

Opera Nova hosts an annual opera festival in Apr featuring performances from Polish and foreign companies. Filarmonia hall holds an early music festival in autumn.

Tourist information

www.visitbydgoszcz.pl; bylot@op.pl; tel: +52 58 58 702

AKADEMIA MUZYCNA IM F NOWOWIEJSKIEGO W BYDGOSZCZY (ACADEMY OF MUSIC BYDGOSZCZ)

ul Slowackiego 7, PL-85-008 Bydgoszcz.
t: +48 052 321 05 82 e: rektor@amuz.
bydgoszcz.pl w: www.amuz.bydgoszcz.pl
Courses Several departments: composition, instrumental, vocal and actors', and choral conducting and music education. As well as performance specialism, options available in complementary subjects, eg ear training, history and literature of music, foreign languages, philosophy, music aesthetics, history of culture. Music facilities 2 faculty buildings in city centre: 53 lecture/practice rooms with pianos, 140-seat concert hall, 100-seat hall, recording studio. Many rooms have audio-visual recording equipment.

Instruments available for rent. Concert series arranged, plus student ensembles such as symphony orchestra, chorus and chamber choir.

GDANSK

City on Baltic coast with a strategic importance, thanks to its port location, dating back to medieval times – it was part of the Hanseatic League trading guild that encompassed various countries along north European coastline. Its shipyards were the epicentre of the popular Solidarnosc (Solidarity) trade union movement which eventually helped lead to fall of communism in the country. Despite this modern association with heavy industry, many attractive buildings from earlier periods can be found throughout the centre. A major education centre, with over 60,000 students at its higher education institutions.

Musical life

Polska Filharmonia Baltycka based at its own concert hall, as is Opera Baltycka at its opera house.

Other cultural information

Gdansk Archipelago of Culture a city-wide cultural network of buildings promoting cultural and performance activities of many kinds. Showcase for modern art at Łazni Centre for Contemporary Art. Baltic Sea Cultural Centre another multi-art organisation based in 2 buildings including a converted church for concerts and other performances.

Festivals and events

International Festival of Organ Music over summer until early autumn, held at Oliwa cathedral. Classical concerts organised over summer.

Tourist information

www.got.gdansk.pl; itpkp@got.gdansk.pl; tel: +48 58 348 13 68

AKADEMIA MUZYCZNA W GDANSKU

uk Lakowa 1/2, PL-80-743 Gdansk.
t: +48 58 300 92 00; +48 58 300 92 13 (foreign enquiries) f: +48 58 300 92 10; +48 58 300 92 10 (foreign enquiries) e: muzyczna@ amuz.gda.pl; brydak@amuz.gda.pl w: www. amuz.gda.pl

Contact Wojslaw Brydak, foreign enquiries. Courses Faculties: composition and music theory; instrumental; vocal and acting; choral conducting, music education, eurythmics and church music Term dates Early Oct-early Feb (winter semester); early Feb-end Sep (summer semester) Fees Free on regular courses; postgrad fees EUR 233-440 per semester, depending on course. Scholarships Some financial aid may be available. Exchange details UK exchange partner institution: Guildhall School of Music. Also partnerships with institutions in Austria, Belgium, Bulgaria, Denmark, Estonia, Finland, France, Germany, Italy, Latvia, Lithuania, Netherlands, Portugal, Sweden, Turkey. Music facilities Academic library with approx 80,000 scores and books etc; sound recording studio Accommodation Student dormitory on campus (2 or 3 bed rooms). No of students Approx 450 students.

KATOWICE

City in an upland area in the southern Polish region of Silesia, with an economy traditionally based on heavy industry. Prevalent architectural feel is modern, with some art nouveau influences among Bauhaus-era modernism and more functional post-war designs.

♪ Musical life

Silesian Philharmonic Symphony Orchestra is regional orchestra based in the city, performing at the Philharmonic Hall. National Polish Radio Symphony Orchestra Katowice also based in the city, performing for the most part at the Silesian Theatre. Spodek is a huge arena hosting rock concerts.

🏛 Other cultural information

City has a number of theatres, ranging from the standard Silesian Theatre to several more experimental companies. Several galleries and museums.

🔗 Festivals and events

Conducting competition named after Polish conductor Grzegorz Fitelberg, held every four years.

ℹ Tourist information

www.um.katowice.pl; ciom@um.katowice.pl; tel: +448 32 259 38 08

AKADEMIA MUZYCZNA IM KAROLA SZYMANOWSKIEGO (KAROL SZYMANOWSKI ACADEMY OF MUSIC)

ul Zacisze 3, PL-40-025 Katowice.
t: +48 32 256 51 48 f: +48 32 256 44 85
e: TokStudiow@am.katowice.pl (rector's office);
J.Mentel@am.katowice.pl (international co-operation) w: www.am.katowice.pl
Courses Full-time and part-time BAs and MA in several division: composition; conducting and music theory; music education; choral conducting; piano; string instruments; organ and harpsichord; wind, brass and percussion; chamber music; accordion; guitar and harp; vocal; composition and music arrangement; jazz instrumental and vocal. Music facilities New concert hall currently in planning.

KRAKOW

Located in the south of the country Krakow's several hundred years of history (it was the country's capital until the 17th century, and counts significant Roman and Jewish influences in its past) have left a rich architectural and cultural legacy, and its city centre has been registered on Unesco's world heritage list. Today, a thriving city with an exciting array of cultural activities including a busy nightlife, its network of underground cellars providing a unique venue for unusual entertainment.

♪ Musical life

One of country's musical centres with very active musical life. The Karol Szymanowski Philarmonic building has resident orchestra (and several chamber groups drawn from its ranks) and choir; Sinfonietta Cracovia a smaller group that performs there also. Several choirs in the city, plus Krakow Opera and Ballet (which have their own orchestra). Busy city for jazz.

🏛 Other cultural information

City houses a number of cultural centres covering a variety of areas: Rotunda Cultural Centre a popular student hangout (jazz, cabaret, film club, venue for bands); Institute of Art Association promotes young performers as part of programme of cultural events; Dworek Białoprądnicki has a strong music presence among its cultural programme. Plentiful art galleries, many of which focus on Polish art (eg Piano Nobile Contemporary Art Galler,

Marian Gołogórski Gallery, Sukiennice Gallery, or the Krakow Poster Gallery).

Festivals and events
Large festival of Jewish culture in summer.

Tourist information
www.krakow.pl; simratusz@infokrakow.pl; tel : +48 12 433 73 10

AKADEMIA MUZYCZNA W KRAKOWIE
ul Sw Tomasza 43, PL-31-027 Krakow.
t: +48 12 422 04 55 e: zbmszlez@cyf-kr.edu.pl (international affairs) w: www.amuz.krakow.pl
Contact Mieczyslaw Szlezer, prorector for international affairs. Courses Courses in instrumental music, vocal music, conducting, theory, composition, education. Application requirements Abitur diploma or equivalent; musical knowledge and skills equal to conservatory higher level diploma. Term dates 1 Oct-10 Jun. Application deadline 25 May. Fees Up to EUR 1000 per semester (Polish & EU students); EUR 4000 (non EU students). Scholarships Scholarships provided by the state and private sponsors. Exchange details Over 60 Socrates-Erasmus partners, plus universities in USA, Chile and S Korea. Music facilities 3 concert halls; library with 50,000 items including audio-visual recordings. Accommodation Student dormitory with 146 places in 2, 3 or 4 bed rooms. No of students 500 national students, plus 35 from overseas.

ŁÓDŹ
Central Polish city with a largely industrial background, particularly textiles. Its people suffered during World War II, particularly its substantial Jewish population who were forced for several years into a ghetto before its destruction in 1944.

Musical life
City's orchestra is Łodz Philharmonic, which has its own strikingly designed concert hall; classical music recitals and other events staged there too.

Other cultural information
Textile museum reflects city's industrial past.

Festivals and events
Film music festival has been running for over 10 years; also ballet festival.

Tourist information
www.cityoflodz.pl; cit@uml.lodz.pl; tel: +48 42 638 59 55

AKADEMIA MUZYCZNA IM GRAZYNY I KIEJSTUTA BACEWICZOW (THE GRAZYNA AND KIEJSTUT BACEWICZ ACADEMY OF MUSIC)
32 Gdanska St, PL-90-716 Lodz.
t: +48 42 662 16 00; +48 42 662 16 15 (international relations) e: international@amuz.lodz.pl w: www.amuz.lodz.pl
Contact Dorota Rossowska, international relations contact. Term dates Oct-early Feb (winter semester); mid Feb-mid Jun (summer semester). Exchange details UK exchange partner institution: Royal Welsh College of Music and Drama. Other partnerships with institutions in Austria, Belgium, Czech Republic, France, Germany, Italy, Lithuania, Netherlands, Slovakia, Sweden, Switzerland; also Chile and China.

POZNAN
City in western Poland, one of the country's oldest – its gothic cathedral is the oldest in the country.

Musical life
Poznan Philharmonic is city's main orchestra; chamber orchestra provided by Aamadeus Chamber Orchestra of the Polish Radio performing in the main hall of the city's Adam Mickiewicz university. Regular opera performances at Theatr Wielki Stanisława Moniuszki.

Other cultural information
Among numerous exhibitions is a musical instrument museum on old market square; both classical instruments and folk instruments from around the world.

Festivals and events
Home to quinquennial Henryk Wieniawski Violin Competion and biennial festival of contemporary Polish music (Apr).

Tourist information
www.poznan.pl; it@cim-poznan.pl; tel: +48 61 852 61 56

AKADEMIA MUZYCZNA IM IGNACEGO JANA PADEREWSKIEGO
ul Swiety Marcin 87, PL-61-808 Poznan.

t: +48 61 856 89 00 *f:* +48 61 853 66 76
e: amuz@amuz.edu.pl *w:* www.amuz.edu.pl
Courses 3-year BA and 2-year MA. Faculties of composition, conducting, theory and eurhythmics; instruments; vocal studies; choral conducting, music education and church music. Only Polish academy with course in violin-making. Also faculties in Szczecin. *Application requirements* B1 certificate in Polish, secondary school qualification. For MA students, audition at end Sep. *Application deadline* Mid May *Fees* BA students from EU/EFTA countries study free; for non-EU/EFTA, EUR 5500, payable mid-Oct. MA fee is EUR 3000, payable by mid Oct. *Language requirements* Polish. *Accommodation* Academy has its own dormitory with double and triple rooms.

WARSAW

Polish capital with a history dating back over seven centuries, little of which remains visible due to massive destruction during World War II bombing, although there have been some restoration projects (notably in the old town area). Its revived Jewish quarter, with its own institute, is a reminder of the Nazi imposed ghetto. City attracts large numbers of students (over a quarter of a million in higher education institutions of varying types and specialisms)

Musical life

City is musically very active. Main institutions: Teatr Wielki is the grand home for Polish National Opera company; Sala Filharmonii (Philharmonic Hall) home of the historic orchestra (and choir) of the same name has a main concert hall and chamber music room. Sinfonia Varsovia a smaller but equally busy group, based in one of the city's most prominent buildings, the Pałac Kulturny. Polish Radio Symphony Orchestra based at Lutosławski Concert Hall in the city. Chamber opera company, Warszawska Opera Kameralna runs several projects, including annual baroque opera festival, and annual Mozart festival (company claims to be the only one featuring the complete Mozart operas in its repertoire). Beethoven festival at easter. Various concert series, such as the summer concerts at the Royal Castle, or those arranged by the Chopin Society based in the city.

Other cultural information

Centre for Contemporary Art features various exhibitions and performances. Among the usual range of art galleries and museums are a poster gallery (Galeria Plakatu) and the Museum of Cartoon and Caricature. Theatre covers the range of genres – for instance, among more serious establishments, Teatr Studio Buffo puts on revues.

Festivals and events

Numerous music events including, early, sacred and contemporary music; Warsaw Autumn the main example of the latter, running for over a week in Sep since 1950s. Chopin Piano Competition takes place every 5 years. Film festival in Oct, as well as the Jazz Jamboree; street art festival in the summer.

Tourist information

www.warsawtour.pl; info@warsawtour.pl; tel: +48 22 94 31

AKADEMII MUZYCZNEJ IM FRYDERYKA CHOPINA (THE FREDERIK CHOPIN ACADEMY OF MUSIC)

2 Okolnik Str, PL-00-368 Warsaw.
t: +48 22 827 72 41; +48 22 827 83 08 (international office) *f:* +48 22 827 83 09
e: zawadzka@chopin.edu.pl *w:* www.chopin.edu.pl
Contact Joanna Zawadzka, international office. *Courses* Level 1 (bachelor's) and level 2 (graduate) courses in several departments: composition, conducting and music theory; piano, harpsichord and organ; instrumental studies (inc accordion and chamber music); vocal studies; music education; sound engineering. Also individual postgrad training in orchestral and keyboard instruments (classes in English, Spanish, German, Italian). *Application requirements* EU nationals required to pass Polish as a Foreign Language exam, level B1. Requirements vary depending on course; for more details, see website. *Term dates* 1 Oct-end Jan (winter semester); early Feb-end May (spring semester); exam sessions may fall outside these dates. *Application deadline* 31 May. *Scholarships* None offered by academy; contact Polish embassies or consulates for information about government grants.

WROCŁAW

Historic city in south west Poland on the river Oder and tributaries – in fact the city is a collection of islands joined together by numerous bridges (over 100). Has a busy, architecturally distinctive market square; city's thousand years of history have left a legacy of mixed architectural styles (baroque, gothic etc). Many students attracted to city's baroque university, but many other institutes besides.

♪ Musical life

Several instrumental groups based in the city, ranging from Witold Lutosławski Philharmonic Orchestra and Wrocław Chamber Orchestra Leopoldinum to chamber and early music ensembles. Ferenc Liszt Society based in the city but organises concerts throughout Poland.

🏛 Other cultural information

Several museum exhibitions on various themes (architectural, archaeological, art and ethnography); a number of contemporary art galleries. Notable artwork is the Racławice Panorama, a 19th century battle depiction created by several artists and housed in its own rotunda building. Plenty of theatres.

🎭 Festivals and events

City hosts a number of music festivals. Wratsilavia Cantans not just singing festival but features performances of all kinds of classical music (one week in Jun, one in Sep). Musica Polonica Nova is a festival of contemporary Polish music every other year; early music at Maj z Muzyką Dawną in May. Guitar and organ festivals (autumn and summer respectively). Various jazz events, and festivals focusing on traditional Polish music .

ℹ Tourist information

www.itwroclaw.pl; info@itwroclaw.pl; +48 71 344 31 11

AKADEMIA MUZYCZNA IM KAROLA LIPINSKIEGO (THE KAROL LIPINSKI ACADEMY OF MUSIC)

pl Jana Pawla II 2, PL-50-043 Wroclaw.
t: +48 71 355 5543 *f:* +48 71 355 2849
e: info@amuz.wroc.pl *w:* www.amuz.wroc.pl
Courses 4 depts: composition, conducting, theory and music therapy (inc computer composition and film music); instrumental studies (inc early music and chamber music); vocal studies (song/oratorio or

stage singing); music education. Details of course requirements on website. 3-year BA programme, 2-year MA programme. *Application requirements* Admission criteria, procedures and application dates vary depending on course; full details available on website. *Term dates* 1 Oct-25 Jan, with exams 26 Jan-10 Feb (winter semester); 16 Feb-31 May, with exams 1-15 Jun (summer semester). *Application deadline* 15 May (EU citizens); 23 Aug (non-EU citizens). *Fees* EUR 2000, plus EUR 200 pa (bachelors and masters studies), EUR 3000, plus EUR 200 (doctoral studies); non-EU citizens only. *Exchange details* Exchanges organised through Erasmus and CEEPUS II *Language requirements* All group classes in Polish; some individual teaching in English and German to overseas students. Language classes available at University of Wroclaw *Music facilities* Chamber music hall, ballet hall, library (over 100,000 titles), audio-visual studio, computer composition studio. Over 200 concerts arranged per year. *No of students* 593 national, 5 overseas students.

MUSIC FESTIVALS

Bydgoszcz Opera Festival ul Marszalka Focha 5, PL-85-070 Bydgoszcz. *w:* www.opera.bydgoszcz.pl

Gaude Mater: International Festival of Sacred Music, Gaude Mater Centre of Culture Promotion, Dabrowskiego 1, PL-42-200 Czestochowa. *t:* +48 34 324 3638; +48 34 365 17 60 *e:* biuro@gaudemater.pl *w:* www.gaudemater.pl *Contact* Malgorzata Zuzanna Nowak, director; Danuta Morawska, secretary; Magdalena Ujma, international co-operation.

International Festival Wratislavia Cantans, Rynek 7, PL-50-106 Wroclaw. *t:* +48 71 3427257 *f:* +48 71 330 52 12 *e:* office@wratislavia.art.pl *w:* www.wratislavia.art.pl

Jewish Culture Festival in Krakow, ul Józefa 36, PL-31-056 Kraków. *t:* +48 12 431 15 17 *f:* +48 12 431 24 27 *e:* office@jewishfestival.pl *w:* www.jewishfestival.pl Music from synagogue, klezmer, Hasidic, classical and Jewish folk music; also films and other presentations.

Ludwig van Beethoven Easter Festival, Chmielna 15/10 St, PL-00-021 Warszawa. *t:* +48 22 331 91 91 *f:* +48 22 313 00 05 *e:* biuro@beethoven.org.pl *w:* www.beethoven.org.pl Festival featuring music of Beethoven and others.

Maj z Muzyka Dawna, ASK WAGANT, skr poczt 2372, PL-50-131 WrocBaw 3. e: biuro@muzyka dawna.pl w: www.muzykadawna.pl Festival of early music.

The Mozart Festival in Warsaw, Warsaw Chamber Opera, ul Nowogrodzka 49, PO-00-695 Warszawa. t: +48 22 628 3096 f: +48 22 627 2212 e: tickets@wok.pol.pl w: www.opera kameralna.pl Annual. Features Mozart's stage works.

Music in Old Krakow, Ul Zwierzyniecka 1, PL-31-103 Krakow. t: +48 12 421 45 66 f: +48 429 43 28 e: biuro@capellacracoviensis.pl w: www. capellacracoviensis.pl Contact Stanislaw Galonski, director. Symphonic, vocal, chamber music, recitals.

Musica Polonica Nova, ul Mazowlecka 17, PL-50-412 WrocBaw. t: +48 71 344 69 66 f: +48 71 344 39 45 e: biuro@MusicaPolonicaNova.pl w: www.musicapolonicanova.pl Biennial festival of contemporary music, focusing on Polish composers.

Organ Day, c/o Philharmonic Orchestra Karol Szymanowski, Zwierniecka 1, PL-31-103 Krakow. t: +48 12 422 0958, also fax e: fk@filharmonia. krakow.pl w: www.filharmonia.krakow.pl Contact Jacek Berwaldt, programme deputy head. Organ recitals, oratorio concerts.

Song of Our Roots, Rynex 6, PL-37-500 Jaroslaw. t: +48 16 621 64 51, also fax e: earlymusic@ poczta.onet.pl w: www.jaroslaw.pl/festiwal Contact Maciej Kazinski, director. Early and traditional music, especially liturgical. Workshops in Gregorian chan, traditional dances, festival choir. Concerts performed by artists and participants together. Lodging in old abbey.

Warsaw Autumn, c/o Polish Composers' Union, Rynek Starego Miasta 27, PL-00-272 Warszawa. t: +48 22 831 1634 ext 32 f: +48 22 8310607 e: festival@warsaw-autumn.art.pl w: www.warsaw-autumn.art.pl Annual. Contemporary music: symphony and chamber music, solo recitals, electronic and computer music, multimedia project.

Nordic Region

NOTE

Nordic Region

Although the countries in the far north of Europe may seem to be distant from the continent's musical heart, geography should not be confused with importance. All five of the countries in this section have thriving classical music scenes.

DENMARK

Professional training in Denmark has followed the Bologna recommendations for several years now (since 2004). Education takes place in specialist music institutions that run parallel to the country's universities, with a degree structure that is the same, save for the fact that a Konservatorium cannot offer PhDs. They may have input into PhDs offered by universities, but it will be the latter who verify and administer them. Around 90% of students progress to the 2nd cycle of studies at masters level. The level of government funding is such that, for EU/EEA students at least, there are no tuition fees.

FINLAND

Although advanced music training in Finland is provided by institutions running a Bologna-compliant system, only one, the Sibelius academy in Helsinki, currently offers masters level as well as the BMus. As a result, graduates of that institution have an advantage in their progression to that higher level – they are automatically accepted without having to take an entrance exam. In terms of qualification, the masters degree is considered the appropriate level certificate for professional performing; the bachelors, however, does entitle a graduate to teach music in schools. All higher education institutions in Finland are state-funded, but the level is higher for music conservatoires (up to 95% of funding).

ICELAND

The 2 advanced level training institutions in Iceland are run on slightly different lines since, by law, the older College of Music is not able to award degrees for the training it gives. In order to rectify this, the Academy of Arts was set up as a private concern (though government-funded) to offer artistic training in performing and visual arts. Its various curricula are designed by the departments themselves, so are not set down by the government. The majority of pre-professional training begins in specialist music schools, partly funded by local government, partly through fees.

NORWAY

There are 3 kinds of higher education institutions providing music training: fully independent state-funded music academy (there is one, the Norwegian Academy of Music), university-affiliated institutions, or private institution such as the Barratt-Due institute. Unlike other degree courses, these institutions are not obliged to provide degrees according to Bologna, so some 4-year 1st cycle degrees are offered; curricula are also independent of central control, with each establishment deciding course content and structure.

SWEDEN

Advanced music training is Sweden is simple to understand since all establishments follow the same degree structure (3 years undergrad + 2 years second cycle); all conservatoires, as with higher education more generally, are centrally funded, with students required to contribute for student welfare and small administration fees only. It has been found that graduates of Swedish conservatoires have good employment prospects, with many able to pursue at least part of their professional career in the field.

Prior to conservatoire level, music education is well embedded within the general education system, with music taught both in schools (compulsory to age 16) and in specialist institutions.

DENMARK

AALBORG

Northern Danish city with an industrial heritage but traces in its architecture of an older past, such as Jens Bang's house, an early 17th century domestic building.

🎼 Musical life

City has its own orchestra, the Aalborg Symfoni-orkester; major classical music performances (concerts and opera) at the Congress and Culture Centre (venue is used for rock and other music too).

🏛 Other cultural information

Utzon Centre is modern art and exhibition centre. Impressive modern art gallery building; also maritime and local history museums.

🎭 Festivals and events

Annual opera festival takes place all over city, with main events at Congress and Culture Centre. City's carnival for a week in May; blues and jazz festival in Aug.

ℹ Tourist information

www.visitaalborg.com; info@visitaalborg.com; tel: +45 9931 7500

NORDJYSK MUSIKKONSERVATORIUM

Ryesgade 52, DK-9000 Aalborg.
t: +45 98127744 e: nordkons.dk w: www.nordkons.dk
Courses 3 year bachelor programme; 2 year master's programme. Studies based on major subject (eg instrumental specialism) with minor subjects (eg music history, aural training). Application requirements Entrance exam; contact academy for details. Applicants must be 18-30 years, although exemptions possible. Application deadline 11 December. No of students Approx 107 students; annual intake approx 20.

AARHUS (ÅRHUS)

Port on Denmark's east coast (Jutland peninsula). Dates back over 1000 years, and city today still features many old buildings – cathedral is 13th century, for example – but also more modern architecture (harbour area is currently being redeveloped). Big student town, with 35,000 at the university alone, and it's estimated that one in five people in the city is a student.

🎼 Musical life

Musikhuset Aarhus is a striking glass dominated concert hall; main hall seats over 1500, chamber hall over 300. Home to Danish National Opera and Aarhus Symoniorkester; another orchestra is Aarhus Sinfonietta.

🏛 Other cultural information

Among range of exhibitions are several reflecting on city's past: a recreation of an old Danish town, a Viking museum, a museum documentint the changing lives of Danish women, and museum of the occupation. Also modern art gallery and thriving theatre scene.

🎭 Festivals and events

Aarhus Festival (Aug-Sep) features different kinds of music and various art forms; jazz festival runs for a week in Jul. SPOR festival in May focuses on contemporary music.

ℹ Tourist information

www.visitaarhus.com; tel: +45 8731 5010.

DET JYSKE MUSIKKONSERVATORIUM (ROYAL ACADEMY OF MUSIC)

Skovgaardsgade 2C, DK-8000 Arhus C.
t: +45 8713 3800 f: +45 8712 3840 e: mail@musik-kons.dk w: www.musik-kons.dk
Contact Keld Hosbond. Courses All levels: classical, rhythmic, electronic; also adult education/refresher courses. Application requirements Generally test on main instrument/voice plus minor subjects (theory, ear tests), as well as piano. Full details of application requirements for each course, and application form, available on website. Term dates Aug/Sep 2009-June 2010. Application deadline 1 Dec. Exchange details Exchanges arranged through Erasmus, Nordplus, Glomus and Nomazz. Language requirements English. Accommodation Help finding accomodation available. No of students 300 students, inc 30 international students.

COPENHAGEN (KØBENHAVN)

Danish capital based on Zealand island at the east of the country, connected to Jutland and Sweden by Oresund Bridge. Characterised by large number of parks and gardens (the most famous being the Tivoli Gardens) and mixture of architectural styles from the medieval old town to a number of new developments, with baroque churches and 18th century town houses in between.

🎼 Musical life

Brand new concert hall opening in 2009 to house DR Radiosymfoniorkest, currently in the DR/ Copenhagen Concert Hall along with the broadcaster's other music ensembles (choir, chamber orchestra, big band). Several other venues: dramatic waterfront opera house with main stage and studio theatre puts on range of opera, plus children's shows and concerts; also experimental music theatre at Musikteater Plex. Tivoli Concert Hall puts on concerts and stage events. The Queen's Hall is a medium-sized concert hall with its own chamber ensemble at the Royal Library's Black Diamond building; smaller is Rundetaarn which stages range of recitals and chamber music from various artists. Copenhagen Philharmonic (Sjællands Symfoniorkester) performs at various venues, including those mentioned. Athelas Sinfonietta a chamber orchestra concentrating on contemporary music. City has a strong jazz tradition.

🏛 Other cultural information

National Museum and National Gallery both in the city. Modern art in particular at Louisiana museum of modern art; Ny Carlsberg Glyptolek, which houses varied collection of philanthropist Carl Jacobsen; Ordrupgaard Museum.

🎭 Festivals and events

City's Golden Days festival, which promotes its cultural activity, includes diverse musical performances; annual jazz festival in Jul.

ℹ Tourist information

www.visitcopenhagen.com; touristinfo@woco.dk; tel: +45 7022 2442

DET KONGELIGE DANSKE MUSIKKONSERVATORIUM

Rosennoernsalle 22, DK-1970 Fredericksberg.
t: +45 7226 7226 *f:* +45 7226 7272
e: dkdm@dkdm.dk *w:* www.dkdm.dk
Courses Bachelors and masters programmes available in 9 departments: strings; woodwind and harp; brass, percussion, orchestral conducting; singing and choral direction; piano, guitar, accordion; church and consort music; educational

theory and aural studies; composition/theory; recording. Also 3 year soloist programme at Opera Academy. New joint study programme, 'Nominem' (Nordic Master in Early Music). *Application requirements* Entrance exam; details and contents of exam available on website. Academy may take into account possibilities for appropriate combination of instruments/voices for ensembles. *Application deadline* 1 Mar for Erasmus/Nordplus applications (through home institution); 15 Feb for Nominem course. *Language requirements* Most classes in Danish; whether courses offered in English is at teacher's discretion. All students expected to have some knowledge of English. Danish language course available through DKDM. *Accommodation* Academy unable to provide housing; 'Jacob Gades Fond' offers housing for music students (see academy website for fund's contact details, and for details of other housing organisations).

RYTMISK MUSIKKONSERVATORIUM

Leo Mathisens Vej 1, Holmen, DK-1437 København K.
t: +45 32 68 67 00 *f:* +45 32 68 67 66
e: aah@rmk.dk *w:* www.rmc.dk
Contact Aage Hagen, head of international relations. *Courses* Government funded institution of higher music education offering degree programmes in contemporary music (eg pop, jazz etc). *Term dates* 2 semesters, Aug-Dec & Jan-Jun. *Application deadline* 1 Dec. *Fees* None. *Scholarships* None. *No of students* 196 students.

ESBJERG

Small, relatively modern city (development began in late 19th century) on the west coast of Denmark's Jutland peninsula. Location makes it good for outdoor activities.

🎼 Musical life

Musikhuset Esbjerg is the city's main venue, with 2 auditoriums (one for chamber performances), staging all music genres.

ℹ Tourist information

www.visitesbjerg.dk; kls@visitesbjerg.dk; tel: +45 76136101

VMK - ACADEMY OF MUSIC AND MUSIC COMMUNICATION

Kirkegade 61, DK-6700 Esbjerg.
t: +45 76 10 43 00 *f:* +45 76 10 43 10
e: info@vmk.dk *w:* www.vmk.dk
Contact Jesper Asp, international co-ord. *Courses* Courses in ensemble music (rhythmic or classical), music communication, church music, electronic music. *Application requirements* Entry exam, application form and CD. *Term dates* Aug-Jun. *Application deadline* Previous Dec. *Fees* Amount depends on nationality. *Scholarships* None. *Exchange details* Several exchange partner institutions. *Language requirements* Danish or English. *Music facilities* Concert hall, music library, recording studio, rehearsal rooms etc. All-Steinway academy. *Accommodation* Student housing guaranteed. *No of students* 110 students in total.

ODENSE

Island-based city in the east of Denmark, one of the oldest in the country and birthplace of Hans Christian Andersen.

♪ Musical life

Odense Symfoniorkester plays a full season of concerts at its home, the Odense Koncerthus.

⏛ Other cultural information

Hans Christian Andersen commemorated with a museum and an exhibition at his childhood home. Art galleries include Kunsthallen Brandts has changing exhibitions focusing on contemporary Danish and international art; Funen Art Museum has a permanent collection of Danish art from 18th century on

🦜 Festivals and events

Main classical festival is Musikhøst (Music Harvest), contemporary music festival at end of Nov. City is venue for Carl Nielsen competitions (violin, clarinet, flute in rotation). Hans Christian Andersen festival in summer; also film and blues festivals.

i Tourist information

www.visitodense.com; otb@visitodense.com; tel: +45 63 75 75 20

DET FYNSKE MUSIKKONSERVATORIUM

Islandsgade 2, DK-5000 Odense C.
t: +45 6611 0663 *f:* +45 6617 7763 *e:* dfm@adm.dfm.dk *w:* www.dfm.dk
Courses Bachelor degree in classical/contemporary music or jazz or folk music, 3-year course including main specialism, ensemble playing and general subjects (eg ear training, piano playing, theory, music history, computer technology). MA in classical/contemporary music or jazz or folk music, 2-year course qualifying students for professional career. Advance postgrad diploma, special additional 2-year course for exceptional students. *Application requirements* Entrance exam (see website for full requirements and set audition items); MA students must have BA degree and recommendation; advanced postgrad diploma students need MA, plus entrance exam. International students accepted as regular students, as exchange students or as guest students with Danish government grant. *Application deadline* 1 Dec (1 Feb for advanced postgrad diploma). *Fees* None for EU/EEA nationals. *Accommodation* Furnished accommodation in hall of residence available for all exchange students. Information for other students at www.studiebyen.odense.dk *No of students* 150 students

MUSIC FESTIVALS

Aalborg Opera Festival Godthåbsgade 8, DK-9400 Nørresundby. *t:* +45 9931 4166 *e:* gft-kultur@aalborg.dk *w:* www.aalborgoperafestival.dk

Aarhus Festival Officersbygningen, Vester Alle 3, DK-8000 Aarhus C. *t:* +45 87 30 83 00 *f:* +45 87 308 319 *w:* www.aarhusfestival.com *Contact* Malco Oliveros, production manager & artistic adviser. Annual festival, largest single collection of cultural events in Scandinavia. Theatre, cabaret, opera, ballet and dance, classical and new music, rock, jazz and folk music. Exhibitions, film and media, sports, symposia, seminars and events for children.

Music Harvest Festival Det Fynske Musikkonservatorium, Islandsgade 2, DK-5000 Odense. *t:* +45 66 110663 *f:* +45 66 177763 *e:* musikhost@adm.dfm.dk *w:* www.musikhost.dk Annual. Held in Odense, concerts and seminars on contemporary music.

Selsø Summer Concerts Langs Hegnet 39, DK-2800 Lyngby. *t:* +45 45 930778, also fax *e:* koncert@flutist.dk *w:* www.flutist.dk *Contact* Mogens Friis, artistic director. Annual. Classical music festival.

Soro International Music Festival Sokovbakkerne 12, DK-440 Kalundborg. *t:* +45 51 36 13 22 *w:* www.soroe-musik.suite.dk

Susaa Festival Skovmarksvej 52, Vetterslev, DK-4100 Ringsted. *t:* +45 57 649164 *w:* www.susaafestival.dk *Contact* Anne Kristine Smith, director; Per Dybro Sörensen, artistic director; Hans-Henrik Nordström, artistic director. Works by Danish composers, including world premieres. Held at Kulturcentret Grönnegade, Nästved.

FINLAND

HELSINKI

Finland's capital, located on the Baltic coast. Although dating back to mid 16th century, biggest developments came in second half of 19th century and post-World War II. City's architecture a mixture of neo-classical and art nouveau styles; there are many distinctive buildings, either civic (such as art nouveau railway station) or religious (Helsinki cathedral, or the Uspenski orthodox cathedral). Coastal location an added attraction: visitors can take trips to the archipelago's various islands, for instance, not to mention the ferry services to Estonia and Sweden.

♪ Musical life

Finlandia Hall, with its marble exterior also a distinctive building, in different style; is the home of the Helsinki Philharmonic Orchestra, but receives visits from other orchestras such as the Finnish Radio Symphony Orchestra, a group that plays in various venues. Kulttuuritalo one such place, a flexible mixed repertoire venue. Good choice of opera: as well as Helsinki City Opera and other small companies, the Finnish national company based in the city. New venue, Helsinki Music Centre, under construction now and will be more focused on classical music. Neighbouring districts of Espoo and Vantaa also have thriving music scenes.

Other cultural information

Good collection of museums and galleries, covering all periods of art and city's history; the Design Museum shows off Finland's strong tradition in this field. Children have their own cultural venue, Annantalo Arts Centre.

Festivals and events

Helsinki Festival runs for a fortnight in Aug, featuring classical, popular and world music. Musica Nova (Feb) has a more eclectic musical outlook, taking in various styles of modern music at venues across the city. More traditional range of classical music at Avanti! Festival in Jun. Again, children well served with several theatre, dance and arts festivals at different points in the year.

ⓘ Tourist information

www.visithelsinki.fi; tourist.info@hel.fi; tel: +358 9 3101 3300

HELSINGIN KONSERVATORIO (HELSINKI CONSERVATORY OF MUSIC)

Ruolahdentori 6, FI-00180 Helsinki.
t: +358 9 5860 580 f: +358 9 5860 5868
e: konservatorio@konservatorio.fi w: www.konservatorio.fi
Courses Vocational (post secondary school) qualifications in music for students aiming to become musicians. Curriculum includes instrumental tuition, solfege, theory of music, orchestral/chamber music/choral studies, conducting. Term dates Mid Aug-end May. Application deadline Mid Mar. Fees None. Music facilities Purpose-built facilities include 520-seat concert hall, chamber music hall, 85 classrooms.

SIBELIUS-AKATEMIA

PO Box 86, FIN-00251 Helsinki.
t: +358 20 753 90; +358 20 753 9400 (international academic affairs) f: +358 20 753 9600 e: info@siba.fi; leena.veijonsuo@siba.fi
w: www.siba.fi
Contact Leena Veijonsuo, contact for international enquiries Courses Degree programmes in church music, composition and theory, folk music, jazz, orchestral and choral conducting, music education, music technology, instrumental performance, vocal music; also degree in arts management. See website for full details. Application requirements Various requirements, depending on course; see website for full details. Term dates Sep-Dec (first semester); Jan-May (second semester) Application deadline Mar 2009 to be confirmed; see website. Fees No tuition fee; EUR 80 Student Union fee only. Exchange details Approx 90 partner institutions. No of students 1500 students.

LAHTI

Lakeside city, though not especially picturesque, with a population of around 100,000.

♪ Musical life

Highly respected Lahti Symphony Orchestra based at the relatively new (completed 2000) 1250-seat Sibelius Hall; also performs for Lahti opera chamber orchestra drawn from the main orchestra also performs there, as do guest artists and occasional non-classical performers.

Other cultural information

Lahti Art and Poster museum has substantial collection of Finnish and international graphic art (for which country is renowned). One institution with musical connection is Finnish Military Music Museum; Ski Museum is a more unusual exhibition. City Theatre is modern designed building with wide range of shows and spectacles.

Festivals and events

Sibelius festival, organised by Lahti Symphony Orchestra, focuses on the composer. Major organ festival in Aug.

Tourist information

www.lahtiguide.fi; tel: +358 20 7281 750

LAHDEN AMMATTIKORKEAKOULU (LAHTI UNIVERSITY OF APPLIED SCIENCES)

Faculty of Music, Svinhufvudinkatu 6 F-G, FIN-15110 Lahti.
t: +358 3828 2996; +358 3828 2995 (international affairs) f: +358 3828 2998
e: music@lamk.fi; w: www.lamk.fi
Contact Marjo Leppä, international co-ord. Courses Professional higher education degree equivalent to a bachelors degree in music performance. Specialisation fields: orchestral instrument (includes principal instrument, orchestra, chamber music, repertoire and literature studies, analysis, orchestral repertoire); voice (voice, secondary instrument - piano, choir and ensemble, lied, basics of acting, repertory and literature studies, analysis); piano (principal study, chamber music/accompaniment, repertory and literature studies, analysis, lied). Application requirements Entrance exam (audition, written theory/solfege/general knowledge test, interview and English language test). Appropriate school-leaving certificate (Finnish, International/European Baccalaureate, or national qualification) and required level of musical ability. Applicants without formal qualifications but with exceptional level of musical ability may be accepted. Term dates 31 Aug-31 May. Application deadline Appiication period end Mar-early Apr. Fees Free tuition; students meet living expenses and cost of educational material. Scholarships None. Exchange details Erasmus and Nordplus exchange programmes. Language requirements Good English language skills (written and spoken). Music facilities New building built especially for music studies. 1 level of rehearsal rooms available for students any time of day. Faculty also has a small chamber music hall and rehearsal theatre. Accommodation Most used accommodation service is Oppilastalot, www.oppilastalo.fi/ No of students Approx 200 students in faculty

TURKU

Old port city (there are regular boats to Stockholm) in south west Finland, originally the capital until Helsinki took over in the 19th century. Home to Finland's oldest university, and still a major educational centre with around 35,000 students in higher education. Nominated European City of Culture for 2011.

Musical life

Turku Philharmonic Orchestra based at its own concert hall (performances from visiting groups too); also gives concerts in Turku Castle and occasionally cathedral. Other city buildings also host regular concerts: Wäinö Aaltonen Museum (changing exhibitions) and the Sibelius museum (charts composer's life and work; there is also display of musical instruments); Brinkkala Mansion cultural centre has a regular concert series.

Other cultural information

As well as those mentioned, city has museums of history and archaeology, as well as modern art. Renovated castle puts on exhibitions alongside museum and restored rooms.

Festivals and events

Classical music festival in Aug. Various festival events (eg jazz, chamber music) in the archipelago surrounding the city.

Tourist information

www.turku.fi; tel: +358 2 262 7444

TURUN AMMATTIKORKEAKOULU TAIDEAKATEMIA (ARTS ACADEMY AT TURKU UNIVERSITY OF APPLIED SCIENCES)

Linnankatu 54-60, FIN-20100 Turku.
t: +358 2 263 350; +358 10 553 5225 (international relations) f: +358 2 2633 5200; +358 1055 35 202 (international relations)
e: antonella.storti@turkuamk.fi w: www. taideakatemia.turkuamk.fi

EUROPE

Courses Courses in instrumental, vocal, orchestral and chamber music, opera, lied, music theory and history. *Application requirements* Upper secondary education with appropriate acceptable qualification. Also audition, including performance and music theory test. *Term dates* 1 Sep-18 Dec (autumn term); 4 Jan-31 May (spring term). *Application deadline* 1 Apr. *Fees* None. *Scholarships* None. *Exchange details* UK exchange partners: Trinity College of Music, Royal Scottish Academy of Music & Drama, Royal Northern College of Music, Leeds College of Art & Design, Falmouth College of Arts, Robert Gordon University, Aberdeen; also partnerships with 41 other European institutions. *No of students* 168 students, inc 8 from overseas.

TURUN KONSERVATORIO
Linnankatu 60, FIN-20100 Turku.
t: +358 2 250 7600 *f:* +358 2 250 7645
e: kanslia@turunkonservatorio.fi *w:* www.turun konservatorio.fi

MUSIC FESTIVALS

April Jazz Espoo Ahertajantie 6 B, FIN-02100 Espoo. *t:* +358 9 455 0003 *f:* +358 9 465172 *e:* april.jazz@kolumbus.fi International jazz festival.

Avanti! Summer Sounds Tallberginkatu 1 B 80, FIN-00180 Helsinki. *t:* +358 9 694 0091 *f:* +358 9694 2208 *e:* avanti@avantimusic.fi *w:* www. avantimusic.fi *Contact* Hannele Markkula, chief executive. Orchestral and chamber music concerts, baroque and contemporary music.

Chamber Music by Lake Tuusula PO Box 41, FIN-04401 Jarvenpaa. *t:* +358 50 302 1669 *f:* +358 9 27 19 2835 *e:* info@tuusulanjarvifestival.fi *w:* www. tuusulanjarvifestival.fi *Contact* Pekka Kuusisto, artistic director. Chamber music in the historical homes of renowned Finnish artists such as Jean Sibelius, Eero Järnefelt and Joonas Kokkonen. The violinist Pekka Kuusisto has compiled a programme in which he will be joined by a host of elite musicians in an intimate and communicative atmosphere.

Crusell Week Uudenkaupungin Kultuuritoimisto, Rauhankatu 10, FIN-23500 Uusikaupunki. *t:* +358 2 8451 5302 *f:* +358 2 8451 5442 *e:* rauno. melos@uusikaupunki.fi *w:* www.crusell.fi *Contact* Rauno Melos. Woodwind music festival.

Finland Festivals Temppelikatu 3-5 A 5, FIN-00100 Helsinki. *t:* +358 9 612 6760 *f:* +358 9 612 67610 *e:* info@festivals.fi *w:* www.festivals. fi *Contact* Kai Amberla, executive director; Minna Salonranta, communication assistant. Various music festivals, including opera, chamber, jazz, rock, dance/theatre, folk music and general music; also visual art.

Gergiev Festival *t:* +358 15 162 076 *f:* +358 15 362 757 *e:* festival@mikkelinmusiikkijuhlat.fi *w:* www.mikkelinmusiikkijuhlat.fi Valery Gergiev and the Orchestra of the Mariinsky Theatre, plus guests.

Helsinki Festival Glass Palace, Mannerheimintie 22-24, FIN-00100 Helsinki. *t:* +358 9 6126 5100 *f:* +358 9 6126 5161 *e:* info@helsinkifestival.fi *w:* www.helsinkifestival.fi *Contact* Risto Nieminen, director. Annual arts festival featuring classical, popular and world music, dance, theatre, visual arts, cinema and city events.

Hetta Music Event Virastotalo, FIN-99300 Enontekio. *t:* +358 1 655 6278 *f:* +358 1 655 6229 *e:* hetan.musiikkipaivat@enontekio.fi *w:* www. hetanmusiikkipaivat.fi Sacred, chamber and choral music.

Imatra Big Band Festival Heikinkatu 1, FIN-55100 Imatra. *t:* +358 20 7479 405 *f:* +358 20 7479 401 *w:* www.ibbf.fi Jazz, blues, funk, world music, rock.

Jaarvenpaa Sibelius Festival PO Box 41, FIN-04401 Jarvenpaa. *t:* +358 9 2719 2201 *f:* +358 9 2719 2727 *e:* juhani.airas@jarvenpaa.fi *w:* www. sibeliuslaulukilpailu.fi

Kaustinen Folk Music Festival PO Box 24, FIN-69601 Kaustinen. *t:* +358 207 2911 *f:* +358 207 291200 *e:* folk.art@kaustinen.fi *w:* www.kaustinen. net *Contact* Jyrki Heiskanen, programme director. Largest annual folk music and dance festival in the Nordic countries. Folk, world, traditional, ethnic, folk-dance.

Klemetti Summer Festival Koulutie 5, FIN-35300 Orivesi. *t:* +358 207 511 550 *f:* +358 207 511 512 *e:* klemettiopisto@kvs.fi *w:* www.klemettiopisto. fi Choral, symphonic, chamber music.

Korsholm Music Festival Frilundintie 2, FIN-65610 Mustasaari. *t:* +358 6 322 2390 *f:* +358 6 322 2393 *w:* www.korsholmmusicfestival.fi *Contact* Dmitri Slobodeniouk, artistic director; Jukka Mäkelaä, executive director. Chamber music with Nordic features.

Kuhmo Chamber Music Festival Torikatu 39, FIN-88900 Kuhmo. *t:* +358 8 652 0936 *f:* +358 8 652

1961 e: kuhmo.festival@kuhmofestival.fi w: www. kuhmofestival.fi Contact Vladimir Mendelssohn, artistic dir. Annual. Chamber music, with over 150 visiting artists.

Lahti Organ Festival Aleksanterinkatu 16, FIN-15140 Lahti. t: +358 3 877230 f: +358 3 877 2320 e: urkuviikko@lahtiorgan.fi w: www. lahtiorgan.fi

Lieksa Brass Week Koski-Jaakonkatu 4, FIN-81700 Lieksa. t: +358 13 6889 4147 f: +358 16 689 4915 e: brass.week@lieksa.fi w: www. lieksabrass.com Brass music festival, master courses. Lieksa International Trumpet Competition.

Musica nova Helsinki c/o The Helsinki Festival, Mannerheimintie 22-24, FIN-00100 Helsinki. t: +358 9 6126 5100 f: +358 9 6126 5161 e: musicanova@musicanova.fi w: www.musicanova. fi Contact Johan Tallgren, artistic dir. Annual international festival of contemporary music. Co-ordinated by Helsinki Festival.

Naantali Music Festival Henrikinkatu 1, PO Box 46, FIN-21101 Naantali. t: +358 2 434 5363 f: +358 2 434 5425 e: info@ naantalinmusiikkijuhlat.fi w: www.naantalimusic. com Contact Tina Tunturi, executive director; Arto Noras, artistic director. Chamber music, orchestras, recitals, masterclasses.

Northern Accordion, Folk Music and Folk Dance Festival Tornio Cultural Office, Keskikatu 22, FIN-95400 Tornio. t: +358 1 643 2424 f: +358 1 643 2612 e: helena.junes@tornio.fi Contact Helena June.

Pori Jazz Festival Pohjoisranta 11 D, FIN-28100 Pori. t: +358 2 626 2200 f: +358 2 626 2225 e: festival@porijazz.fi w: www.porijazz.fi Annual. International jazz festival. Major open-air concerts in Kirjurinluoto concert park by the Kokemaki river, plus jam sessions in more intimate settings.

Riihimaki Summer Concerts Valtakatu 10, FIN-11130 Riihimaki. t: +358 20 758 5040 f: +358 1 973 2626 e: riihimaen.kesakonsertit@riihimaki. fi w: www.riihimaenkesakonsertit.fi Recitals and chamber music.

Sata Hame soi International Accordion Festival PO Box 33, FIN-39501 Ikaalinen. t: +358 3 440 0224 f: +358 3 4501 264 e: juhlat@satahamesoi. fi w: www.satahamesoi.fi Contact Kimmo Mattila, artistic director; Sirpa Sippola, general director. Annual. Focus on traditional Finnish accordion music; programme features accordion and related

instruments in various settings from concert halls to outdoor events. Also international light and classical music.

Savonlinna Opera Festival Olavinkatu 27, FIN-57130 Savonlinna. t: +358 15 476750 f: +358 15 4767540 e: info@operafestival.fi w: www. operafestival.fi Contact Jan Hultin, general director; Jari Hämäläinen, artistic director. Annual. Opera, recitals, concerts.

Tampere Biennale Tullikamarinaukio aukio 2, FIN-33100 Tampere. t: +358 50 405 5225 f: +358 3 223 0121 e: music@tampere.fi w: www.tampere.fi/ biennale Contact Minnakaisa Kuivalainen. Biennial. 5-day contemporary classical music festival, mainly Finnish music.

Tampere Jazz Happening Tullikamarin aukio 2, FIN-33100 Tampere. t: +358 50 530 8777 f: +358 3 223 0121 e: music@tampere.fi w: www. tampere.fi/jazz Contact Juhamatti Kauppinen Festival of modern jazz, improvised music and related genres.

Tampere Vocal Music Festival Tullikamarin aukio 2, FIN-33100 Tampere. t: +358 3 5656 6172 f: +358 3 223 0121 e: music@tampere.fi w: www. tampere.fi/vocal Contact Eija Koivusalo, producer; Minnakaisa Kuivalainen, executive director. Biennial. Festival includes international chorus review, a contest for vocal ensembles; training for choir conductors and singers; concerts in choral and vocal ensemble music, vocal world music.

Turku Music Festival Uudenmaankatu 1, FIN-20500 Turku. t: +358 2 251 1162 f: +358 2 231 3316 e: info@turkumusicfestival.fi w: www. turkumusicfestival.fi Annual. Orchestral, early, contemporary and chamber music.

Vantaa Baroque PO Box 10, FIN-01301 Vantaa. t: +358 9 8392 5073 f: +358 9 8392 5072 w: www.vantaanbarokki.fi Contact Håkan Wikman, artistic director. Annual.

Lahti Sibelius Festival Sibeliustalo, Ankkurikatu 7, FIN-15140 Lahti. t: +358 3 814 4460 f: +358 3 814 4451 e: sinfonialahti@lahti.fi w: www. sinfonialahti.fi Weekend of concerts centred around Sibelius.

ICELAND

REYKJAVIK

Main city in Iceland, characterised by its dramatic geographical setting, result of many thousands of years of volcanic activity. Geology plays a major part in daily life, with most domestic heating exploiting geothermal activity; residents also take advantage of naturally heated water for outdoor swimming. Today, city's nightlife has wide reputation, or even notoriety; for a country of its size it has a vibrant cultural life.

♪ Musical life

Iceland Symphony Orchestra is focus of classical music; currently gives concerts in the university cinema building (as well as numerous performances overseas), but a new hall, Tónlistarhus, is due for completion in 2009. Many orchestra members also play for Icelandic Opera, a small company with its own building.

🏛 Other cultural information

Centre for Icelandic art is main promoter of visual art, but a substantial number of independent galleries across city. Theatre also prominent — National Theatre stages shows in a range of genres, from drama to musicals; City Theatre also looks beyond presentation of plays, with concerts and discussions also on its programme.

🎭 Festivals and events

Reykjavik Arts Festival every other year in May; Dark Music Days (Feb), run by Society of Icelandic Composers, focuses on contemporary music; summer Festival of Sacred Arts includes music, but other art forms too. More sacred music, plus early music at Skálholt cathedral in the Skálholt Summer Concerts festival (about 50 km to the east of Reykjavik). Jazz festival in autumn.

ℹ Tourist information

www.visitreykjavik.is; info@visitreykjavik.is; tel: +354 590 1550

TONLISTARSKOLINN I REYKJAVIK (REYKJAVIK COLLEGE OF MUSIC)

Skipholt 33, IS-105 Reykjavik.
t: +353 553 0625 f: +353 553 9240 e: tono@tono.is w: www.tono.is

LISTAHASKOLI ISLANDS (ICELAND ACADEMY OF THE ARTS)

Solvholsgata 13, IS-101 Reykjavik.
t: +354 552 4000; +354 545 2205 (international co-ordinator) f: +354 562 3629 e: lhi@lhi.is; alma@lhi.is w: www.lhi.is
Contact Alma Ragnasdottir, international co-ordinator Courses BMus degrees in instrumental/vocal performance (piano, strings/winds, voice, other); Diploma in instrumental/vocal performance; BA degrees in musicology, music education, composition (general, new media, film music, stage music, production). Exchange students should contact international co-ordinator for further information. Application requirements Secondary school exam (Icelandic 'studentsprof') or equivalent. Applicants who do not meet this general requirement must demonstrate maturity and knowledge which can be evaluated as equivalent to the missing education (detailed explanation to be enclosed with application form). Term dates Late Aug-mid Dec (autumn semester); early Jan-early May (spring semester). Application deadline 15 Apr (for autumn semester/whole year); 15 Oct (for spring semester). Fees ISK 142.5 per semester (ISK 285 for whole year). Scholarships Via LLP Socrates or Nordplus for students within those organisations. Exchange details Active within LLP Socrates and Nordplus networks in music, dance, design, architecture and fine arts. Member of AEC; also member of ELIA (art), Cumulus (design), EAAE (architecture). No of students 74 students in dept of music, of whom 4 from overseas; 376 academy students in total.

MUSIC FESTIVALS

Dark Music Days Society of Icelandic Composers, Lauf svegi 4, IS-101 Reykjavik. t: +354 5 524 972 f: +354 5 562 6273 w: www.listir.is Annual. Contemporary music.

Festival of Sacred Arts Hallgrimskirkja Skolavorduholt, IS-101 Reykjavik. t: +354 510 1000 f: +354 510 1010 e: kirkjulistahatid@kirkjan.is w: www.kirkjan.is Biennial festival focusing on the spiritual in the arts.

Reykjavik Arts Festival Laekjargata 3b, PO Box 88, IS-121 Reykjavik. t: +354 5 612 444 f: +354 5 622 350 w: www.artfest.is Contact Hrefna Haraldsdottir, artistic director. Multi-arts festival.

Skalholt Summer Concerts Laufasvegur 4, IS-101 Reykjavik. t: +354 866 4600 e: siha@ismennt.is w: www.sumartonleikar.is Contact Sigurður Halldórsson, director. Annual. Baroque and contemporary sacred music.

BERGEN

City on North Sea coast, encompassed by mountains; second largest in the country with a population of a quarter of a million. Its national importance dates back to medieval period when it was a key port as part of the Hanseatic League; now its historic harbourside is on Unesco world heritage list. Numerous wooden buildings are characteristic of the city (the city has suffered from fires throughout its history).

♪ Musical life

City is home to one of world's oldest, and well-regarded, orchestras in the Bergen Philharmonic Orchestra (tours internationally as well). Grieghallen is home to the orchestra (the composer used to be its music director), but stages other music too, not least opera. USF Verftet a more visual performing arts venue, but music performed there too. BIT20 Ensemble is a small, contemporary music ensemble performing in the city and on tour. Grieg celebrated in a museum dedicated to him at Troldhaugen; museum also contains a small recital room, the Troldsalen.

Other cultural information

City is home to a large number of museums and attractions. Hanseatic Museum charts city's importance at the time; city's role during World War II explained at Theta Museum; others focus on local arts and crafts (eg Horda Museum), history of education (Bergen School Museum). Art galleries on so-called 'Art Gallery Street'.

Festivals and events

Bergen International Festival (May-Jun) covers classical music plus literature, dance, theatre, opera and visual arts, focusing on work from Nordic and Baltic countries. Jazz festival in May also.

i Tourist information

www.visitbergen.com; info@visitbergen.com; tel: +47 55 55 20 00

GRIEGAKADEMIET, INSTITUTT FOR MUSIKK

Lars Hillesgate 3, N-5015 Bergen.
t: +47 55 58 69 50 *f:* +47 55 58 69 60
e: grieg@hffa.uib.no; bjorn.halvorsen@grieg.
uib.no *w:* www.grieg.uib.no
Contact Bjorn Halvorsen, enquiries. *Courses* Bachelor programmes in performance, composition and pedagogy/music education; master's programmes in performance or composition, ethnomusicology, music therapy. Also offers 1-year international diploma in performance or composition (for international students), and Nominem (Nordic Master in Early Music). *Application requirements* Norwegian language proficiency test required (exchange students exempt). Applicants assessed on musical and academic ability, inc written aural skills and music theory test; requirements vary, contact academy for further details. *Term dates* Mid Aug -end Jun. *Application deadline* 15 Dec for performance or composition courses; 1 Jun for ethnomusicology or music therapy courses. *Fees* No tuition fees. *No of students* Approx 160.

OSLO

Norwegian capital, towards the southern tip of the country and at the northern end of a long bay (the Oslofjord). Once known as Kristiania (Oslo only adopted definitively in early 20th century), city dates back to middle ages, but began developing more importance in early 19th century when Swedish ownership ended – the large Royal Palace dates from this time. Norway's main centre for higher education with many institutions covering various disciplines. Benefits from a location close to forests and hills, so ideal for outdoor activities.

♪ Musical life

City has a new opera house for its national opera and ballet companies; has its own house orchestra too, which gives a few concerts in its own right. As well as stage performances, visiting soloists and orchestras come to perform. Several other orchestral groups based in Oslo: Oslo Philharmonic (based at Oslo Philharmonic Hall) the best known; Norwegian Radio Orchestra and Norwegian Chamber Orchestra play at university's concert hall.

Other cultural information

National Gallery is country's main art gallery, with a diverse range of artworks. Institutions devoted to Viking history (eg Viking Ship Museum) as well as other aspects of Norwegian culture (Norwegian Museum of Cultural History, Norwegian Folk Museum) and activity (Ski Museum). City's new House of Literature – combination of bookshop, place for discussion, writers' workshops and accommodation for visiting writers.

Festivals and events

Well served for festivals. Apart from city's summer festival featuring a range of entertainment in main square and other venues, there is an international festival of church music in Mar; chamber music festival and jazz festival in Aug; contemporary music festival in Sep (the Ultima festival); world music festival in Oct. Also biennial Queen Sonja Music Competition (Aug).

Tourist information

www.visitoslo.com; info@visitoslo.com; tel: +47 815 30 555

BARRATT DUE MUSIKKINSTITUUT

Postboks 5344 Majorstuen, N-0304 Oslo.
t: +47 22 06 86 86 e: post@bdm.no w: www.barrattdue.no
Courses 4-year BA (240 credits) in music performance; final year students specialise in either performance or instrumental/voice tuition with practical teacher training. Masters course offered in co-operation of Norwegian Academy of Music. Application deadline 5 Jan, bachelors; 15 Dec, masters. Auditions early Mar for bachelors, mid Feb for masters.

NORGESMUSIKKHØLE (NORWEGIAN ACADEMY OF MUSIC)

PO Box 5190 Majorstua, NO-0302 Oslo.
t: +47 23 36 70 00 f: +47 23 36 70 01
e: mh@nmh.no w: www.nmh.no
Contact Knut Myhre (international enquiries). Courses 4-year undergrad courses in music performance, music education, church music, composition, individual programme. Postgrad courses: advanced studies for solo instrumentalists or chamber music ensembles, advanced studies in composition; masters degrees in performance, church music, music theory, conducting, music education, music therapy. More details on postgrad programmes available on the website. Application requirements A level qualification or equivalent, plus audition (see website for details of repertoire and other information). Term dates End Aug-end Jun. Application deadline 15 Dec. Fees None. Exchange details Affiliated to Socrates and Nordtran. Language requirements Classroom tuition in Norwegian; individual tuition may be in another language, mostly English. Music facilities Approx

300 concerts organised each year. Applicants must show proficiency in Norwegian for admission. Accommodation No student housing facilities. For more information on accommodation, see www.sio.no No of students 475 students in total.

STAVANGER

Norwegian port city on south west coast; location means it is closely associated with oil industry (previously had been a fishing town), but it retains a certain amount of charm, particularly in the Old Town. City used by visitors as a base for skiing, hiking and mountain sports.

Musical life

Stavanger Symfoniorkester at the Bjergsted Music Park and Konserthus; building for new 2-hall concert hall for 2011 is under way.

Other cultural information

Visiting exhibitions at the Rogaland Museum of Fine Arts, a combination of Norwegian and international artists. Its nomination as one of the European Cities of Culture in 2008 has left a legacy in the number of cultural initiatives

Festivals and events

Main classical music festival is the International Chamber Music Festival (Aug); there is also an annual jazz festival (May)

Tourist information

www.regionstavanger.com; info@regionstavanger.com; tel: +47 51 85 92 00

UNIVERSITY OF STAVANGER

Dept of Music and Dance, Postbox 8002, N-4036 Stavanger.
t: +47 51 83 40 00/29 f: +47 51 83 40 50
e: hilde.skare@uis.no w: www.uis.no
Contact Jens T Larsen, head of dept; Hilde Skare, head of office/international co-ord. Courses Bachelor in music performance (classical or jazz), master in music performance (classical), extension courses in music performance; also music production & recording. Application requirements Entrance exam/audition; completed BA in music, plus entrance exam/audition for masters courses. Special entrance requirements for each programme. Term dates Mid Aug-mid Jun. Application deadline 1 Mar

(international students). *Fees* Approx EUR 87 per semester. *Scholarships* None. *Exchange details* Exchanges arranged through Erasmus, Nordplus/ Espansiva. *Language requirements* Norwegian required for bachelors programme; all others, Norwegian or English. *Music facilities* Modern buildings with concert halls located in Bjergsted Music Park; good facilities for teaching and practice; recording studios. *Accommodation* Assistance available through university student welfare organisation. *No of students* 200 students in total, including 50 from overseas.

TROMSØ

Small northern Norwegian city (around 60,000 people), based largely on an island just off the North Sea coast a substantial distance north of arctic circle (city linked to mainland by bridge). Natural surroundings are spectacular, and its northerly location means it is dark for most of the day during deepest winter months and light all day during summer. However, also means that its geographically isolated, with nearest station 4 hours away; access possible by road, air or boat. Despite size and location, city has a vibrant nightlife.

♪ Musical life

There is a professional orchestra, Tromsø Symphony Orchestra, though it is currently small in size, tending to focus on chamber music and small-scale orchestral work. Main cultural venue is the Kulturhuset, with music and a varied range of other performances.

🏛 Other cultural information

Main sights are city's 2 cathedrals, the old wooden Tromsø cathedral and the 1960s built Arctic cathedral. A handful of museums and galleries.

🦎 Festivals and events

Nordlysfestivalen (Northern Lights Festival – the city is perfectly placed for seeing the aurora borealis display), a Jan music festival featuring classical and folk performances from local and visiting artists. Annual film festival, also Jan, attracts a large audience.

ℹ Tourist information

www.destinasjontromso.no; info@visittromso.no; tel: +47 77 61 00 00

MUSIC CONSERVATORY OF TROMSØ UNIVERSITY COLLEGE
Krognessveien 33, N-9293 Tromsø.
t: +47 77 66 03 04 *f:* +47 77 61 88 99
e: kunst@hitos.no *w:* www.hitos.no

MUSIC FESTIVALS

Arts Festival of North Norway PO Box 294, N-9489 Harstad. *t:* +47 77 041230 *f:* +47 77 067363 *e:* firmapost@festspillnn.no *w:* www. festspillnn.no Concerts, theatre, dance, art exhibitions, literature and film, seminars, children's festival and youth festival.

Bergen International Festival PO Box 183 Sentrum, N-5804 Bergen. *t:* +47 55 210630 *f:* +47 55 210640 *e:* info@fib.no *w:* www.fib.no *Contact* Per Boye Hansend, festival director; Marit Eikemo, information manager. Nordic impulses in music theatre, opera, dance, literature and visual art. Approximately 180 events in more than 14 venues in and around Bergen.

Forde Folk Music Festival PO Box 395, Fordehuset, Angedalsvn 5, N-6801 Forde. *t:* +47 57 721940 *f:* +47 57 721941 *e:* info@ fordefestival.no *w:* www.fordefestival.no *Contact* Hilde Bjørkum, festival director. Traditional and world music from all over the world. Concerts, workshops, exhibitions, children's events. Approx 80 events, 250 artists, 30,000 visits each year.

Ilios Festival for Contemporary Music NY Musikk, Box 244, N-9483 Harstad. *t:* +47 913 94 673 *e:* post@ilios.no *w:* www.ilios.no

International Chamber Music Festival, Stavanger Sandviga 27, N-4007 Stavanger. *t:* +47 51 846670 *f:* +47 51 846650 *e:* mail@icmf.no *w:* www.icmf. no *Contact* Emilie Labarchède, managing director; The Grieg Trio, artistic directors. Annual.

Lofoten Internasjonale Kammermusikkfest Vaaganveien 30, NO-8310 Kabelvag. *e:* knut@ lofotenfestival.com *w:* www.lofotenfestival.com *Contact* Knut Kirkesaether.

Nordlysfestivalen (Northern Lights Festival) Pb 966, N-9260 Tromso. *t:* +47 77 68 90 70 *e:* post@ nordlysfestivalen.no *w:* www.nordlysfestivalen.no Annual music festival.

Oslo Chamber Music Festival Grev Wedels Plass 2, N-0151 Oslo. *t:* +47 23 100730 *f:* +47 23 100731 *e:* post@oslokammusikkfestival.no *w:* www.oslokammusikkfestival.no *Contact* Arve Tellefsen, artistic director. Annual.

Oslo International Church Music Festival Konens gate 4, N-0153 Oslo. *t:* +47 22 41 81 13 *f:* +47 22 41 81 14 *e:* info@oicmf.no *w:* www. oslokirkemusikkfestival.no Annual festival bringing renowned choirse, orchestras and church musicians from Norway and abroad.

The Risor Festival of Chamber Music PO Box 304, N-4953 Risor. *t:* +47 37 153250 *f:* +47 37 151440 *e:* info@kammermusikkfest.no *w:* www. kammermusikkfest.no *Contact* Leif Ove Andsnes, Lars Anders Tomter, artistic leaders; Turid Birkeland, festival director. Annual chamber music festival.

St Olav Festival of Trondheim PO Box 2045, N-7410 Trondheim. *t:* +47 73 841450 *f:* +47 73 841451 *e:* info@olavsfestdagene.no *w:* www. olavsfestdagene.no *Contact* Per Kvistad Uddu, director. Church services, concerts, lectures, guided tours, exhibitions, activites for children, chamber music courses and early music projects. Traditional market.

Ultima Oslo Contemporary Music Festival Kongensgate 4, N-0153 Oslo. *t:* +47 22 429999 *f:* +47 22 424218 *e:* info@ultima.no *w:* www. ultima.no Annual. Contemporary music, including concerts and performances, sound-installations, multimedia concerts, films, educational arrangements and seminars.

Vestfold International Festival PO Box 500, N-3101 Tonsberg. *t:* +47 33 308850 *f:* +47 33 308859 *w:* www.vestfoldspillene.no Classical music, early music, jazz, world music, dance, theatre.

ARVIKA

Small town in south west of the country, with a population of around 15,000.

MUSIKHÖGSKOLAN INGESUND

SE-671 91 Arvika.
t: +46 570 385 00 *f:* +46 570 804 38
e: info@imh.kau.se *w:* www.imh.kau.se

GOTHENBURG (GÖTEBORG)

City on south west coast of Sweden. Historical significance in trade with Asia, and port is still busy today. Home to a number of higher education institutions, so large student population in the city.

♪ Musical life

Two main venues, the opera house and concert hall. Opera house is home to opera and ballet, with diverse repertoire (includes music theatre), and has own orchestra (who also perform concerts in the city and elsewhere). Göteborgs Symfoniker based at the concert hall, but venue has a broad programming policy, with chamber music, recitals, visiting orchestras, jazz and more.

⌂ Other cultural information

A number of museums, with a wide range of subjects covered: museums reflecting city's history as a trading port, such as East India house, and the Göteborg Maritime Centre; Museum of World Culture. Various science and industry-related places such as Volvo Museum, Radio Museum, Museum of Medical History, and Universeum science centre. Göteborg Art Hall focuses on contemporary art and visual culture

❀ Festivals and events

Free entertainment events at the annual Göteborg Culture Festival. Major film festival in Jan-Feb, short jazz festival in Aug.

ⓘ Tourist information

www.goteborg.com; turistinfo@goteborg.com; tel: +46 31 61 25 00

GÖTEBORGS UNIVERSITET HÖGSKOLAN FOR SCEN OCH MUSIC (ACADEMY OF MUSIC AND DRAMA, GOTHENBURG UNIVERSITY)

Box 210, SE-405 30 Göteborg.
t: +46 31 786 4020; +46 31 7864103

(international co-ordinator) *f:* +46 31 786 4030
e: Margareta.Hanning@hsm.gu.se *w:* www.hsm.gu.se
Contact Margareta Hanning, international co-ordinator. *Term dates* 1 Sep-20 Dec; 8 Jan-1 Jun. *Application deadline* 15 Jan; exchange students 1 Mar. *Fees* None

MALMÖ

City at southernmost tip of Sweden, linked to Denmark (Copenhagen) by the Øresund Bridge. Dates back to medieval times, and general layout of the city reflects this, although buildings are in the main from much later periods (especially 19th century onwards). Added attractions are the city's beaches; harbour area has also been recently redeveloped and is now a popular area for visitors and residents.

♪ Musical life

Opera house is base for Malmö Opera (although repertoire also includes musicals) and its orchestra; separate orchestra is Malmö Symfoniorkester at city's 1200-seat Konserthuset. Receives visiting orchestras etc, but concert hall not just for classical music.

⌂ Other cultural information

Art Museum focuses on Nordic art. Many smaller exhibitions on various topic such as toys, sport, theatre, fishing.

❀ Festivals and events

Malmö Festival (Aug) is city's main celebration featuring entertainment, culinary events etc.

ⓘ Tourist information

www.malmo.se; malmo.turism@malmo.se; tel: +46 40 34 12 00

MUSIKHÖGSKOLAN I MALMÖ (MALMO ACADEMY OF MUSIC)

Box 8203, SE-200 41 Malmo.
t: +46 40 32 54 50 *f:* +46 40 32 54 60
e: joakim.nilsson@mhm.lu.se *w:* www.mhm.lu.se
Contact Joakim Nilsson, director of international affairs *Application deadline* 15 Apr.

SWEDEN

ÖREBRO

City in southern Sweden dating back to middle ages – notable remnant is the castle, and old town contains a number of characteristic 18th and 19th century wooden houses.

♪ Musical life

There is a 700-seat concert hall in the city, with performances from the up and coming Swedish Chamber Orchestra – has a wide repertoire, with contemporary music a key focus. Group tours widely outside the city as well as running its own subscriber and open concerts.

🏛 Other cultural information

Small collection of museums and galleries.

ℹ Tourist information

www.orebrokompaniet.se; info@orebrokompaniet.se; +46 19 21 21 21

ÖREBRO UNIVERSITET MUSIKHÖGSKOLAN (OREBRO UNIVERSITY SCHOOL OF MUSIC)

Musikhogskolan vid Örebro, SE-701 82 Örebro.
t: +46 19 30 33 50 f: +46 19 30 34 85
e: karin.tornblom@musik.oru.se w: www.oru.se

STOCKHOLM

Swedish capital, located on an archipelago on the east coast of the country. Developed in importance around 700 years ago as part of wealthy north European trading cartel the Hanseatic League. Old town retains medieval layout of narrow streets. Its geographical situation means water dominates, with numerous waterways between the islands; as well as trips to the many islands in the archipelago, there are also sea connections to Finland and Baltic countries.

♪ Musical life

Several concert venues. Berwaldhallen is home of Swedish Radio Symphony Orchestra and its associated choirs; Royal Stockholm Philharmonic Orchestra based at Stockholm Concert Hall, a 3-hall venue therefore able to host everything from solo recitals to symphony concerts. More popular music events at the modern-design arts centre Kulturhuset Stockholm. Variety of opera houses: Drottningholms Slottstheater a small renovated 18th century theatre at the Royal Palace; Folkoperan another intimate venue, in contrast to the neo-classical (actually late 19th century) Kungliga Operan building and its company.

🏛 Other cultural information

Waterfron Nationalmuseum is main art collection, featuring European masters and a substantial collection of Swedish art. Also a modern art museum (Moderna Museet). Many other galleries and museums besides. Several theatres such as art nouveau Royal Dramatic Theatre. Kulturhuset's programme encompasses all kinds of art (exhibitions, films, theatre, dance, literary events etc).

🐟 Festivals and events

Early Music Festival (early Jun) in the Old Town. Berwaldhallen hosts the annual Baltic Sea Festival focusing on classical music and performers from countries surrounding the Baltic; also events at Royal Palace and Konserthuset. Stockholms Kulturfestival (Aug) is a mix of events such as open air concerts, children's events, art and photography exhibitions, film shows etc.

ℹ Tourist information

www.stockholmtown.com; info@svb.stockholm.se; +46 8 508 28 500

KUNGL MUSIKHÖGSKOLAN (ROYAL COLLEGE OF MUSIC)

Valhallavagen 105, Box 27711, SE-115 91 Stockholm.
t: +46 8 16 18 00; +46 8 16 32 00 (international co-operation) f: +46 8 664 14 24
e: info@kmh.se w: www.kmh.se
Contact Johan Falk, Anders Oman. Courses Undergrad courses in performance, composition, conducting, music education, piano tuner studies; also individually tailored courses with classical music, jazz, folk music, music from other cultures as well as music and media technology. Master's programmes: music, music therapy, music education. Application requirements Official language is Swedish, except for Nordic Master in Folk Music and Nordic Master in Jazz courses (offered in English only); for guest/exchange and postgrad students, courses can be given in English at professor's discretion. Auditions held in person in Mar. Term dates Late Aug-mid Dec; early Jan-mid Jun 2010. Application deadline 10 Jan (regular students); 15 Feb (Erasmus/guest students). Fees

Small student union fee only. *Scholarships* No institutional scholarships available for overseas students. *Exchange details* Exchange programmes arranged through Erasmus, Nordplus, Linnaeus-Palme (with certain third world institutions). *Language requirements* Official language is music, except for Nordic master in folk music and Nordic master in jazz (English only); for guest/exchange and postgrad students, courses can be given in English at professor's discretion. *Music facilities* Concert halls, computer music studios, church organs, period instruments. *Accommodation* Exchange students are usually helped with accommodations *No of students* 700.

MUSIC FESTIVALS

Confidencen Ulriksdals Slottstheater, SE-170 79 Solna. *t:* +46 8 85 70 16 *f:* +46 8 85 61 21 *e:* info@confidencen.se *w:* www.confidencen.se

Drottningholms Slottsteater Festival PO Box 15417, SE-10465 Stockholm. *t:* +46 8 556 93100 *f:* +46 8 556 93101 *e:* dst@dtm.se *w:* www.dtm. se *Contact* Per Forsstrom, general manager; Mark Tatlow, artistic director. Annual. 17th and 18th century opera and ballet, period productions.

Göteborg International Organ Academy Ebbe Lieberathsgatan 25, SE-0412 65 Göteborg. *t:* +46 31 773 5211 *f:* +46 31 773 5200 *e:* organ. academy@hsm.gu.se *w:* www.goart.gu.se/gioa *Contact* Hans Davidsson, artistic director. Biennial. Includes concerts, workshops, seminars, lectures, discussions and services. Theme for 2009: Handel, Haydn.

Gotland Organ Festival Gotlands Orgelvecka, Visby Domkyrkoförsamling, V Kyrkog 5, SE-621 56 Visby. *t:* +46 498 20 68 00 *f:* +46 468 20 68 12 *e:* thomas.fors@visbydf.se Organ, choral and harpsichord music.

International Music Week Geijerskolan, SE-684 93 Ransater. *t:* +46 552 302 50 *f:* +46 552 304 48 *e:* expedition@geijerskolan.se *w:* www. geijerskolan.se Choirs, recorders, orchestras.

ISCM World Music Days 2009 c/o ISCM Swedish Section, SE-450 46 Hunnebostrand. *t:* +46 523 91210 *f:* +46 738 210004 *e:* magnus.lemark@ glocalnet.net *w:* www.iscm.a.se *Contact* Magnues Lemark, president. Contemporary music concerts, meetings, symposium.

Nordic Music Days Nordic Composers' Council, Box 27327, SE-102 54 Stockholm. *t:* +46 76 171 56 00 *e:* info@nordicmusicdays.com *w:* www. nordicmusicdays.com *Contact* Stina Lyles, secretary general Collaborative festival of contemporary Nordic music, rotating between Denmark, Finland, Iceland, Norway and Sweden. 2009 festival in Oslo.

Osthammars Musikvecka (The Osthammar Music Festival) Box 66, S-74221 Osthammar. *t:* +46 1 738 6147 *f:* +46 731 7537 *e:* musik veckan@osthammar.se *w:* www.musikveckan.nu Folk and world music, choirs, jazz and classics to rock and salsa. Includes music workshops and family concerts.

Stockholm Early Music Festival Tångvägen 9, 1 tr, SE-126 38 Hägersten. *t:* +46 70 460 03 90 *e:* info@semf.se *w:* www.semf.se Baroque, renaissance and medieval music in Stockholm's Old Town.

Stockholm International Composer Festival Stockholm Concert Hall, PO Box 7083, S-10387 Stockholm. *t:* +46 8 786 0200 *f:* +46 8 5066 7720 *e:* info@konserthuset *w:* www.konserthuset. se

Vadstena Academy Opera Festival Bergsgatan 57, S-11231 Stockholm. *t:* +46 8 545 51 880 *f:* +46 8 545 51 887 *e:* info@vadstena-akademien. org *w:* www.vadstena-akademien.org *Contact* Nils Spangenburg, artistic leader. Annual. Rare early operas, newly commissioned works and concerts at the castle and old theatre in historic setting of Vadstena's medieval town.

Russia and the Baltic Region

Russia and the Baltic Region

Of all the places to study music, Russia probably has the most forbidding reputation. But if you have the ability, self-discipline, not to mention the thick skin, spending time at a Russian conservatoire will give you access to one of the most uncompromising music education traditions and put you in a long line among the great musicians who have passed through it. And as historical and cultural locations, Moscow and St Petersburg take some beating. The three Baltic states, though previously part of the USSR, offer something different, being to the average western eye relatively young countries (though this is, of course, far from the historical truth) which are keen to welcome visitors from overseas to observe and participate in their cultural life.

RUSSIA

The Russian system of higher music education does not easily fit with the 5-year bachelors-plus-masters scheme that is coming to the fore in Europe, with diploma courses (the undergraduate equivalent) lasting 5 years and postgrad programmes up to 3 further years. Other shorter courses are available, however – at St Petersburg, there are various 1-year non-degree programmes, particularly suitable for international students since these can be individually tailored and can start at any point in the academic year.

ESTONIA

The main music academy (which has university status) in Estonia is in the capital Tallinn, and students follow the Europe-wide system of bachelors and masters degrees, just as the rest of Estonia's higher education system does. Unlike the majority of Estonian higher education institutions, the academy authorities elected to make it a 4+1 system (ie 4-year bachelors followed by 1-year masters). It is estimated that 90% of students progress to masters level. Students arrive having spent time at extra-curricular primary and secondary music schools (there is also a music school providing specialist music education as part of a wider curriculum). Unusually, it is not necessary for students to attend the academy to gain professional qualification since this is also available through the regional music schools (those leaving are granted a professional diploma), though most do; singers entering the academy will have had the chance to attend 2 years of preparatory classes.

LATVIA

Advanced professional, musicological and music teacher training is provided by the sole institution set up for the purpose. The state-run, state-funded Latvian Academy of Music runs a 4-year bachelors programme followed by a 2-year masters in all areas; there is also the possibility to study for a doctorate (2-year course) in musicology, or possibly a specialist performance area such as piano accompaniment. Plans to increase the scope of doctoral studies are currently being investigated. Access to masters level courses are by possession of a professional bachelor's degree plus audition, exam and discussion; and the number of students progressing to this level is determined partly by budgetary considerations.

LITHUANIA

The Lithuanian Academy of Music and Theatre is the main music performance training institution, with teacher training provided in universities elsewhere, although the academy itself also has university status. As elsewhere in the Baltic states, the bachelors level degree is awarded after 4 years of successful study, after which students can progress to a 2-year masters. Doctorates are reserved for students of musicology, ethnomusicology and history; performers, however, can follow a 2-year course leading to the higher performing qualification. Funding comes from the state for half the student body, with the other half contributing a fee.

MOSCOW

Russian capital with architecture all its own. As well as the famous St Basil's cathedral and the Kremlin building, visitors will find ornate buildings throughout the city, even in the underground system in which rococo ceilings and great chandeliers can be seen.

♪ Musical life

Large number of major venues. Most famous is Bolshoi Theatre, principally an opera house showcasing Russian opera and ballet but also stages concerts from its orchestra. More opera at the Galina Vishnevskaya centre. Much newer building is Moscow International Performance Arts Centre with 2 concert halls (1753-seat Svetlanov Hall and 575-seat Chamber Hall; there is also a theatre for plays etc). Other notable venues include the chamber music hall at the Pavel Slobodkin centre; concert hall at the Pushkin museum; daily concerts in the 2 halls of the Moscow House of Composers. Many other venues besides. Conservatoire concert halls are also prestigious venues in life of the city; conservatoire Great Hall a regular venue for Russian National Orchestra, the best known in the city, along with Tchaikovsky Symphony Orchestra of Moscow. Moscow Chamber Orchestra and Chamber Orchestra Kremlin are 2 smaller groups.

🏛 Other cultural information

Moscow State Circus is world-renowned venue and troupe of performers. Wide range of museums and galleries: Pushkin Museum of Fine Arts a collection of paintings from various eras, plus other historic artefaces from around the world; Tretyakov Gallery displays the private collection of a patron of art; Museum of Contemporary Russian History focuses on events surrounding 1917 revolution, among other things. Dostoyevsky House Museum recreates domestic situation of the time, plus some ephemera from the writer's life; literary theme continued at the Tolstoy Museum.

🎭 Festivals and events

Golden Mask festival focuses on stage work of all kinds, including opera, music theatre and operetta.

ℹ Tourist information

www.moscow-city.ru; info@moscow-city.ru

MOSCOW PI TCHAIKOVSKY CONSERVATORY

Bolshaya Nikitskaya Street 13/6, 125009 Moscow.
t: +7 495 629 20 60; +7 495 629 73 18 (dept for foreign students) f: +7 495 627 72 71 (dept for foreign students) e: international@mosconsv. ru; foreign@mosconsv.ru w: www.mosconsv.ru
Courses Undergrad preparatory course, including study of Russian; main undergrad course (exams in specialism, ear tests and harmony, Russian, piano). Postgrad courses available in organ; accompaniment; string, wind and brass instruments; opera and orchestral conducting, choral direction; chamber music; solo singing; composition. Application requirements Entrance exams include Russian (written and oral) and specialism. Term dates 15 Sep 2009-25 Jan 2010; 15 Feb-15 Jul 2010.

GNESINS' ACADEMY OF MUSIC

Povarskaya st 30/36, 121069 Moscow.
e: mailbox@gnesin-academy.ru w: www.gnesin-academy.ru
Courses Private music college providing music education at 4 levels: elementary school, primary school, secondary school, academy. Awards bachelors, masters and professional degrees.

MOSCOW PI TCHAIKOVSKY CONSERVATORY

Bolshaya Nikitskaya Street 13/6, 125009 Moscow.
t: +7 495 629 20 60; +7 495 629 73 18 (dept for foreign students) f: +7 495 627 72 71 (dept for foreign students) e: international@mosconsv. ru; foreign@mosconsv.ru w: www.mosconsv.ru
Courses Undergrad preparatory course, including study of Russian; main undergrad course (exams in specialism, ear tests and harmony, Russian, piano). Postgrad courses available in organ; accompaniment; string, wind and brass instruments; opera and orchestral conducting, choral direction; chamber music; solo singing; composition. Application requirements Entrance exams include Russian (written and oral) and specialism. Term dates 15 Sep-25 Jan; 15 Feb-15 Jul.

ST PETERSBURG

Russian city on the river Neva near the Baltic coast near borders with Finland and Estonia. Its predominant architectural styles, in the centre of the city, are baroque and neo-classical. Known over the years variously as Petrograd and Leningrad until the fall of communism in 1991 when it was given back its historic name. Petrograd was at the heart of the 1905 uprising as well as the 1917 October Revolution when Lenin came to power. Suffered greatly during World War II thanks to the German siege of Leningrad that became a motivation behind Shostakovich's seventh symphony, whose Leningrad premiere (after performances in Moscow, London and New York) took place under extraordinarily defiant circumstances during the siege.

Musical life

2 major performing companies perhaps best known under other names: Mariinsky Theatre (formerly the Kirov) a major opera and ballet company; the Leningrad Philharmonic Orchestra now the Saint Petersburg Philharmonic. Both now still major organisations, the theatre (and its orchestra, which does not restrict itself to opera performance) under Valery Gergiev, the orchestra under Yuri Temirkanov. St Petersburg Academic Symphony Orchestra another prominent orchestra in the city; more opera at the Mussorgsky Opera Theatre (another renamed establishment, formerly the Mikhailovsky and Maly Theatre); for lighter music theatre, the Musical Comedy Theatre programmes traditional operetta; Teatro Buffo for cabaret and children's comedy. Oktabrsky hall for rock and pop events.

Other cultural information

Home to the world famous Hermitage Museum and Winter Palace and its extensive collection of art from around Europe. Russian Museum focuses more on Russian art. Kunstkamera founded by Peter the Great is a history and archaeology museum.

Festivals and events

Winter Festival Arts Square is a classical music festival in Dec featuring groups based in the city plus visitors from elsewhere. Musical Olympus festival invites young competition winners from around the world to perform during second half of May. 'Stars of the White Nights' festival at the Mariinsky over the summer. Ballet festival also at the Mariinsky in Mar, also separate event 'Dance Open' in the same month. Early music festival in Sep.

Tourist information

www.st-petersburg.ru;

THE RIMSKY-KORSAKOV ST PETERSBURG STATE CONSERVATOIRE

3 Teatralnaya Square, 190000 St Petersburg. *t:* +7 812 312 2129; +7 812 314 9693 (international student office) *f:* +7 812 571 6389; +7 812 571 8288 (international student office) *e:* foreigndep@conservatory.ru *w:* www. conservatory.ru
Contact Natalia Agababova, dean for international student affairs; Olga Makarova, admissions officer. *Courses* 5 year Diploma course in music performance: piano, organ, orchestral instruments, folk instruments, vocal music, composition, conducting, musicology; also choreography. Postgrad (PhD) course in music performance. Non-degree special training course (1-10 months). 1 year preparatory course. *Application requirements* Certificate of completed secondary education and suitable performance ability. Candidates must be age 18+. Knowledge of Russian at pre-intermediate level or above for students enrolling in 5 year Diploma course. *Term dates* 1 Sep-30 Jun. *Application deadline* 1 Jul. *Fees* EUR 5500 pa (Diploma course); EUR 4000 (preparatory course); EUR 500 pm (special training course). *Scholarships* None. *Exchange details* UK exchange partner institution: Royal Scottish Academy of Music. Also partnerships with 14 institutions across Europe, Asia and USA. *No of students* 1300 national students and 250 from overseas.

MUSIC FESTIVALS

AD Sakharov International Art Festival The Nizhny Novgorod State Academic Philharmony, Rostropovich Kremlin, Build 2, 603082 Nizhny Novgorod. *t:* +7 8312 391623 *f:* +7 8312 391608 *e:* otomina@philharmony.nnov.ru *w:* www. sakharov.innov.ru *Contact* Olga Tomina, artistic director. Symphonic, chamber, choral music, theatre and art exhibitions.

Golden Mask *t:* +7 495 662 53 52 *f:* +7 495 629 92 42 *w:* www.goldenmask.ru Festival of staged performances including opera, music theatre and operetta.

Moscow International Music Festival RosinterFest, 12 Sadovaya Triumfalnaya Str, 103006 Moscow. *t:* +7 495 510 26 92, also fax *e:* rosinterfest@ rosinterfest.ru 2 weeks programme of masterclasses, lessons, recitals and concerts.

Musical Olympus International Festival Korablestroiteley st 14, 199226 St Petersburg.

t: +7 812 356 5042 *f:* +7 812 356 6104 *e:* mo@musicalolympus.ru *w:* www.musicalolympus.ru Parade of winners; winners of biggest and most prestigious competitions invited to perform in major St Petersburg venues.

Stars of the White Nights 1 Theatre Square, 190000 St Petersburg. *t:* +7 812 326 4141 *f:* +7 812 314 1744 *e:* post@mariinsky.ru *w:* www.mariinsky.ru 3-month long summer festival featuring Mariinsky Theatre productions and orchestral works

ESTONIA

TALLINN

Capital of Estonia on the coast across the Gulf of Finland from Helsinki. Became independent of USSR in 1991 since when it has become a popular destination for visitors. Based round a medieval old town (a Unesco world heritage site) which is well preserved today and features a number of prominent buildings, including church, civic (eg the guild hall) and state buildings (eg the gothic town hall), narrow cobbled streets as well as market square, from the period. Part of city walls with distinctive conical towers, still exist.

♪ Musical life

Centres of musical life are Estonia Concert Hall (approx 900 seats) for classical music, with major concerts by Estonian National Symphony Orchestra (sometimes with Estonian Philharmonic Chamber Choir), and Estonia National Opera. Opera house includes a 'winter gardens' holding informal recitals of classical and lighter music. Regular events elsewhere, such as medieval town hall or Art Museum of Estonia; Linnahall for wider range of musical styles. Unusual outdoor venue, the Tallinn Song Stage, built in 1959 for mass national Song Festival, but holds other popular concerts too. City is an attractive destination for visiting amateur choirs, youth orchestras etc.

Other cultural information

Theatre and music museum displays antique instruments, music machines and curiosities; otherwise a large choice of galleries and exhibitions, particularly reflecting city's and country's history. Kumu is a brand new, award-winning art gallery focusing on both Estonian art and more general trends. Several theatres, as well as mainstream, there are puppet theatres, a Russian language theatre, revue and cabaret, dance etc.

Festivals and events

Numerous music events. International choir festival (Apr); organ festival and chamber music festival in Aug; also early music festival (Jan-Feb); annual contemporary music festival in Oct; short winter festival of concerts in Dec-Jan. Sacred music the focus of Credo festival of orthodox music (Sep). Several city fairs, markets and festivals.

ℹ Tourist information

www.tourism.tallinn.ee; turismiinfo@tallinnlv.ee; tel: +372 645 7777

EESTI MUUSIKA - JA TEATRIAKADEEMIA (ESTONIAN ACADEMY OF MUSIC AND THEATRE)

Rävala pst 16, EE-10143 Tallinn.
t: +372 6675 700; +372 6675 760 (international relations) f: +372 6675 800; +372 675 e: ema@ema.edu.ee; katrin@ema.edu.ee w: www.ema.edu.ee
Contact Katrin Makarov, international relations co-ordinator. Courses International bachelor studies (only available if 10+ students enrol) and International Masters Studies programmes, taught in English. Course specialisms: piano, organ, harpsichord, strings (inc harp and guitar), brass and woodwind (inc baroque flute and saxophone), percussion, voice, conducting, church music, music teacher studies, jazz studies, traditional music, composition, electronic music, musicology; accompaniment, chamber music, cultural music also available for Masters. Application requirements Entrance exam. Fees EU students can apply for state-funded courses and fee-based courses; non-EU students can only apply for fee-paying courses. See website for fee scales. Exchange details UK partner institutions for SOCRATES/ERASMUS: City University London, Guildhall School of Music and Drama, Rose Bruford College, Royal Northern College of Music, Royal Scottish Academy of Music and Drama, Royal Welsh College of Music and Drama Music facilities 60 classrooms plus 14 rehearsal rooms where classes can be held; chamber music hall seating up to 200; choir class with auditorium for 77 students; audition room with baroque organ; electronic music lab; recording studio; library with music listening and computer facilities. 95 pianos in total. No of students 690 students.

VILJANDI

Small town (population of around 20,000) in south of Estonia. Festival events include an early music festival, folk festival and dance festivals.

ℹ Tourist information

www.viljandimaa.ee; +372 43 30 442

TARTU ULIKOOLI VILJANDI KULTUURIAKADEEMIA (UNIVERSITY OF TARTU VILJANDI CULTURE ACADEMY)
Posti 1, EE-71004 Viljandi.
t: +372 435 5254 (international relations)
f: +372 435 5231 *e:* kool@kultuur.edu.ee; margot@ut.ee; international@ut.ee *w:* www.kultuur.edu.ee
Contact Margot Must, international relations co-ord; Ulle Tensing, snr specialist for international studies. *Courses* Jazz, classical and church music, traditional music; school music at BA level. From 2009, traditional music and school music will also be available at MA level. *Application requirements* Admission on the basis of results of state exams/final exams (international tests are converted to Estonian system) and entrance exam (solfeggio and test in applicant's specialism). Non-Estonian applicants must complete the Intensive Estonian language course (offered by University of Tartu Language Centre). *Term dates* 1 Sep-end Jan (autumn term); mid Feb-end June (spring term). *Application deadline* 1 Jun (EU applicants); 1 May (non EU applicants). Entrance exam end Jul. *Fees* EUR 900 per term (EEK 15,000), subject to confirmation *Scholarships* Limited number of scholarships available (see website for details) *Exchange details* Exchange partnerships with institutions in Finland, Sweden, Norway and Austria. Also member of NORTRAD, an association of higher schools in nordic countries that provide traditional music education. *No of students* 98 national students, 1 or 2 from overseas.

MUSIC FESTIVALS

International Festival of New Music NYD Eesti Kontsert, Estonia Avenue 4, EE-10148 Tallinn. *t:* +372 614 7700 *f:* +372 614 7709 *e:* neeme.punder@concert.ee *w:* www.concert.ee *Contact* Neeme Punder, manager. Biennial.

International Pianists' Festival Eesti Kontsert, Estonia Avenue 4, EE-10148 Tallinn. *t:* +372 614 7700 *f:* +372 614 7709 *w:* www.concert.ee

The International Pianists Festival KLAVER Eesti Kontsert, Estonia Avenue 4, EE-10148 Tallinn. *t:* +372 614 7700 *f:* +372 614 7709 *e:* neeme.punder@concert.ee *w:* www.concert.ee *Contact* Neeme Punde, manager. Biennial.

Viljandi Early Music Festival Kevade 7-4, EE-10137 Tallinn. *t:* +372 6621 819 *f:* +372 614 7709 *e:* neeme.punder@concert.ee *w:* www.viljandimaa.ee/vanamusa *Contact* Neeme Punder, manager.

LATVIA

RIGA

City (country's capital) of fluctuating fortunes whose position on the Baltic coast and role as a trading port led to its rise in the 12th and 13th centuries; subsequently occupied by Germany and Russia between periods of independence, finally gaining independence from USSR in 1991. The historic old town displays a clear German influence; elsewhere there are a number of art nouveau creations (Alberta, Elizabetes and Strelnieku streets in particular).

♪ Musical life

Historic opera house, the Latvian National Opera, is a company performing a full season from autumn-early summer with its full-time orchestra and chorus; also a ballet company based in the building. Construction of new concert hall scheduled to begin soon. Orchestras include New Chamber Orchestra of Riga, which collaborates with Latvian National Theatre as well as putting on its own concerts; Sinfonietta Riga a small but ambitious orchestra performing a number of premieres each season. City's cathedral is home to what was once the world's largest organ

🏛 Other cultural activities

Literature, Theatre and Music Museum has aim of displaying and archiving those aspects of Latvian cultural life. Several historical institutions: Occupation Museum looks at country's history of invasion; other institutions focus on other aspects, either general history or more specific such as museum exploring role of Jews in country's history. Just outside city is a large 'museum reserve', with castle museums, 'folksong park' and sculpture garden. Art galleries.

🕸 Festivals and events

Opera Festival closes National Opera's season, reprising season's performances and bringing in guest companies and conductors. Choral music of sacred nature, both small and large-scale in various city locations (Aug-Sep), organised by country's state choir. Sound Forest festival features experimental music of various types. Every 3rd year, the multi-country Baltic Folklore Festival comes to Riga. Various non-music events: animation festival (Apr), book fair (Feb)

i Tourist information

www.rigatourism.lv; tourinfo@riga.lv; tel: +371 67037900

LATVIAN ACADEMY OF MUSIC

1 Kr Barona St, LV-1050 Riga.
t: +371 7228684; +371 67223522
(international relations) f: +371 7820271
e: ms@music.lv (international relations) w: www.jvlma.lv
Contact Maija Sipola, vice rector for international relations Courses Professional bachelor's and masters degree programmes in keyboard, string, woodwind, brass or percussion performance, conducting (choral and orchestral), vocal music; also bachelors in music teaching, musicology and ethnomusicology. Application requirements Entrance exams take place end Jun/beginning Jul in music literature, solfeggio and music theory, plus interview and audition. Term dates Sep-Jun. Application deadline Jun. Fees Contact for details. Scholarships None. Exchange details UK exchange partner: Royal Scottish Academy of Music & Drama; also partnerships with 34 other institutions throughout Europe. No of students 600.

VILNIUS

Lithuanian capital is built up around a typical medieval old town, with narrow streets and numerous historic buildings, especially in the area around Cathedral Square (there are several other squares, Town Hall Square being the place for fairs and celebrations). Architecturally diverse – there are churches in various styles, gothic, renaissance, classic and baroque. Has a large student population of over 60,000 in higher education. 2009 Capital of European Culture (with Linz in Austria).

Musical life

2 main concert venues, National Philharmonic Hall and Palace of Congresses. Former has concerts from Lithuanian National Symphony Orchestra and the highly respected Lithuanian Chamber Orchestra; latter is home to the Lithanian State Symphony Orchestra. National opera and ballet companies share their own venue and have their own dedicated orchestra. City's numerous churches are regular concert venues.

Other cultural information

Contemporary Art Centre holds exhibitions, conferences and lectures (as well as music events). Various museums on different themes: Pushkin Museum on literature; Museum of Theatre, Music and Cinema (includes collections of mechanical instruments and recordings). Also art galleries and Lithuanian national museum.

Festivals and events

Banchetto Musicale has early music concerts in city's churches (Sep-Oct); 'Gaida' contemporary music festival in Oct; jazz festival in Nov . Modern dance festival in May; tango festival in Jun. St Christopher's Summer Festival features music in accessible areas around the city.

Tourist information

www.vilnius-tourism.lt; tic@vilnius.lt; tel: +370 5 262 9660

LIETUVOS MUZIKOS IR TEATRO AKADEMIJA (LITHUANIAN ACADEMY OF MUSIC AND THEATRE)

Gedimino pr 42, LT-01110 Vilnius.
t: +370 5 2612691; +370 5 212 4967 (international relations) f: +370 5 2126982
e: rektoratas@lmta.lt (rectorate); rima.rimsaite@lmta.lt (international relations); avida@lmta.lt (academic affairs). w: www.lmta.lt
Contact Povilas Gylys, vice-rector of studies; Rima Rimsaite, international relations; Vida Augutiene, academic affairs. Courses Music courses offered for international students: piano, organ, harpsichord, string instruments, wind and percussion instruments, accordion, conducting (choral, orchestral, military band), vocal performance, jazz, composition. Study programmes in 3 cycles offered: art of music performance, composition, music pedagogy, musicology, ethnomusicology. Application requirements 1 exam in area of principal study consisting of performance and interview. Contact admissions office for details of exam requirements. Term dates 1 Sep-15 Jan (autumn semester); 2 Feb-15 Jun (spring semester). Application deadline 25 Jun (national/EU applicants); 15 Jan (overseas applicants). Fees EU students pay same fees as national students (contact for details); LTL 19000-34000 (non EU students), depending on level. Scholarships None available for overseas students. Exchange details UK partner institutions: Royal Academy of Music, Royal College of Music, Dartington College of Arts, University of Glamorgan, University of Nottingham, Royal Scottish Academy of Music & Drama, Royal Northern College of Music. Also over 70 partnerships with institutions in almost all EU countries. Language requirements Lithuanian or English. Music facilities 40 rooms with pianos for individual practice, library, recording library. Accommodation Student dormitory; assistance in finding private accommodation is provided. No of students 1110 national students, plus 24 from overseas.

MUSIC FESTIVALS

Banchetto Musicale S Konarskio g 49, LT-03123 Vilnius. t: +370 5 2333997 e: info@bmfestival.lt w: www.bmfestival.lt Contact contact Early music festival, including performances and master-classes.

Contemporary Music Festival GAIDA Lithuanian Composers Union, Mickeviciaus 29, LT-08117 Vilnius. t: +370 5 2123611 f: +370 5 2120939 e: gaida@lks.lt w: www.mic.lt Annual. Performances by leading new music ensembles, soloists, chamber and symphony orchestras; selection of programmes, including new works by international and Lithuanian composers. Pre-concerts talks, masterclasses, etc.

Jauna Muzika – New Music Festival Lithuanian
Composers Union, Mickeviciaus 29, LT-08117 Vilnius.
t: +370 5 2721727 *f:* +370 5 2120939
e: jaunamuzika@lks.lt Annual. New contemporary
music, mostly electroacoustic and electronic; various
multimedia projects. Young composers from Lithuania
and other countries as well as well-known authors.

Vilnius Festival Klaipedos g 6, LT-01117 Vilnius.
e: info@vilniusfestivals.lt *w:* www.vilniusfestivals.lt
Classical music festival.

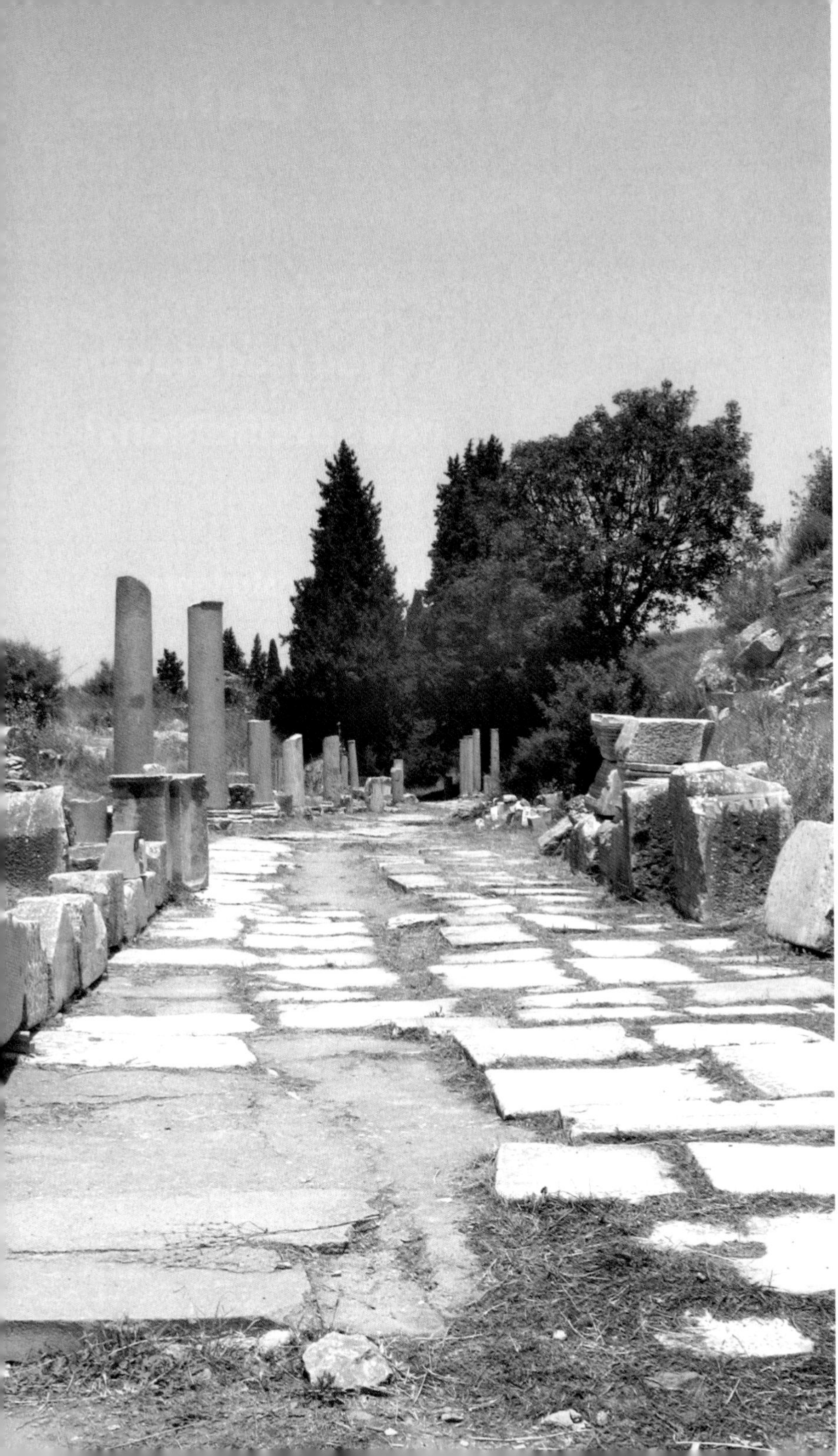

Greece and Turkey

Greece and Turkey

Although the two countries have been (often bitter) rivals, both have at various points been influential in the development of western civilisation – indeed, until independence in the mid 19th century, Greece was part of the Ottoman Empire, the precursor of modern-day Turkey (the current republic was established in 1923). Consequently, visitors with a keen interest in cultural history will find much to interest them.

Over its long history, the geographic location of what is now called Turkey, straddling the border between Europe and Asia, has meant it has absorbed aspects from east and west. Over the past century, it has developed especially strong links with Germany – the Ottoman Empire signed an alliance with Germany at the start of World War I; more recently, Turks migrated to Germany in large numbers during the 1960s helping the then West Germany overcome a labour shortage during its 'economic miracle' period of economic growth.

In Greece, the country more generally makes for an attractive place to stay, although cultural life and classical music is more restricted to the major cities. In more provincial and rural areas, however, there are several strong folk music traditions, some dating back hundreds of years. And of course, Greece was where many of our theoretical concepts – modes, acoustic properties and so on – were first articulated.

GREECE

Conservatoires in Greece are, in the main, private institutions (the exception is the State Conservory in Thessaloniki) so are not considered as having the same status as other higher education establishments – they are not obliged to participate in the quality assurance systems which universities are subject to, for instance, although the universities tend to concentrate on musicology and music education rather than professional training. As a result, the qualifications the conservatoires offer may not be

TURKEY

And one less well-known connection, this time a musical one, is the fact that Turkey's classical music education system was devised and put in place by the German composer Paul Hindemith at the invitation of the Turkish government in 1935. His recommendations remained in place until 1982, when conservatoires were attached to universities.

The conservatoires in Turkey offer a 2-cycle system (4 years + 2 years), with curricula that are at least 60% in common with each other and which are state approved.

GREECE

ATHENS

Capital of Greece and one of the world's oldest cities, birthplace of many well-known philosophers and writers. Evidence of its importance as a classical city state is still present, with numerous examples of architecture of the time throughout the city; most obvious example is the acropolis (literally, 'top of the city') with the remains of the Parthenon temple overlooking the city.

♪ Musical life
Main concert venue is the Megaron Moussikis; several performance spaces: main concert hall seats just under 2000, and Mitropoulos Hall (just under 500); opera/ballet theatre (Alexandra Trianti Hall). Chamber orchestra (Camerata-Friends of Music Orchestra) based there; various other orchestras include Athens State Orchestra and the Orchestra of Colours. National opera has its own orchestra.

▥ Other cultural information
Very large number of sites of archaeological and historical interest – new acropolis museum opens in 2009. Exhibition with a musical theme at the Museum of Greek Traditional Instruments (over 1200 examples).

⚄ Festivals and events
Athens Festival has various theatre, music and other cultural events in venues throughout the city.

ℹ Tourist information
www.breathtakingathens.com.

HELLENIC CONSERVATORY
53 Didotou str, GR-10681 Athens.
t: +30 210 3818335 *f:* +30 210 3834485
e: eo@conservatory.gr *w:* www.conservatory.gr
Courses Taught courses in classical music, Byzantine music, jazz, Greek music, popular music, music technology, music kinetics.

THESSALONIKI
Main city in the province of Macedonia (not to be confused with the country, the Republic of Macedonia) in the northern part of Greece.

♪ Musical life
Concert hall hosts concerts from Greek and international performers; also opera and ballet, and various jazz, world music and other performances. City's main orchestra is Thessaloniki State Symphony Orchestra.

⚄ Festivals and events
Dimitria festival an all-round arts event including classical music.

ℹ Tourist information
www.thessalonikicity.gr

CONSERVATORY OF NORTHERN GREECE
16 Heronias Str, Zardinidis Villa, GR-546 55 Thessaloniki.
t: +30 2310 422742 *e:* info@conservatoire.gr
w: www.conservatoire.gr

STATE CONSERVATORY OF THESSALONIKI
15 Fragon Str, GR-54625 Thessaloniki.
t: +30 2310 510551 *f:* +30 2310 510558
e: odiokrat@otenet.gr *w:* www.odiokrat.gr
Courses Courses in the following schools/departments: piano, harp, string instruments, guitar, woodwind, brass, percussion; monody, melodrama, Byzantine music; composition, wind orchestration, advanced theory. *Music facilities* 200-seat concert hall with 2 Steinway pianos, harpsichord

MUSIC FESTIVALS
Hermopoulis Guitar Festival Byzantiou 88, GR-142 34 Kalogzeza. *t:* +30 210 275 5466 *e:* and@akroama.net *w:* www.guitarfestival.gr Concerts, guitar competition, master class, guitar ensemble

ANKARA

Capital of Turkey, located in the centre of the country, with a population approaching 4 million. Like much of the country, the city has a long and interesting history, ruled over the centuries by various regimes until modern Turkey was founded in 1923 (it was at this point the city became capital, taking over from Istanbul). This has left a varied architectural legacy today.

Musical life

City is hope to state opera and ballet companies, based mainly at Ankara Opera House though 2 other opera venues there (Leyla Gencer Sahnesi and Operet Sahnesi). CSO Concert Hall and Bilkent Concert Hall are 2 main concert venues; latter is home to Bilkent Symphony Orchestra, the former to the Presidential Symphony Orchestra (CSO).

Other cultural information

Various museums and exhibitions, many focusing on country's history and art.

Festivals and events

International Ankara Music Festival runs every April covering wide range of music. International children's festival during same month.

Tourist information

www.ankara.bel.tr

ANKARA DEVLET KONSERVATUVARI (ANKARA STATE CONSERVATORY)

Bahriye Ucok Caddesi 4, TR-06500 Ankara.
t: +90 312 212 62 10 1112 13 f: +90 312 215 84 66 e: hudevkon@hacettepe.edu.tr
w: www.konser.hacettepe.edu.tr

BILKENT UNIVERSITY

Faculty of Music and Performing Arts, TR-06800 Bilkent Ankara.
t: +90 312 290 1777; +90 312 290 2944 (international centre) f: +90 312 266 4539
e: intcent@bilkent.edu.tr (international centre)
w: www.bilkent.edu.tr
Contact Berna Orge, International Centre co-ordinator

ISTANBUL

Turkey's largest city, though not capital (though historically, as Byzantium and Constantinople, it had been), and one of largest in the world (population around 12 million). Located at an important strategic point straddling the Bosphorus, the stretch of water linking Black Sea to Mediterranean; it is also the stretch of water separating Europe from Asia, meaning the city effectively located on 2 continents. Selected as one of European Capitals of Culture in 2010.

Musical life

City is home to Istanbul State Opera and Ballet and Istanbul State Symphony Orchestra (based at Caddebostan Cultural Centre); Cema Resit Rey hall is another major venue. Sanat Arts and Culture centre has concerts in a range of musical styles.

Other cultural information

Istanbul Modern is a contemporary art gallery with permanent and changing exhibitions. Institutions focusing on aspects of Turkish and associated culture and society include archaeology museum and museum of Islamic arts.

Festivals and events

Annual international music festival in summer (Jun); international film festival (Apr); jazz festival (Jul); biennial art festival (Sep-Nov, even years).

Tourist information

www.ibb.gov.tr

STATE CONSERVATORY AT 'MIMAR SINAN' FINE ARTS UNIVERSITY

Dolmabahce Caddesi, Akaretler Duragi, TR-34357 Besiktas - Istanbul.
t: +90 2122616110 f: +90 2122610041
e: kons@msu.edu.tr; metin.ulku@hotmail.com
w: www.msgsu.edu.tr
Contact Metin Ulku Courses Programmes in composition and conducting, piano, string instruments, wind and percussion instruments, musicology, ethnomusicology and folklore; also opera (part of performing arts dept). See website for further details. Application requirements Differ for each programme and for level of entry; see website for details. Term dates 5 Oct-31 Dec (autumn semester); 1 Feb-7 May (summer semester). Application

TURKEY

EUROPE

deadline Late Aug-early Sep. *Fees* YTL 700 (approx EUR 350). *Scholarships* None. *Exchange details* Exchange partnerships with institutions in Austria, Belgium, Estonia, Germany, Italy, Lithuania. *No of students* Approx 320; also approx 100 full time students at pre-college stage.

MUSIC FESTIVALS

International Ankara Music Festival SCA Music Foundation, Tunali Hilmi Cad 114/43, TR-06700 Ankara. *t:* +90 312 427 0855 *f:* +90 312 467 3159 *e:* sca@ankarafestival.com *w:* www.ankara festival.com Annual. Classical music, baroque, early music, ballet, dance, jazz.

International Istanbul Music Festival Istanbul Foundation for Culture and Arts, Istiklal Caddesi 64, Beyoglu, TR-34435 Istanbul. *t:* +90 212 334 07 74 *f:* +90 212 334 0705 *w:* www.iksv.org *Contact* Yesim Gurer, director. Annual. Orchestra, chamber, recitals, opera, vocal, dance, traditional music.

International Izmir Festival Izmir Foundation for Culture, Arts and Education, Mithalpasa Caddesi no 138, Karatas, TR-35420 Izmir. *t:* +90 232 482 00 90 *f:* +90 232 482 01 66 *e:* info@iksev.org; izmirfestival@iksev.org *w:* www.iksev.org *Contact* Ceyda Berk, foreign affairs co-ordinator; Filiz Sarper, president. Annual. Classical, traditional and contemporary music, ballet, theatre and opera. Venues include the Great Theatre of Ephesus and the Library of Celsus.

NORTH AMERICA

United States

United States

Although it is one country, the USA offers a huge range of possibilities for the visiting student. It means, in a way, it is not enough simply to decide to go to the USA to study. Not only are there the obvious differences in courses and type of study, but each city, each state, each region has its own character. In the north east, the historic states of New England contrast with the highly urbanised; in the south west, San Francisco is not the same as its neighbour Los Angeles; lovers of the outdoors can choose the mountainous Rocky Mountain states or the Pacific coast; some cities are famous for their homegrown traditions, others pride themselves on the great range of cultural backgrounds of the people living there.

As in Europe, professional music training in the USA is carried out in several types of educational establishment but which can broadly be defined as specialist music colleges or conservatoires based within universities with several faculties. The range of musical education taught depends on the institution: some place a strong emphasis on practical performance study, others include a substantial academic component, others still offer a number of joint degrees. In many cases, this weighting is reflected in the kind of qualification offered, with the bachelors-masters-doctorate stream providing practical courses in the liberal arts tradition on one hand; diplomas and licentiates rewarding more specialist practical study, but without the academic reputation that degree courses convey.

Course length is akin to the Bologna Process model, with a 4-year bachelors degree leading to the possibility of 1 or 2-year masters. This increasing harmonisation makes exchange between the continents increasingly attractive to students in either area. Unlike many places in Europe where doctorates tend to be awarded for study in the academic or pedagogical fields, it is possible to earn a doctorate for performance-based work. However, the existence of artist diplomas means that these more specialist practical courses may be more appropriate.

The other difference between the USA and most of Europe is the cost of tuition which usually reaches tens of thousands of dollars per year. There are, however, substantial scholarships and other awards – some governmental, some institutional, some from private sources – available to help with these costs. The extent of this aid does vary from institution to institution, however.

BALTIMORE

Principal city in Maryland and major seaport on east coast of USA, a little upstream from Chesapeake Bay. Harbour area has seen much redevelopment recently, changing from a predominantly industrial zone to an area popular among visitors. City's buildings display variety of architectural styles reflecting mixed nature (historic industrial but redeveloped) of the place.

Musical life

Baltimore Symphony Orchestra based at Joseph Meyerhoff Symphony Hall (though also has a base elsewhere in Maryland), a 2400-seat hall that also puts on numerous concerts from visiting artists. A chamber music society promotes various concerts, including commissions and new work.

Other cultural information

Museum dedicated to Edgar Allan Poe, a Baltimorean. City also birthplace of baseball legend Babe Ruth and there is museum about him too. Harbourside National Aquarium features various exhibits but also has a conservation mission; several exhibitions also reflect city's maritime and industrial heritage as well as art galleries such as Baltimore Museum of Art (changing and touring exhibitions)

Festivals and events

Artscape festival is a free festival of performing arts, crafts, and visual arts in Jul. Annual book festival in Sep.

i Tourist information

www.baltimorecity.gov

THE PEABODY INSTITUTE OF THE JOHNS HOPKINS UNIVERSITY

1 East Mount Vernon Place, Baltimore, MD 21202.
t: +1 410 659 8100 w: www.peabody.jhu.edu
Courses 3 undergrad programmes: music performance, music education, recording arts and sciences. Application requirements Applicants for all undergrad programmes must audition in a performance major (composition, computer music, early music instruments, guitar, jazz, keyboard instruments, orchestral instruments, voice). Application deadline 1 Dec. Fees $33,000 per year tuition (degree programmes); $27,500 tuition (artist diploma and graduate performance diploma programmes) Scholarships Various scholarships and forms of financial aid available Music facilities 695-seat concert hall, 150-seat concert/rehearsal space with concert organ, 95-seat theatre; several recording studios, computer music studio. Collection of instruments, including early music instruments, available for students. Library with over 100,000 items, audio-visual centre. Accommodation Hall of residence spaces for 165 students; all 1st and 2nd year students required to stay on campus, unless excepted.

BLOOMINGTON

City in the state of Indiana in northern part of Midwest. Local and community arts well supported, with Bloomington Arts and Entertainment District a community organisation promoting art and cultural activity reflecting the needs of the city.

Festivals and events

All-round performing arts festival at Indiana University in Feb and summer music festival in Jun-Aug. Early music festival in May; festival of world music in Sep.

i Tourist information

www.visitbloomington.gov

INDIANA UNIVERSITY – JACOBS SCHOOL OF MUSIC

1201 E Third Street, Merrill Hall 003, Bloomington, IN 47405-2200.
t: +1 812 855 7998 f: +1 812 856 6086
e: musicadm@indiana.edu w: www.music.indiana.edu
Courses Bachelor of music in composition, early music, jazz studies, performance (orch instruments, pno, sax, voice), also available as major with study in outside field; bachelor of music education; master of arts in musicology; master of music in composition, computer music composition, conducting, early music, jazz studies, music theory, organ & church music, performance; doctorate in music; artist diploma; performer diploma. Other courses available; see website for full details of all courses. Application requirements Audition and in some cases interview; recorded auditions may be acceptable. See website for details of requirements and audition dates. Term

dates Aug-May. *Application deadline* 1 Dec. *Fees* Full details of fees available on website. *Scholarships* All undergrad applicants automatically considered for merit-based financial aid. Merit-based awards also available for postgrad students, as well as small number of instructorships and assistantships. *Music facilities* Over 170 full-time faculty members. Facilities included recital halls, over 170 practice rooms, choral and instrumental rehearsal rooms, over 100 studios and offices; Musical Arts Center performance venue. *No of students* 1600 students in total.

BOSTON

City on the north east coast of USA in the area known as New England. One of the country's oldest, with a key role in both the founding of the country by English settlers in the 17th century and its eventual independence from Britain (hence events such as Boston Tea Party revolt). As a result, Boston is strongly associated with historic patriotism. Throughout 19th century, significant numbers of Irish immigrants settled in the city, and today Boston closely identified with Irish and Irish-Americans (hence Boston Celtics basketball team). A number of higher education institutions based in and around the city reinforce the city's tradition for intellectual and academic activity.

♪ Musical life

Boston Symphony Orchestra probably the most prominent performing organisation in the city, performing in the city and, every summer, at Tanglewood summer music academy; the Boston Pops, specialising in lighter classical music, is drawn from its members. Boston Philharmonic is the other main large-scale group. Boston Ballet company has its own orchestra, and is highly regarded; 2 well established opera companies, Boston Lyric Opera performs at Schubert Theatre (part of Citi Performing Arts Centre), and Opera Boston at the 1200-seat Cutler Theatre. City a notable centre for early music: Handel and Haydn Society originally a choral society (founded 1815) that has evolved to become chorus and orchestra performing music up to classical period; Boston Baroque a smaller group concentrating on that period.

▥ Other cultural information

Strong for theatre; 'theatre district' includes opera house and City Performing Arts Centre (not just opera and ballet, but plays, lectures etc). Institute of Contemporary Art on riverfront has art exhibitions, films, discussions, readings and other activities. Various institutions with exhibitions about city's heritage, eg Commonwealth Museum, Paul Revere House celebrating him and his role in American Revolution, or properties looked after by Historic New England; also wider interest, such as Museum of Afro-American History or Museum of Science.

▨ Festivals and events

City hosts annual early music festival which also encompasses a trade show. Also annual celtic music festival in Jan. Civic events include Patriot's Day celebrations (20 Apr) and traditional reading of Declaration of Independence (4 Jul).

ℹ Tourist information

www.bostonusa.com; tel: +1 617 536 4100

BERKLEE COLLEGE OF MUSIC

1140 Boylston St, Boston, MA 02215.
t: +1 617 266 1400 *e:* admissions@berklee.edu; registrar@berklee.edu *w:* www.berklee.edu
Application requirements Live audition and interview. Audition locations in Greece, Spain, Ireland, Germany, Finland, France, Ghana, South Africa, Japan, Malaysia, India, South Korea, Israel, Australia, Barbados, Mexico, Panama, Ecuador, Brazil. Audition dates depend on country; see website for details. *Application deadline* Application and auditi *Fees* $150 non-refundable application fee; $500 tuition deposit; $13,750 tuition (degree programme), $11,850 tuition (diploma programme). Fees per semester. *Scholarships* All students considered for scholarships as part of audition/interview process. Berklee International Grant available for overseas students. *Music facilities* Berklee Performance Center (seats 1212) for student and professional performances; 4 recital halls in various locations (capacity ranges from 80-180); 3 electronic piano rooms (40 keyboards in each); 50 ensemble rooms; film scoring lab; 8 music synthesis labs (over 250 types of synthesizer); 300 private practice rooms, including special units for percussionists and pianists; recording studios including 12 professional production facilities. Also library and media centre. *Accommodation* 800

places in halls of residence; Berklee Student Activities Center provides advice for off-campus living.

THE BOSTON CONSERVATORY

8 The Fenway, Boston, MA 02215.
t: +1 617 536 6340 *f:* +1 617 912 9101
e: admissions@bostonconservatory.edu *w:* www.bostonconservatory.edu
Courses Bachelors and masters degrees, graduate performance diploma, artist diploma. 25 curricula offered in several depts: piano, strings, voice and opera, woodwind, brass, harp and guitar, percussion/marimba, composition. Website gives full details of bachelors and masters course content. *Term dates* Early Sep-early Dec (fall semester); mid Jan-end Apr (spring semester). *Fees* $30,400, full time bachelors degree programme; $28,700, full time master program, except $30,400 masters in opera performance and music theatre. See website for details of other fees. *Scholarships* All applicants considered for scholarships on basis of merit. See website for details of grants and financial aid available. *No of students* Total of 350 students in music division.

NEW ENGLAND CONSERVATORY

290 Huntington Ave, Boston, MA 02115.
t: +1 617 585 1100 *f:* +1 617 585 1115
e: admission@newenglandconservatory.edu
w: www.newenglandconservatory.edu
Courses Undergrad diploma, bachelor of music, double degree programmes, master of music, graduate diploma, doctor of musical arts, artist diploma; also professional string quartet and piano trio training programmes *Application deadline* 1 Dec for priority admission to fall semester and for financial aid applications. Once admitted students have until 15 Apr to accept offer. *Fees* $32,900 undergrad tuition per year (bachelors, diploma, master of music, doctor of musical arts); $30,000 graduate diploma. *Language requirements* TOEFL required for non-native English speakers (61 iBT, 500 paper-based); some exemptions may be granted. *Accommodation* Hall of residence with double rooms and small number of single rooms. All undergrads live in hall of residence in first year unless living with parents, aged 21 or over, or married.

BOULDER

City in the western US state Colorado at the eastern edge of the Rocky Mountains. Location means there are numerous opportunities for outdoor activity (rock climbing, biking etc). City also attracts many to its higher education and research institutions, one of which, Naropa, is a Buddhist institution combining western scholarship and eastern contemplative traditions.

Musical life

One of world's best chamber groups, the Takács Quartet, is based at University of Colorado at Boulder. For orchestral music, Boulder Philharmonic the main group, performing at Macky Auditorium on university campus.

Other cultural information

Boulder Museum of Contemporary Art has changing programme of exhibitions; many smaller galleries and workshops besides. Theatre and dance performance, plus exhibitions, at Dairy Center for the Arts; other theatres on university campus

Festivals and events

Colorado Music Festival runs for 6 weeks every summer. Annual MahlerFest in May features recitals, discussions etc and culminates in a performance of a Mahler symphony. Another composer featured in festival is Bach at the Boulder Bach Festival (various dates throughout the year). Main non-music events are Boulder International Film Festival (Feb) and summer Shakespeare Festival in open-air Mary Rippon Theater at Colorado University.

Tourist information

www.bouldercoloradousa.com; visitor@bouldercvb.com; tel: +1 303 442 2911

UNIVERSITY OF COLORADO AT BOULDER – COLLEGE OF MUSIC

301 UCB, Boulder, CO 80309-0301.
t: +1 303 492 6352 *w:* www.colorado.edu
Courses Bachelors and masters degrees in music and music education; doctor of musical arts; also post-masters professional certificates in opera and solo vocal performance, string quartet performance (for pre-established groups), woodwind performance. *Application requirements* Application by application form, letter of recommendation and

audition; postgrad application includes *Application deadline* 15 Jan. *Scholarships* Wide range of scholarships at undergrad and postgrad level; also assistantships etc. Postgrad applicants automatically considered for scholarships, assistantships and other financial aid. *Music facilities* Entrerpreneurship Center for Music gives career advice and courses in making the most of music marketplace (business and communication skills etc). Takács Quartet is ensemble in residence.

CAMBRIDGE

Part of greater Boston area, across the Charles River from Boston itself. Boasts a vibrant, youthful attitude. Home of Harvard University and Massachusetts Institute of Technology.

♪ Musical life

Radius Ensemble another small group with an eclectic programme

🏛 Other cultural information

Varied theatres and entertainment venues: eg American Repertory Theatre for varied programme including classics and new work; Central Square Theater houses 2 professional companies; Cambridge Multicultural Arts Center stages a range of interdisciplinary performance events and exhibitions. Large number of galleries: Carpenter Center for the Visual Arts (at Harvard) a large example, but other smaller establishments with interesting range of exhibitions.

ℹ Tourist information

www.cambridge-usa.org; info@cambridge-usa.org; tel: +1 617 441 2884

LONGY SCHOOL OF MUSIC

1 Follen St, Cambridge, MA 02138.
t: +1 617 876 0956 ext 1251 *f:* +1 617 876 9326 *e:* admission@longy.edu *w:* www.longy.edu
Contact Alex Powell, dir of admissions & student services. *Courses* Master of music degree, graduate performance diploma, artist diploma, Dalcroze certificate & licence, undergrad diploma, bachelor of music degree (from Emerson College). *Application requirements* Application form and audition (live or recorded). *Term dates* Sep-mid May. *Application deadline* 1 Dec for priority scholarships consideration; late applications also accepted. *Fees*

$100 application fee. *Scholarships* Generous merit scholarships based on audition and file review *Language requirements* TOEFL examination. *Music facilities* Edward Pickman Concert Hall, Wolfinsohn Recital Room, numerous teaching studios, classrooms and practice rooms in 2 historic buildings in Cambridge MA. *Accommodation* Hall of residence space near campus; school also operates a housing network to help students find apartments and roommates. *No of students* Approx 200 students, 35% of whom are from more than 20 overseas countries.

CHICAGO

City in Illinois, north of the USA, on the edge of Lake Michigan (the location helped it earn its nickname the 'windy city'). Developed rapidly in the late 19th century, partly thanks to a city-wide fire in 1871, leading to first US experiments in skyscrapers; today Chicago's skyline is renowned because of the large numbers of high-rise buildings. City has had a major input into history of jazz, with many African American musicians arriving from southern states in early part of 20th century.

♪ Musical life

Symphony Center is the main venue for classical music with regular performances from Chicago Symphony Orchestra. Also regular venue (though the group plays in a variety of locations in the city) for Chicago Sinfonietta which explicitly aims to be as culturally diverse as possible in its make-up and artistic activity. Cube Ensemble is Chicago-based new music group. Chicago Opera Theater promises fresh approach to opera at its base, the Harris Theater for Music and Dance; music theatre at Light Opera Works. Chicago Chamber Musicians promotes wide range of chamber music events from a variety of city-based artists and guests. Outside of classical, city has a very strong tradition of jazz and blues music that remains today.

🏛 Other cultural information

Chicago Cultural center, once a library, now a municipal arts venue with performances and exhibitions across a range of disciplines. Known for its tradition of theatre, in particular social and political theatre (Steppenwolf company is perhaps best known), and improvised theatre.

Festivals and events

Grant Park Music Festival has around 30 free outdoor concerts around Millennium Park, many by the festival's own orchestra and chorus.

i Tourist information

www.choosechicago.com

CHICAGO COLLEGE OF PERFORMING ARTS – THE MUSIC CONSERVATORY

430 S Michigan Ave, Chicago, IL 60605.
t: +1 312 341 3500 *w:* http://ccpa.roosevelt.edu

Courses Bachelor of music in composition, jazz studies, music education or performance; 5-year double major in music education and performance; master of music in composition, performance, orchestral studies (woodwind, brass, percussion only); professional diploma in orchestra studies (woodwind, brass, percussion only) or opera; performance diploma. *Application requirements* Audition, music theory diagnostic exam. See website for audition requirements for each discipline. *Application deadline* 15 Jan (fall entry); 1 Dec (spring entry; at discretion of admissions office). *Fees* $75 application fee ($100 if postmarked after 15 Jan). Undergrad tuition fees $624 per hour, $3487-6685 per term,or $19,000 per year, depending on number of hours received; postgrad fees $737 per hour, or $13,640-14,730 per year. *Music facilities* Performing Arts Library, soundproof practice studios, 195-seat recital hall, concert facilities, orchestra rehearsal room, electro-acoustic facilities, technology lab, piano lab with digital pianos. Concerts in Roosevelt University's 3700-seat Auditorium Theatre, 1400-seat Harris Theater (off-campus). *Accommodation* Student accommodation available.

CLEVELAND

City in Ohio on the shore of Lake Erie. Developed as an industrial city, but suffered a decline after immediate post-war prosperity; recently has benefitted from various redevelopment projects. Many of the educational establishments, including music school, situated just outside the city in an area called University Circle.

Musical life

Cleveland Orchestra traditionally one of the figurehead US orchestras, with concerts at Severance Hall (in University Circle area). Opera Cleveland performs a short season at the State Theatre. Rock and Roll Hall of Fame located in the city. Pops orchestra performs at Severance Hall, as well as holiday series at Playhouse Square. Oberlin Conservatory in nearby city of Oberlin has many concerts too.

Other cultural information

Theatre district (including opera theatre) based round Playhouse Square Center with its diverse range of entertainment and performance in several venues. For art, Cleveland Museum of Art a prominent gallery with wide range of exhibits; Museum of Contemporary Art Cleveland has variety of changing exhibitions. Several dance companies (eg Ohio Dance Theatre, Dance Cleveland)

Festivals and events

Blossom Festival features Cleveland Orchestra in summer outdoor concerts at a purpose-built venue outside the city in a national park location. Biennial international piano competition (odd years). Great Lakes Theater Festival in fact a regular theatre season (Sep-May).

i Tourist information

www.positivelycleveland.com; visinfo@positively cleveland.com; +1 216 875 6600

CLEVELAND INSTITUTE OF MUSIC

11021 East Boulevard, Cleveland, OH 44106.
t: +1 216 791 5000 *f:* +1 216 791 3063
e: admission@cim.edu *w:* www.cim.edu

Courses Bachelor of music, master of music, doctor of musical arts offered; non-degrees include artist certificate (undergrad), artist diploma or professional studies diploma (postgrad). Distance learning programmes available through high-speed videoconferencing. *Application requirements* Audition held in Cleveland; DVD recorded applications may be accepted for some disciplines. Apply online at www.unifiedapps.org; application must include paper letter of recommendation. *Application deadline* 1 Dec (fall application); 1 Oct (spring application) *Fees* $100 application fee; rises after 1 Dec. *Scholarships* Application for financial aid and scholarships is part of general application process. *Language requirements* TOEFL test for non-native English speakers. *Music facilities* 540-seat Kulas Hall; library with 52,000 scores and music books, also 23,000 AV materials. Teaching studios and practice rooms in main building and annex. Technology learning centre, audio recording studios. *Accommodation* Dormitory for 100 students. *No of students* 427 conservatory students.

COLUMBUS

Capital of Ohio in American Midwest. City has a substantial number of students at higher education level (around 100,000), being the location of Ohio State University

Musical life

City has an active musical life. Main orchestra is Columbus Symphony at the Ohio Theater (over 2700 seats); ProMusica Chamber Orchestra a much smaller group performing at various venues in the city. Ohio Theatre is also venue for city's opera company Opera Columbus. Capital Theater (900+ seats) has a range of music performance, particularly world and folk, jazz, musicals etc. Various classical music promoters such as Chamber Music Columbus.

Other cultural information

As well as for a Jack Nicklaus Museum, Ohio State University is location for Wexner Center for the Arts, an institution promoting live performance (including some music), films and exhibitions, with a focus on contemporary work. Elsewhere, Columbus Museum of Art has its own collection and hosts special exhibitions. Several theatre venues run by Columbus Association for the Performing Arts. King Arts Complex focuses on African American performance, visual art and cultural awareness.

Festivals and events

Columbus Arts Festival in Jun primarily craft and art fair, but music and other performance also involved. Opera Columbus runs an annual international singing competition (Mar). Various cultural and community events throughout the year.

Tourist information

www.ExperienceColumbus.com; VisitorInfo@ExperienceColumbus.com; tel: +1 614 221 6623

CAPITAL UNIVERSITY CONSERVATORY OF MUSIC

1 College and Main, Columbus, OH 43209-2394.
t: +1 614 236 6101 *e:* visit@capital.edu
w: www.capital.edu
Fees $27,680 for undergrad students. *Scholarships* Nearly all students receive some form of financial aid, either through scholarships awarded on merit or financial assistance loans and grants. *Music facilities* 950-seat auditorium with 3-manual organ; 180-seat recital hall; 30 practice rooms, various sizes; electronic/recording studio; music technology space; range of acoustic and electronic instruments; *Accommodation* 6 halls of residence.

DENVER

Capital of Colorado, originally a mining town in the second half of the 19th century; underwent significant development during 1970-80s due to oil boom. Known as the Mile High City due to its height above sea level, although not actually situated in mountainous region — Rockies are some 25km to the west of the city — being located on the High Plains region of the US prairie area. A centre of the US brewing industry (with a beer festival in Sep).

Musical life

Opera Colorado puts on a short season of standard opera at the Ellie Caulkins Opera House. Colorado Symphony Orchestra performs at Boettcher Concert Hall, unusual in being designed in the round. Both venues are part of Denver Performing Arts Complex (DPAC).

Other cultural information

Various theatre spaces at DPAC; Denver Center for the Performing Arts a tenant organisation at DPAC, focusing on plays and musicals, plus cabaret and student performances. Denver Art Museum has a large collection of native American art and has recently added a striking modern-style building designed by Daniel Liebeskind.

Festivals and events

Central City Opera is a festival running Jun-Aug in Central City, a town a short distance to west of Denver; 3 or 4 productions each year. Jazz Festival in Mar.

i Tourist information

www.denver.org; VisitorInfo@visitdenver.com; tel: +1 303 892 1505

UNIVERSITY OF DENVER - LAMONT SCHOOL OF MUSIC

2344 E Iliff Ave, Denver, CO 80208.
t: +1 303 871 6400 *f:* +1 303 871 3118
w: www.du.edu/lamont/
Courses Music courses arranged in 4 programmes: conservatory programme (professional training in western classical music); jazz & commercial music programme; university programme (academic focus); community programme (community outreach and non-traditional education opportunities). *Application deadline* 1 Nov for early applicants; 15 Jan for regular decision applicants. *Fees* $50 non-refundable application fee ($60 for postgrad applicants). *Language requirements* Non-native international applicants must submit TOEFL scores with application. *Music facilities* Robert and Judi Newman Center for the Performing Arts houses concert hall/opera theatre and flexible performance space. School also has teaching, rehearsal and practice studios, music library with computer lab, recording studio, small performance spaces, individual practice rooms; rehearsal spaces include vocal arts room, instrumental room, jazz room and virtual practice rooms (with computer-generated reverberation effects to mimic acoustics of different types of performance space). All-Steinway school.

EUGENE

City in Pacific coastal state of Oregon, known for its scenic location and prevalence of outdoor activities but also its artistic atmostphere – as well as its traditional performing arts, the city has a reputation for alternative art and lifestyles).

🎼 Musical life

Eugene Symphony based at Hult Center for the Performing Arts; also home to opera and ballet company. The Shedd Institute includes a classical concert series among its variety of performing arts events.

🏛 Other cultural information

Hult Center has a 500-seat theatre as well as the concert hall, plus art gallery. Range of theatre companies, galleries etc across the city.

🎭 Festivals and events

Oregon Bach Festival (Jun-Jul) based at University of Oregon, focuses on music and musical influence of Bach. Oregon Festival of American Music annual event in Aug taking in a variety of American idioms eg jazz, folk and art music. Summer series of outdoor concerts in city's parks.

i Tourist information

www.eugene-or.gov

UNIVERSITY OF OREGON SCHOOL OF MUSIC AND DANCE

1225 University of Oregon, Eugene, OR 97403-1225.
t: +1 541 346 3761 *f:* +1 541 346 0723
e: audition@uorgeon.edu *w:* http://music.uoregon.edu
Music facilities 540-seat concert hall, electro-acoustic music studios, piano lab with digital keyboards, computer lab with 24 MIDI keyboards,

GAINESVILLE

City in northern Florida, home to one of USA's largest universities (University of Florida).

i Tourist information

www.visitgainesville.com; tel: +1 352 374 5260

UNIVERSITY OF FLORIDA – SCHOOL OF MUSIC

101 Fine Arts Building A, PO Box 115800, Gainesville, FL-32611-5800.
t: +1 352 392 0223 *f:* +1 352 392 0461
e: music@arts.ufl.edu *w:* www.arts.ufl.edu
Application requirements Bachelors and masters in choral conducting, composition/theory, music education, instrumental conducting, musicology/ethnomusicology, brass, keyboard, percussion, string, woodwind, voice, sacred music. *Music facilities* University Auditorium concert hall (900 seats) with large organ. 3-storey building housing practice rooms, teaching studios, classrooms, ensemble rehearsal rooms, electronic music lab, music library; university also has 61-bell carillon.

HOUSTON

City on the coast of the Gulf of Mexico in Texas. Success over the years in several industries makes it a relatively wealthy place with knock-on effects for well-supported arts provision. A unique urban feature of the city is its tunnel system, a 10km network linking various buildings; tunnels are air conditioned so are a means of escaping Houston's long periods of hot weather. City is famous as the location for NASA's Mission Control.

♪ Musical life

Houston Grand Opera at Wortham Theater Center has its own orchestra; Houston Ballet another full-time professional company based at the theatre, performing in each of its 2 spaces. Houston Symphony Orchestra (with associated chorus) based at Jones Hall for the Performing Arts with a substantial series (many concerts repeated 2 or 3 times). Other visiting artists and ensembles perform there also. Hobby Center for Performing Arts is home to a professional string orchestra called Maggini.

⬛ Other cultural information

Hobby Center for the Perfoming Arts with its 2 halls, is a venue for local performers as well as visiting artists. Part of theatre district along with Wortham Theater and Alley Theater (2 spaces, 800+ seater and 310 seater), the latter being the main repertory theatre in the city. As well as theatre district, city has a museum district including an extensive fine arts museum and a contemporary arts museum. Nearby is Rothko Chapel, a modern contemplation space containing a number of works by Mark Rothko; venue was the inspiration for Morton Feldman's piece of the same name for viola and choir.

🎎 Festivals and events

Various short events, particularly folk and world music and events celebrating different national cultures represented in the city.

ℹ Tourist information

www.visithoustontexas.com; tel: +1 713 437 5200

THE SHEPHERD SCHOOL OF MUSIC

MS 532, Rice University, PO Box 1892, Houston, TX 77251-1892.

t: +1 713 348 4854 e: music@rice.edu w: www.rice.edu

Courses Music students accepted according to needs of school's ensembles, so specific numbers of voice types and orchestral instruments. Undergrad performance majors required to study at least 4 semesters of chamber music. *Application requirements* Most applicants must audition in person, and it is responsibility of applicant to arrange audition time and date. *Application deadline* 2 Jan. *Scholarships* Merit awards available, renewable annually upon review. No financial need-based aid available for international students. *Music facilities* Alice Pratt Brown Hall includes 1000-seat auditorium, 250-seat recital hall, organ recital room, opera studio, 65 practice rooms, 7 classrooms, rehearsal/ensemble spaces, 54 teaching studios. *Accommodation* All 1st years at Rice University encouraged to live on campus; halls of residence arranged into 9 colleges of approx 230 residential places. *No of students* Approx 120 each undergrad and masters students and 50+ doctoral students at Shepherd School.

LOS ANGELES

With a population of nearly 4 million, the west coast city is country's second largest, despite the precarious geological location (on the San Andreas Fault) making it vulnerable to earthquakes. Most famous, arguably, for its central role in the film industry, an industry which has in the past attracted large numbers of classical composers to the city, particularly European émigrés and exiles, Stravinsky, Schoenberg, Korngold being 3 of the best known.

♪ Musical life

The unusually shaped Walt Disney Concert Hall (designed by Frank Gehry) is home to Los Angeles Philharmonic and its associated chorus. Orchestra formerly based at 3200-seat Dorothy Chandler Pavilion where LA Opera resident; numerous other concerts there from recitals to orchestral. Both venues part of Performing Arts Center of Los Angeles. Performance spaces at universities, eg UCLA has 4-hall arts complex with 2 concert halls (one large, one medium-sized). Hollywood Bowl probably the world's best known outdoor venue; has its own orchestra for light classical type music, and has performances from LA Phil during year, especially during summer. City is a centre for the music recording industry, so it attracts many musicians from fields of pop, rock, rap etc.

Other cultural information

Performing Arts Center includes theatrical venues as well as opera and music (Ahmanson Theatre, recently renovated Mark Taper Forum). Skirball Cultural Centre provides a mix of modern art forms, including film, readings, plays, exhibitions (as well as music). LA home to many well-known paintings, especially modern art Galleries include LA County Museum of Art and Getty Center; Hammer Museum has both permanent collection and regular changing exhibitions of contemporary art. The entertainment industry attracts visitors too, whether to the big studios such as Universal, Disneyland theme park or locations associated with film industry.

i Tourist information

www.discoverlosangeles.com

THE COLBURN SCHOOL

200 South Grand Ave, Los Angeles, CA 90012.
t: +1 213 621 2200 f: +1 213 625 0371
e: admissions@colburnschool.edu w: www.colburnschool.edu
Contact Kathleen Tesar, assoc dean for admissions. Courses Bachelor of music, performance diploma, artist diploma, professional studies certificate. Application requirements Prescreening recording, live audition for selected applicants. Term dates Late Aug-May. Application deadline Mid-Jan. Fees $100 application fee; $500 enrolment fee (once accepted). Scholarships All students receive full tuition, room and board scholarships. Language requirements Strong English skills (TOEFL score of 500+). Music facilities 415-seat concert hall, 200-seat hall, 85-seat hall; 45 practice rooms with 24 hr access, teaching studios. School is located across the street from Walt Disney Concert Hall, home of LA Philharmonic, and near home of LA Opera. Accommodation All students housed in school residence hall on campus. No of students c 35% of students are from overseas.

USC THORNTON SCHOOL OF MUSIC

Los Angeles, CA-90089-0851.
t: +1 213 740 6935 f: +1 213 740 3217
e: uscmusic@usc.edu w: www.usc.edu
Courses Academic programmes in several areas: choral music, classical guitar, composition, early music performance, jazz studies, keyboard studies, keyboard collaborative arts, music education, musicology, music industry, organ studies, popular music, scoring for film and TV, strings, studio/jazz guitar, vocal arts & opera, winds & percussion. BM degrees are 4 years, MM degrees are 2 years; graduate certificate 2 years. Application requirements Application by audition; some courses require pre-screening. Application deadline Applications to be received by 1 Dec. Music facilities Main performance venues: Bovard Auditorium (1220 seats), 3 recital halls (1 with 280, 2 with 90 seats); also proscenium theatre (590 seats). Various rehearsal spaces. Music library with over 90,000 items. No of students 1072 students in total, 627 of whom undergrad. Students come from approx 40 countries.

MADISON

City in northern US Midwest state of Wisconsin; combines plentiful green space with attractive urban environment and proximity to outdoor activities outside the city.

Musical life

Madison Symphony Orchestra performs its concert series at 2200+ seater Overture Hall; also provides accompaniment for Madison Opera's 2-opera season. Wisconsin Chamber Orchestra performs concert series throughout year, plus short summer outdoor season.

Other cultural information

As well as orchestra, Overture Center houses various theatre spaces and Madison Museum of Contemporary Art.

Festivals and events

Various rock and pop festivals, plus jazz, world and folk music.

i Tourist information

www.visitmadison.com; gmcvb@visitmadison.com; tel: +1 608 255 2537

UNIVERSITY OF WISCONSIN-MADISON – SCHOOL OF MUSIC

3561 Humanities, 455 North Park Street, Madison, WI 53706-1483.
t: +1 608 263 1900 *f:* +1 608 262 8876
e: music@music.wisc.edu *w:* www.music.wisc.edu
Courses Bachelors degrees in composition, music education, music performance, musicology and ethnomusicology, music theory; also available as part of double major. *Application requirements* Online application. Audition is 10-15 minute performance in chosen specialism, plus theory and piano tests. *Scholarships* Applicants who audition in person are eligible to apply for scholarships. Scholarships are tenable upon certain conditions (participation in performing organisations, satisfactory level of achievement and progress). *Music facilities* 9 classrooms; 3 large rehearsal rooms for choral, band and orchestra rehearsals; 111 practice rooms, some suitable for small ensembles; 3 concert halls (700-seat main hall, 170-seat recital hall, 160-seat organ recital hall).

NASHVILLE

Capital city of Tennessee. Known as 'music city', but another nickname ('Athens of the South') relates to the large number of higher education institutions in the city.

Musical life

Schermerhorn Symphony Center the relatively recently completed home of the Nashville Symphony, the orchestra performing around 100 concerts a year there. City's musical heritage lies more with country music (city is location for Country Music Hall of Fame) and rock and roll. Tennessee Performing Arts Centre, previous home for the orchestra, now concentrates on opera (Nashville Opera Association runs small number of productions each year), musicals, rock etc, with occasional classical events. Perhaps best known for Grand Ole Opry radio broadcast, unique in having its own dedicated venue (Grand Ole Opry House).

Other cultural information

City's art museum based at the full-scale reproduction of the Greek Parthenon in Centennial Park. State Museum explores Tennessee's history, not least its involvement in Civil War.

Festivals and events

Annual book festival and film festival.

Tourist information

www.visitmusiccity.com; tel: +1 800 657 6910

BLAIR SCHOOL OF MUSIC – VANDERBILT UNIVERSITY

2400 Blakemore Ave, Nashville, TN 37212-3499.
t: +1 615 322 7651 *f:* +1 615 343 0324
e: Blair-web@vanderbilt.edu *w:* www.vanderbilt.edu
Music facilities Over 60 teaching studios; over 50 practice rooms; 3 electronic labs; 3 interactive practice rooms; 286-seat recital hall; performing arts centre with 618-seat hall (inc pit, scene shop and dock, dressing rooms), choral rehearsal hall, instrumental rehearsal hall, audio recording studio; music library with over 40,000 volumes and scores, 5500 CDs, 14,500 LPs.

NEW HAVEN

Small harbour city in north eastern state of Connecticut closely linked with Yale University.

Musical life

New Haven Symphony Orchestra is one of the country's oldest, performing at Yale's Woolsey Hall or Shubert Theatre (for its pops series). School of Music a focus for much of the area's classical music.

Other cultural information

University is location for several museums, including a collection of historic musical instruments and a gallery concentrating on British art.

Festivals and events

Chamber music festival during summer.

Tourist information

www.newhavencvb.org; tel: +1 800 332 7829

YALE SCHOOL OF MUSIC

PO Box 208246, New Haven, CT 06520-8246.
t: +1 203 432 4155 (admissions) *f:* +1 203 432 7448 *e:* gradmusic.admissions@yale.edu
w: http://music.yale.edu
Courses Graduate professional school within Yale

University. Certificate in performance; BA/MM programme for performance or composition; MM (2-year postgrad); master of musical arts (3-year predoctoral programme); DMA. *Application requirements* All applicants must submit prescreening recordings and 3 letters of recommendation. *Application deadline* 1 Dec. *Fees* $100 application fee. *Scholarships* Full tuition award and fellowship made to all students, except those receiving awards from other agencies. International students may apply for student loans. *Music facilities* Woolsey Hall (seats 2695), includes pipe organ; Sprague Memorial Hall building, for chamber music and recitals (seats 680), also houses recording studio, music technology centre, multimedia room, practice rooms; music faculty studios. All-Steinway school.

NEW YORK

The largest city in the USA (population of over 8 million), though not the capital (in fact, it is not even capital of New York State). Its history as a gateway for immigrants from around the world means many diverse cultures are now well established there, something reflected in the pan-global nature of New York cuisine. Has a diverse architecture, ranging from skyscrapers for which it is famous to 'brownstone' terraces and townhouses, stretching across its five boroughs. Perhaps one of the world's best known cities, its landmarks and locations familiar to many through their appearance in countless films.

♪ Musical life

One of foremost musical cities in the world, with New York Philharmonic one of the foremost orchestras, performing concerts at its home in the Lincoln Center, Avery Fisher Hall, as well as Carnegie Hall (actually main stage, recital hall and medium sized hall, so a venue for performers of all kinds, and not just classical) and on tour. Other main orchestra is the Met Orchestra, the accompanists for Metropolitan Opera, the major city opera house. American Symphony Orchestra presents fewer concerts, but still a large group. Prestigious chamber orchestras include Orpheus Chamber Orchestra, notable for performing without conductor or fixed principals; Orchestra of St Luke's a versatile group of up to 55 musicians, but often performing in different sized groups; Jupiter Symphony Chamber Players has a season of about 40 concerts

in the city. Much opera besides the Met, eg New York City Opera, performing in various venues across city. Jazz at Lincoln Center the country's most prominent jazz promoter and has its own orchestra; the centre is a major music venue with several performance spaces.

🏛 Other cultural information

Performing arts of all kinds are plentiful, from experimental to mainstream. Theatre district on Broadway with more experimental or intimate performances 'off-Broadway'. Some of world's greatest art galleries and museums, particularly on 'museum mile': Metropolitan Museum of Art and Guggenheim Museum with its distinctive spiral are best known there; MoMA (Museum of Modern Art) another popular destination.

🎭 Festivals and events

As well as its year-round events, Lincoln Center promotes various festivals, eg Mostly Mozart Festival (Jul-Aug). Music and other events in Central Park during summer months. Music Theatre festival in autumn.

ℹ Tourist information

www.nycgo.com; visitorinfo@nycgo.com; tel: +1 212 484 1200

AARON COPLAND SCHOOL OF MUSIC

Room 203, Queens College CUNY, 65-30 Kissena Blvd, Flushing, NY 11367.
t: +1 718 997 3800 *f:* +1 718 997 3849
w: http://qcpages.qc.cuny.edu/music
Application requirements Audition and qualifying exam (including listening exam). *Application deadline* 31 Jan. *Music facilities* Concert hall with organ, theatrical lighting, professional quality audio and visual equipment; 487-seat recital hall; music library with 50,000 books and scores, 12,000 recordings, 65,000 items of performance music; media centre; 169-seat choral room/recital hall; orchestral rehearsal room; 40 practice rooms; recording studio overlooking concert hall, orchestral and choral rooms; 3 electronic music studios (computer studio, synthesizer room, editing studio).

THE JUILLIARD SCHOOL

60 Lincoln Center Plaza, New York, NY 10023-6588.

t: +1 212 799 5000 *e:* admissions@juilliard.edu
w: www.juilliard.edu

Courses 4-year bachelor of fine arts degree or 3-year diploma available in classical disciplines or jazz; 2-year artist diploma in opera studies; artist diploma in string quartet studies for pre-formed quartets; doctoral degree availabl in collaborative piano, composition, keyboard instruments, orchestral instruments, voice. *Application requirements* In-person audition for all applicants; overseas students may supply recording with application for pre-screening. *Fees* Tuition $28,640; non-refundable application fee (amount varies according to course) and miscellaneous admin fees also payable. *Scholarships* Financial aid (Juilliard scholarships, loans and work-study aid) available for international applicants. All doctor of musical arts students receive full-tuition scholarships. *Language requirements* TOEFL required for all non-native English speakers, regardless of citizenship. *Music facilities* Most floors in halls of residence have 2 practice rooms with pianos; 84 practice rooms in addition; rehearsal rooms, classrooms and 35 private teaching studios; more than 200 pianos; Alice Tully Hall for concerts, 1000-seat theatre, 200-seat drama theatre, 278-seat recital hall; 2 smaller recital/masterclass halls. Library with approx 68,000 scores and 20,000 books plus LPs, CDS, tapes and videos; orchestral library with complete collection of standard repertoire; media centre with 32 listening stations. *Accommodation* All first-time college students required to live in hall of residence; housing not guaranteed for complete period of study.

MANHATTAN SCHOOL OF MUSIC

120 Claremont Avenue, New York, NY 10027.

t: +1 212 749 2802 *e:* administration@msmnyc.edu; admission@msmnyc.edu *w:* www.msmnyc.edu

Courses Majors in classical or jazz; orchestral performance programme at postgrad level. Pinchas Zukerman Performance Program for exceptionally gifted violinists and violists. Special programmes available outside curriculum. *Application requirements* Application via www.unifiedapps.org only. Certain instruments require prescreening by CD; also audition and online essay. *Application deadline* 1 Dec. *Fees* $100 non-refundable application fee. *Scholarships* Manhattan School of Music Scholarships and President's Awards available to international students; awarded in varying amounts to highly qualified students on basis of audition and financial need. *Language requirements* TOEFL for non-native English speakers; min score depends on level of degree programme (some exceptions may be granted). *Music facilities* 846 auditorium, 281-seat recital hall, 35-seat performance space, 58 practice rooms; 2 spaces for student recitals, lectures etc. 2 new performance spaces (recital hall and flexible space). *Accommodation* 12 storeys of student residences, with total 550 beds.

OBERLIN

Small town in Ohio in the north of USA near Lake Erie; nearest major city is Cleveland.

i Tourist information
www.cityofoberlin.com

OBERLIN COLLEGE – CONSERVATORY OF MUSIC

39 W College St, Oberlin, OH 44074-1588.

t: +1 440 775 8413 *f:* +1 440 775 6972
e: conservatory.admissions@oberlin.edu *w:* www.oberlin.edu/con

Courses Bachelor of music; performance diploma; double degree programme; bachelor of arts; combined bachelor/masters programme in opera, conducting, historical performance; masters programme in historical performance; masters in music teaching; artist diploma. *Application requirements* Auditions on campus, at regional audition sites and in Asia; candidates living more than 600 miles from campus and 200 miles from regional centre may submit recording. Under 15% of international applicants accepted each year. *Fees* $38,012 tuition; $268 other required fees. *Scholarships* Over 80% of international students receive financial aid (scholarships or loans); average aid package is approx 75% of cost of attendance. *Music facilities* 5 concert halls (including 696-seat auditorium with organ, 144-seat Kulas Hall); 150 practice rooms; 40 studios; 10 classrooms; 200 Steinway grand pianos; 14 practice organs; over 1500 musical instruments for student use.

Library has over 121,000 books and scores, 47,000 sound recordings, 43 listening stations.Over 500 concerts promoted staged per year. *No of students* 615 students in total.

PHILADELPHIA

Located on Atlantic coast in north east USA, city was a major 19th century industrial city having also played a key role in America's successful fight for independence (it is the city where the Liberty Bell, symbolic of American independence, is kept). Centre for higher education with over 120,000 students at institutions (covering many disciplines) in the city. City gave its name to a style of soul music (the Philadelphia sound or Philadelphia soul) in 1970s.

Musical life

Philadelphia Orchestra is one of main US symphony orchestras, with a long tradition. Based at modern Kimmel Center for the Performing Arts, with its 2 concert halls (2500-seater and 650-seater) and 4-manual organ; building also home to the Chamber Orchestra of Philadephia. Chamber music concerts promoted at Kimmel Center and elsewhere by Philadelphia Chamber Music Society. Annenberg Center for the Performing Arts has more eclectic selection of modern music styles. Opera from Opera Company of Philadelphia, with varied season at Academy of Music.

Other cultural information

Pennsylvania Academy of the Fine Arts holds important collections of American arts. Musuem of Art has various changing exhibitions as well as its own varied collection; Rodin Museum, owned by Musuem, is dedicated to the French sculptor and has largest collection of his work outside France. African American Museum has collection of African American art and objects, the oldest of its kind. Walnut Street Theatre has been in constant use since 1809, supposedly the longest in English-speaking world.

Festivals and events

Annual folk festival in Aug; summer season of outdoor concerts by Philadelphia Orchestra at Mann Center for the Performing Arts.

Tourist information

www.independencevisitorcenter.com; inforequest@ independencevisitorcenter.com; tel: +1 800 537 7676

THE CURTIS INSTITUTE OF MUSIC

1726 Locust St, Philadelphia, PA 19103-6187. *t:* +1 215 893 5252 *f:* +1 215 893 9065 *e:* admissions@curtis.edu *w:* www.curtis.edu *Courses* Diploma or bachelor of music degree; master of music or professional studies certificate open to vocal students. *Application requirements* Auditions in Feb-Mar. *Term dates* Sep-May. *Application deadline* 11 Dec. *Fees* $150 application fee; $350 if postmarked after deadline. *Scholarships* All-scholarship policy to undergrad and postgrad students, regardless of financial situation (worth $33,500 and $46,000 per year respectively). *Language requirements* Min level of English required (written TOEFL 550). *Music facilities* 240-seat concert hall for recitals and faculty concerts, organ lessons, masterclasses etc. Opera studio black box theatre, seating 125. Resource centre has over 57,000 scores and books; orchestra library has over 1000 sets of parts. Instrument loans available, especially keyboard instruments for specialist students and conductors. *Accommodation* 13 2-bed apartments available, with priority to new students. *No of students* Over 160 students in total.

ROCHESTER

Mid-sized city in the north of New York State south of Lake Ontario, known for offering a high quality of life. Close to wine-growing region, and various wine-related attractions in or near the city.

Musical life

Conservatoire is main focus for city's classical music – Rochester Philharmonic performs substantial concert series there.

Other cultural information

Rochester Contemporary Art Center has exhibitions and contemporary performing arts events. Geva Theatre Center has 2 stages and put on wide variety of work, including premiers and comedy.

Festivals and events

Jazz festival in Jun includes free outdoor concerts.

NORTH AMERICA

Deaf Rochester Film Festival (Mar) – city has a large deaf community.

ℹ Tourist information
www.visitrochester.com; info@visitrochester.com; tel: +1 585 279 8300

EASTMAN SCHOOL OF MUSIC
26 Gibbs Street, Rochester, NY 14604.
t: +1 585 274 1000; +1 585 274 1060 (admissions) e: admissions@esm.rochester.edu
w: www.esm.rochester.edu
Courses As well as degrees, various specialist diplomas and certificates available: performer's certificate, artist's certificate, arts leadership certificate, certificate in college/community teaching, world music certificate, ethnomusicology. Application requirements Audition at Eastman, at US regional centre, by recording, or by audition in Asia (South Korea, Taiwan, Singapore, Hong Kong, Thailand; some majors and degree programmes require applicants to submit recording for prescreening). Overseas students must send 3 letters of recommendation. Application deadline 1 Dec. Fees $34,860 undergrad tuition fee (2008 figure); graduate fees depend on course. Language requirements Min proficiency in English required. Music facilities Eastman Theatre for large ensembles, Kilbourn Hall for recitals; 2 smaller venues, black box theatre for small opera, organ recital hall. No of students Approx 25% of students from overseas.

SALT LAKE CITY
Capital city of state of Utah, founded in mid 19th century by religious figure Brigham Young, a leader in the Mormon (Latter Day Saint) movement.

ℹ Tourist information
www.visitsaltlake.com; tel: +1 801 534 4900

UNIVERSITY OF UTAH - SCHOOL OF MUSIC
204 David P Gardner Hall, 1375 E Presidents Circle, Salt Lake City, UT 84112-0030.
t: +1 801 581 6762 f: +1 801 581 5683
w: www.music.utah.edu
Application deadline 15 Feb. Scholarships Undergrad scholarships and graduate assistantships available. Language requirements TOEFL score of 500 minimum for international students. Music facilities 2 concert halls, recital hall, chamber music room, music library. No of students 425 students in total.

SAN FRANCISCO
City on the Pacific coast of the USA that developed in the late 19th century during the gold rush when population numbers exploded. It recovered quickly from catastrophic earthquake in 1906, establishing strong footing as a financial centre allowing construction of projects such as the Golden Gate bridge in aftermath of the great depression that hit other cities in the USA. Many distinctive features (steep hills, cable cars and tramways, Victorian architecture) and noted for its seafood cuisine. Politically liberal in outlook, city was central in 60s alternative culture and a pioneer in fighting for gay rights.

♪ Musical life
Major arts venue is War Memorial and Performing Arts Center: holds San Francisco Opera and Ballet (over 3000 seats); San Francisco Symphony in the neighbouring Louise M Davies Symphony Hall, its sweeping elegant interior seating over 2700; Herbst Theater, with over 900 seats is a large venue for recitals and chamber music. San Francisco Chamber Orchestra gives numerous concerts in SF and nearby Californian cities. Other orchestras include San Francisco Composers Chamber Orchestra made up of composer-performers and concentrating on new music, as do San Francisco Contemporary Music Players; Kronos Quartet based in city, enhancing its contemporary credentials. Concert promoting organisations include San Francisco Performances which puts on events (especially chamber music and recitals) in many of city's main venues; Old First Concerts brings wide range of classical music to church that gives the series its name. Some contemporary music at Yerba Buena Center for the Arts.

▥ Other cultural information
Dance, particularly folk/ethnic-originating, at World Arts West centre and Yerba Buena Center. Unusual building of the San Francisco Musuem of Modern Art has works by numerous major 20th century artists; de Young Museum, also a striking modern design, is another important gallery. Prominence of gay communities in the city reflected

in cultural activities from Pride March to organisations and societies, and theatre and performance events.

 Festivals and events

Mozart festival in Jul, various locations. Range of performance at International Arts Festival in May. Various events celebrating city's multi-cultural make-up, eg Chinese moon festival in early autumn (city has a Chinatown and Chinese have been notable part of city's demographics from days of the goldrush).

i Tourist information

www.onlyinsanfrancisco.com; tourismsales@sfcvb.org; tel: +1 415 391 2000

SAN FRANCISCO CONSERVATORY OF MUSIC

50 Oak St, San Francisco, CA 94102-6011.
t: +1 415 503 6231 *f:* +1 415 503 6299
e: admit@sfcm.edu *w:* www.sfcm.edu
Contact Melissa Cocco-Mitten, admissions. *Courses* Performance-related instruction, theory, musicianship, history etc. *Application requirements* By audition only. *Term dates* Aug-May. *Application deadline* 1 Dec. *Fees* $100 application fee. *Scholarships* 94% of students currently on scholarship; average award is half-tuition. *Language requirements* TOEFL IBT: 61. *Music facilities* £80 million building in the civic centre area of San Francisco, a short distance from SF Symphony, Ballet and Opera. *No of students* 28% of students are from overseas.

TALLAHASSEE

Capital city of state of Florida.

i Tourist information

http://talgov.com

FLORIDA STATE UNIVERSITY – COLLEGE OF MUSIC

Tallahassee, FL 32306-1180.
t: +1 850 644 3424 *f:* +1 850 644 2033
w: www.music.fsu.edu
Courses Bachelors in music (general, commercial music, jazz, sacred music), composition, music education, music in performance, music therapy, music theory. Master of music (music theory, music therapy, musicology); also master of music in composition, music education, opera production,

music in performance. Doctorate in music composition, music in performance, music education, musicology, music therapy. *Application deadline* 4 Aug-1 Dec; later applications accepted if space available. *Scholarships* Scholarships available for US citizens or residents. *Language requirements* Min level of English required (TOEFL 550 or higher). *No of students* 750 undergrad students, 400 postgrad; includes students from approx 20 countries.

WINCHESTER

Small city in the state of Virginia in eastern USA. Area was heavily involved in fighting during American Civil War.

i Tourist information

www.visitwinchesterva.com; info@visiwinchesterva.com; tel: +1 540 542 1326

SHENANDOAH CONSERVATORY

Shenandoah University, 1460 University, Winchester, VA 22601.
t: +1 540 665 4569 *w:* www.su.edu/conservatory
Courses 64 degree programme choices in several areas: arts management, arts studies, church music, collaborative piano, composition, dance, ethnomusicology, jazz studies, music education, music performance, music production and recording technology, music therapy, theatre and music theatre. *Application requirements* Applications must include letter of recommendation. *Music facilities* Facilities include teaching and performing venues, dance space, recording studio, piano lab, individual practice facilities, small and large rehearsal rooms, MIDI lab, media centre, music education/therapy lab, voice lab.

MUSIC FESTIVALS

American Festival of Microtonal Music 318 East 70th St, Suite 5FW, New York, NY-10021. *t:* +1 212 517 3550 *e:* afmmjr@aol.com *w:* www.afmm.org *Contact* Johnny Reinhard, director.

American Landmark Festivals Federal Hall National Memorial, 26 Wall St, New York, NY 10005. *t:* +1 212 866 2086 *f:* +1 212 864 1665 *e:* AmLandmarkFstvls@aol.com *w:* www.americanlandmarkfestivals.org *Contact* Gena Rangel. Cultural and performing arts events in landmark venues. Solo and chmbr mus, opera and operetta, poetry reading, historic film with live music and commentary.

Aspen Music School and Festival 2 Music School Rd, Aspen, CO 81611. *t:* +1 970 925 3254 *f:* +1 970 925 8077 *e:* festival@aspenmusic.org *w:* www.aspenmusicfestival.com Annual. Orchestra, chamber music, opera.

Bang on a Can Summer Music Festival 80 Hanson Place #701, Brooklyn, New York, NY 11217. *t:* +1 718 852 7755 *e:* info@bangonacan.org *w:* www.bangonacan.org Residency for composers, performers and conductors of contemporary music at one of the foremost US contemporary art museums. Faculty includes Bang on a Can founders Michael Gordon, David Lang and Julia Wolfe.

Bloomington Early Music Festival Early Music Associates Inc, PO Box 734, Bloomington, IN 47402. *t:* +1 812 331 1263, also fax *w:* www.blemf.org Concerts, opera, talks, education events. Exceptional musicians from around the world. Performance on period instruments.

Blossom Festival The Cleveland Orchestra, Severance Hall, 11001 Euclid Ave, Cleveland, OH 44106-1796. *t:* +1 216 231 7300 *e:* info@clevelandorchestra.com *w:* www.clevelandorchestra.com Weekend concerts by the Cleveland Orchestra at large outdoor venue in national park outside Cleveland.

Boston Early Music Festival 161 First Street, Suite 202, Cambridge, MA 02142-1207. *t:* +1 617 661 1812 *f:* +1 617 661 1816 *e:* bemf@bemf.org *w:* www.bemf.org *Contact* Kathleen Fay, executive director; Paul O'Dette & Stephen Stubbs, artistic co-directors. Biennial. The week includes around-the-clock performances of mediaeval, renaissance and baroque music, public discussions, nearly 100 fringe concerts, performance masterclasses, dance workshops, the world-famous trade show of instrument makers and exhibitors from all over the world, Family Day programs, and more.

Boulder Bach Festival PO Box 1896, Boulder, CO 80306. *t:* +1 303 776 9666 *e:* info@boulderbachfestival.org *w:* http://boulderbachfestival.org Local professional orchestra, volunteer chorus and nationally known soloists.

Bowdoin International Music Festival Bowdoin College, 6300 College Station, Brunswick, ME 04011-8463. *t:* +1 207 373 1400 *f:* +1 207 373 1441 *e:* info@bowdoinfestival.org *w:* www.bowdoinfestival.org *Contact* Lewis Kaplan, artistic dir; Peter Simmons, executive dir.

Central City Opera Festival 400 S Colorado Blvd, Suite 530, Denver, CO 80246. *t:* +1 303 292 6500 *f:* +1 303 292 4958 *e:* admin@centralcityopera.org *w:* www.centralcityopera.org *Contact* Valerie Hamlin, publicist Annual. Four productions in the Central City Opera House, in the Rocky Mountains.

Chautauqua Institution PO Box 28, Chautauqua, NY 14722. *t:* +1 716 357 6217; +1 716 357 6200 (information) *f:* +1 716 357 9014 *e:* mmerkley@ciweb.org *w:* www.ciweb.org *Contact* Marty W Merkley, vice president & director of programming.

Colorado MahlerFest PO Box 1314, Boulder, CO 80306-1314. *t:* +1 303 530 2646 *e:* info@mahlerfest.org *w:* www.mahlerfest.org Festival dedicated to life and times of Mahler and culminates in a performance of one of his symphonies.

Colorado Music Festival 900 Baseline Rd, Cottage 100, Boulder, CO 80302. *t:* +1 303 449 1397 *e:* cmf@coloradomusicfest.com *w:* www.coloradomusicfest.org Annual 6 week summer festival at Chautauqua Auditorium, Boulder. Well known classical music repertoire, world music and works by modern composers.

Festival Miami University of Miami, 1320 South Dixie Hwy, Suite 731, Coral Gables, FL 33146. *t:* +1 305 284 4940 *f:* +1 305 284 3901 *e:* festivalmiami.music@miami.edu *w:* www.festivalmiami.com Annual. Orchestral, choral, chamber music, jazz, musical theatre, solo artists.

Florida International Festival PO Box 1310, Daytona Beach, FL 32115-1310. *t:* +1 386 257 7790 *f:* +1 386 238 1663 *w:* www.fif-lso.org Biennial. Classical, jazz, dance, chamber, masterclasses. 60 performances, plus free public events.

Gilmore International Keyboard Festival 359 Kalamazoo Mall, Suite 101, Kalamazoo, MI-49007. *t:* +1 269 342 1166 *e:* dhoke@gilmore.org *w:* www.thegilmore.org *Contact* Daniel R Gustin, dir. Biennial festival celebrating keyboard music. Concerts, recitals, lectures, chamber music, master classes and film.

Glimmerglass Opera Festival Box 191, Cooperstown, NY 13326. *t:* +1 607 547 5700 *f:* +1 607 547 6030 *e:* tickets@glimmerglass.org Operas, recitals, symposia.

Grand Teton Music Festival 40125 W Lake Creek Drive 1, Wilston, WY 83014. *t:* +1 307 733 3050 *f:* +1 307 739 9043 *e:* gtmf@gtmf.org *w:* www.gtmf.org Annual. The nation's finest classical musicians in orchestras and chamber music concerts.

Grant Park Music Festival 205 East Randolph Drive, Chicago, IL 60601. *t:* +1 312 742 7638 *e:* info@grantparkmusicfestival.com *w:* www. grantparkmusicfestival.com Festival with free outdoor concerts around Millennium Park, many by the festival's own orchestra and chorus.

The International Festival at Round Top PO Drawer 89, Round Top, TX 78954-0089. *t:* +1 979 249 3129 *f:* +1 979 249 3100 *e:* jamesd@ festivalhill.org *w:* www.festivalhill.org *Contact* James Dick, Alain Declert, contacts. Classical, orchestral, chamber, solo. Young artists studying and performing with faculty, all studying on full scholarship.

International Trumpet Guild Conference 410 Second Ave NE, Carmel, IN 46032. *t:* +1 317 844 4341 *f:* +1 317 844 2126 *e:* pr@trumpetguild. org *w:* www.trumpetguild.org 4 day festival featuring concerts and clinics by the world's finest trumpet players and teachers.

Marlboro Music Festival and Music 1616 Walnut St, Suite1600, Philadelphia, PA 19103. *t:* +1 215 569 4690 *f:* +1 215 569 9497 *e:* info@marlboro music.org *w:* www.marlboromusic.org Festival in Vermont with performances from young musicians and established artists who have worked together exploring a variety of chamber music.

The MasterWorks Festival The Christian Artists' Fellowship, PO Box 700, Winona Lake, IN 46590. *t:* +1 574 267 5973 *f:* +1 574 267 8315 *e:* cpaf@christianperformingart.org *w:* www. masterworksfestival.org *Contact* Stephanie Terranova. Classical performing arts camp for dedicated individuals aged 14-26 in a Christian setting. Orchestra and chamber music; intensive study, private lessons, masterclasses, rehearsals, recitals; concerto competition; classical guitar, piano, dance, opera and theatre; bible studies.

Midsummer Mozart Festival 760 Market St # 749, San Francisco, CA 94102. *t:* +1 415 627 9141 *f:* +1 415 627 9142 *w:* www.midsummer mozart.org Concerts featuring renowned soloists and local performers.

Mostly Mozart Festival Lincoln Center for the Performing Arts, 70 Lincoln Center Plaza, 9th Floor, New York, NY 10023. *t:* +1 212 875 5456 *e:* customerservice@lincolncenter.org *w:* www. lincolncenter.org

Newport Music Festival PO Box 3300, Newport, RI 02840. *t:* +1 401 846 1133 *f:* +1 401 849 1857 *e:* staff@newportmusic.org *w:* www. newportmusic.org *Contact* Mark P Malkovich III, general director; Mark Malkovich IV, marketing director. Classical chamber music in the Gilded Age Newport mansions, with America debut recitals of international artists. Composer Series features select chamber music of a major composer. 67 concerts featuring music from the romantic era.

Norfolk Chamber Music Festival Woolsey Hall, 500 College St, Ste 301, New Haven, CT 06520. *t:* +1 860 542 3000 *e:* norfolk@yale.edu *w:* www. yale.edu/norfolk

Ojai Music Festival 201 South Signal St, Ojai CA 93023. *e:* info@ojaifestival.org *w:* www.ojaifestival. org

Opera Theatre of St Louis PO Box 191910, 210 Hazel Ave, St Louis, MO 63119-7910. *t:* +1 314 961 0171 *f:* +1 314 961 7463 *e:* info@opera-stl. org *w:* www.opera-stl.org

Oregon Bach Festival 1257 University of Oregon, Eugene, OR 97403-1257. *t:* +1 800 457 1486 *f:* +1 541 346 5669 *e:* gevano@uoregon.edu *w:* www.oregonbachfestival.com *Contact* Helmuth Rilling, artistic dir & cond; John Evans, exec dir; George Evano, dir of communications. Choral-orchestral concerts focusing on the music and influence of JS Bach. Also chamber music, conducting masterclass, family events, educational programme.

Oregon Festival of American Music PO Box 1497, Eugene, OR 97440-1497. *t:* +1 541 687 6526 *e:* info@ofam.net *w:* www.theshedd.org Festival of a variety of American music; different theme each year.

Other Minds Festival 333 Valencia St, Suite 303, San Francisco, CA 94103-3552. *t:* +1 415 934 8134 *f:* +1 415 934 8136 *e:* otherminds@ otherminds.org *w:* www.otherminds.org *Contact* Charles Amirkhanian, executive & artistic director. Experimental and avant-garde contemporary music plus panel discussions.

Princeton Festival PO Box 2063, Princeton, NJ 08543. *t:* +1 609 537 0071 *w:* www.princeton festival.org

Sarasota Music Festival 709 North Tamiami Trail, Sarasota, FL 34236. *t:* +1 941 952 9634 *f:* +1 941 953 3059 *w:* www.sarasotamusicfestival.org *Contact* Robert Levin, artistic director; RoseAnn McCabe, admin director. Masterclasses and performances of a wide variety of chamber music.

Tanglewood 297 West St, Lenox. *e:* bhorgan@bso.org *w:* www.bso.org

Canada

Canada

Canada's major cities are some of the best reputed for quality of life – the country is often seen as the ideal place for visitors who wish to experience the scale of North America but are not attracted by its neighbour to the south. And even though the cliché of the country is of the chilly north (certainly true during winter!), the cities by the Great Lakes are on the same latitude as the Mediterranean Sea. And we shouldn't forget that the country is bilingual, or rather, that while most of the country speak English, the north east province of Québec is French-speaking, and proudly so.

In many respects, the situation regarding music education in Canada is similar to that in the US – training comes through specialist institutions and universities with practical music faculties; honours degrees at bachelors level come after 4 years' study, for instance (although masters degrees can take up to 2 years to complete); students will be expected to pay sizeable tuition fees (although in general not as much as in the US), but again with the possibility of significant financial support.

One difference that interested students will have to note is that Canada has two official languages, with French the official language in the north eastern province of Québec (which includes Montréal), English elsewhere. Non-native speakers of those languages will be expected to pass a language test or be able to demonstrate sufficient proficiency. That said, McGill University in Montréal is an anglophone institution. So, as with everything, students are advised to make full enquiries as to entrance requirements; but as North American college websites are very well maintained, and most include comprehensive information for international students.

MONTREAL

Largest city in province of Québec, located on confluence of St Lawrence and Ottawa rivers. Its importance in 19th and early 20th century, along with its previous incarnation as a port city, have left a historic architectural legacy which, combined with new building more recently means the city's built environment is diverse – the Old Montreal area around the old port has a characteristic atmosphere, but other districts have their own character too. City has a large amount of green space, especially around the Mount Royal (from where the city gets its name); as this might suggest, the official language is French.

Musical life

Place des Arts arts complex is home to 3 orchestras: Orchestre Symphonique de Montréal and Orchestre Métropolitain du Grand Montréal are the largest city orchestras; I Musici de Montréal a small chamber group also performs at other venues such as Salle Pollack at McGill University and Salle Claude Champagne at Université de Montréal (both venues with substantial musical programmes). Opéra de Montréal and city's ballet company also at Place des Arts (both OSM and OMGM provide orchestral accompaniment, depending on the show). Contemporary music promoted by Société de Musique Contemporaine de Québec (SMCQ) through its regular concert series.

Other cultural information

Musée d'Art Contemporain de Montréal has permanent collection of over 7000 pieces; also visiting and special exhibitions. Thriving contemporary dance scene; city is home base for Cirque du Soleil. Centre Pierre Péladeau includes 2 rehearsal rooms as well as auditorium (Salle Pierre-Mercure); Segal Centre for the Performing Arts includes 2 theatre spaces and cinema, plus company dedicated to Yiddish theatre.

Festivals and events

Annual chamber music festival in May, with performances in various venues across the city. New music festival run by SMCQ in late winter. International music competition annually in May (disciplines change from year to year). Just for Laughs festival is world's largest comedy festival; also international jazz festival.

Tourist information

www.tourisme-montreal.org; info@tourisme-gouv. qc.ca; tel: +1 514 873 2015

SCHULICH SCHOOL OF MUSIC - MCGILL UNIVERSITY

Strathcona Music Building, 555 Sherbrooke St West, Montreal, QC H3A 1E3.
t: +1 514 398 4546 f: +1 514 398 8873
e: conservatory.music@mcgill.ca w: www.mcgill.ca/music
Courses BMus available in composition, music education, music history, music theory, performance (keyboard, voice, orchestral), performance (church music), early music performances, jazz. Also diploma programmes: licentiate for instrumentalists/singers wishing to focus on performance rather than theory; artist diploma for students of advanced level who already have bachelor or licentiate. MA, MMus, DMus and PhD available in various areas. Students studying orchestral instrument included in orchestral training programme. Application requirements 15-20 min audition in Feb. Applications must include statement of intent explaining reasons for applying to the school. Application deadline 15 Jan, for entry and scholarships. Fees CAN $85 application fee, CAN $60 audition fee, both non-refundable; for postgrad, fee is CAN $100. Scholarships Various scholarships available: approx 40 Schulich Scholarships of CAN $5000-10,000; entrance scholarships; limited number of string scholarships (CAN $10,000).

UNIVERSITÉ DE MONTRÉAL – FACULTÉ DE MUSIQUE

PO Box 6128, Station Centre-ville, Montréal QC, H3C 3J7.
t: +1 514 343 6427 f: +1 514 343 5727
e: musique@umontreal.ca w: www.umontreal.ca
Application requirements Applicants for performance course required to have technical ability and knowledge of repertoire, theory and solfege. Examples of tests available on website. Fees International students: CAN $419.77 per credit (undergrad); CAN $6296.55 (full time masters). Scholarships No university scholarships for international students; some government awards for students from developing countries. Language requirements Language of instruction and administration is French.

NORTH AMERICA

QUEBEC CITY

City in north east Canada, capital of the province of the same name, overlooking (with some spectacular views) the St Lawrence River. One of the oldest settled cities in the country, and much of its architecture is north European in flavour. First language is French.

Musical life

Orchestra Symphonique de Québec the principal orchestra (has associated choir), performing in city at the Grand Théâtre de Québec; theatre's 2 halls (one 1875 seats, one with approx 500) stage various other music events including some opera. Les Violons du Roy a well-known string ensemble performing music from baroque to present day music, associated with choir La Chapelle de Québec; main venue in city is Palais Montcalm (main hall has 1100+ seats). Traditional/folk music strongly influenced by French traditions.

Other cultural information

Musée National des Beaux-Arts has a collection spanning several centuries of art; also hosts touring and special exhibitions. Of particular interest to area is Musée de l'Amérique Française (the oldest museum in Canada) with various collections of artefacts, botanical samples, books etc, plus exhibitions examining development of French culture on the continent. L'Institut Canadien de Québec predominantly promoter of French Canadian literature but also has visual and performing arts activities. Contemporary dance at La Rotonde from various small local and international companies.

Festivals and events

Summer festival has various kinds of performance, with music covering various styles, principally non-classical.

Tourist information

www.quebecregion.com; tel: +1 418 641 6654

CONSERVATOIRE DE MUSIQUE DE QUÉBEC

270 rue Saint-Amable, Québec, Québec G1R 5G1.
t: +1 418 643 2190 f: +1 418 644 9658
e: CMQ@conservatoire.gouv.qc.ca
w: www.conservatoire.gouv.qc.ca

Fees Max tuition fees for overseas students: CAN $2480 (undergrad), CAN $7440 (masters), CAN $9300 (doctorate); other annual fees apply. *Language requirements* All courses given in French.

TORONTO

City in province of Ontario on the shores of the Lake Ontario. Although city began growing in importance at the start of 19th century and there are older areas, the predominant architectural styles are more modern; CN Tower a distinctive feature, was world's tallest structure for many years. Population of approx 2.5 million, with very diverse multicultural profile.

Musical life

Major centre for performing arts in Canada. Toronto Symphony Orchestra based at distinctively designed purpose-built hall (Roy Thompson Hall); Toronto Philharmonia is smaller group based at Toronto Centre for the Arts (George Weston Recital Hall; non-professional Orchestra Toronto also resident at the centre). New music, especially Canadian, from chamber-sized Esprit Orchestra. Canadian Opera Company is country's largest; has its own orchestra and venue at Four Seasons Centre, shared with National Ballet of Canada. Chamber music promotions from Music Toronto at St Lawrence Centre for the Arts; centre has other resident music groups, Opera in Concert, Operetta Theatre and brass band (as well as Esprit Orchestra). City has its own early music centre, reflecting the large amount of period music in the city; centre promotes concerts, runs workshops and raises awareness of early music. Sony Centre has a varied programme of entertainment events.

Other cultural information

Various theatres: Princess of Wales Theatre purpose-built for musicals. Elgin and Winter Gardens complex unusual in being a double-decker theatre (has 2 rooms, one above the other); has range of shows. Young Centre for the Performing Arts has resident company (Soulpepper) but visited by many others.

Festivals and events

Main arts event is LuminaTO (Jun), with various art forms and styles across the city. Summer Music

Festival focuses more on classical (Jul-Aug), including opera. Prestigious comedy festival; jazz festival (Jun-Jul); various ethnic cultural events.

i Tourist information
www.seetorontonow.com; toronto@torcvb.com; +1 416 203 2500

THE ROYAL CONSERVATORY – THE GLENN GOULD SCHOOL

273 Bloor Street West, Toronto ON, M5S 1W2.
t: +1 416 408 2824 f: +1 416 406 3096
e: glenngouldschool@rcmusic.ca w: www.rcmusic.ca

Courses School is part of The Royal Conservatory, a larger community-based music education organisation. Course programmes: performance diploma program (PDP) has practical focus; bachelor of music degree in performance allows PDP students to obtain accredited degree; artist diploma programmes in solo, piano, orchestral instruments *Scholarships* All students eligible for some financial aid; also full tuition awards, scholarships (renewable depending on progress and performance), assistantships, bursaries for those in financial need. All awards subject to conditions. *Music facilities* Based at TELUS Centre; facilities include 1140-seat concert hall, smaller hall, multipurpose rehearsal hall, chamber/recital room, 77 practice studios, 20 classrooms, music tech lab, library. *Accommodation* No on-campus housing facilities; website gives details of accommodation organisations. *No of students* 130 students in total.

VANCOUVER

Canada's main port, on west coast in British Columbia.

♪ Musical life
City's main orchestra is Vancouver Symphony Orchestra, although Vancouver Opera also has its own professional group for its 4 annual productions. City Opera of Vancouver a company producing chamber opera. Early Music Vancouver promotes appreciation of early music through educational events, performance opportunities, sponsorship etc. Active world music scene with various intercultural collaborations and folk groups/events.

🏛 Other cultural information
Vancouver Playhouse and Arts Club Theatre for standard theatrical performance. Main gallery is Vancouver Art Gallery.

🎭 Festivals and events
PuSh International Performing Arts Festival (Jan-Feb) has all-round programme of live performance, including music, dance, theatre. Vancouver Early Music Festival in Jul-Aug has concert, workshops and lecture/presentations. International folk and jazz festivals. Shakespeare festival overlooking the main bay; alternative theatre events at Vancouver Fringe.

i Tourist information
www.vancouvertourist.com

UNIVERSITY OF BRITISH COLUMBIA SCHOOL OF MUSIC

Music Building, 6361 Memorial Rd, Vancouver BC, V6T 1Z2.
t: +1 604 822 3113 f: +1 604 822 4884
e: musicoff@interchange.ubc.ca w: www.music.ubc.ca

Courses 4-year BMus, MMus, MA, DMA, PhD qualifications available. *Application requirements* For BMus, candidates must audition and meet minimum academic requirements for entry into university. Auditions in Jan/Feb or Apr; audition in person preferred, but recordings acceptable in some circumstances. *Fees* International students: CAN $20,623 (undergraduate); additional fees apply. *Scholarships* CAN $3 million spent on scholarships for international students (across university as a whole). Various other awards and financial aid available. *Language requirements* Minimum level of English required; see website for details of conditions. *Music facilities* 289-seat recital hall in department; Chan Centre for the Performing Arts has 1400-seat hall plus 200-seat theatre. Old auditorium currently being restored and will be an additional performance space resource.

MUSIC FESTIVALS

Banff Summer Arts Festival The Banff Centre, PO Box 1020, Banff AB, T1L 1H5. t: +1 403 762 6100 f: +1 403 762 6444 e: arts_info@banffcentre.ca w: www.banff.ca Annual festival of concerts, performances, exhibitions, art walks, readings, lectures etc.

Canada's National Arts Centre Summer Music Institute National Arts Centre, Music Dept, 53 Elgin St, Ottawa Ontario K1P 5W1. *t:* +1 613 947 7000 ext 568 *f:* +1 613 943 1400 *e:* charris@nac-cna. ca *w:* www.nac.cna.ca/smi *Contact* Christy Harris, mgr NAC SMI Young Artists Programme: Pinchas Zukerman and an exceptional faculty provide private instruction and chamber music coaching for over 65 highly talented students. All perform in chamber ensemble concerts. Senior and junior levels. Conductors Programme: intense workshops with dedicated professional ensemble directed by Kenneth Kiesler. Conductors conduct NAC orchestra in final concert. Young Composers Programme: opportunity to workshop new music with dedicated chamber musicians directed by NAC Award composer Gary Kulesha.

Canterbury International Choral Festival Arts Bureau for the Continents, c/o 350 Sparks St, Suite #207a, Ottawa Ontario K1R 7S8. *t:* +1 613 234 3360 *f:* +1 613 236 2636 *e:* abc@abc.ca *w:* www. abc.ca

The Elora Festival – A Celebration in Song PO Box 370, Elora, Ontario N0B 1S0. *t:* +1 519 846 0331 *f:* +1 519 846 5947 *e:* info@elorafestival. com *w:* www.elorafestival.com *Contact* Jurgen Petrenko, general manager. Primarily classical choral music; also chamber music and contemporary series.

Festival de Musique de Chambre de Montréal 5560 Sherbrooke St W, Montréal QC, H4A 1W3. *t:* +1 514 489 7444 *f:* +1 514 481 6270 *e:* administration@festivalmontreal.org *w:* www. festivalmontreal.org Performances in historic sites by renowned artists and rising stars.

Festival International de Lanaudière 1500 Base-de-Roc Boulevard, Joliette PQ J6E 3Z1. *t:* +1 450 759 7636; +1 800 561 4343 (tickets during festival) *f:* +1 450 759 3082 *w:* www.lanaudiere. org *Contact* François Bédard, general manager. Largest classical music festival in Canada located 30 minutes from the eastern tip of the island of Montreal. Concerts in covered 2000-seat amphitheatre in forest surroundings.

Festival International de Musique Actuelle de Victoriaville CP 460, Victoriaville PQ G6P 6T3. *t:* +1 819 752 7912 *f:* +1 819 758 4370 *e:* info@ fimav.qc.ca *w:* www.fimav.qc.ca *Contact* Michel

Levasseur, artistic director. New music festival, jazz, improvised rock, contemporary and electroacoustic music.

Festival Orford 3165 Chemin du Parc, Orford, Quebec J1X 7A2. *t:* +1 819 843 9871 *f:* +1 819 843 7274 *e:* centre@arts-orford.org *w:* www.arts-orford.org Chamber and symphonic music, opera, sacred music with musicians of international repute.

Montreal/New Music International Festival Société de Musique Contemporaine de Québec, Centre Pierre-Péladeau, 300 blvd de Maisonneuve Eest, Montréal QC, H2X 3X6. *t:* +1 514 843 9305 *e:* smcq@smcq.qc.ca *w:* www.smcq.qc.ca

Niagara International Music Festival Arts Bureau for the Continents, c/o 815 Taylor Creek Drive, Suite #200, Ottawa, Ontario K1C 1T1. *t:* +1 613 234 3360 *f:* +1 613 236 2636 *e:* abc@abc.ca *w:* www.abc.ca Annual choral festival for groups of all ages hosted in the Niagara Falls area of Ontario.

Ottawa International Music Festival Arts Bureau for the Continents, 350 Sparks St, Suite #207a, Ottawa, Ontario K1R 7S8. *t:* +1 613 234 3360 *f:* +1 613 236 2636 *e:* abc@abc.ca *w:* www.abc. ca For world choirs, bands and orchestras.

PuSh International Performing Arts Festivals 300-640 West Broadway, Vancouver, BC V57 1G4. *t:* +1 604 605 8284 *f:* +1 604 874 7874 *e:* info@ pushfestival.ca *w:* http://pushfestival.ca Live performing arts: theatre, dance, music and interdisciplinary performance.

Summer Music from the Comox Valley PO Box 3056, Courtenay BC V9N 5NS. *t:* +1 250 338 7463 *f:* +1 250 703 2251 *e:* info@cymc.ca *w:* www.cymc.ca *Contact* BA Hampton, general manager. International youth music camp and festival. Jazz, chamber music, orchestra, concert band, opera, musical theatre. Student and faculty performances in venues on Vancouver Island.

Toronto International Choral Festival Arts Bureau for the Continents, 350 Sparks St, Suite #207a, Ottawa, Ontario K1R 7S8. *t:* +1 613 234 3360 *f:* +1 613 236 2636 *e:* abc@abc.ca *w:* www. abc.ca For world choirs.

Toronto Summer Music 720 Bathurst St, Suite 501, Toronto, ON M5S 2R4. *t:* +1 647 430 5699 *e:* info@torontosummermusic.com *w:* www. torontosummermusic.com Canadian and international musicians in concerts, opera, workshops, lectures.

Unisong Festival, Ottawa Arts Bureau for the Continents, 350 Sparks St, Suite #207a, Ottawa, Ontario K1R 7S8. *t:* +1 613 234 3360 *f:* +1 613 236 2636 *e:* abc@abc.ca *w:* www.abc.ca For Canadian choirs singing en masse on Canada Day.

Vancouver Early Music Festival 1254 West 7th Avenue, Vancouver BC V6H 1B6. *t:* +1 604 732 1610 *f:* +1 604 732 1602 *e:* workshops@ earlymusic.bc.ca *w:* www.earlymusic.bc.ca *Contact* Jose Verstappen, executive director; Melissa Duchak, assoc programme dir. Series of summer courses and early music concerts.

WSO International New Music Festival 555 Main St, Suite 101, Winnipeg, Manitoba R3B 1C3. *t:* +1 204 949 3950 *f:* +1 204 956 4271 *e:* wso@ wso.mb.ca *w:* www.wso.mb.ca *Contact* Alexander Mickelthwaite, music director; Vincent Ho, composer-in-residence. WSO welcomes guest composers and artists from round the world to present a broad range of musical styles.

NORTH AMERICA

NOTES

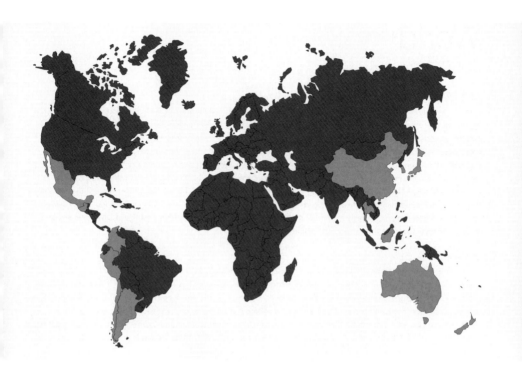

WORLD

World

AUSTRALIA & NEW ZEALAND

Australia's music conservatoires are all faculties of universities and are therefore fully integrated within the national higher education system, and the structure of degree programmes closely matches the anglo-saxon model (bachelors, masters, doctorate). The slight difference is that Australian institutions offer a degree after 3 years' study; successful completion of this entitles students to move to a 4th 'honours' year. A more significant difference is that, being a southern hemisphere country (winter during the northern hemisphere's summer and so on) the academic year is reversed. While this may cause a difficulty for exchange programmes, for those looking to study at postgraduate level it would simply be a question of taking a break between the end of the bachelor's degree at home and the beginning of the masters in Australia (beginning in February). The same is true of New Zealand, and here also practical advanced music training is provided at universities, incorporated within traditional university academic music departments rather than specialist faculties.

WORLD

The majority of this guide has focused on institutions in countries in the west with a long tradition of providing music training. But as many western conservatoires are realising, the opportunities for establishing links elsewhere are great – China in particular is proving willing to build contacts in western countries (several US institutions, for instance, hold entrance auditions in China), just as it is raising the profile of classical music in the country. Elsewhere – Palestine, for example, or India – the infrastructure for classical music education is only now being put in place. In the remainder of this section, we provide contact details for a selection of institutions in various locations around the world.

Australia and New Zealand

AUSTRALIA

ADELAIDE

ℹ **Tourist information**
www.adelaidecitycouncil.com; visitor@adelaide
citycouncil.com; tel: +61 8 8203 7611

ELDER CONSERVATORIUM OF MUSIC

The University of Adelaide, Adelaide SA 5005.
t: +61 8 8303 5995 *f:* +61 8 8303 4423
e: music@adelaide.edu.au *w:* www.music.
adelaide.edu.au
Courses Bachelor of music (performance) is 1-year
supplement to bachelors in music studies (3 years).
Application requirements International students apply
direct to university or through international
representatives across the world. Audition process
involves audition, interview, portfolio plus aural and
theory test. Master of music and PhD available in
performance, as well as ethnomusicology/musicology,
composition, music education, music technology.
Graduate diploma for performance-focused
Application deadline 30 Sep for local and international
students; auditions early Dec (some late auditions may
be scheduled). *Fees* AUS $19,000, international
undergrad tuition; AUS $22000, international
postgrad tuition. *Music facilities* Elder Hall auditorium,
with organ; electronic music unit; music library.

BRISBANE

ℹ **Tourist information**
www.brisbane.qld.gov.au

QUEENSLAND CONSERVATORIUM

PO Box 3428, South Brisbane QLD 4101.
t: +61 7 3735 6111 *f:* +61 7 3735 6262
e: qcgu_enquiry@griffith.edu.au *w:* www.griffith.
edu.au/music
Courses Range of undergrad and postgrad courses.
Music facilities 2 campuses (South Bank and Gold
Coast). 615 seat concert hall, music technology
studios and music library (South Bank); pop music
studios (South Bank). Various performers in
residence. *No of students* Nearly 700 students from
over 20 countries internationally.

CANBERRA

ℹ **Tourist information**
www.visitcanberra.com.au; crvc@act.gov.au; tel:
+61 2 6205 0044

CANBERRA SCHOOL OF MUSIC

The Australian National University, Canberra ACT
0200.
t: +61 2 6125 5111 *e:* schoolofmusic@anu.edu.
au *w:* www.anu.edu.au/music
Courses Bachelor of arts and bachelor of music
degrees; successful completion of 3-year bachelor
of music gives access to 4th year specialisation.
1-year master of music in performance (including
jazz), musicology or composition; graduate diploma
and graduate certificate also available for students
wishing to advance their technical or musical skills.
School is home to university Keyboard Institute,
focusing on keyboard-related activity in
performance, teaching, research and instrument-
making/restoration. *Scholarships* ANU scholarships
available for students in all faculties, including
international students. *Music facilities* Llewellyn Hall,
seats over 1300, is also venue for visiting professional
groups; band room, seats 120; rehearsal room,
seats 120. *Accommodation* International students
guaranteed accommodation if they accept academic
offer and apply for accommodation by 21 Jan.

HOBART

ℹ **Tourist information**
www.welcometohobart.com.au; info@vibetasmania.
co.au; tel: +61 3 6234 4666

UNIVERSITY OF TASMANIA
CONSERVATORIUM OF MUSIC

University of Tasmania, Private Bag 63, Hobart
TAS 7001.
t: +61 3 6226 7314 *e:* international.office@
utas.edu.au *w:* www.utas.edu.au/music
Courses BMus is 3-year professional training degree,
with option to progress to 1-year advanced honours
degree. Masters and graduate diploma qualifications
for specialist performers. *Application requirements*
Written test on music theory and history, plus aural
test and general writing ability; performance audition
comprising 3 contrasting pieces; interview. Overseas
applicants may be able to supply recording. *Fees*
Undergrad music degrees AUS $15,370; masters
degree, graduate diploma etc approx AUS $15,000.
Scholarships Various scholarships available. *Music
facilities* 200 seat recital hall with 4 pianos, computer
lab, recording room/digital streaming studio, DVD
authoring studio, piano lab, percussion room, lecture
theatre with piano, music library.

SYDNEY

i Tourist information
www.sydneyaustralia.com.au

AUSTRALIAN INTERNATIONAL CONSERVATORIUM OF MUSIC

114 Victoria Rd, Rozelle, Sydney NSW 2039.
t: +61 2 9637 0777 *f:* +61 2 9637 0222
e: admin@aicm.edu.au *w:* www.aicm.edu.au
Contact Katrina Quintal. *Courses* Bachelor of music (perf), diploma of music (perf); postgrad pathways; also perf arts high school (yrs 7-12). *Application requirements* Entrance by audition and interview. *Term dates* Mid Feb-early Jul (semester 1); end Jul-early Dec (semester 2). *Application deadline* 12 Feb (semester 1); 10 Jul (semester 2). *Fees* AUS $16,800 (local), AUS $19,600 (international). *Scholarships* Check website for details. *Language requirements* IELTS score 6.0 for international students. *Music facilities* Performance hall, practice studios, classrooms, recording facilities, computers and technology, various instruments. *Accommodation* Homestay accommodation available. *No of students* 20% of student body from overseas.

SYDNEY CONSERVATORIUM OF MUSIC

The University of Sydney, Sydney NSW 2006.
t: +61 9351 1222 *f:* +61 2 9351 1264 *e:* con.international@usyd.edu.au *w:* www.music.usyd.edu.au
Contact Elaine Chia. *Courses* Diploma of music, bachelor of music studies, bachelor of music (performance, musicology, composition, music education), advanced diploma of opera, graduate diploma of music, master of music studies (performance, pedagogy, creative sound production), master of music (performance, musicology, composition, music education), DMA, PhD. *Application requirements* Must meet minimum university entry and pass audition and/or interview. *Term dates* Late Feb-Jun (semester 1); Jul to end Nov (semester 2). *Application deadline* 31 Oct (for Feb entry); 30 Apr (for Jul entry). *Fees* Undergraduate from AUS $22,855; postgraduate from AUS $19,920 *Scholarships* Over AUS $5 million in scholarships awarded each year. Merit-based scholarships assessed on audition. No separate application necessary. *Exchange details* Exchange agreements with Royal Academy of Music, Royal College of Music, Royal Northern College of Music (UK); Hochschule für Musik Freiburg, Hochschule für Kunste Bremen (Germany); Shanghai Conservatory of Music (China); also many other destinations in Asia, Europe and USA through the University of Sydney's university-wide programme. *Language requirements* English (IELTS minimum 6.5). *Music facilities* 5 performance halls (inc 500-seat concert hall), 69 practice rooms, 130 teaching studios and offices, music technology and recording facilities, extensive library. Close to Sydney Opera House, in heart of Sydney's cultural precinct. *Accommodation* On-campus accommodation at University of Sydney; accommodation service available through international office. *No of students* 830 students, inc 80 international students.

MUSIC FESTIVALS

Adelaide Festival of the Arts PO Box 8221, Station Arcade, Adelaide SA 5000. *t:* +61 8 8216 4444 *f:* +61 8 8216 4455 *e:* info@adelaidefestival.com.au *w:* www.adelaidefestival.com.au Biennial. Multi-arts festival. Opera, dance, classical and contemporary music, theatre, visual arts, new media events, literature, outdoor, masterclasses, forums, etc

Australian Festival of Chamber Music PO Box 5871, Townsville Qld 4810. *t:* +61 7 4771 4144 *f:* +61 7 4771 4122 *e:* info@afcm.com.au *w:* www.afcm.com.au Concert season of chamber music; chamber music seminar.

Australian International Music Festival Sydney World Projects, 195 Glen Cove Marina Rd, Suite 201, Vallejo, CA 94591. *t:* +1 707 556 5885 *f:* +1 707 556 5896 *e:* deborah-gibbs@world-projects.com *w:* www.world-projects.com *Contact* Deborah Gibbs, World Projects CEO. Annual. Brings together best school, university, community musicians, with opportunity at Sydney Opera House and join in a wide variety of music and social activities.

Perth International Arts Festival M418, University of Western Australia, 3 Crawley Ave, Crawley WA 6009. *t:* +61 8 6488 2000 *f:* +61 8 6488 8555 *e:* festival@perthfestival.com.au *w:* www.perthfestival.com.au *Contact* Shelagh Magadza, artistic director; Julian Donaldson, general manager. Oldest annual international multi-arts festival in the southern hemisphere. Offers some of the world's best theatre, music, film, visual arts, street arts, literature and free community events.

NEW ZEALAND

AUCKLAND
ℹ Tourist information
www.aucklandnz.com; nz@aucklandnz.com; tel: +64 9 307 0616

NATIONAL INSTITUTE OF CREATIVE ARTS AND INDUSTRIES
The University of Auckland, Building 520, 6 Symonds St, Auckland.
t: +64 9 373 7599 ext 87409 *e:* info-music@auckland.ac.nz *w:* www.creative.auckland.ac.nz
Courses Bachelor of music, 3-year course in composition, history and literature of music, jazz, classical performance, popular music; available as honours degree with 1 extra year's study. Postgrad diploma and master of music both 1-year courses; master of music available in performance, composition, musicology. Doctor of music arts an advanced performance-centred programme. *Term dates* Classes start early March (semester 1) and mid Jul (semester 2). *Application deadline* 1 Oct (semester 1), 1 May (semester 2). *Fees* For international students: NZ $23,290 (BA), NZ $24,390 (BA honours), NZ $24,390 (MM), NZ $27,680 (doctor of musical arts); further administrative fees also apply. *Scholarships* Scholarships available for international students at both undergrad and postgrad levels. *Language requirements* English required. *Music facilities* 155-seat music theatre used for staged productions and concerts; practice spaces, recording facilities. *Accommodation* Student residences available in Auckland, including full-board halls of residence, self-catering university flats and private accommodation.

WELLINGTON
ℹ Tourist information
www.wellingtonnz.com; bookings@WellingtonNZ.com; tel: +64 4 802 4860

TE KOKI - THE NEW ZEALAND SCHOOL OF MUSIC
PO Box 2332, Wellington.
t: +64 4 463 5369 *f:* +64 4 463 5157
e: info@nzsm.ac.nz *w:* www.nzsm.ac.nz
Courses Majors in arranging, classical performance, ethnomusicology, instrumental/vocal composition, jazz, music studies, music therapy, musicology, sonic arts *Application requirements* International students

apply through Victoria University of Wellington *Application deadline* Mid Sep. *Fees* NZ $ 19,878, international undergrad tuition; NZ $22,035, international postgrad tuition; various non-tuition fees also apply. *Scholarships* Scholarships available but must be applied for; see website for details of prizes available, including music prizes as well as scholarships. *Music facilities* Concert room, concert hall, small theatre; instrument collection includes period instruments (originals and copies); keyboard lab with 12 digital pianos (at Kelburn campus) and with 22 keyboards (at Mt Cook campus); practice rooms available. Artists in residence are New Zealand Piano Quartet, the New Zealand String Quartet, Chrome (period instrument group).

MUSIC FESTIVALS
Adam International Cello Festival and Competition PO Box 3770, Christchurch. *t:* +64 3355 4054 *f:* +64 3 365 0318 *e:* catherine@artscentre.org.nz *w:* www.adaminternationalcellofest.com Competition, daily masterclasses, concerts, recitals, workshops and finals gala concert.
New Zealand International Arts Festival PO Box 10-113, Wellington. *t:* +64 4 473 0149 *f:* +64 4 471 1164 *e:* nzfestival@festival.co.nz *w:* www.nzfestival.co.nz *Contact* Lissa Twomey, artistic director; David Inns, chief executive.
Otago Festival of the Arts PO Box 5710, Dunedin 9058. *t:* +64 3 477 7600 *f:* +64 3 474 5431 *e:* info@otagofestival.co.nz *w:* www.otagofestival.co.nz *Contact* Nicholas McBryde, director. Biennial. Festival celebrating the very best in the performing, visual and related arts.

Far East

CHINA

BEIJING
i Tourist information
www.ebeijing.gov.cn

CENTRAL CONSERVATORY OF MUSIC
43 Baokia Street, Xicheng District, Beijing 100031.
t: +86 10 66425597 *e:* contactus@ccom.edu.cn
w: www.ccom.edu.cn
Courses 4 year bachelors (5 year for composition, musicology, conducting, music education, vocal/opera); 2-3 year masters, includes thesis and viva. Non-degree study programmes available. *Application deadline* Beginning of Dec; auditions in Feb *Fees* Application fee 200 yuan preliminary + 60 yuan, next round (undergrad); 900 yuan (postgrad). Tuition: 33,000 yuan (undergrad), 38,000 yuan (masters), 42,000 yuan (doctorate). *Language requirements* Degree students must meet minimum standard of Mandarin; those who do not must study for a year at International Music Exchange Centre. *Music facilities* Concert hall and recital hall *No of students* Approx 1900 students in total, of whom 40 from overseas.

CHENGDU
i Tourist information
www.chengdu.gov.cn

SICHUAN CONSERVATORY OF MUSIC
6 Xinsheng Road, Chengdu 610021.
t: +86 28 85430297 *f:* +86 28 85430712
e: sccmws@126.com *w:* www.sccm.cn
Courses Courses in composition; music performance (conducting, piano, accordion, wind and string instruments, traditional Chinese instruments, voice, opera, music theatre, classical Chinese dancing); marketing and management; musicology; music education; film & TV; piano tuning and violin-making. Undergrad degrees 4-5 years, depending on course. *Application requirements* Entrance exam in Mar. *Fees* 21,000 yuan (undergrad); 27,000 yuan (masters). *Language requirements* Entrance exam in Mandarin.

SHANGHAI
i Tourist information
http://lyw.sh.gov.cn

SHANGHAI CONSERVATORY OF MUSIC
No 20 Fenyang Road, Xuhui District, Shanghai 200031.
t: +86 10 64370137 *f:* +86 10 64330866
w: www.shcmusic.edu.cn

WORLD

HONG KONG
i Tourist information
www.discoverhongkong.com

HONG KONG ACADEMY OF PERFORMING ARTS
School of Music, 1 Gloucester Road, Wanchai.
t: +852 2584 8500 *f:* +852 2827 5823
w: www.hkapa.edu
Courses Bachelor of music degree (3 years) provides training to professional level plus historical/theoretical knowledge. Advanced diploma (2 years) focuses on performing and performance issues. Professional diploma (usually 1 year) for post-diploma or post-degree professional training. Master of Music available in performance or composition (2 years in either case). Courses provided in several departments: Chinese music; composition & electronic music; keyboard; opera & vocal studies; strings; woodwind, brass and percussion; academic studies. *Application requirements* 2-round audition: preliminary performance followed by audition and theory test. *Music facilities* 3 purpose-built performance venues: concert hall and recital hall at Wanchai campus, theatre at new Bethanie campus. 12 teaching rooms, 17 practice rooms. Electronic music studio, keyboard lab. Instruments include pipe organ, chamber organ, harpsichords, fortepiano, 8 concert pianos, various string instruments (including baroque). Large orchestral music collection.

MUSIC FESTIVALS
Hong Kong Arts Festival c/o International Programme Office, 35 Little Russell St, London.
t: +44 20 7637 5661 *f:* +44 20 7323 1151
e: joseph.seelig@easynet.co.uk *Contact* Joseph Seelig, international programme consultant. Features all types of music, but mainly classical, world music and jazz.

JAPAN

TOKYO
i Tourist information
www.metro.tokyo.jp

TOKYO COLLEGE OF MUSIC
3-4-5 Minami-Ikebukuro, Toshima-ku, Tokyo 171-8540.
t: +81 3 3982 3196 *f:* +81 3 3982 8440
e: admissions@tokyo-ondai.ac.jp *w:* www.tokyo-ondai.ac.jp
Courses 4-year degree programmes available in music education, vocal music, instrumental music, composition (including film scoring), conducting. Non-degree programmes in traditional Japanes music (instruments and composition), jazz improvisation, Indonesian gamelan. *Music facilities* Main campus includes concert hall; 12-storey classroom/studio building with recital hall and pipe organ; practice room facility; graduate school with performance space and recording studio; 2-storey ensemble rehearsal building.

MUSIC FESTIVALS
Japan Contemporary Music Festival c/o Japan International League of Artists, 1-34-8 Shinjuku Gyoen-mae Bldg 2F, Shinjuku-ku, Tokyo. *t:* +81 3 3356 4033 *f:* + 81 3 3356 5780 *e:* music@jila.co.jp *w:* www.jila.co.jp Annual. The festival features the winning works of the Tokyo International Competition for Chamber Music Composition held in November every year.

Japan International Youth Musicale in Shizuoka Tokoha Gakuen Educational Institute, 1 22 1 Sena Aoi-ku, Shizuoka City, Shizuoka Prefecture 420-0911. *t:* +81 54 261 1356 *f:* +81 54 261 5601 *e:* jiym@tokoha.ac.jp *w:* www.tokoha.ac.jp/jiym/jiym.html *Contact* Kenji Kimiya, director, Tokoha Gakuen; Tsutomu Asaba, director, organising committee, JIYM. Triennial international youth music festival.

Kitakyushu International Music Festival 2-1-1 Chuo, Yahatahigashi-ku, Kitakyushu 802-0019. *t:* +81 93 663 6567 *f:* +81 93 662 3028 *e:* info@kimfes.com *w:* www.kimfes.com

Osaka International Festival New Asahi Building, 2-3-18 Nakanoshima, Kita-ku, Osaka 530-0005. *t:* +81 6 6227 1061 *f:* +81 6 6227 1262 Annual. Classical music, concertos, piano recitals, ballet, traditional Japanese music and dance.

Pacific Music Festival Sumitomo Seimei Sapporo

Chuo Building 1F, 1-14 Minami 2-jo, Higashi 1-chome, Chuo-ku, Sapporo 060-0052. *t:* +81 11 242 2211 *f:* +81 11 242 1687 *e:* webmaster@pmf.jp *w:* www.pmf.jp International educational music festival. Orchestra with chamber music, string quartet and composition courses.

SINGAPORE
i Tourist information
www.visitsingapore.com

YONG SIEW TOH CONSERVATORY OF MUSIC
National University of Singapore, 3 Estate Office Drive, Singapore 117485.
t: +65 6516 1167 *f:* +65 6872 6915
e: music@nus.edu.sg *w:* www.nus.edu.sg
Courses 4-year bachelor of music degree, majoring in either performance (piano or orchestral instruments) or composition; core curriculum includes theory, history, repertoire studies, conducting, music technology. 2-year graduate diploma has a limited number of places; modules to be passed include major study, large ensemble/accompanying, chamber ensemble, recital. *Application requirements* Regional auditions in Singapore, Malaysia, China, Hong Kong, Taiwan, Thailand, New Zealand. Recordings acceptable for those who do not live close to audition locations; must include a spoken self-introduction on why they wish to study at the conservatoire. *Fees* S\$59,520 total annual tuition for international students; additional fees also apply. *Scholarships* Partial or full scholarships may be awarded based on student's ability or on conservatoire's instrumental requirements. All students automatically considered. *Language requirements* All classes conducted in English; intensive language support available for successful non-native speaking applicants. *Music facilities* Various performance opportunities in various concert series run by conservatoire.

DAEGU
i Tourist information
http://english.daegu.kr

KEIMYUNG UNIVERSITY COLLEGE OF MUSIC AND PERFORMING ARTS
2800 Dalgubeoldaero, Dalseo-Gu, Daegu 704-701.
e: intl@kmu.ac.kr *w:* www.kmu.ac.kr
Courses Departments of orchestral instruments, voice, composition, piano, organ. *Music facilities* Multimedia studio, acting room, film editing room, computer/MIDI studio, sound recording studio, listening room.

SEOUL
i Tourist information
www.visitseoul.net; senglish@visitseoul.net; tel: +82 2 2171 2461

KOREA NATIONAL UNIVERSITY OF ARTS
Seongbuk-gu, Seoul, 136-716.
t: +82 2 7469 042 *e:* admissions@knua.ac.kr
w: www.knua.ac.kr
Courses Broad range of courses in several departments: vocal music, opera, lied & oratorio, instrumental music, composition, music technology, conducting, musicology. Bachelors and masters degrees, 3-year artist diploma. *Term dates* 1 Sep-mid Dec (fall semester); 2 Mar-mid Jun (spring semester).

BANGKOK
i Tourist information
www.bangkoktourist.com

MAHIDOL UNIVERSITY COLLEGE OF MUSIC
25/25 Phutthamonthon Sai 4 Rd, Salaya, Photthamonthon, Nakhonpathom, 73170.
e: mswww@mahidol.ac.th *w:* www.mahidol.ac.th
Courses Undergrad courses in 7areas: music performance,Thai and oriental music, jazz, music technology, music industry, pop music, composition; all follow courses in music theory, music history, music technology. Masters degrees in musicology, music education, music performance. *Music facilities* 353-seat music auditorium, recital hall (approx 200 seats), outdoor performance areas; rehearsal rooms, teaching studios, audiovisual room, music library.music arboretum made up of trees used for making instruments, but is also used for special music performances. *Accommodation* Dormitories and other on-campus accommodation available.

Americas

ARGENTINA

CONSERVATORIO DE MÚSICA JULIÁN AGUIRRE
Av H Yrigoyen 7652, 1828 Banfield.
t: +54 4242 4879 *e:* consaguirre@yahoo.com.ar *w:* www.consaguirre.com.ar

DEPARTAMENTO DE ARTES MUSICALES Y SONORAS 'CARLOS LOPEZ BUCHARDO'-IUNA
Av Córdoba 2445, C1120AAG Buenos Aires.
t: +54 4 964 5593 *f:* +54 4961 9618
e: departamento@artesmusicales.org *w:* www.artesmusicales.org

CONSERVATORIO DE MÚSICA GILARDO GILARDI
Palacio Servente, Calle 12 y 523, Tolosa.
t: +54 221 4 21 1696 *w:* http://abc.gov.ar/

paginaescuela/0001AM0001
Music facilities 150-seat auditorium, chamber music hall, 40 classrooms, recording studio, sound lab, orchestra hall,

MUSIC FESTIVALS
International Encuentros Festival Fundacion Encuentros Internacionales de Musica Contemporanea, Santa Fe 3269-4b, 1425 Buenos Aires. *t:* +54 11 4822 1383, also fax *w:* www.aliciaterzian.com.ar *Contact* Alicia Terzian, artistic director. Concerts, masterclasses, symposium, electronic music, experimental theatre, lectures (contemporary music only). Education forum introducing ancient and contemporary music. Annual national competition (2008: string quartet; 2009: violoncello; 2010: piano)

COLOMBIA

UNIVERSIDAD NACIONAL DE COLOMBIA - CONSERVATORIO DE MÚSICA
Avenida Carrera 30 no 45-03, Edificio 305.
t: +57 1 3165000 ext 12506 *e:* consermu_farbog@unal.edu.co *w:* www.facartes.unal.edu.co

CHILE

CONSERVATORIO DE MÚSICA UNIVERSIDAD AUSTRAL DE CHILE
General Lagos 1107, Valdivia.
t: +56 63 22 19 16 *f:* +56 63 21 38 13
e: comusica@uach.cl *w:* www.uach.cl/conservatorio

GUATEMALA

UNIVERSIDAD DEL VALLE DE GUATEMALA
Departamento de Música, BA Isabel Ciudad-
Real, Guatemala City.
t: +502 2364 03 36 ext 541 *e:* isabelcr@uvg.
edu.gt *w:* www.uvg.edu.gt

MEXICO

CONSERVATORIO NACIONAL DE MÚSICA DE MÉXICO
Presidente Mazaryk 582, Colonia Polanco.
t: +52 80 63 47 *e:* cnm@correo.inba.gob.mx
w: www.conservatorianos.com.mx

Courses Licentiates in harp, opera/recital singing, harpsichord, composition, choral/orchestral conducting, guitar, string instruments, woodwind instruments, brass instruments, organ, percussion, piano, composition.

PUERTO RICO

CONSERVATORIO DE MÚSICA DE PUERTO RICO
350 Rafael Lamar St, San Juan, 00918.
t: +787 751 0160 *f:* +787 758 8268
w: www.cmpr.edu

PERU

CONSERVATORIO NACIONAL DE MÚSICA
Jr Carabaya 421-435, Lima.
t: +51 426 9677 *f:* +51 426 5658
e: informes@cnm.edu.pe *w:* www.cnm.edu.pe

Middle East

ISRAEL

THE JERUSALEM ACADEMY OF MUSIC AND DANCE

w: www.jamd.ac.il
Courses Bachelors and masters courses in 3 faculties: performing arts; composition, conducting and music education; dance, movement and movement notation. *No of students* Over 600 students in total.

BUCHMANN-MEHTA SCHOOL OF MUSIC

Tel Aviv University, Tel Aviv 69978.
t: +972 36408415 *f:* +972 36409174
e: music1@post.tau.ac.il *w:* www.tau.ac.il/arts/music
Courses BMus focusing on practical studies; BA is joint study with one course in music school, one from another department. Postgrad courses include masters and artist diplomas. *Application requirements* Auditions include keyboard proficiency exam as well as live audition; applicants are recommended to attend in person (recordings may be submitted for informal assessment). Postgrad students are accepted at discretion of faculty. *Scholarships* Scholarships available for outstanding students and those in financial hardship; school's excellence programme pays tuition for selected students. *Music facilities* 450-seat concert hall with 2 Steinway concert pianos, recording studio (connected to hall); smaller, flexible auditorium (120); baroque room with harpsichord, clavichord, fortepiano and pipe organ.

MUSIC FESTIVALS

Felicja Blumental International Music Festival addressall. *w:* www.blumentalfestival.com *Contact* Annette Celine, artistic dir; Avigail Arnheim, exec dir. Musicians from around the globe and talents from Israel. Recitals, musical spectaculars, specially commissioned ballet; lectures, films.

Israel Festival, Jerusalem Jerusalem Theatre, PO Box 4409, 91044 Jerusalem. *t:* +972 2 561 1450 *f:* +972 2 566 9850 *e:* israel_f@smile.net.il *w:* www.israel-festival.org.il *Contact* Yossi Tal-Gan, general director; Gil Shohat, classical music adviser. Annual. Opera, symphonic and chamber music, contemporary and early music, recitals, theatre, ballet and contemporary dance, ethnic music, jazz, rock, multidisciplinary.

Red Sea Jazz Festival 6 Rabin Square, 64951 Tel Aviv. *t:* +972 3 695 9355 *f:* +972 3 696 3528 *e:* eilam@netvision.net.il *w:* www.redseajazzeilant.com/EN Annual. 40 concerts featuring top jazz ensembles, masterclasses and evening jam sessions.

Zimriya-World Assembly of Choirs 4 Aharonowitz St, 64951 Tel Aviv. *t:* +972 3 528 0233 *f:* +972 3 629 9524 *e:* harzimco@netvision.net.il *w:* www.zimriya.org.il Workshops, concerts, opera.

ECOLE DE MUSIQUE GHASSAN YAMMINE

PO Box 7, Bikfaya Metn, Beirut.
t: +961 3304455 *f:* +961 4980656 *e:* info@
edmgy.com *w:* www.edmgy.com
Contact Ghassan Yammine, pres. *Courses* Instruments,
singing, music education, composition, choral music,
music technology. *Fees* $400-1800 per year.
Scholarships Scholarships available. *Exchange
details* Exchanges with Boulogne-Billancourt local
conservatoire, Ecole Normale de Musique (Paris).
Language requirements French or English.
Accommodation Help finding accommodation
available. *No of students* 500.

MUSIC FESTIVALS

**Al Bustan International Festival of Music and
the Arts** Mail Box 343, 56 Gloucester Rd, London.
f: +44 20 7937 2633 *e:* festival@albustan.co.uk
w: www.albustanfestival.com *Contact* Myrna Bustani,
president; Melinda Hughes, assistant.

PALESTINIAN TERRITORY

EDWARD SAID NATIONAL CONSERVATORY

PO Box 66676, Regent Hotel, 20 Azzahra'
Street, Jerusalem 91666.
t: +972 2 627 1711 *f:* +972 2 627 1710
e: info@ncm.birzeit.edu *w:* www.ncm.birzeit.edu
Courses Branches in Jerusalem, Ramallah, Bethlehem;
pre-conservatoire training leading to diploma that
will qualify students for entry into forthcoming
university level programme at ESNCM.

Atelier Lyrique – Opéra National de Paris 120 rue de Lyon, F-75012 Paris, France. t: +33 1 40 01 17 52 f: +33 1 40 01 17 87 e: atelierlyrique@operadeparis.fr w: www.operadeparis.fr For singers: repertoire workshops; role study; special classes (pronunciation, diction, vocal control, theatre workshops etc; possible participation in Opéra de Paris productions and other concerts. Also opportunities for répétiteurs. *Application requirements* Applicants must be aged at least 18 and no more than 30. Auditions in Paris in Mar. *Course dates* Oct-Jun. *Application deadline* Mid Feb.

Cardiff International Academy of Voice. t: 02920 481753 e: HillJ5@cardiff.ac.uk w: www.cardiff.ac.uk/ciav *Contact* Jennifer Hill, artistic admin.

Houston Grand Opera Studio 510 Preston St, Houston, TX 77002, USA. t: +1 713 546 0227 e: studio@houstongrandopera.org w: www.houstongrandopera.org 8-12 singers accepted each year. Classes in voice, acting, stage movement, diction, languages; also special classes (fight choreography, audition techniques, financial advice, PR, agent representation). Singers assigned supporting roles in HGO mainstage productions; various other performance opportunities. *Application requirements* Auditions in Nov.

Internationales Opernstudio Köln Offenbach-platz, D-50667 Köln, Germany. t: +49 221 221 28391 e: rupert.burleigh@stadt-koeln.de w: www.buehnenkoeln.de/opernstudio.php

The Metropolitan Opera Lindemann Young Artist Development Program Lincoln Center, New York, NY 10023, USA t: +1 212 799 3100 w: www.metoperafamily.org

Specialised training in music, language, movement and dramatic coaching. Access to rehearsals at Met productions. Places are for one year, renewable for up to 3 years for singers, 2 years for pianists; young artists receive annual stipend for living expenses.

National Opera Studio The Clore Building, 2 Chapel Yard, Wandsworth High St, London. t: +44 20 8874 8811 f: +44 20 8875 0404 e: info@nationaloperastudio.org.uk w: www.nationalopera-studio.org.uk 1-year intensive course providing opera training to singers and repetiteurs at an international level. The course adds dramatic, language and interpretative skills to trainees, preparing them for a professional career in opera.

10-15 coaching sessions per week with music, language, movement and stagecraft coaches. Trainees perform concerts throughout the year directed by internationally renowned directors, and normally attend residencies with 2 of the 6 main British opera companies during the 2nd term. Course culminates in an annual showcase in which trainees perform in fully staged excerpts from various operas; attended by casting directors, agents and press. *Application requirements* Audition. *Course dates* Sep-Dec, Mar-Apr, Apr-Jun. *Application deadline* Dec.

Opera Studio Nederland Kloveniersburgwal 87-89, NL-1011 KA Amsterdam, Netherlands. t: +31 20 420 05 62 f: +31 20 42 25 05 e: info@operastudio.nl w: www.operastudio.nl Programme bridges gap between conservatoire training and professional stage. Maximum of 8 singers; Dutch candidates given priority.

Oper Frankfurt Opera Studio Unitermainanlage 11, D-60311 Frankfurt am Main, Germany. e: opernstudio@buehnen-frankfurt.de w: www.oper-frankfurt.com Professional tuition in learning new roles, acting, language coaching, phonetics lessons, dialogue, improvisation, make-up. Master-classes with renowned singers, plus opportunity to perform in small roles in the opera house. *Application requirements* Applicants must have completed singing studies; age limit 30 or younger for women, 32 or young for men. *Application deadline* February.

Orlando Opera Studio 1111 N Orange Ave, Orlando, FL 32804. t: +1 407 426 1717 f: +1 407 426 1700 w: www.orlandoopera.org Opportunities for a limited number of young talented singers. Professional training (voice, acting, language, movement, fencing, masterclasses); also main stage performance opportunities. Occasional spaces for répétiteurs

Portland Opera Studio The Hampton Opera Center, 211 SE Caruthers St, Portland, OR 97214, USA. t: +1 503 241 1407 f: +1 503 241 4212 w: www.portlandopera.org Vocal coaching, language training, acting classes, masterclasses. Students feature in their own production as well as in supporting roles for mainstage season. *Application requirements* Auditions in New York. *Application deadline* Applications open late summer for entry into subsequent year's programme.

Royal Northern College of Music Opera Studio

124 Oxford Rd, Manchester. *t:* +44 161 907 5200 *e:* info@rncm.ac.uk *w:* www.rncm.ac.uk New course leading to RNCM international artist diploma. Students perform principal roles in RNCM operas; other performance opportunities. *Application requirements* Applicants must have completed undergrad and postgrad vocal and opera studies, plus stage experience. *Course dates* Sep-Apr (2 terms).

San Francisco Opera Center 301 Van Ness Ave, San Francisco, CA 94102, USA. *t:* +1 415 861 4008 *e:* mop@sfopera.com (Merola Opera Program) *w:* http://sfopera.com Adler fellowships for advanced singers and répétiteurs offer intensive training and roles in SFO's main stage season. *Application requirements* Applicants must have attended Merola Opera Program, 11-week summer training programme.

Santa Fe Opera Apprentice Singer Program The Santa Fe Opera, 17053 US Highway 84/285, Santa Fe, NM 87506, USA *t:* +1 505 986 5955 *e:* artsadmin@santafeopera.org *w:* www.santafeopera.org Apprenticeship at summer opera festival, working side by side with international artists; opportunities for performance on mainstage cast and auditions in front of major opera companies. Apprentices regularly invited to return to Santa Fe opera during main season. *Application deadline* Aug-Sep (for entry in subsequent year).

Seattle Opera Young Artist Program PO Box 9248, Seattle, WA 9109-0248 *t:* +1 206 389 7600 *w:* seattleopera.org 20-week career guidance and training for singers aged 22-32; includes acting training, masterclasses, auditions, role study. Each artists performs a complete role in a fully produced opera.

Staatsoper Unter den Linden – Opernstudio Unter den Linden 7, D-10117 Berlin, Germany. *t:* +49 30 20354635 *f:* +49 30 20354668 *e:* b.anifantakis@staatsoper-berlin.de *w:* www.staatsoper-berlin.de 2-year programme. Students learn supporting roles for main stage; also classes in ensemble singing, stage movement, diction etc. *Application requirements* Age limit 32; application by CV with repertoire list and photo. *Application deadline* End Sep.

Swiss Opera Studio Bern University of the Arts, Jakob-Rosius-Str 16, CH-2502 Biel/Bienne, Switzerland. *t:* +41 32 322 84 13 *f:* +41 32 322 84 34 *e:* opernstudio@hkb.bfh.ch *w:* www.hkb.bfh. ch *Contact* Mathias Behrends, head of studies. 2-year course leading to an opera degree. *Application requirements* Open to those studying at BUA or in music dept at Zurich School of Music; all must have completed 1st year of opera class at these institutions.

Zurich Opera House – International Opera Studio Falkenstr 1, CH-8008 Zurich, Switzerland. *t:* +41 44 268 66 01 *f:* +41 44 268 64 37 *e:* ios@opernhaus.ch *w:* www.opernhaus.ch *Contact* Renata Blum. Prepares exceptionally talented young singers and pianists for an international operatic career. Training includes musical interpretation, acting, style, ensemble singing, vocal interpretation, diction. Students are given small parts in Zurich Opera productions, attend performances, workshops and masterclasses. Also course for répétiteurs. *Application requirements* Age limit 30 (women), 31 (men). See website for details and application form. *Course dates* Academic year Sep-mid July.

ORGANISATIONS

Association Européenne de Conservatoires, Académies de Musique et Musikhochschulen (AEC) PO Box 805, NL-3500 AV Utrecht, The Netherlands. t: +31 30 2361242 f: +31 30 2361290 e: aecinfo@aecinfo.org w: www.aecinfo.org European cultural and educational network with 238 member institutions in professional music training in 55 countries. Aims to stimulate and support international collaboration; represents the interests of the professional music training sector on national, European and international level.

British Council t: +44 161 957 7755 f: +44 161 957 7762 e: general.enquiries@britishcouncil.org w: www.britishcouncil.org The UK's international organisation for cultural relations and educational opportunities. UK offices in London, Manchester, Edinburgh, Cardiff, Belfast; overseas offices in 110 countries.

Conservatoires UK Admissions Service (CUKAS) Rosehill, New Barn Lane, Cheltenham GL52 3LZ, United Kingdom t: +44 871 468 0470 w: www.cukas.ac.uk Provides facilities to research and apply for practice-based music courses at the following UK conservatoires: Birmingham Conservatoire, Leeds College of Music, Royal College of Music, Royal Northern College of Music, Royal Scottish Academy of Music and Drama, Royal Welsh College of Music and Drama, Trinity College of Music.

European League of Institutes of the Arts (ELIA) Keizersgracht 105, NL-1015 CH Amsterdam, The Netherlands. t: +31 877 875 244 f: +31 877 875 344 e: elia@elia-artschools.org w: www.elia-artschools.org Independent network of approx 315 arts educations institutes covering all arts disciplines (dance, design, theatre, fine art, music, media arts, architectures) from 47 countries.

European Music School Union Postbus 265, NL-3500 AJ Utrecht, Netherlands. t: +31 30 2303740 f: +31 30 2303749 e: office@musicschoolunion.eu w: www.musicschoolunion.eu Umbrella organisation of national music school associations with 26 countries affiliated. Non-governmental and non-profit organisation.

International Association of Music Information Centres Steentstraat 25, B-1000 Brussels, Belgium. t: +32 2 504 90 90 f: +32 2 502 81 03 e: iamic@iamic.net w: www.iamic.net Worldwide network of organisations promoting new music; 41 member organisations in 38 countries.

Jeunesses Musicales International Palais des Beaux-Arts, rue Baron Horta 13, B-1000 Bruxelles, Belgium. t: +32 2 513 97 74 f: +32 2 514 4755 e: mail@jmi.net w: www.jmi.net Set up in 1945 to enable young people to develop through music across all boundaries. Member organisations in 45 countries.

Mundus Musicalis - Study Music in Europe AEC, PO Box 805, NL-3500 AV Utrecht, Netherlands. t: +31 30 2361242 f: +31 30 2361290 e: aecinfo@aecinfo.org w: www.studymusicineurope.org Information website for students (particularly those from outside EU) wishing to study music in Europe.

National Association of Schools of Music 11250 Roger Bacon Drive, Suite 21, Reston, VA 20190-5248, USA. t: +1 703 437 0700 f: +1 703 437 6312 e: info@arts-accredit.org w: http://nasm.arts-accredit.org Organisation of schools, conservatoires, colleges and universities in USA. Establishes national standards, provides information to potential students and parents.

Project Visa w: http://projectvisa.com/ Information on visa requirements around the world; also details of embassies.

UK Erasmus Council UK Erasmus National Agency, British Council, 28 Park Place, Cardiff CF10 3QE, United Kingdom t: +44 29 2039 7405 f: +44 29 2023 7494 European Commission exchange programme that enables students in 31 countries to study for part of their degree in another Incorporated into the Socrates programme which covers education from school to university to lifelong learning.

Unesco International Music Council 1 rue Miollis, F-75732 Paris Cedex 15, France. t: +33 1 45 68 48 50 f: +33 1 45 68 48 66 w: www.unesco.org/imc Global network of expert organisations and individuals working in the field of music.

CONSERVATOIRES

Birmingham Conservatoire (p 25) Paradise Place, Birmingham B3 3HG, United Kingdom *t:* +44 121 331 5901 *f:* +44 121 331 5906 *e:* conservatoire@bcu.ac.uk *w:* www.conservatoire.bcu.uk

Cork Institute of Technology School of Music (p 66) Union Quay, Cork, Ireland *t:* +353 21 480 7300 *f:* +353 21 454 7601 *e:* bmus@cit.ie *w:* www.cit.ie

Hochschule für Musik 'Franz Liszt' Weimar (p 101) Postfach 2552, D-99406 Weimar, Germany *t:* +49 3643 555 0 *f:* +49 3643 555 147 *e:* hans-peter.hoffmann@hfm.weimar.de *w:* www.hfm.weimar.de

Royal Academy of Music (inside front cover; see advertising feature p 38–39) Marylebone Rd, London NW1H 5HT, United Kingdom *t:* +44 20 7873 7373 *f:* +44 20 7873 7374 *e:* registry@ram.ac.uk *w:* www.ram.ac.uk

Royal College of Music (p 41) Prince Consort Rd, London SW7 2BS, United Kingdom *t:* +44 20 7589 3643 *f:* +44 20 7589 7740 *e:* info@rcm.ac.uk *w:* www.rcm.ac.uk

Royal Northern College of Music (p 46) 124 Oxford Rd, Manchester M13 9RD, United Kingdom *t:* +44 161 907 5200 *w:* +44 161 273 7611 *e:* admissions@rncm.ac.uk *w:* www.rncm.ac.uk

Royal Scottish Academy of Music and Drama (p 28) 100 Renfrew St, Glasgow G2 3DB, United Kingdom *t:* +44 141 332 4101 *f:* +44 141 332 8909 *e:* registry@rsamd.ac.uk *w:* www.rsamd.ac.uk

Royal Welsh College of Music (p 26) Castle Grounds, Cathays Park, Cardiff CF10 3ER, United Kingdom *t:* +44 2920 391361 *f:* +44 2920 391305 *e:* music.admissions@rwcmd.ac.uk *w:* www.rwcmd.ac.uk

Trinity College of Music (p 44–45) King Charles Court, Old Royal Naval College, London SE10 9JF, United Kingdom *t:* +44 20 8305 4444 *f:* +44 20 8305 9444 *e:* enquiries@tcm.ac.uk *w:* www.tcm.ac.uk

EVENTS

Chetham's International Summer School and Festival for Pianists (p 50) Chetham's School of Music, Long Millgate, Manchester M3 1SB, United Kingdom *t:* +44 1625 266899 *e:* info@pianosummerschool.com *w:* www.pianosummerschool.com

The John Kerr English Song Award (p 61) Clifton Coach House, Camden Park, Tunbridge Wells, TN2 5AA, United Kingdom *t:* +44 1892 530049 *e:* maureen.lyle@googlemail.com *w:* www.johnkerraward.org.uk

Manchester International Piano Competition for Young Pianists (p 50) Chetham's School of Music, Long Millgate, Manchester M3 1SB, United Kingdom *t:* +44 1625 266899 *f:* +44 1265 266899 *e:* info@pianoconcertocompetition.com *w:* www.pianoconcertocompetition.com

Queen Elisabeth International Music Competition (p 154) 20 Rue aux Laines, B-1000 Bruxelles, Belgium *t:* +32 2 213 4050 *f:* +32 2 514 3297 *e:* info@

qeimc.be *w:* www.queimc.be

Tunbridge Wells International Young Concert Artists Competition (p 60) Competition Office, PO Box 10, Tunbridge Wells, United Kingdom *t:* + 44 1892 616844, also fax *e:* info@twiyca.org *w:* www.twiyca.org

INSTRUMENT MANUFACTURERS & DEALERS

Florian Leonhard Fine Violins (p 41) 3 Frognal Lane, London NW3 7DY, United Kingdom *t:* +44 20 7813 3307 *f:* +44 20 7813 3308 *e:* violins@florianleonhard.com *w:* www.florianleonhard.com

Frederick Phelps Ltd – Dealers in Fine Violins (p 42) 34 Conway Rd, London N14 7BA, United Kingdom *t:* +44 20 8482 3887 *f:* +44 20 8882 2006 *e:* office@phelpsviolins.com *w:* www.phelpsviolins.com

Stringers of Edinburgh (p 30) 13 York Place, Edinburgh EH1 3EB, United Kingdom *t:* +44 131 557 5432 *f:* +44 131 557 6999 *e:* info@stringersmusic.com *w:* www.stringersmusic.com

Tom Woods Cellos (p 4; outside back cover) (London) *t:* +44 20 7362 1812 *e:* tom@tomwoodscellos.com *w:* www.tomwoodscellos.com

Top Wind Flute Specialists (p 42) 2 Lower Marsh, London SE1 7RJ, United Kingdom *t:* +44 20 7401 8787 *f:* +44 20 7401 8788 *e:* topwind@topwind.com *w:* www.topwind.com

INSURANCE SERVICES

Allianz Musical Insurance (p 60) Allianz House, 6 Vale Ave, Tunbridge Wells TN1 1EH, United Kingdom *t:* +44 870 2400 303 *w:* www.allianzmusicalinsurance.co.uk

ONLINE SHEET MUSIC SUPPLIERS

Inter-Note Music (p 218) Siebenbürgerhof 6, D-69493 Hirschberg, Germany *t:* +49 6201 6505 623 *e:* info@inter-note.com *w:* www.inter-note.com

Scorestore Music (p 22) Redwood, Swallowfield Rd, Arborfield, Reading RG2 9JY, United Kingdom *t:* +44 118 976 2020 *f:* +44 118 976 1185 *e:* info@scorestore.co.uk *w:* www.scorestore.co.uk

VENUES

Cadogan Hall (p 37) 5 Sloane Terrace, London SW1X 9DQ, United Kingdom *t:* + 44 20 7730 5744 *f:* +44 20 7881 0634 *e:* info@cadoganhall.com *w:* www.cadoganhall.com

For details of thousands more organisations, summer schools, educational establishments, suppliers and support services, plus performers and agents, see the British & International Music Yearbook 2009. Buy your copy by visiting www.rhinegold.co.uk or calling +44 20 7333 1720.